Creating Couture Embellishment

LAURENCE KING

Published in 2017 by
Laurence King Publishing Ltd
361–373 City Road, London,
EC1V 1LR, United Kingdom
T +44 (0)20 7841 6900
F + 44 (0)20 7841 6910
enquiries@laurenceking.com
www.laurenceking.com

This book was produced by Laurence King
Publishing Ltd, London

A catalog record for this book is available from
the British Library

ISBN: 978-1-78067-949-5

Printed in China

Ellen W. Miller

Creating

Couture

Embellishment

Laurence King Publishing

Contents

Introduction

Welcome to *Creating Couture Embellishment*.

Different embellishments go in and out of style in the fashion world. No matter. Because so many different kinds of embellishment techniques are presented here, the current trend or the next, as well as traditional styles, are all contained in this one book. Maybe your designs featuring a particular embellishment technique will spark the next fashion trend. If one of these techniques inspires you, the bibliography at the back of the book will help you find other books about it.

Each chapter opens with a full-scale bodice, photographed on a store mannequin, that demonstrates one of the techniques in that chapter. The other techniques in each chapter have been worked on sleeves and photographed as finished examples to accompany each exercise. All these images have been gathered at the beginning of the book in a visual index to inspire you and help you think about your garment design: Do you want to add fullness to your garment? Consider ruffles or pleats. Do you want to add flat decoration? Consider bias or appliqué. Do you want to add three-dimensional decoration? Consider passementerie or decorative ribbons. Do you want to add sparkle? Consider crystals and nailheads, or beads and sequins.

Once you have decided which technique you wish to master, read through the chapter introduction for general information about the various fabrics, threads, and other tools you will need to create the embellishments. Many of the embellishments can be made in multiple ways: for example, crystals can be applied with prong sets, glue, or Hotfix; all three methods are shown, allowing you to choose your favorite.

Please practice the technique several times before attempting to create it in your garment's fashion fabric. Couture sewing implies mastery of the technique, and mastery comes only with practice. Learning which fabrics or ribbons are suitable for a particular technique takes experimentation. For example, how loosely or tightly you gather fabric to create a flower depends on your fabric and flower choices; adding a bead or a button to the center of the flower is a matter of personal style. I have offered suggestions for fabric and ribbon choices, how tightly to gather the fabric, and ideas for different centers, but you must try all of the possibilities yourself before you will become an expert: a couture sewer.

When writing *Creating Couture Embellishment*, I assumed the reader had a basic knowledge of sewing. If you are a beginner sewer I recommend the *Reader's Digest Complete Guide to Sewing*, but any book with basic hand and machine sewing techniques is fine. Most of the techniques in *Creating Couture Embellishment* involve hand sewing, but a simple sewing machine is all that is required for the machine-based techniques. In my sewing room I have a straight stitch sewing machine, a zigzag sewing machine, and a serger—nothing too fancy, as I like to concentrate on mastering techniques, not fussing with lots of settings on the sewing machine.

This book is not about how to design with embellishments; it is a book about how to make beautiful embellishments. It is up to you to imagine elegantly decorated garments. This book will teach you how to make the luxurious ornaments that will transform your garment from plain to polished. While most of the photographs show restrained embellishments for instructional purposes, the world is full of beautiful colors, textures, and patterns waiting to be celebrated by your fanciful, embellished creations.

Ellen W. Miller

Visual index

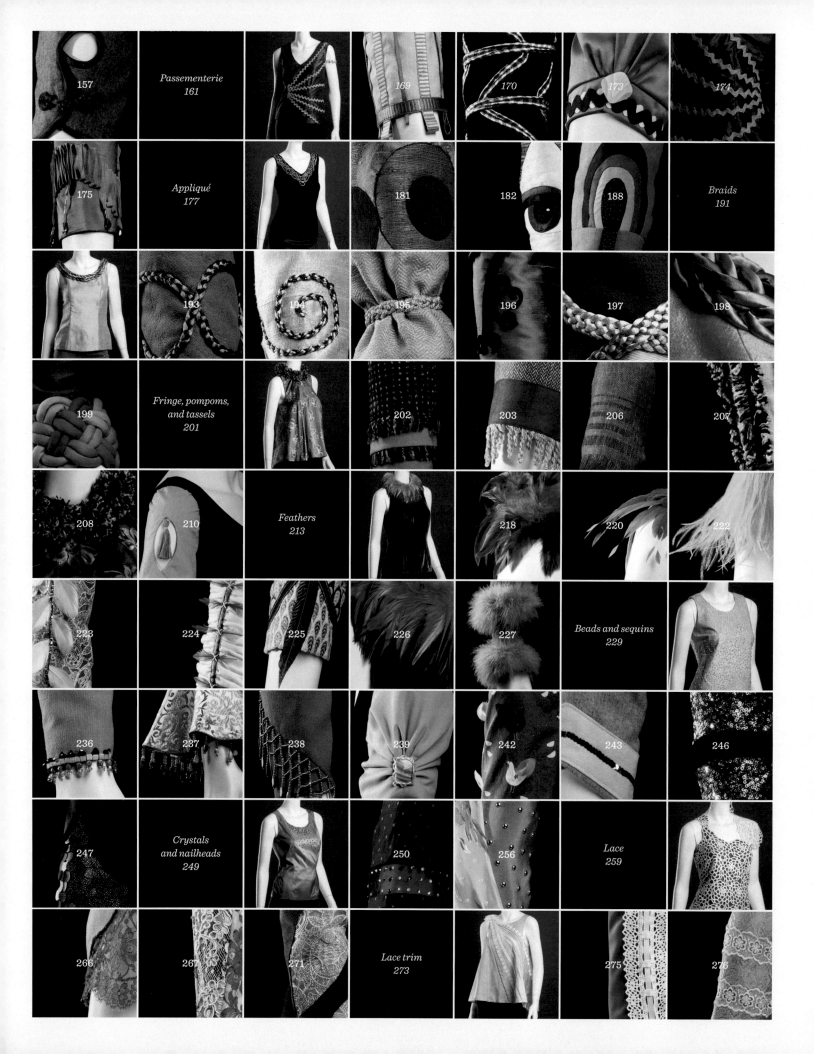

157

Passementerie
161

169

170

173

174

175

Appliqué
177

181

182

188

Braids
191

193

194

195

196

197

198

199

*Fringe, pompoms,
and tassels*
201

202

203

206

207

208

210

Feathers
213

218

220

222

223

224

225

226

227

Beads and sequins
229

236

237

238

239

242

243

246

247

*Crystals
and nailheads*
249

250

256

Lace
259

266

267

271

Lace trim
273

275

276

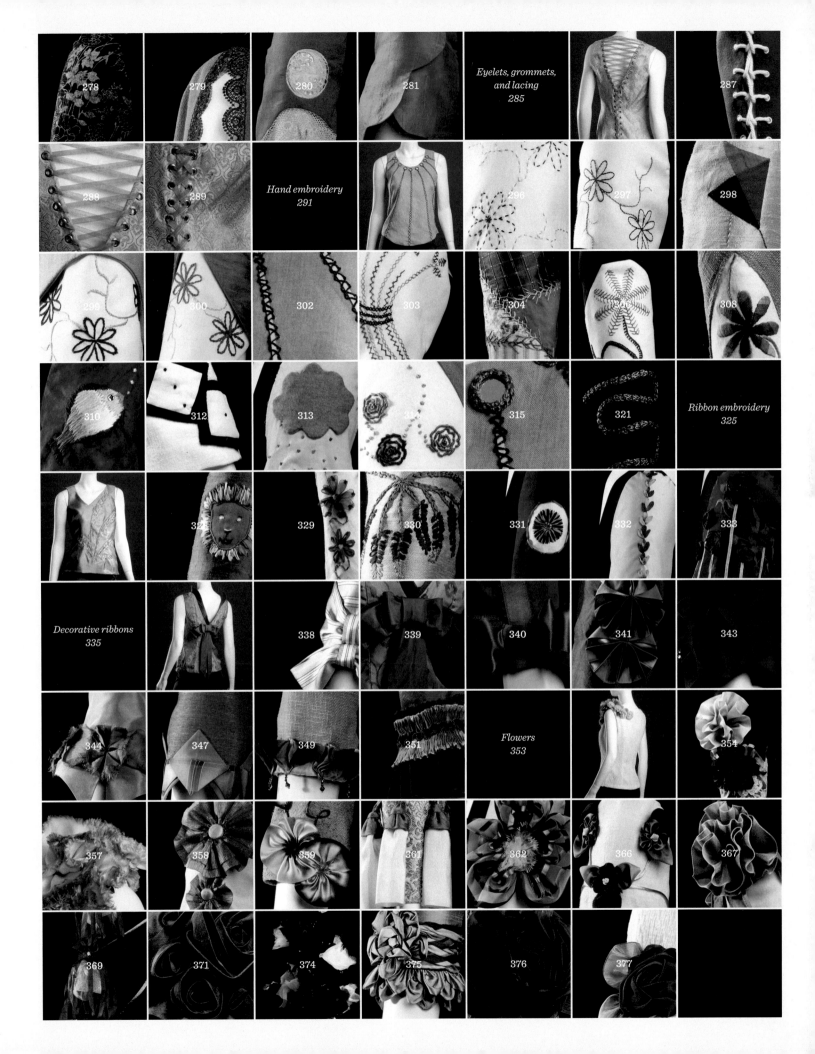

278

279

280

281

Eyelets, grommets, and lacing
285

287

288

289

Hand embroidery
291

296

297

298

299

300

302

303

304

306

308

310

312

313

315

321

Ribbon embroidery
325

328

329

330

331

332

333

Decorative ribbons
335

338

339

340

341

343

344

347

349

351

Flowers
353

354

357

358

359

361

362

366

367

369

371

374

375

376

377

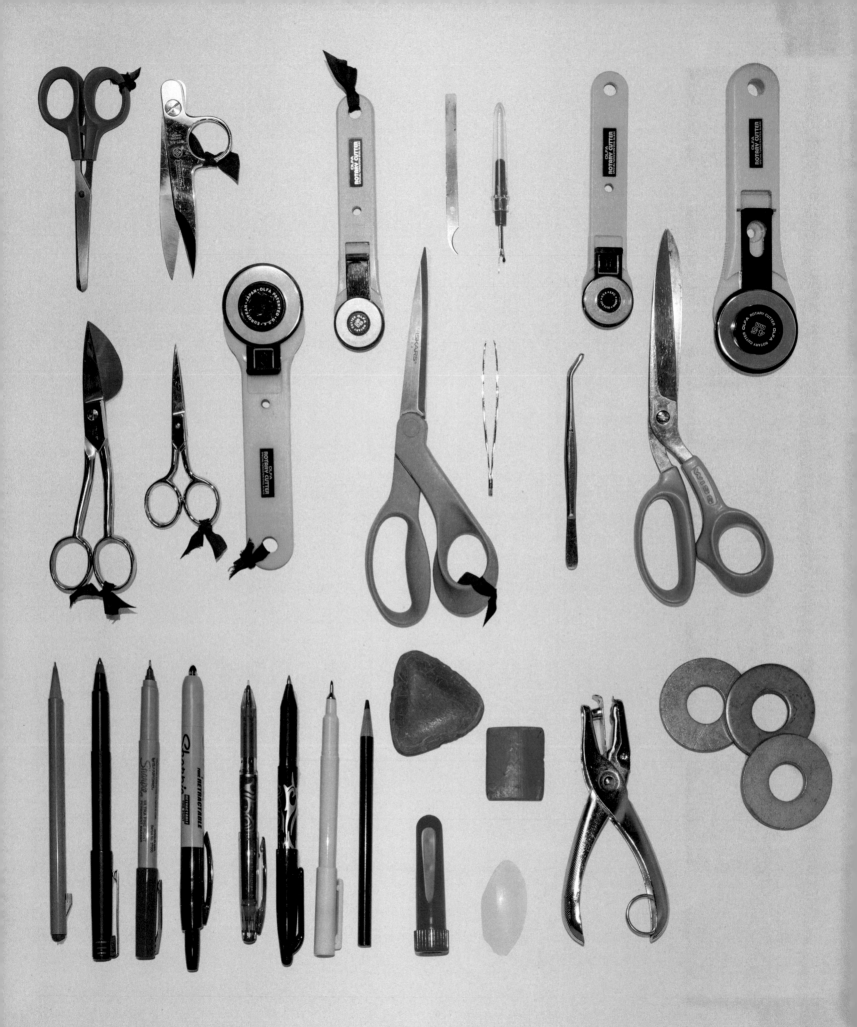

1
Basic tools and techniques

Tools

Scissors

It is best to keep a pair of dressmaker's shears and some rotary cutters for cutting fabric, and a separate pair of basic scissors for cutting paper. Once scissors have cut paper they will not cut fabric as well. To distinguish between the two sets, tie a piece of ribbon around those used for cutting fabric.

1. **Appliqué scissors** have a duckbill-shaped blade that slides under the fabric up to the stitching line. The bent handles help minimize the movement of the fabric as you cut.
2. **Blunt-ended scissors** can be used if you want to avoid accidentally cutting through a stitching line, for example, but they are still sharp enough to cut thread and fabric.
3. **Embroidery scissors** are small, very sharp scissors, good for clipping and grading.
4. **Snips** are good for cutting thread tails.
5. **45mm and 18mm rotary cutters** can be used to cut fabric; they work like a pizza cutter, rolling along on fabric laid on a self-healing cutting mat. The smaller rotary cutter is for cutting small curves, like armholes and necklines.
6. **8in (20cm) dressmaker's shears** are also used for cutting fabric. The difference between shears and scissors is that scissors are 2–6in (5–15cm) long and have equally sized, round finger holes, while shears are longer and have a small hole for the thumb and a larger hole for multiple fingers.
7. A **serger ripper** is small scalpel-like knife that is very sharp and perfect for cutting the multiple threads of a serger seam.
8. A **seam ripper** is used for unpicking seams.
9. **Tweezers, both straight and bent**, are helpful in threading the serger, grabbing or holding beads and other small items, and pulling thread tails.

Marking tools

A range of specialist tools and standard stationery items can be used to mark fabric.

1. A **quilt pounce** holds finely ground chalk for pattern transfers.
2. **Mechanical pencils** are ideal because they are always sharp.
3. A **razor-point pen** bleeds through fabric when marking multiple muslin layers.
4. **Fine- and large-point permanent pens** bleed through fabric layers, but will not wash off.
5. **Fine- and medium-point heat-erasable pens** have ink that disappears with steam; sometimes they leave a residue, so test on a scrap.
6. **Air-erasable pens** have ink that disappears with exposure to air—from 12 hours to never, so test on a fabric scrap.
7. **Dressmaker's pencils** come in a variety of colors: white for dark fabric, blue for light fabric, etc.
8. A **hem gauge** is a small ruler with an inset triangular piece that can be positioned along the ruler when making recurring marks.
9. A **point turner** will get into the points of corners to turn them right side out without poking through the fabric.
10. **Chalk** comes finely ground for a **wheeled dispenser** or quilt pounce, or compressed in **triangles** and pencils. Wheeled dispenser chalk brushes away; other forms are more permanent.
11. Plain **soap slivers** leave a mark that can be wiped off with a washcloth; soap with moisturizers leaves a permanent greasy mark.
12. **Tailor's wax** is a colored wax that is permanent.
13. A **hole punch** and a safety pin are handy for attaching notes to samples: labeling them as preshrunk, detailing stitch length, etc.
14. An **awl and serrated pattern wheel** make individual holes or a line of holes, respectively. The awl can also be used to ease trim under the sewing machine's presser foot.
15. **Pattern weights** can be used to hold down anything from a pattern paper to a feather boa. Large washers like these from a hardware store may be covered in grease, so wash them before use.

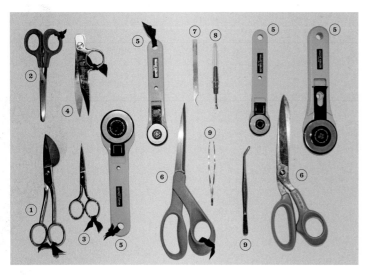

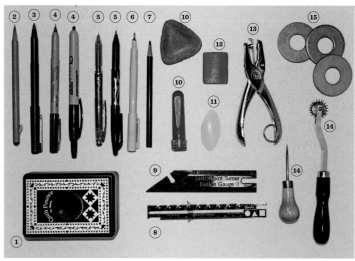

Rulers

A range of rulers is indispensable for tackling different jobs.

1. A **vary form curve ruler** has a numbered edge designed to mimic an armhole and neckline, making it ideal for pattern making.
2. A **small clear plastic ruler** is useful for quick measurements.
3. A **large clear plastic ruler** has holes along the centerline that are handy for drawing large circles (see Steps 1 and 2, p. 40).
4. A **cloth tape measure** is used for measuring the human form and other three-dimensional objects.
5. A **metal-edged clear plastic ruler** can be used for measuring and for cutting small things with a rotary cutter, as the metal will protect the plastic from the cutter's blade.
6. An **L square** keeps lines perpendicular to one other.
7. A **large metal ruler**, 2in (5cm) wide x 48in (122cm) long, can be used for larger tasks, and helps keep rotary cutters on a straight path.

Pins and needles

Very sharp pins and needles are essential when working with fine fabrics; replace them when they become bent or dull. Needles are sized by wire width; the thinner the wire, the higher the gauge number. Think of it this way: if only one needle is cut from a length of wire, it is a one-gauge needle; if you stretch the same piece of wire, making it longer but thinner to cut three needles, then each needle will be a three-gauge needle.

1. **Flowerhead pins** have large heads that prevent the pins from slipping through net, lace, and other loosely woven fabrics.
2. $1^3/_4$in (4.5cm) **quilting pins** are sharp, with easy-to-grab heads.
3. $1^1/_2$in (3.8cm) **glass-head pins** are shorter and easy to handle.
4. $1^1/_4$in (3cm) **dressmaker's pins** are very thin and sharp, sliding easily into any fabric.
5. **Toothpicks** have squared-off bodies, making them perfect for sitting on top of a button when making a shank.

6. **Betweens** or **quilting needles**, sizes 10, 7, 5, are short with small eyes.
7. **Sharps**, sizes 12, 10, 7, 2, are all-purpose hand-sewing needles.
8. An **easy-thread needle** or **self-threading needle** allows you to pull the thread into the eye from the top, which is useful when burying the thread tail between layers of fabric (see Trapunto, Step 3, p. 117).
9. A **ballpoint** needle is used for sewing knit fabrics. Rather than piercing the fibers like a regular needle, the ballpoint needle slides between them; if you pierce the fibers of a knit fabric it can run.
10. **Embroidery (or crewel) needles**, sizes 10, 7, 5, 3, have long eyes for holding multiple-stranded embroidery thread, which makes them easy to thread. They can also be used for quick hand-sewing projects.
11. A **chenille needle** has a very long eye, perfect for ribbon embroidery; the ribbon can lie flat in the eye, reducing stress on the ribbon.
12. A **darning needle** has a round eye and a long shaft, making it ideal for basting larger projects.
13. A **tapestry needle** has a blunt tip and large eye for holding multiple-stranded thread.
14. A **double-eyed needle** is perfect for threading serger thread tails back through the serging at the end of a seam. Protecting the thread tails from abrasion keeps the serger's stitching from unraveling.
15. **Thimbles**, designed to protect the pointer or middle fingers, are available in several materials, shapes, and sizes. **Leather thimbles** are sized from small to large. **Metal thimbles**, sized from 6 to 15, are available with closed ends, open ends, and as a **ring version** designed to sit below the fingernail.
16. A **needle threader** helps thread the needle when the eye is tiny, as on a quilting needle, or if the thread frays easily, as in metallic threads.
17. A $1^3/_8$in (3.5cm) round **rubber needle grabber** helps to pull needle and thread through several layers of fabric.
18. A cake of **beeswax** can be used to strengthen hand-sewing thread and help keep it from tangling; pull the thread through it twice. You can then iron the thread, sandwiched between layers of muslin, to melt the wax into the thread and remove any extra wax if you wish.

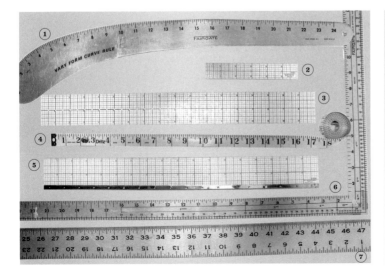

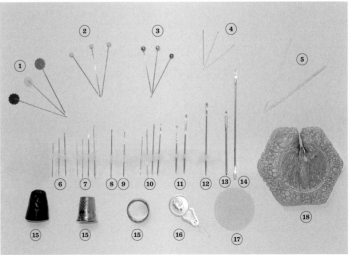

Sewing machine feet

Having the proper sewing machine foot can turn a tedious, difficult project into a quick and easy one. There are hundreds of sewing machine feet to choose from, but before you invest in additional feet, ascertain whether your sewing machine takes low-shank, high-shank, or slant-shank feet. Shown here are some high-shank feet.

1. A **regular straight stitch foot** with a finger guard; the toes are each $1/4$in (6mm) wide.
2. A **right cording foot**, also used as a **zipper foot**.
3 A **little foot**; the toes are each $1/8$in (3mm) wide.
4. An $1/8$in **(3mm) edgestitching foot**; if you place the edge of the fabric against the offset metal guide the stitching will be $1/8$in (3mm) from the fabric edge.
5. A **roller foot** is helpful when sewing velvets, leather, vinyl, and plastics as the rollers help to ease the fabrics out from the needle.
6. An **invisible zipper foot** has two channels on the underside of the foot and a hole in between them for the needle. Place one side of the invisible zipper coil in one channel, and the sewing machine will accurately sew the zipper in place. Repeat, using the other channel for the other coil.
7. Like an invisible zipper foot, a **piping foot** has a channel underneath and a hole for the needle. When used with the correct width of filler the piping foot produces evenly sewn piping. Unfortunately, these feet only work well with the specific filler to fit the channel, requiring purchase of multiple feet for different piping sizes.
8. A **satin stitch foot** has a flat channel just behind the needle hole to allow the thicker thread of a dense satin stitch to slide under the foot.

Pressing tools

Proper ironing and pressing helps give your sewing project a couture finish.

1. A **wooden pressing block** provides a surface for hard-to-reach, tricky parts of a garment. The straight, narrow surface on the top, for example, is perfect for pressing open a seam without leaving an impression on the right side of the fabric. A set of padded covers (not shown) enhances the pressing block.
2. A **needle board** keeps a velvet or corduroy pile from being crushed when pressed.
3. A **ham** is placed under curved seams for pressing.
4. An industrial gravity-fed **iron** is designed to be "on" all day. The water-bottle reservoir can be refilled any time the water runs low, and steam is produced when the iron is horizontal or vertical.
5. A small **table-top ironing board** sits on a work table. A large ironing mat can also be placed on the table when ironing and preshrinking large pieces of fabric.
6. This **work table** is 44in (112cm) wide x 66in (168cm) long, and 38in (97cm) tall, so that the user does not have to stoop too much while working.
7. A **Teflon sheet** (not shown) acts as press cloth when working with fusibles, keeping the iron's soleplate clean.

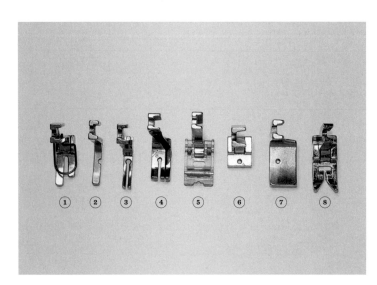

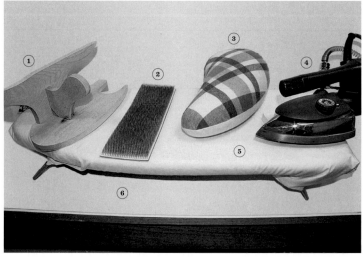

Interfacings and stabilizers

The terms "interfacing" and "stabilizer" are often used interchangeably. Although the materials are ever evolving, here are some guidelines to help you make sense of these products.

Originally, interfacings were created to add shaping and support to garments: for the roll of a collar or to stiffen a corset, for instance. Once always woven—from lightweight organza to heavyweight horsehair canvas—now knit and mesh web interfacings are available, some of which can work without limiting stretch fabrics. Most interfacings are designed to stay in a garment forever and can be divided into two groups: sew-in and fusible. Sew-in interfacings are sewn into a garment at the seam line. Fusible interfacings have a resin or glue on the wrong side that is melted with the heat of an iron. When using fusibles, always use a press cloth between the interfacing and the iron; the resin or glue can seep between the fibers and gum up the iron's soleplate. Some interfacings need to be preshrunk before using; some fuse better with a dry iron; some fuse better with a damp press cloth or steam. Make sure you read any specific usage instructions that come with your interfacing.

Stabilizers steady a fashion fabric against the force of sewing machine stitches, particularly in machine embroidery and free-motion quilting. Stabilizers are not woven; they are extruded fibers that may have a discernible warp and weft pattern, or a mesh web. Some stabilizers are paper products. Most are designed to be removed once the stitching is completed. Temporary stabilizers have specific methods of removal: tear-away, wash-away, or heat-away. Fusible stabilizers can be fused to fabric on one or both sides, depending on the product. Again, make sure you read the manufacturer's instructions.

Interfacings

Woven sew-in: These traditional interfacings range from silk organza to hair canvas. They need to be sewn into the garment.

Woven fusibles: These are newer versions of woven interfacings with resin or glue on the wrong side, which melts when ironed, fusing the interfacing to the fabric. Often they use the same fabrics as non-fusible interfacings but with resin dots added to one side.

Knits: Like woven fusibles but generally with a softer hand. Many knit interfacings are designed to stretch with knit fabric even after fusing. Knit interfacings work well with woven fabrics, too, and are thin enough to be used in multiple layers to achieve the right support.

Paper fusibles: Not recommended for use in garments; during laundering the paper may fail, wadding up like a tissue that has been through the washing machine.

IRONING WRINKLES FROM FUSIBLE INTERFACING

If fusible interfacing gets wrinkled, place a sheet of kitchen parchment paper or a Teflon pressing sheet under it against the glue, and use a cool iron to slowly smooth out the wrinkles.

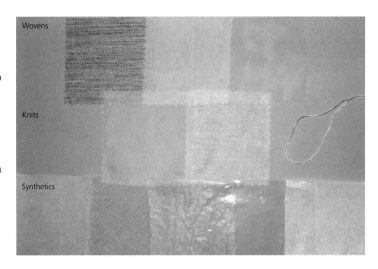

Top row: Wovens—hair canvas, lightweight interfacing, silk organza.
Middle row: Knits—knit interfacing, weft insertion interfacing and fusible thread.
Bottom row: Synthetics—fusible mesh with paper backing, fusible mesh without paper backing, wash-away interfacing, heat-away interfacing, tear-away interfacing.

Stabilizers

Paper non-fusibles, specifically tear-away and cut-away: These work well for pattern transfers and as temporary stabilizers. Tear-away comes in different weights or strengths to match different weight fabrics. Most stores carry only one weight; multiple weights can be found online. To use as a pattern-transfer medium, run a sheet through a desktop printer to print directly on the interfacing. Pin the printed design onto the fabric, sew the embellishment on top, then tear away the interfacing, leaving the embellishment on the fabric. Cut-away stabilizers are "permanent": excess stabilizer is cut away, but remains under the embellishment.

Synthetic mesh non-fusibles: Wash-away and iron-away stabilizers are ideal for delicate fabrics; they offer support during sewing then dissolve with water or heat. Wash-away stabilizers can be used as pattern-tracing aids, but have not yet advanced enough to be able to go through a printer. They come in multiple weights to suit different embellishment and fabric weights. Iron-away stabilizers come in one weight, so far, and are designed for pattern tracing and to keep machine threads from becoming ensnarled in the fabric. Both the fabric and the embellishment must be able to withstand immersion in water or prolonged heat from an iron while these meshes are removed. Follow the manufacturer's directions to remove them.

Synthetic mesh fusibles: These are mesh sheets that fuse two fabrics with ironing: for example, an appliqué to a base fabric. Wonder-Under® has a paper backing that allows you to fuse it to the appliqué and then peel off the backing to fuse the appliqué to the base fabric. Stitch Witchery® has no paper backing, so you must position both fabrics before fusing.

A subset of this group is fusible thread; use it in a needle or bobbin to create a thin "line" of resin or glue when stitching. After sewing, press the piece to the base fabric to fuse it in place along the stitched line.

Transferring patterns

Heat-erasable and air-erasable pens

Heat-erasable pens have ink that disappears when exposed to the heat of an iron. Air-erasable pens have ink that fades over time—a couple of hours to two days. Both pens may leave a faint residue on fabric, so check them on a fabric scrap. Here a heat-erasable pen is used to mark guidelines on fabric for a cross-stitch pattern.

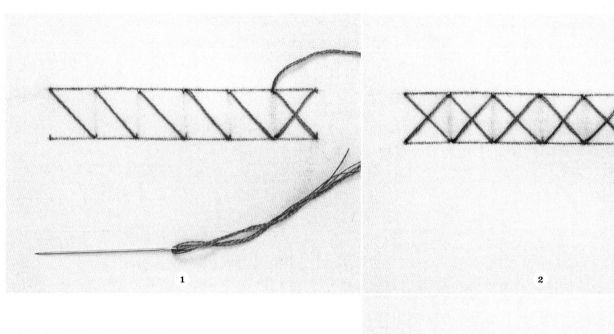

1 Use the heat-erasable or air-erasable pen to mark the stitch placement.

2 Complete the stitching.

3 Steam the fabric with the stitching; be sure to follow the manufacturer's instructions. The heat-erasable pen marks will disappear.

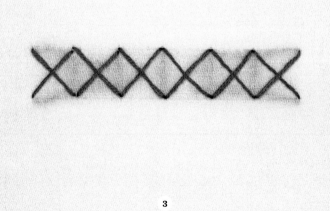

Tear-away interfacing or tissue paper

Tear-away interfacing comes in a variety of weights; lightweight is suitable for most of the techniques shown in this book. Tear-away interfacing can be drawn on directly or used in a home printer; this allows you to adjust a design on your computer to fit your garment and then print it out. Tissue paper can also be used, but may not work well in the printer. Here tear-away interfacing is used to transfer a computer-designed pattern for a piece of decorative braid to fabric.

PRINTING ON TEAR-AWAY INTERFACING

Use your desktop printer to print your design onto tear-away interfacing:

1. Cut the tear-away interfacing to fit on a piece of paper that will fit through your printer.

2. Place several pieces of double-sided sticky tape across the top of the piece of plain paper. Stick the interfacing to the double-sided sticky tape.

3. Feed the piece of interfacing attached to the plain paper into your printer as a single unit and print your design.

1

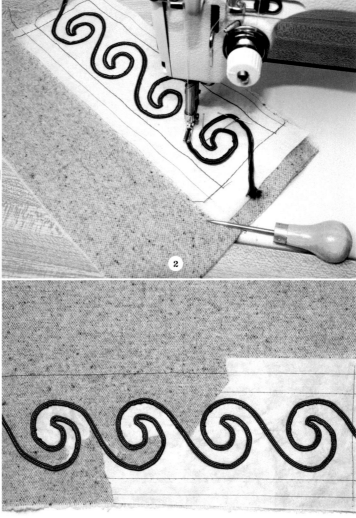

2

3

1 Print the pattern onto tear-away interfacing (see box above right), then peel away the regular paper. Pin the braid to the pattern on the tear-away interfacing.

2 Baste the interfacing to the fabric (here, basted in red thread). Sew the braid to the fabric through the interfacing.

3 Once the pattern is complete, remove the tear-away interfacing from the fabric.

Chalk and oak tag

Chalk or heat-erasable pens can be used to draw around a pattern drawn on oak tag or card stock. When cutting out the pattern, consider whether to use the positive space or the negative space as your guide. Here chalk and oak tag are used to transfer a pattern for appliqué pieces to fabric.

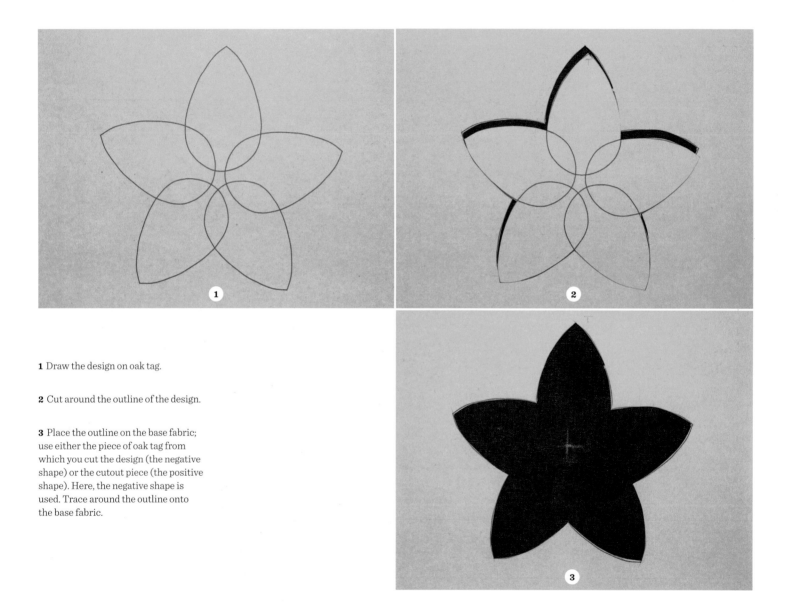

1 Draw the design on oak tag.

2 Cut around the outline of the design.

3 Place the outline on the base fabric; use either the piece of oak tag from which you cut the design (the negative shape) or the cutout piece (the positive shape). Here, the negative shape is used. Trace around the outline onto the base fabric.

Machine basting

Machine basting can be used to mark a seam line for turning under or pressing with great accuracy, or as an aid for turning the seam allowance on lightweight fabrics. This technique can also be used to mark hemlines accurately. Before you begin, make sure the machine stitching does not leave permanent holes in the fabric. Here machine basting is used to mark a seam allowance in reverse appliqué.

1 Machine-stitch the seam line. Here, the pattern was transferred using an oak tag pattern traced with chalk; the pattern was then machine-basted as the chalk line disappeared too quickly to be useful.

2 Turn the seam allowance under and pin or press in place. Sew.

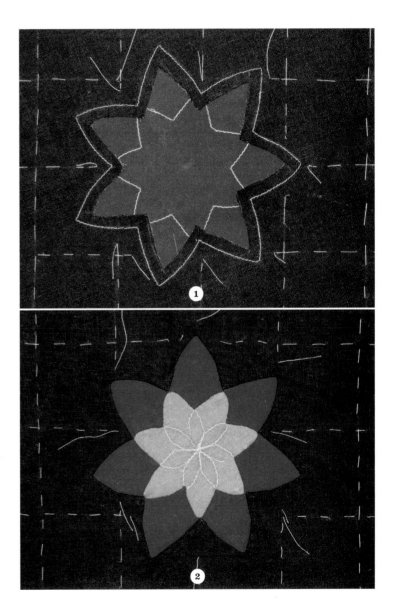

Pouncing

Pouncing involves transferring a pattern onto fabric by forcing finely ground chalk through holes punched in the design lines of the pattern. This method allows you to sew a pattern directly onto fabric rather than through interfacing. Here an appliqué pattern is transferred onto fabric.

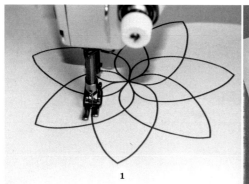

1 Print or draw your design on a piece of heavy paper or card stock. Change your sewing machine needle to a heavy-duty needle (e.g., #16/100). Remove all thread from the machine. Sew along the design lines so that the needle makes holes in the paper.

2 Pin the punched paper to the fabric.

3 Shake a little powered chalk onto the paper and use a finger to smear it along the line of holes.

4 Continue smearing the chalk until all the lines have been covered. Lift off the paper. Shake excess chalk into a folded piece of paper and return it to the container. Do not shake off the fabric, as this may dislodge the chalked design.

5 The completed chalk-drawn design.

MACHINE SEWING ON PAPER

When you have finished sewing the paper, put this needle aside and label it "paper sewing needle." Once a needle has been used to sew paper it will not sew fabric well.

POWDERED CHALK

You will need some powdered chalk for this method. Powdered dressmaker's chalk is available as refills for Chaco liner tools. You can also make your own by crushing chalkboard chalk or tailor's chalk in a small bag to produce a fine powder.

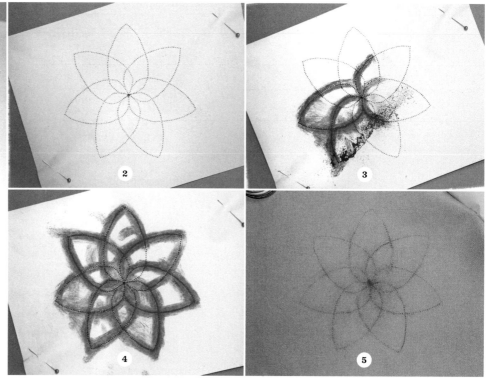

USING A QUILT POUNCE

A quilt pounce, or pounce pad, holds ground chalk in a box. Using a quilt pounce to pat chalk over punched design lines is much neater than smearing the chalk with your fingers, though both methods give the same result.

A quilt pounce ready to be patted over a punched design.

The transferred design with the underside of the quilt pounce.

Pattern paper

Designs can be drawn on plain pattern paper and pinned to fabric.
The fabric can then be cut out around the pattern, or seam lines
and allowances can be marked with chalk or a dressmaker's pencil.
Here an appliqué pattern is transferred onto fabric.

1 Transfer the design to pattern paper.
(Here a non-fusible paper web product
was used.) Pin the pattern to the fabric.
Cut the fabric along the cutting line.

2 Using chalk or a dressmaker's pencil,
mark the seam line. You can either cut
away the seam allowance from the
paper pattern and use the new pattern
edge as a guide (as shown here) or you
can remove the pattern and mark the
seam line by measuring in from the
fabric edges.

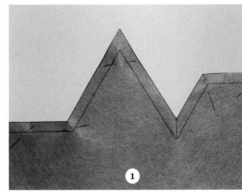
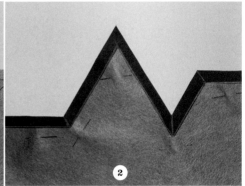

Freezer paper

Freezer paper is coated with plastic on one side that melts slightly when
ironed. This sticks to fabric, yet the paper can be easily peeled off and
reused, making it very useful for marking designs on fabric. Here freezer
paper is used to transfer a pattern for appliqué pieces onto fabric.

1 Print or draw the design elements
onto the matte side of a sheet of freezer
paper. Place the freezer paper, shiny
side down, on the wrong side of the
fabric and iron the two layers to lightly
adhere the freezer paper to the fabric.

2 Cut out the shapes (here the shapes
in the bottom row still need some
trimming). Peel the freezer paper off
the fabric pieces.

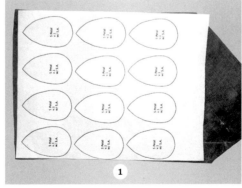
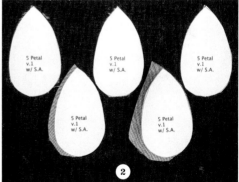

PRINTING ON FREEZER PAPER

Use your desktop printer to print your design onto freezer paper:

1. Cut the freezer paper to fit onto a piece of paper that will fit through your printer.

*2. Stick the freezer paper to the plain paper with double-sided sticky tape, with the shiny side against
the plain paper and the matte side facing out. This will prevent the plastic on the freezer paper from
melting slightly, and gumming up the printer as it passes through.*

3. Feed the piece of freezer paper attached to the plain paper into your printer and print your design.

Basic stitches

Balanced sewing machine stitch

A balanced sewing machine stitch has the proper tension adjustments for both the needle and bobbin threads. For all sewing machine stitches, the needle and bobbin threads should meet and intertwine in between the two layers of fabric.

Most sewing machines arrive from the factory properly set for sewing with plain thread: polyester, or cotton-wrapped polyester core. When you sew with a thinner thread (like monofilament thread) or a thicker thread (like button thread), you will need to adjust the tension settings. The thinner the thread, the harder the tension disks must grip it to control the thread properly; thicker threads require less tension.

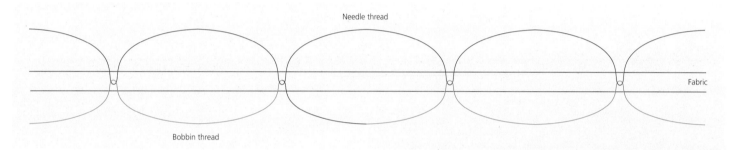

Needle thread

Fabric

Bobbin thread

ADJUSTING THE NEEDLE THREAD TENSION

If your tension dial does not have numbers marked on it, draw a line on it; think of the line as a clock hand and note the "time." Always adjust the tension settings a quarter-turn at a time. Turn the tension dial clockwise to tighten the tension and counterclockwise to loosen it. Using different colors of thread in the needle and bobbin when balancing the tensions will help you see which thread is which; use the same brand and type of threads and fabric in the tension samples as you will be using for the final garment.

ADJUSTING THE BOBBIN THREAD TENSION

To gauge if the tension is set properly on your bobbin casing, pass the thread through the casing's tension disk normally. Pull out 6–12in (15–30cm) of thread; the thread should glide out easily. Now hang the bobbin casing in the air; the bobbin should not unwind when held still. If you jerk the thread, as if the bobbin casing were a yoyo, the thread should unspool a couple of inches.

If the tension is too tight, loosen the tension screw on the bobbin casing— the larger of the two screws holding the tension disks. You can also buy extra bobbin casings, adjust them, and reserve them to use with thinner or thicker threads.

Machine gathering stitch

When gathering a single layer of fabric, set the stitch length to 5mm (5 spi). The needle thread will loop to the wrong side of the fabric, as shown in the diagram below. The bobbin thread is not pulled up to form a tight stitch, but sits at the bottom of the loops formed by the needle thread. After stitching two rows of gathering stitches, gently pull on the bobbin threads and the fabric will gather up. If you pull the needle thread by mistake, each of those long loops will need to be pulled up in order to be successfully gathered; the needle thread will likely jam before the gathering is complete. Placing white thread in the bobbin whenever you sew gathering stitches will remind you which is the bobbin thread.

STITCH LENGTH	
Stitches per inch (spi)	Millimeters (mm)
50 spi	0.5mm
25 spi	1mm
20 spi	1.3mm
15 spi	1.5mm
12 spi	2mm
10 spi	2.5mm
8 spi	3mm
6 spi	4mm
5 spi	5mm

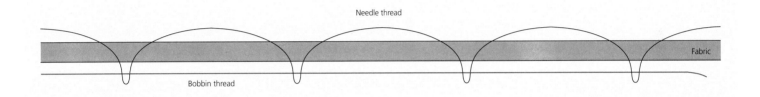

Needle thread

Fabric

Bobbin thread

Balanced zigzag stitch

When sewing with zigzag stitch, check the appearance of your stitches on both the right and wrong sides of the fabric to make sure your needle and bobbin threads are set at the correct tension.

1. Too tight: The needle tension is too tight; the bobbin thread is pulled through to the right side of the fabric.
2. Too loose: On the right side of the fabric, the zigzags form nice triangles and the bobbin thread is not showing, but on the wrong side the needle thread is showing through at the stitch points.
3. Just right: On the right side of the fabric, the zigzags form nice triangles and the bobbin thread is just showing at the stitch points; on the wrong side, the needle thread is just showing at the stitch points.

Right side

Wrong side

USING TISSUE PAPER TO PREVENT TUNNELING

Sometimes a zigzag stitch will cause fabric to curl up slightly underneath the stitches, forming a "tunnel." Placing tissue paper under the fabric, against the feed dogs, may help to prevent this.

Without tissue paper, there is some minor tunneling of the fabric.

With tissue paper, the stitches and the fabric pucker less.

Sewing with monofilament thread

Monofilament thread, also known as invisible thread, is useful for sewing multicolored trim where sewing with one color would be too prominent and would negatively affect the design.

Monofilament thread is available in polyester and nylon. Polyester thread will not discolor with age and has a higher melting point; nylon thread may melt when pressed with a hot iron. Both polyester and nylon threads are available in "Clear" for use with light-colored fabric and "Smoke" for use with darker colors.

When sewing with monofilament threads, samples should be made to test the needle and bobbin tensions and to be sure the thread will spool off properly. Often, too much thread reels off the spool and twists around itself, causing thread loops or knots along the thread path; the thread will then jam and the sample will bunch up. Try using a mesh thread net or make one from an old nylon stocking. Place the mesh or stocking around the spool of thread, with the thread threaded through the top and then threaded through the machine normally. Similarly, a piece of sticky tape at the top of the thread stand may keep the thread from jumping off the spool and out of the thread guides.

Monofilament thread can be used in the needle or the bobbin. As the thread is very thin, you can use a very thin needle, like a Microtex; you can use a regular sewing machine needle too. Because the thread is so thin, you will need to tighten the tension disk (see p. 24). If you are using monofilament thread in the bobbin, wind it slowly, and do not fill the bobbin all the way. You might want to get a second bobbin case just for monofilament, as it is very hard to accurately change the tension of the bobbin case as you switch threads. Recording exactly where the tension disks are set on a perfectly stitched sample will also save you time when you next use monofilament thread.

Polyester monofilament thread in "Clear" and "Smoke."

A mesh thread net can help monofilament thread to spool off properly, preventing twists and knots.

It is important to test the tension of the needle and bobbin thread before you begin a project using monofilament thread, to make sure you have your settings just right.

The samples below have been sewn with monofilament thread in the needle (Smoke in lines 1, 2, and 3; Clear in line 4) and regular thread in the bobbin. The photographs show the stitch line from the right side and the wrong side.

Right side   Wrong side

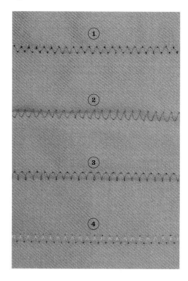 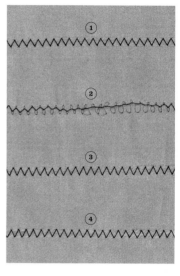

1. Too tight: The needle tension is too tight; the bobbin thread is pulled from the wrong side to the right side.
2. Too loose: The zigzags are nice triangles and the bobbin thread is not showing on the right side at the stitch points, but on the wrong side the monofilament thread is showing through.
3. Just right: The zigzags are nice triangles and the bobbin thread is just showing on the right side at the stitch points.
4. Just right: When sewn with Clear monofilament thread, the sewing line disappears. On the wrong side, the threads are well balanced and the bobbin thread makes a neat stitch.

Basting

Grid basting

Grid basting is a good way to hold two fabrics together so they function as one. Here a pink mesh with flocked black spots is backed with a darker pink lining fabric. Grid basting can be used on long lengths of fabric or on individual pattern pieces after they have been cut out.

SEWING DIRECTION

Work all the basting lines in the same direction. If you sew the lines going up the fabric and then down it, you can unintentionally push the fabric up and then down with each row of basting, forming a sort of herringbone pattern.

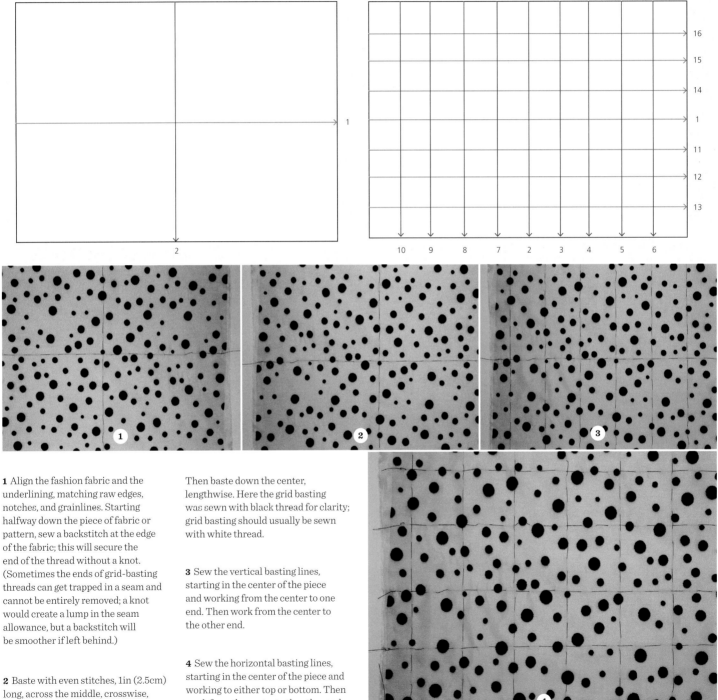

1 Align the fashion fabric and the underlining, matching raw edges, notches, and grainlines. Starting halfway down the piece of fabric or pattern, sew a backstitch at the edge of the fabric; this will secure the end of the thread without a knot. (Sometimes the ends of grid-basting threads can get trapped in a seam and cannot be entirely removed; a knot would create a lump in the seam allowance, but a backstitch will be smoother if left behind.)

2 Baste with even stitches, 1in (2.5cm) long, across the middle, crosswise, of the fabric or pattern piece.

Then baste down the center, lengthwise. Here the grid basting was sewn with black thread for clarity; grid basting should usually be sewn with white thread.

3 Sew the vertical basting lines, starting in the center of the piece and working from the center to one end. Then work from the center to the other end.

4 Sew the horizontal basting lines, starting in the center of the piece and working to either top or bottom. Then work from the center to the other end.

Diagonal basting

A diagonal basting stitch can be used to baste bulky pieces of trim and items such as zippers in place. The completed stitch looks like a Z, with the diagonal stitch showing on one side of the fabric and two horizontal stitches showing on the other side. When sewn as a permanent stitch, it is called a pad stitch and is used extensively in tailoring.

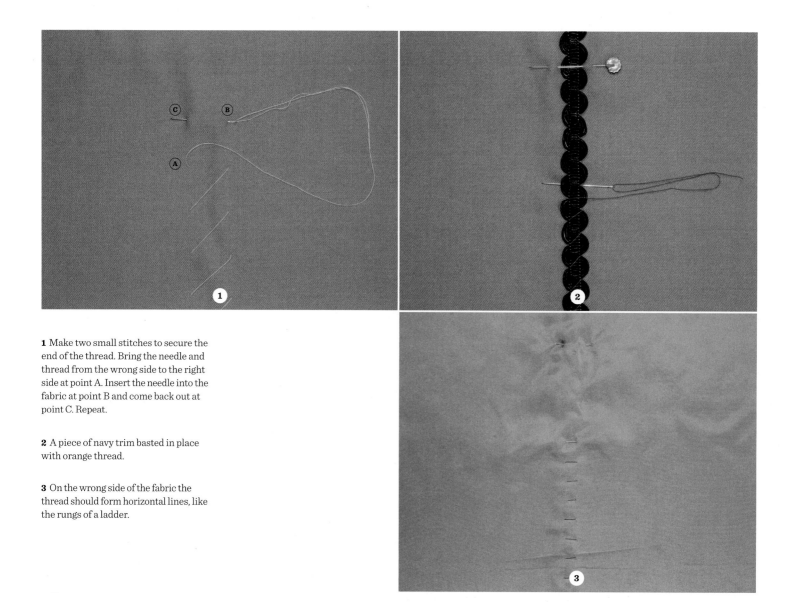

1 Make two small stitches to secure the end of the thread. Bring the needle and thread from the wrong side to the right side at point A. Insert the needle into the fabric at point B and come back out at point C. Repeat.

2 A piece of navy trim basted in place with orange thread.

3 On the wrong side of the fabric the thread should form horizontal lines, like the rungs of a ladder.

Knotting thread ends

Making a knot for hand sewing

You can knot a thread by looping the thread around a finger and then rolling the loop down and off the finger; this makes a lumpy knot, which can be useful. There are occasions, however, when you need a smaller knot, which is shown below.

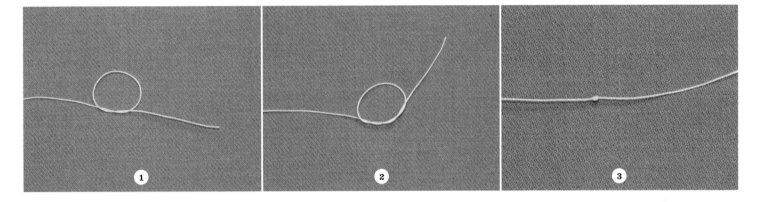

1 Make a loop in the end of the thread. Slide the end of the thread through the loop.

2 Slide the end of the thread through the loop a second time. If a larger knot is needed you can slide the end of the thread through the loop a third time.

3 Pull the loop closed to finish the knot.

Hiding the knot at the beginning of sewing

When sewing two or more layers together, it is often necessary to hide the knot at the beginning and end of your stitching so that the knot is not seen from either the right or wrong side of the fabric.

CUTTING THE THREAD TAIL

When making a knot in the end of the thread do not cut the thread right next to the knot: the thread end will unravel slightly and the knot will come undone. Trim the thread tail to ½in (1.3cm). When you bury the knot between the fabric layers, the thread tail should disappear too.

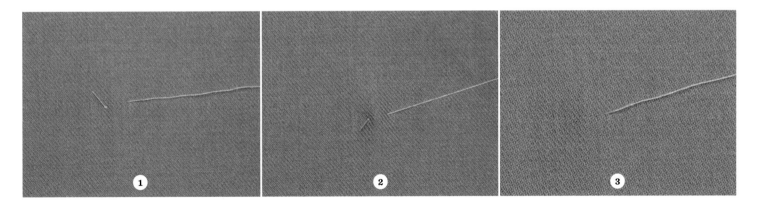

1 Make a small knot at the end of the thread. Insert the needle into the top fabric ½–1in (1.3–2.5cm) away from where your first stitch will start. Slide the needle and thread between the layers of fabric and come up where your first stitch will start.

2 Wrap the thread around your finger and pull gently until you hear a pop as the knot goes through the top fabric. The knot will catch between the layers, and the thread tail should disappear.

3 The knot buried between the layers.

Hiding the knot at the end of sewing

When you reach the end of your sewing, you can hide the knot between the layers of fabric, just as you did at the start.

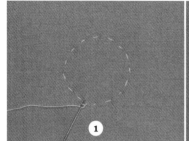 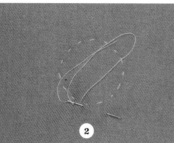 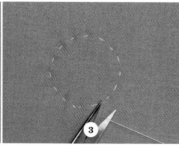 

1 Make a knot in the thread before completing the last stitch.

2 Complete the stitch. Slide the needle and thread between the layers of fabric and come back up ½–1in (1.3–2.5cm) away from your last stitch, pulling gently until the knot pops through the fabric.

3 Pulling slightly on the needle and thread, cut the thread close to the fabric surface. When the thread is snipped the new end of the thread should disappear back between the fabric layers.

4 The knot and the end of the thread are hidden between the layers of fabric.

Knotting threads after machine stitching

If you do not want to backstitch when machine stitching, you can hand-knot the threads instead.

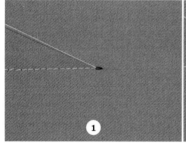 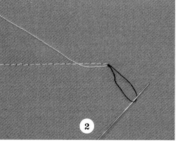 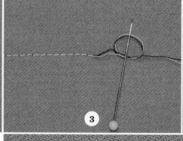 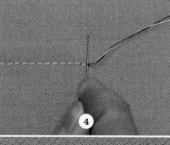

1 Working from the wrong side, tug on the bobbin thread (here white) to pull the needle thread (here magenta) through to the wrong side.

2 Once the needle thread can be grasped, insert a pin into the loop to help pull it all the way through.

3 Knot the needle thread with the corresponding bobbin thread using an overhand knot. Insert a pin into the loop to guide the knot down the length of the thread.

4 Bring the knot to the fabric surface.

5 The completed knot on the wrong side of the fabric.

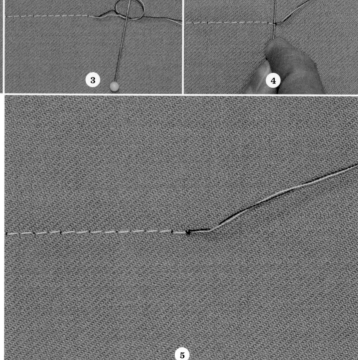

Pressing seams

It is a good idea to press seams straight after sewing them, sometimes called "sandwich pressing." After sewing, the stitches that make up the seam sit on top of the fabric, creating a small ridge of thread. Pressing directly on top of the seam helps to embed the thread into the yarns of the fabric.

Once a new seam has been pressed, it can be further pressed as needed, with the seam allowances open or to one side.

PRESS CLOTHS

An unhemmed piece of lightweight natural or white silk organza makes an excellent press cloth. Lightweight organza is sheer enough to see through but sturdy enough to keep fashion fabric from becoming shiny when pressed.

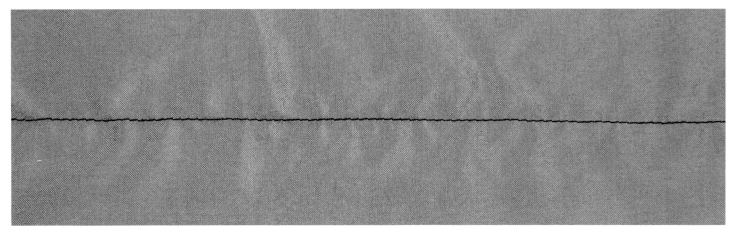

The newly sewn seam.

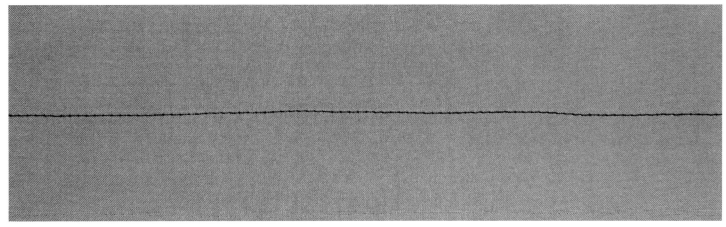

The seam after being pressed.

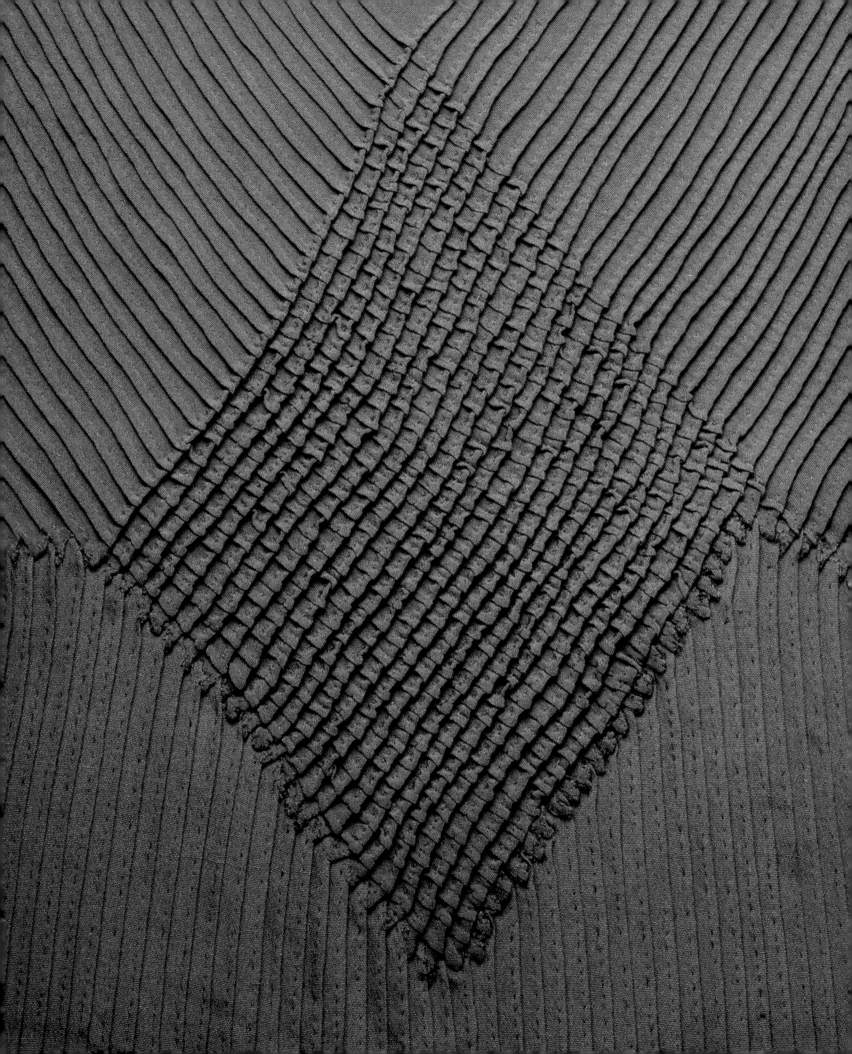

2
Fabric manipulation

Ruffles and flounces may conjure up images of pinafores and tiered skirts, but they can add elegant, even opulent, touches to a garment. The terms are often confused: ruffles are gathered along one edge before being attached to a base fabric, while flounces are sewn flat to a base fabric. The flare of flounces is created by the cut of the fabric used to create them.

Ruffles and flounces can be added to almost any part of a garment. They can be used to edge a hem, a neckline, or a cuff, while some parts of a garment, such as a peplum, are actually a form of flounce in themselves. Both can also be used to create decorative patterns and add texture to a plain fabric. There are several choices to make when creating ruffles and flounces, the most basic of which are the width, length, and density of the gathering.

2.1
Ruffles and flounces

A narrower ruffle or flounce will tend to stand proud of the base fabric, while the weight of a deeper ruffle will fall closer to the body. A tightly gathered ruffle will also stand away from the base, but a more loosely gathered ruffle might have a less prominent shape. Try a basic ruffle, then experiment with different styles.

Flounces can be circular or regular in width, or cut in a spiral to create a change in width from one end to the other. In addition to the decorative effect, a graded width is also useful for avoiding bulk in certain areas—for example, with a flounce that encircles an armhole, the narrower end can be positioned in the underarm area. Again, the width of the flounce and the size of the circle from which it is cut will affect the look.

Finally, hems can be given a ruffled effect by using fishing line in the hem or by stretching the fabric as it is run through a serger.

Basic ruffles

When gathering a light- to medium-weight fabric, a ratio of 2:1 (two times the gathered fabric to the base fabric) is good place to start. Here a piece of lightweight silk fabric 20in (50cm) long was gathered and sewn into a base fabric 10in (25cm) long.

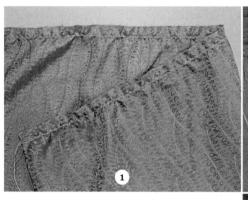

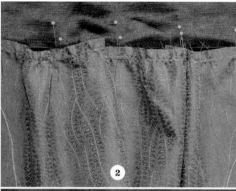

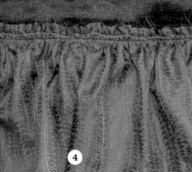

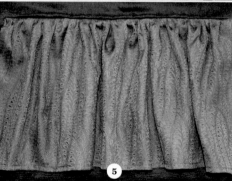

1 Hem the ruffle with the most suitable technique. Place a white threaded bobbin in the sewing machine and set the stitch length to very long. Assuming a $1/2$in (1.3cm) allowance, sew two lines of gathering stitches: the first line at $3/8$in (1cm) and the second line $1/16$in (1mm) from the seam line (see Machine Gathering Stitch, pp. 25).

2 Divide the gathered edge into four or more equal sections and place a pin at the start of each section. Divide the base fabric into the same number of sections and mark with pins. Pin the gathered fabric to the base fabric, matching section to section.

3 Gently pull on the white bobbin thread; the fabric should gather easily. When each section of the gathered fabric fits onto the base fabric, twist both the white bobbin thread and the needle thread around the end pins in a figure of eight to secure the gathering at the correct length. Distribute the gathers evenly within each section, releasing the thread around the pins if the gathering is too tight or too loose.

4 Hand-baste the gathered fabric to the base fabric and check the gathers from the right side to make sure they are even before stitching by machine. Here the basting thread is white and the sewing machine thread is orange. Press the seam allowance only.

5 The finished gathered piece.

VARIATION

Try tighter gathers. Here a piece of lightweight silk 40in (100cm) long is gathered to 10in (25cm)—a ratio of 4:1.

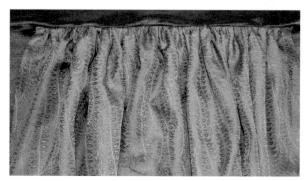

Gathering fabric over a cord

Gathering a thick fabric is easy if you use a machine to zigzag over a cord and then gather the fabric along the cord.

1

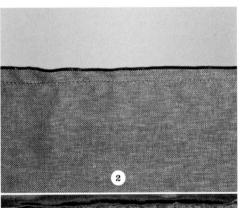

2

3

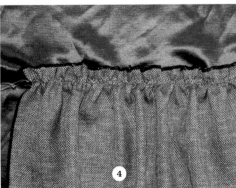

4

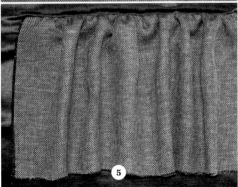

5

1 Set up the sewing machine with a zigzag stitch just wide enough to cover and hold the cord, but without catching the sides of the cord. The "cord" can be made from a range of fibers: bug tail—$^1/_{16}$in (1mm) to $^5/_8$in (1.5cm)—rayon cord or thread, heavy beading thread like C-Lon or S-Lon, or pearl cotton. Here pearl rayon cord was used.

2 Place the cord on the fabric at the gathering line, using pins to secure it. Sew over the cord with zigzag stitch.

3 Gather the fabric by sliding it along the cord. Place pins at each end of the gathering, and wrap the ends of the cord around the pins in a figure of eight to secure the gathering at the correct length.

4 Pin, hand-baste, and machine-sew the ruffle to the base fabric as described in Basic Ruffles (opposite).

5 The finished fabric gathered over a cord.

FINISHING THE RAW EDGES BEFORE GATHERING

If using a fabric that frays easily, clean-finish the edges (e.g., by serging) on all sides before gathering.

Double ruffles

A double ruffle is gathered in the center of the fabric to form two ruffles, one on either side. The fabric width will make a dramatic difference to the finished look—a narrow piece of fabric will form a V-shape standing proud of the garment, like the ruffles on a dress shirt; a wide piece will form two ruffles that fall in folds from the line of gathering stitches. A wide ruffle will also show both right and wrong sides, so choose your fabric carefully.

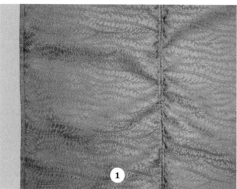

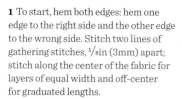

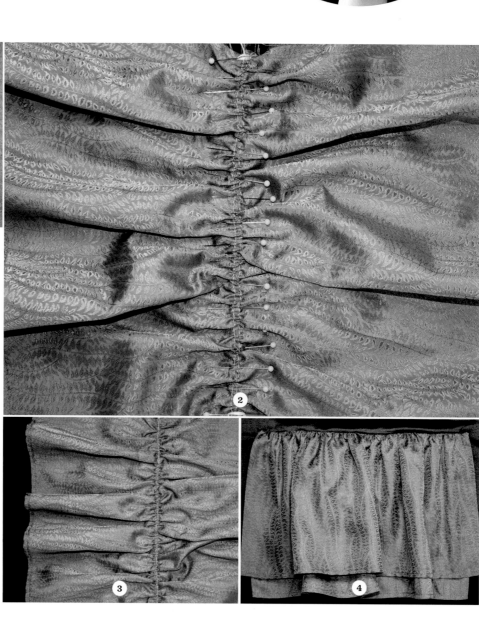

1 To start, hem both edges: hem one edge to the right side and the other edge to the wrong side. Stitch two lines of gathering stitches, 1/8 in (3mm) apart; stitch along the center of the fabric for layers of equal width and off-center for graduated lengths.

2 Gather the fabric to the correct length and pin in place on the base fabric. Hand-baste the ruffle, then remove the pins.

3 Sew the ruffle to the base fabric, stitching between the two lines of gathering stitches.

4 The finished double ruffle.

Circular flounces

Circular flounces are made from ring-shaped pieces of fabric. They are a little tricky because they can be dramatically affected by small changes in the size of the fabric pieces, and the placement of the cut from the inner circle (seam line) to the outer edge (hem). Changing the placement of the cut will affect the grainlines of the flounce. Changing the size of either the inner or outer circle will affect the size and depth of the flounce, as well as the length of the seam line.

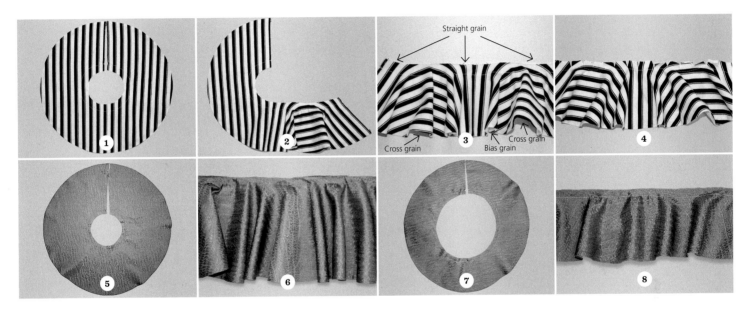

1 This circle has been cut from striped fabric, with the stripes following the straight grain. Note that the radius is cut along the straight grain at the top of the circle.

2 As the inner edge of the circle is straightened, the frills begin to form.

3 When the inner circle is pulled straight, the portions of the circle on the straight grain, at the ends and the center of the flounce, lie flat on the table, and will lie flat against the body, too. The cross-grain sections of the flounce, where the stripes are nearly horizontal, flare away from the table, just as they will flare away from the body.

4 If the seam allowance of the inner circle is clipped almost to the staystitching, along the seam line, the staystitching lies flat against the table. The flare in the cross-grain area is slightly reduced, while bias areas are allowed to ripple more.

5 Changing the size of the circles also affects the amount of frill. Here a circle with an outer diameter of 18in (46cm) has an inner circle with a diameter of 4$^1/_2$in (11.5cm).

6 As the inner edge of the circle is straightened along the seam line, note the fullness of the ruffle and length of the seam line, which is 16in (40.5cm).

7 This circle also has an outer diameter of 18in (46cm), but the diameter of the inner circle is 8in (20cm).

8 As the inner circle is straightened along the seam line, note the smaller amount of flare but the longer length of the seam line, which is 29in (73.5cm).

LINING A FLOUNCE

If lining the circle of fabric, cut the lining on the same grainline as the fashion fabric. If it is cut on a different grain, the two layers will fight and negate the frill. Stitch the fashion fabric and lining together along the circle's hemline at the outer edge. Turn the circles right sides out, then staystitch the two layers together along the seam line at the inner edge.

Sewing circular flounces

Circular flounces can be sewn onto a
garment horizontally or vertically, with
quite different results.

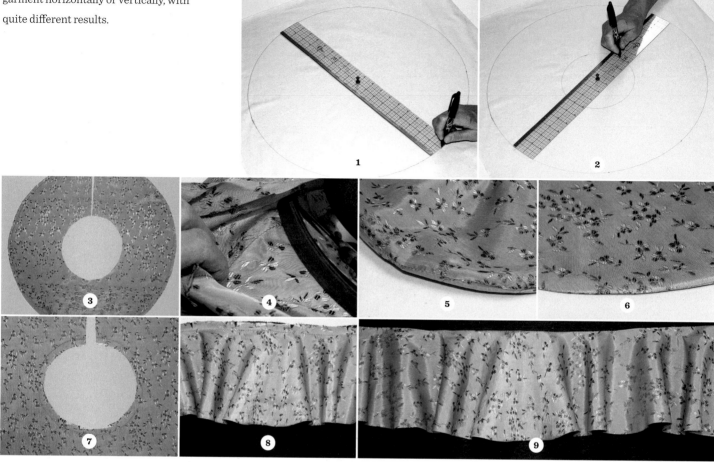

1 Draw a pattern on paper or muslin.
To draw a large circle, use a string or a
ruler with the pivot point in the center
and a pencil at the end. This ruler has
holes along the centerline through
which a pushpin can anchor the pivot
point. Keep the pencil at the end of the
ruler while turning the ruler around the
pivot point. Here the circle has a 9in
(22.5cm) radius.

2 To mark the smaller inner circle,
push the pencil in front of a set point
on the ruler as the ruler pivots, or insert
the pencil's point into one of the centerline holes. Here the pencil is at the 3in
(7.5cm) mark from the pivot point.

3 Cut the two circles out of fashion
fabric and cut the radius along the
straight grain. With right sides
together, stitch together the outer
circumferences of the two circles.
Press the seam to embed the stitches.

4 Open out the circles to expose a small
portion of the seam. Working vertically
across the seam, on the wrong side of
the fabric, press the seam, pushing the
tip of the iron just beyond the seam
allowance. This will push out the seam
line to the right side. Carefully work
your way around the inside of the
circle, pressing the seam without
introducing any unwanted creases.

5 When you have finished pressing the
inside of the circle, it will look like an
inflated pita bread.

6 Press the circles flat together, with
the seam line at the edge or rolled
slightly to the wrong side.

7 Sew the seam allowances of the
smaller, center circle together, wrong
sides together.

8 Open out the inner circle and sew its
edge to the base fabric, clipping the
seam allowance when necessary so it
lies flat. If you are sandwiching the
flounce between two layers of fabric,
sew the flounce to the bottom layer
first, so you can see how the flounce
drapes as you stitch.

9 The circular flounce sewn into
a seam.

VARIATION

Rotate the base fabric so that the
circular flounce hangs vertically to
create a different arrangement.

Spiral flounces

Spiral flounces use circles of fabric to create different flounce shapes.

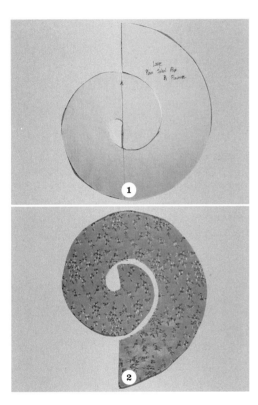

Left to right: Circular flounce, spiral flounce, graduated spiral flounce.

1 Draw a pattern on paper or muslin. Starting at the center of a large circle, draw a spiral toward the outer edge; here the spiral starts and finishes on the straight grain, but that is optional. The spiral should be of equal width along its length.

2 Cut out two spiral flounces and sew them together, right sides together, along the edges of the spiral, leaving the wide end open. Turn right side out, then sew the end closed; the center and the end of the spiral can be left out of the garment's seam to form a bell-like end. The finished seam line of this spiral flounce is 18in (46cm).

VARIATION

Make a graduated spiral flounce by cutting out a pattern with the width of the spiral decreasing toward the center of the circle. The finished seam line of this graduated spiral flounce is 27in (68.5cm) long.

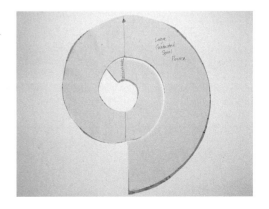

Fishing-line hems

Fishing line is a monofilament that can be sewn into a hem to create ruffles. It is classed by the strength of the line under tension—20lb test line is fairly lightweight and thin, while 80lb test line is stronger and thicker. Fishing line is stored on a spool and so has a tendency to curl; this is what creates the ruffle. You can alter the curliness with heat. Fabrics such as organza, voile, chiffon, and georgette work best with this hem technique, although a strong fishing line made extra curly can ruffle a lightweight cotton nicely. Cut hemlines on the bias for a frillier hem.

To make fishing line curlier, wind a length around a wooden rod (right). Be careful to wind with the existing curl. Tape the ends down. Place the wrapped wood in a pot of boiling water and boil for 3 minutes. Remove and cool thoroughly before unwinding the line.

For a looser curl, steam the fishing line with an iron. After winding the fishing line around the wood, steam it with an iron for a full minute. Let it cool completely on the wood.

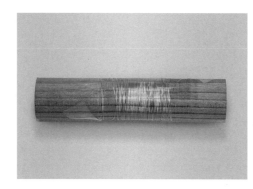

Wind fishing line around a wooden rod in preparation for boiling to tighten the curl. A large dowel, a piece of closet pole, or an old thread spool all work well.

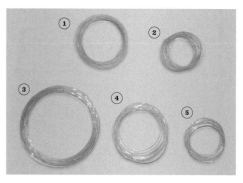

1. 20lb test fishing line as it comes off the spool.
2. The 20lb line after it has been boiled to tighten the curl.
3. 80lb test fishing line as it comes off the spool.
4. The 80lb line after it has been steamed.
5. The 80lb line after it has been boiled.

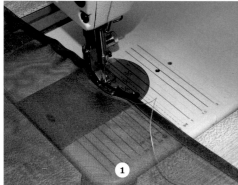

A double ruffle in polyester georgette, finished with a 20lb test line on the left and a boiled 20lb line on the right.

On the left: an 80lb test line; on the right: a boiled 80lb line.

1 On a piece of lightweight fabric (here polyester georgette is used), sew a tiny turned hem. With a 1in (2.5cm) hem allowance, sew a line of stitches with a regular stitch length ³/₄in (2cm) from the raw edge. Fold the hem allowance along the stitched line toward the wrong side of the fabric and press. Trim the hem allowance to ¹/₄in (6mm). The line of stitches will run near the center of the hem allowance facing you. Fold the fabric again, enclosing the raw edge, so that the stitched line is now pointing up, away from the finished edge. Press.

Slide the fishing line into the hem fold, all the way to the edge, so that it is not caught in the stitching. Sew the hem in the middle of the folded fabric, being sure to keep the fishing line inside the hem fold.

2 The finished hem.

Serger lettuce hems

Stitching a narrow turned hem with wooly nylon thread in the upper looper of a serger can create a curled hem. When you stretch the fabric as you guide it over the feed dogs, the hem will ruffle into a "lettuce edge." Usually this technique is used with knit fabrics, but if a lightweight woven fabric is cut on the bias and gathered, it can also be given a lettuce-edged hem.

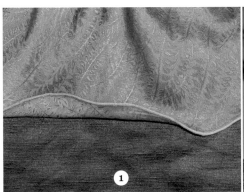

1 Set up the serger for a rolled hem. Place wooly nylon thread in the upper looper and regular serger thread in the lower looper and needle. Adjust the looper tensions: the upper looper should be quite loose and the lower looper quite tight. Set the needle tension to normal. Test the settings on scraps of garment fabric; the wooly nylon should cover both the right and wrong sides of the rolled hem. Decrease the stitch length so the stitches are close enough together that the wooly nylon covers the fabric beneath.

2 While guiding the fabric through the serger, pull down on the fabric in front of the feed dogs to stretch it as it goes under the foot. Be careful not to pull too hard on the fabric or the machine's timing mechanisms will have to be reset.

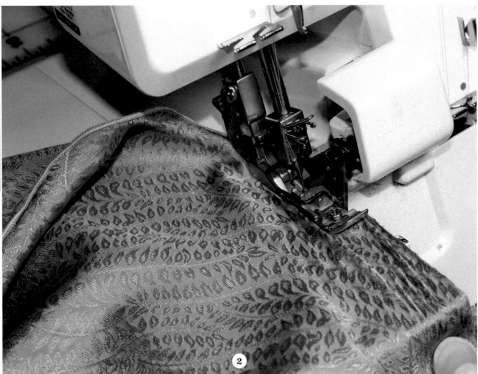

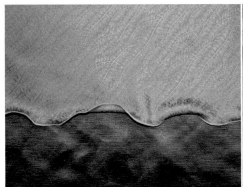

The lettuce hem with the fabric flat against the base fabric.

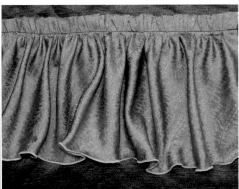

The sample gathered and sewn to the base fabric.

Tucks are small sections of fabric that are folded out and stitched along their length. They create a decorative effect that is both three-dimensional and regimented. Tucks can be released at the ends to add fullness to a garment for fitting, or can be included as panels of fabric sewn into a garment with the ends confined.

While tucks are generally spaced evenly across an area, varying the spacing can create different effects. Blind tucks have no space between them and create a more dense area of fabric. Centered tucks and centered double tucks create a columnar look, while crossed tucks give a quilted look. Pin tucks add fine detail; they can also be made even more decorative by using stitching lines to alter the direction in which they lie along their length, creating rippled patterns.

2.2
Tucks

Illusion tucks are not, strictly speaking, tucks at all, but pieces of bias fabric sewn to a base fabric to resemble a tuck. The flexibility of bias strips allows more exaggerated patterns than can be created by manipulating the base fabric alone.

Light- and medium-weight fabrics create the best tucks, especially if you want to add an area of fine detailing to a garment. Heavyweight fabrics can sculpted into different shapes with the use of a few judiciously placed tucks.

The structure of a tuck

Tucks are made by folding fabric, and then stitching along the base of the folds. There are many possible folds producing many different tucks, but the same basic structure underlies each.

1 The tuck is designed with both sides (A and B) the
same length.

2 The tuck is pinched out of the fabric.

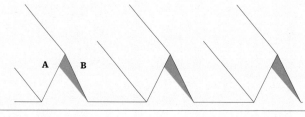

3 Then the sides of the tuck are closed and sewn
together along the folds at the base.

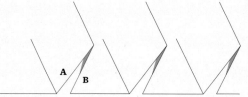

4 Finally, the tuck is pressed to one side.

Spaced tucks

Spaced tucks have flat fabric between them. First decide where the tucks will be placed, then decide on their width and frequency. Often the easiest way to experiment is by folding paper, so that you do not waste fashion fabric. The width, frequency, and spacing of tucks all affect how much fabric will be needed.

Calculating fabric for spaced tucks

For spaced tucks, the tuck face (A) is the same width as each fold behind it (B, C), with added space (D) between each tuck. One spaced tuck = A+B+C+D.

In this pattern, A+B+C+D = 1+1+1+1 = 4in (10cm). Each spaced tuck therefore needs 4in (10cm) of fabric but shows a face (A) of 1in (2.5cm) plus a space (D) of 1in (2.5cm), a total visible width of A+D = 2in (5cm).

Multiply the total fabric needed for each tuck by the number of tucks required. This pattern is for ten tucks, so 10 x 4in (10cm) = 40in (100cm) of fabric is required. Multiply the number of tucks by the total visible width of each tuck (A+D) to find the finished width of the tucks. In this pattern, 40in (100cm) of fabric gives 20in (50cm) of finished spaced tucks. You will need an additional 1in (2.5cm) to create the space before the first tuck.

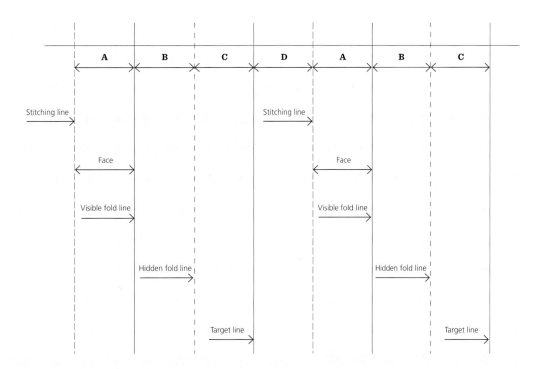

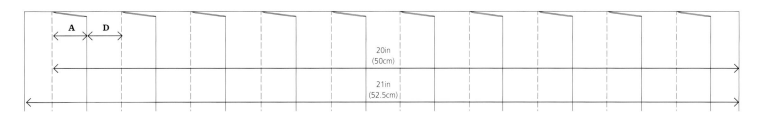

Marking and folding spaced tucks

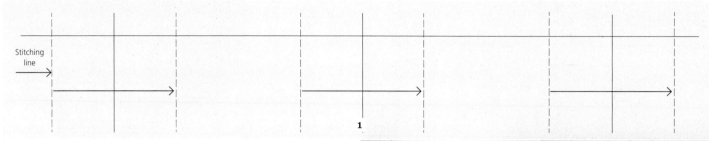

Stitching
line

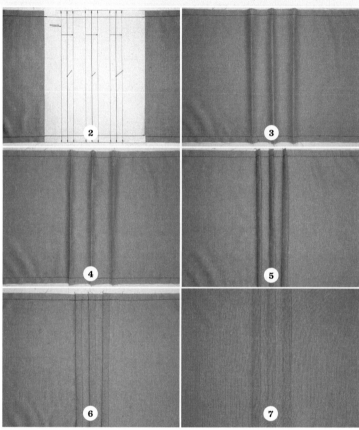

1 Create a paper pattern for the spaced tucks. The horizontal staystitching lines are drawn at top and bottom, vertical stitching lines are drawn in red, visible fold lines are drawn in black, and arrows point in the direction the tuck is to be folded after stitching. This pattern shows three tucks, each 1in (2.5cm) wide when sewn, which requires 3in (7.5cm) per tuck. There is a 1in (2.5cm) space between tucks. Notch both ends of each stitching line and the visible and hidden fold lines.

2 Working with the fabric and pattern facing right side up, mark the ends of the tucks on the fabric within the notches with chalk or dressmaker's pencil. If you need a guide along the length of any line, punch a hole in the middle of the line on the paper pattern with an awl. Place the pattern on the fabric. Poke a pin through the hole. Remove the pattern, leaving the pin in the fabric. Mark the pin placement with a tailor's tack or removable chalk mark.

3 Fold the fabric between the visible fold line marks, making one fold at a time. Soft-press the tucks by holding the iron just above the folds and briefly steaming the fabric. Remove pins as you go to avoid leaving pin marks in the fabric.

Soft-pressing the folds forms the pleats without permanent creases so corrections can be made if any of the folds are off grain or improperly placed. Stop to check that the folds are straight and parallel after a number of folds have been soft-pressed.

4 Hard-press the folds.

5 Sew the tucks, using the markings on the sewing machine's throat plate for guidance. Use a stitch length of 1.5mm (15 spi) at the beginning and end of each tuck, and 2.5mm (10 spi) between; this will keep each tuck stitching from unraveling without knotting each pair of thread tails. Continue stitching until all the tucks are complete. Press each tuck as sewn.

6 Press the tucks flat. Staystitch the tuck ends down within the seam allowance. Set the tucks with lots of pressure and steam from the iron. Lay a damp cloth over the tucks, then place a hot iron (as hot as the fabric can stand) on top. Leave the iron in place until the press cloth beneath is dry. Pick up the iron and move it to another section of the damp press cloth; do not slide the iron over as that may disturb the tucks beneath. Let the tucks rest undisturbed on the ironing board until the fabric has completely cooled.

Placing pieces of oak tag or brown paper between the layers of fabric will prevent imprints of the fold lines forming on other layers.

7 The spaced tucks sewn in a matching thread.

MARKING TUCKS USING OAK TAG

Tucks can also be marked using oak tag and an iron (see Marking and Folding Knife Pleats—Oak Tag Method, pp. 64–65).

FOLD TUCKS ON THE GRAINLINE

Care must be taken to fold each tuck and pleat on the grain; any fold line slightly off grain will look uneven. Once the fold line is pressed it will be difficult, if not impossible, to remove.

SETTING TUCKS

Before pressing, lay a press cloth dampened with a mixture of ten parts water to one part 5% distilled white vinegar over the tucks; this will help set them.

Blind tucks

Blind tucks are positioned so that there is no empty space between them; the visible folded edge of each tuck covers the stitching line of the next. A target line is not needed for this type of tuck but can be added to the pattern for clarity. As with spaced tucks, work with the right side facing up.

Calculating fabric for blind tucks

When making blind tucks, it is necessary to figure in the loss of fabric due to the next tuck starting $\frac{1}{8}$in (3mm) before the previous tuck ends. If tucks show a 1in (2.5cm) face, the beginning tuck (A1 and B1) is 1in (2.5cm) wide, with the space between the target line and stitching line (C1) of the second tuck $\frac{7}{8}$in (2.3cm) away. However, in all subsequent tucks, both A and B measure $1\frac{1}{8}$in (2.8cm) and C measures 1in (2.5cm). The extra $\frac{1}{8}$in (3mm) is hidden under the previous tuck.

This pattern is for ten blind tucks with each tuck face equal to 1in (2.5cm), overlapping the next tuck by $\frac{1}{8}$in (3mm). For ten blind tucks, you will need $34\frac{1}{8}$in (86.3cm) of fabric to create 10in (25cm) of finished tucks, with an additional 2in (5cm) to create the space before the first and after the last tucks.

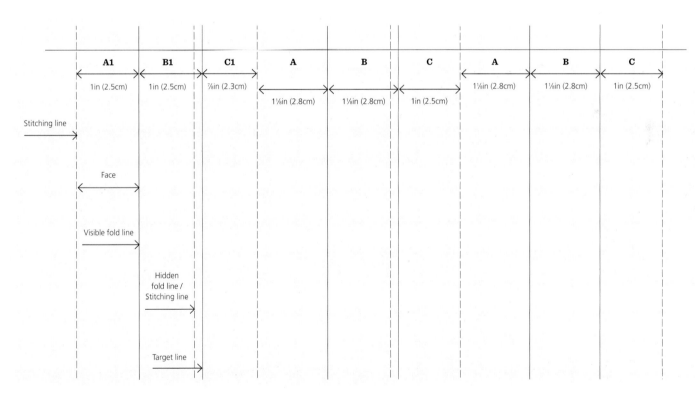

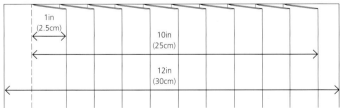

Marking and folding blind tucks

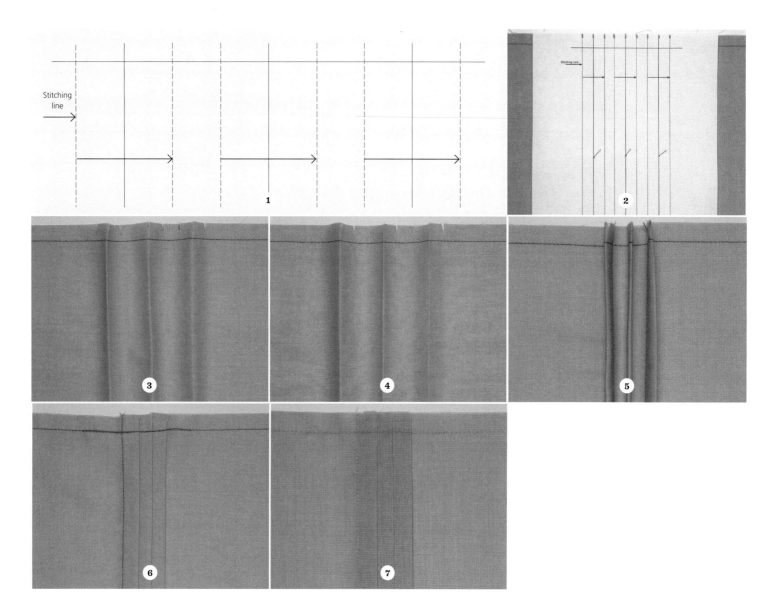

1 Draw the pattern on paper. A pattern for blind tucks is often drawn without target lines. Notch both ends of each stitching line and the visible and hidden fold lines.

MARKING TUCKS USING OAK TAG

Tucks can also be marked using oak tag and an iron (see Marking and Folding Knife Pleats—Oak Tag Method, pp. 64–65).

2 Working with the fabric and pattern facing right side up, mark the ends of the tucks on the fabric within the notches with chalk or dressmaker's pencil. If you need a guide along the length of any line, punch a hole in the middle of the line on the paper pattern with an awl. Place the pattern on the fabric. Poke a pin through the hole. Remove the pattern, leaving the pin in the fabric. Mark the pin placement with a tailor's tack or removable chalk mark.

3 Fold the fabric between the visible fold line marks, making one fold at a time. Soft-press the fold (see Marking and Folding Spaced Tucks, Step 3, p. 48). Stop to check that the folds are straight and parallel after a number of folds have been soft-pressed.

4 Hard-press the folds. Sew the tucks, using the marks on the sewing machine's throat plate for guidance.

5 Press each tuck as sewn.

6 Press the tucks flat. Staystitch the tuck ends down, stitching within the seam allowance.

7 The same blind tucks sewn in matching thread.

Centered tucks

Centered tucks are pressed with the centerline of the tuck positioned over the tuck's stitching line, rather than pressed to one side. As with other tucks, work with the right side of the fabric facing up.

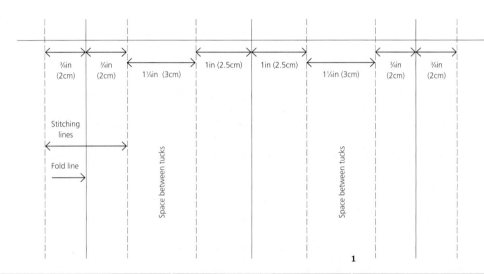
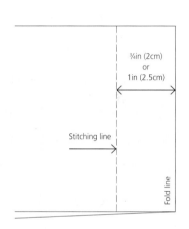

¾in (2cm) ¾in (2cm) 1¼in (3cm) 1in (2.5cm) 1in (2.5cm) 1¼in (3cm) ¾in (2cm) ¾in (2cm)

Stitching lines

Fold line

Space between tucks

Space between tucks

¾in (2cm) or 1in (2.5cm)

Stitching line

Fold line

1

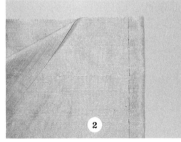

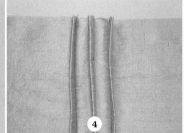

2   **3**   **4**   **5**

6

1 Draw the pattern and transfer the markings to the fabric, working with the right side up. Here a series of three tucks is made: the first tuck is ³/₄in (2cm) wide, followed by a 1¹/₄in (3cm) space; the center tuck is 1in (2.5cm) wide, followed by a 1¹/₄in (3cm) space; the final tuck is ³/₄in (2cm) wide.

2 Fold each tuck on the fold line, matching sewing lines.

3 Sew each tuck.

4 Press the seam line only; be careful not to press a crease into the tuck.

5 Cut a strip of oak tag the same width as the tuck. Cut the tip of the oak tag strip into a rounded shape and slide it through the tuck, carefully lining up the fabric fold line over the tuck seam; a centerline drawn on the oak tag strip can help with this. Press the tuck with the oak tag strip still inside. Remove it and press again, as shown with the tuck on the right.

6 The pressed centered tucks.

Centered double tucks

Centered double tucks consist of two centered tucks, one sitting on top of the other, with the upper one slightly narrower than the lower.

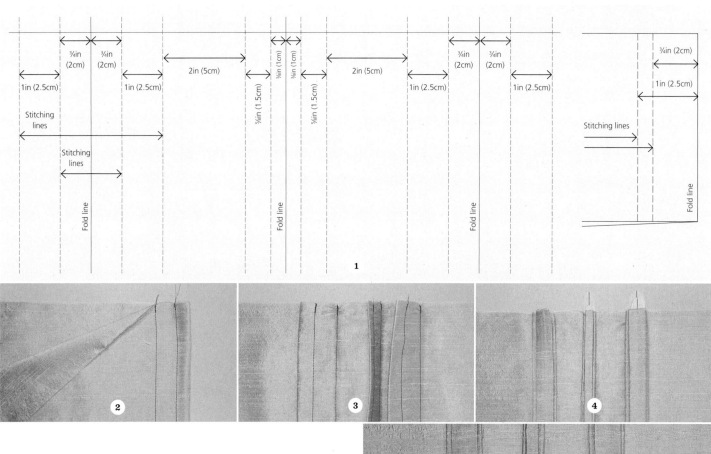

1 Make the pattern and transfer the markings to the fabric, working on the right side of the fabric. Here the first tuck is ³⁄₄in (2cm) wide, centered over a 1in (2.5cm) tuck, followed by a 2in (5cm) space; the second tuck is ³⁄₄in (1cm) wide, centered over a ⁵⁄₈in (1.5cm) tuck, followed by a 2in (5cm) space; the third tuck is ³⁄₄in (2cm) wide, centered over a 1in (2.5cm) tuck.

2 Working with the right side up, match the pairs of seams and stitch.

3 Press the seam lines only, being careful not to press a crease into the tucks.

4 Cut strips of oak tag equal to the width of the tucks. Cut the tips of the oak tag strips into a rounded shape and slide them through the tucks, carefully lining up the fabric fold line over the tuck seam; a centerline drawn on the oak tag strip can help with this.

Press the tuck with the oak tag strip still inside. Remove the oak tag strip and press again, as shown with the tuck on the left.

5 The finished centered doubled tucks.

Pin tucks

Pin tucks are very narrow tucks. They can be used on any type of garment, although they are most commonly used on dress shirt fronts and lingerie. As with other tucks, work with the right side of the fabric facing up.

Calculating fabric for pin tucks

For pin tucks, the tuck face (A) is the same width as each fold behind it (B, C), with added space (D) between each tuck. One pin tuck = A+B+C+D.

In this pattern, $A+B+C+D = \frac{1}{4}+\frac{1}{4}+\frac{1}{4}+1 = 1\frac{3}{4}$in (0.6+0.6+0.6+ 2.5 = 4.3cm). Each tuck needs $1\frac{3}{4}$in (4.3cm) but shows a face of $\frac{1}{4}$in (0.6cm) plus a space (D) of 1in (2.5cm), a total visible width of $A+D = 1\frac{1}{4}$in (3.1cm).

This pattern has ten spaced pin tucks, each requiring $1\frac{3}{4}$in (4.3cm) of fabric, so $17\frac{1}{2}$in (43cm) of fabric is required to create $12\frac{1}{2}$in (31cm) of finished pin tucks, plus an additional 1in (2.5cm) to create the space before the first tuck and after the last tuck.

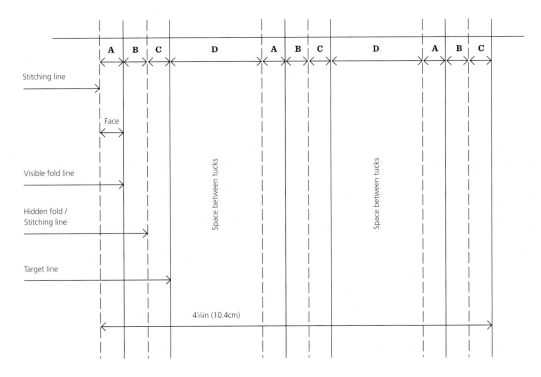

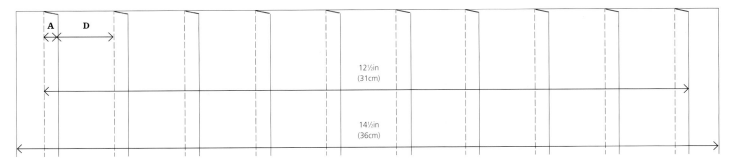

Marking and folding pin tucks

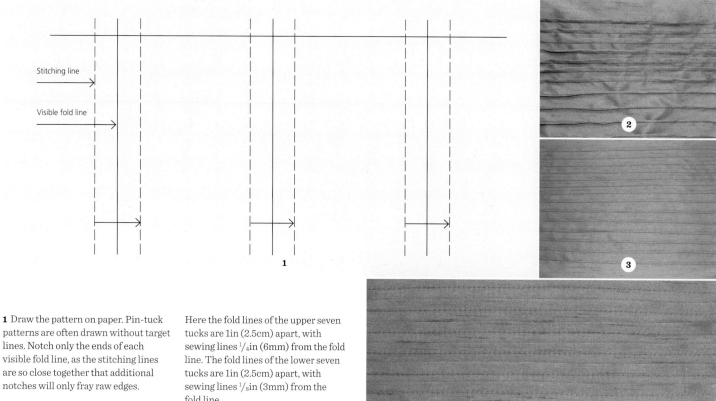

Stitching line

Visible fold line

1

1 Draw the pattern on paper. Pin-tuck patterns are often drawn without target lines. Notch only the ends of each visible fold line, as the stitching lines are so close together that additional notches will only fray raw edges.

Fold the fabric along each visible fold line, making one fold at a time. Soft-press the fold (see Marking and Folding Spaced Tucks, Step 3, p. 48). Check that the folds are straight and parallel after a number of folds have been soft-pressed, then hard-press the folds.

2 Sew the tucks, using the markings on the sewing machine's throat plate for guidance. Measure from the pressed fold line.

Here the fold lines of the upper seven tucks are 1in (2.5cm) apart, with sewing lines $1/4$in (6mm) from the fold line. The fold lines of the lower seven tucks are 1in (2.5cm) apart, with sewing lines $1/8$in (3mm) from the fold line.

3 Press the pin tucks as stitched and then press them all flat.

4 Pin tucks stitched at $1/4$in (6mm) and $1/8$in (3mm) from the fold line in matching thread.

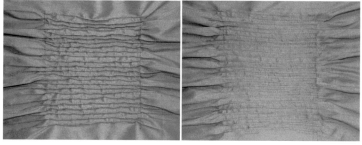

Using pin tucks to constrain fabric

Pin tucks can be used as an alternative to darts—for example, by taking in the fabric through the waist area and releasing it over the bust and hips. Here, 13in (33cm) of fabric has been pin-tucked and reduced down to a 7in (17.5cm) section.

The pin tucks stitched.

The pin tucks pressed.

Crossed pin tucks

Pin tucks can also be sewn into a variety of decorative patterns. Here, the tucks were sewn first horizontally and then vertically to create a boxlike surface pattern.

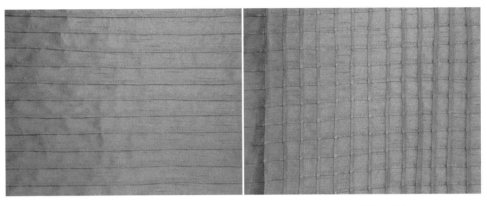

Pin tucks stitched horizontally at ⅛in (3mm) wide and pressed flat.

A second set of pin tucks ⅛in (3mm) wide is stitched vertically across the first and pressed flat.

Rippled tucks

Pin tucks can also be sewn down in alternating directions along their length to create a wave effect.

1 Sew a series of pin tucks. Here the pin tucks are sewn ¼in (6mm) wide, with ¾in (2cm) between them. Soft-press the tucks so the stitches are embedded into the fabric and the tucks lie nearly flat, with spaces between unrumpled.

2 Push the tucks up and down with your hands to find the rippling effect that works best for your design. Draw stitching guidelines, with a heat-erasable pen or chalk, through the center of the ripples.

3 Press the tucks and stitch to the base fabric on each guideline. Do not back tack; pull the thread tails to the wrong side of the fabric and knot.

4 The finished rippled tucks.

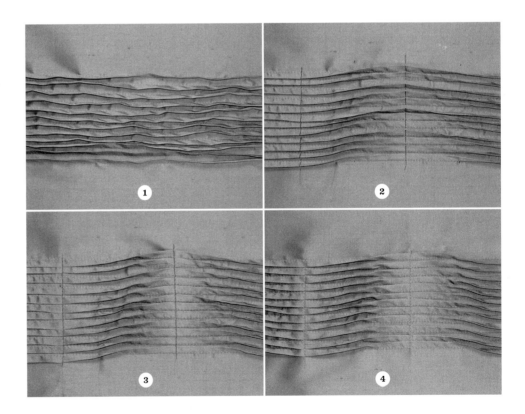

VARIATION

You can vary the width of tucks for dramatically different results.

Here, tucks 1in (2.5cm) wide have been stitched with 1in (2.5cm) between them and sewn down to the base fabric with four lines of stitching.

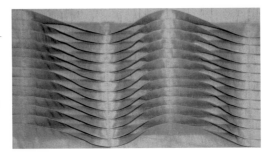

Illusion tucks

Illusion tucks are made of bias strips appliquéd onto a matching base fabric, creating the illusion that the base fabric is tucked. (See pp. 128–32 for how to make and shape bias strips.) Sew the bias strips to the base fabric right sides together and press down toward the hem of the garment, forming the tuck. When groups of tucks intersect, one group is sewn over the ends of the other; this dictates the sewing order—tucks to go underneath must be sewn to the base fabric first.

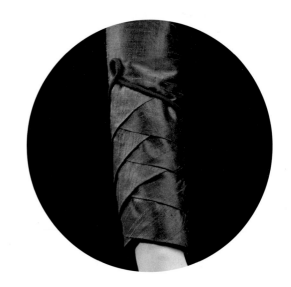

1 Print the pattern on tear-away interfacing and machine-baste it to the base fabric. Here the bias strip placement is colored brown and a $1/4$in (6mm) seam allowance has been marked inside the strip. (See Transferring Patterns, pp. 18–23).

2 Cut the bias strips. The strips should be twice the width of the visible tuck plus seam allowance. Here the sizes of finished strips are $1/2$in (1.3cm) wide and 1in (2.5cm) wide. The seam allowance is $1/4$in (6mm) so the strips were cut $1\,1/2$in (3.8cm) wide and $2\,1/2$in (6.2cm). Fold the strips in half, wrong sides together, and press.

3 Place the raw edge of a folded bias strip along the seam allowance guideline. Overlap the strips on the pattern that will be sewn on top by $3/8$in (1cm).

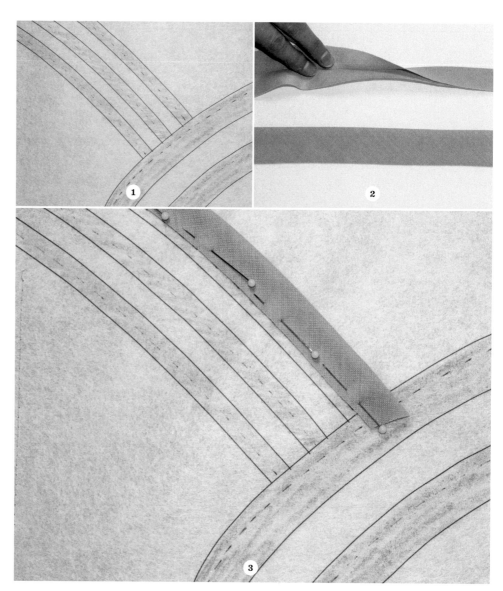

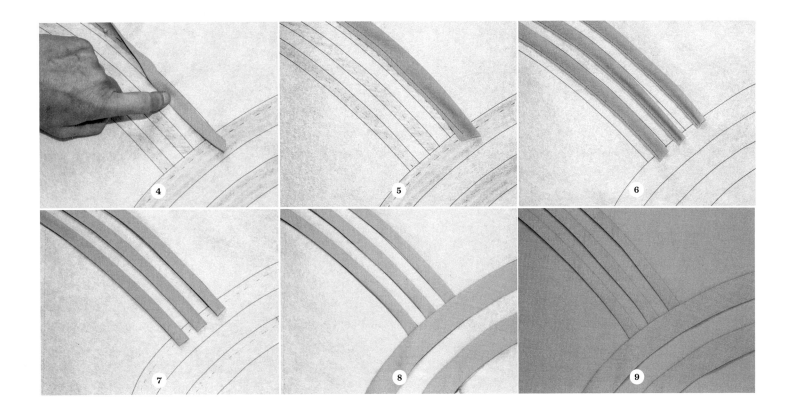

4 Check that the bias strip folds over the pins in the proper direction on the garment before sewing. The strips should smooth down the body like the nap on a velvet garment.

5 Stitch the bias strip to the base fabric on top of the pattern. Pull the thread tails to the wrong side and knot.

6 Sew the other bias strips of the group to the base fabric. Trim the seam allowance closest to the base fabric to reduce the bulk under the tuck.

7 Fold the strips down over the seam line and press into place. Steam with a damp press cloth if needed.

8 Repeat Steps 3–7 for the remaining tucks. Remove the tear-away interfacing and gently press the strips.

9 The finished illusion tucks.

STEAM CURVING BIAS STRIPS INTO SHAPE

If the tuck is curved, use steam from the iron to shape the bias strip before stitching in place. Fold and pin the strip into place along the guideline.

Fold the strip over the pins. Steam the entire strip as it will be sewn. Let the strip cool and dry before removing pins and stitching.

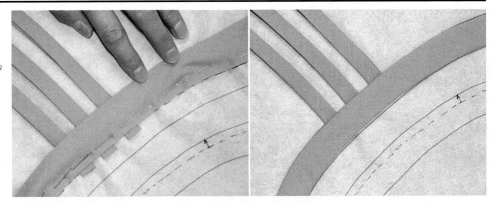

Pleating is the art of folding fabric to reduce its visible surface and allow the full fabric width to expand elsewhere in the garment. Pleated forms are found in many settings, from architecture to product design, taking inspiration from the underside of a mushroom or a scallop's shell. In fashion, pleats are often an integral part of many garments—from Scottish kilts to the sleek, form-fitting, columnar dresses of Mariano Fortuny and Madame Grès.

Pleats can be decorative as well as functional. A pleated skirt that fits at the waist, flows snugly down the hips, and flares over the legs allows movement, while a pleat folded to conceal a brightly colored inner fabric allows a flash of color with each stride.

2.3
Pleats

There are two categories of pleats: flat and standing. Flat pleats lie flat against the body, while standing pleats stand proud. Knife, kick, box, inverted, centered, and multi-pleats are flat. Cartridge, accordion, mushroom, and sunburst pleats are standing. While flat pleats can be reset after a garment is cleaned, standing pleats are harder to reform and reset. An iron or a commercial flat-press will press flat pleats flat, but standing pleats are usually set with molds made of cardboard or metal, which are often custom made and unavailable to retail dry cleaners.

Couturier Mariano Fortuny created a unique hand-pleating process on silk fabric that died with him. During Fortuny's lifetime, his garments were returned to his workshops to be cleaned and re-pleated when needed. Modern professional pleating companies offer a similar-looking pleating service but often prefer to work in polyester, as some polyesters hold their pleated shapes longer than silk.

The structure of a pleat

There are myriad variations of pleats, all of which derive from one or more of three basic styles: accordion, knife, and box. The accordion pleat is a standing pleat; it stands away from the work table. Variations of accordion pleats include cartridge, mushroom, and sunburst pleats. Knife pleats—also known as side pleats—and box pleats are flat pleats; they lie flat on the work table.

When fabric is evenly folded, with each fold having an up side (A) and a down side (B), it makes an accordion pleat.

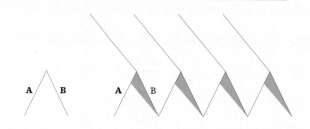

Pushing the accordion pleat to the side to flatten it creates a knife or side pleat. In this drawing the sides of the pleats are equal lengths. If sides A and B both equal 1in (2.5cm) then three pleats requires 6in (15cm); the pleats sit directly on top of one another.

The sides do not, however, need to be equal; B can be shorter than A, as shown in this drawing, where B is half the length of A. If side A equals 1in (2.5cm) and side B equals $\frac{1}{2}$in (1.3cm), then three pleats require $4\frac{1}{2}$in (11.4cm) and the pleats overlap each other.

A box pleat is two knife pleats folded facing each other and meeting under the face "box." Shown here at top left is the familiar knife pleat, below are two knife pleats facing each other to form a box pleat, as shown at far right.

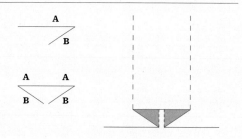

An inverted pleat has a similar folding pattern to the box pleat, except that the pleats are folded with the box underneath, so it resembles a box pleat seen from the wrong side—hence the name "inverted."

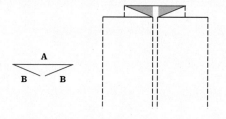

Knife pleats

Knife pleats are flat pleats, folded to one side, usually with all the pleats folded in the same direction.

Calculating fabric for knife pleats

For knife pleats that butt up to each other with no space between them, the pleat face (A) is the same width as each fold behind it (B, C). One knife pleat = A+B+C.

In this pattern, A+B+C = 1+1+1 = 3in (2.5+2.5+2.5 = 7.5cm). Each pleat needs 3in (7.5cm) of fabric but shows a face (A) of 1in (2.5cm). The fabric to pleat ratio is 3:1—3 yards (meters) of flat fabric for 1 yard (meter) of pleated fabric.

This pattern has ten pleats each requiring 3in (7.5cm) of fabric, so 30in (75cm) of fabric is needed. When pleated, the piece of fabric will be 10in (25cm) long.

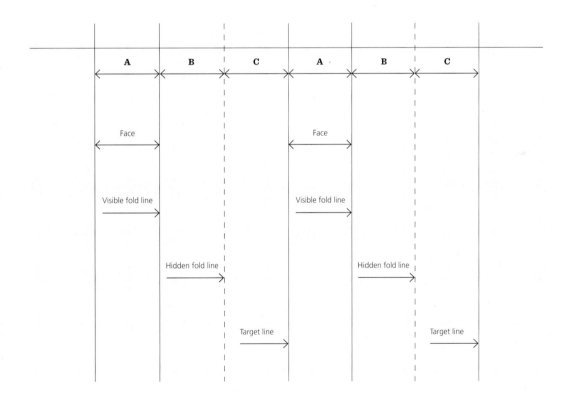

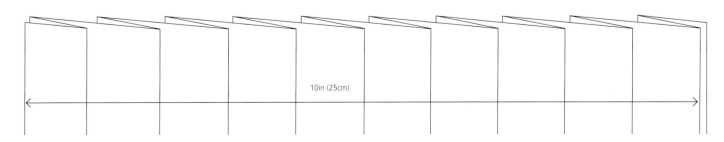

Knife pleats that have flat fabric visible between each pleat are measured the same way as continuous knife pleats, with added space (D) between the pleats. One spaced knife pleat = A+B+C+D.

In this pattern, A+B+C+D = 1+1+1+1 = 4in (2.5+2.5+2.5+2.5 = 10cm). Each spaced pleat needs 4in (10cm) of fabric but shows a face (A) of 1in (2.5cm) plus a space (D) of 1in (2.5cm), a total width of A+D = 2in (5cm). The fabric to pleat ratio is 4:2 or 2:1— 4 yards (meters) of flat fabric for 2 yards (meters) of pleated fabric.

This pattern has ten spaced pleats each requiring 4in (10cm) of fabric, so 40in (100cm) of fabric is needed. When pleated, the piece of fabric will be 10in (25cm) long.

CALCULATING PLEATS FOR A SKIRT

To calculate the number of pleats needed for a skirt, divide the hip measurement by the width of one pleat.

If one pleat has a width (A) of 1in (2.5cm), and a space (D) of 1in (2.5cm) between each pleat, the total pleat width is A+D = 2in (5cm).

If the hip measurement is 36in (90cm), then 36÷2in (90÷5cm) = 18 pleats.

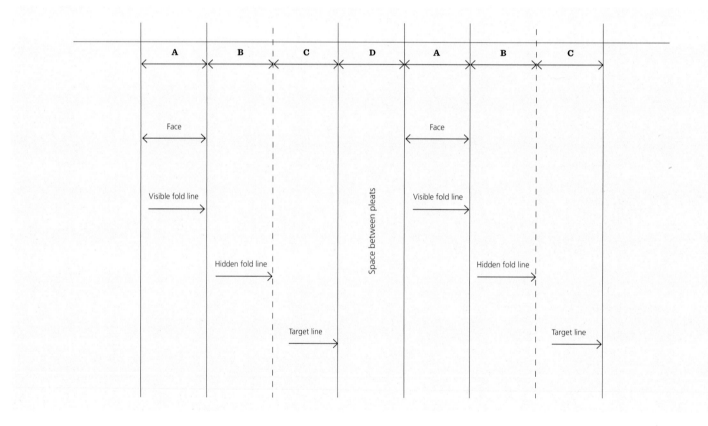

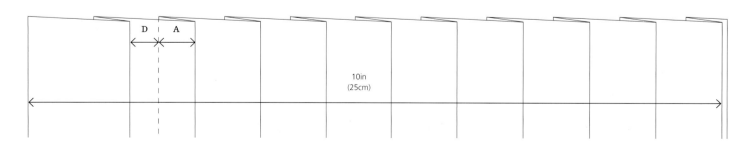

Marking and folding knife pleats—
Pin method

Pin marking is the most common method of marking and folding pleats, demonstrated here on a simple knife pleat.

TRANSFERRING PLEAT FOLD LINES TO FABRIC

For clarity, the fabric is shown right side up. Often pleat fold lines are transferred to the wrong side of the fabric, with the pleats folded accordingly.

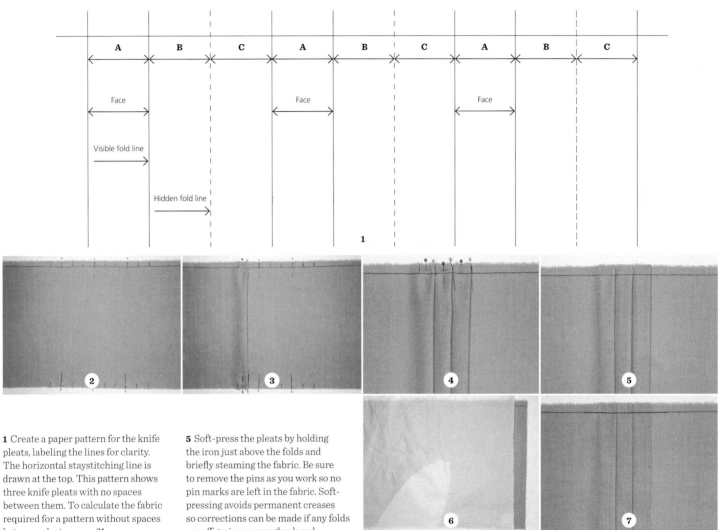

1 Create a paper pattern for the knife pleats, labeling the lines for clarity. The horizontal staystitching line is drawn at the top. This pattern shows three knife pleats with no spaces between them. To calculate the fabric required for a pattern without spaces between pleats, see p. 61.

2 Transfer the pleat marks to the fabric. Place pins at the top and bottom of the visible fold lines.

3 Place pins on the target line. Pinch the fabric at the pins on the visible fold line and bring them over to meet the pins on the target line. Pin the pleat in place.

4 Place pins on the next target line and bring the next pleat over to meet them. Repeat Steps 3–4 across the fabric.

5 Soft-press the pleats by holding the iron just above the folds and briefly steaming the fabric. Be sure to remove the pins as you work so no pin marks are left in the fabric. Soft-pressing avoids permanent creases so corrections can be made if any folds are off grain or wrongly placed.

6 Set the pleats by pressing with lots of steam and pressure from the iron. Lay a damp cloth over the pleats and place a hot iron (as hot as the fabric can stand) on top. Leave the iron in place until the press cloth beneath is dry. Pick up the iron and move it to another area of the damp press cloth; do not slide the iron across as it may disturb the pleats beneath. Let the pleats rest undisturbed on the ironing board until the fabric is completely cool.

Placing pieces of oak tag or brown paper between the layers of fabric will prevent imprints of the fold lines forming on the other layers.

7 Staystitch the top of the pleats within the seam allowance to hold the pleats in place. The bottom of the pleats can be basted "shut" if needed.

SETTING PLEATS

Before pressing, lay a press cloth dampened with a mixture of ten parts water to one part 5% distilled white vinegar over the tucks; this will help to set the tucks.

Marking and folding knife pleats— Oak tag method

This method of marking and folding pleats is useful when you are pleating an entire piece of fabric, rather than just making one or two pleats. Here it is demonstrated on knife pleats with space between them, but it can be adapted to create box, inverted, and multiple pleats too.

In this pattern, each knife pleat shows a face (A) of 1in (2.5cm) plus a space (D) of 1in (2.5cm) before the next pleat, a total visible width of 2in (5cm). There are a total of four knife pleats in the pattern, using 16in (40cm) of fabric, which pleats to 8in (20cm), including an extra 1in (2.5cm) for the space after the last pleat.

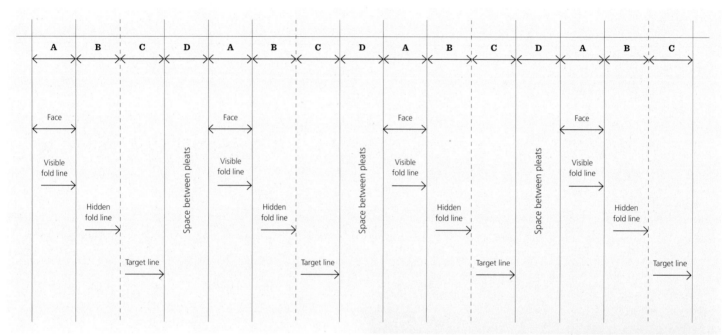

1 Cut two strips of oak tag the width of the fabric plus 2in (5cm), by double the width of a single pleat. Here the strips are 18in (46cm) long by 2in (5cm) wide, to create knife pleats 1in (2.5cm) wide. Draw a line down the center of one oak tag strip to mark the pleat width. Pin this strip near the edge of an ironing board. Pin the other strip below it, leaving a gap between strips equal to the width of the space between the pleats, here 1in (2.5cm).

2 Slide the fabric under the top strip of oak tag with the wrong side of the fabric facing up. The staystitching on the right indicates the fabric edge that will be joined to the rest of the garment.

3 Fold the fabric down over the top strip of oak tag. Press along the top edge of the oak tag to create the visible fold line. Use a piece of organza for a press cloth if needed.

4 Flip the fabric up to expose the oak tag and refold it along the drawn line, without disturbing the crease made in Step 3, to create the hidden fold line. Soft-press this fold line. With this method, only the visible and hidden fold lines are pressed; the target fold line is not marked.

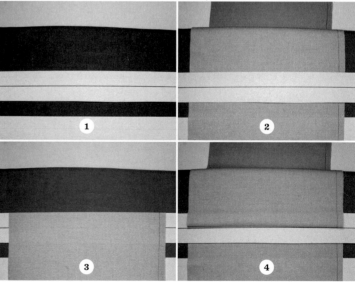

5 Unfold the fabric and pull it toward you until the second crease, the hidden fold line crease, lies directly on top of the upper edge of the lower strip of oak tag. The hidden fold line crease should be a mountain fold crease, while the visible fold crease should be a valley fold crease (see Mountain and Valley Folds box, p. 79).

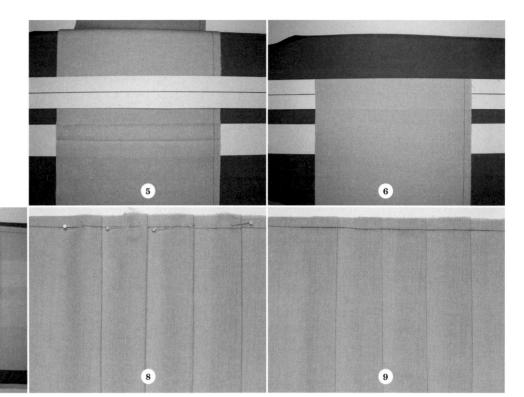

6 Fold the fabric over the top strip of the oak tag and repeat Steps 3–5 until the fabric is completely pressed for pleating.

7 Once all the pleats are folded, remove the fabric from the oak tag strips and check that all the pleats are straight and evenly spaced.

8 Fold the pleats to the side and soft-press them (see Marking and Folding Spaced Tucks, Step 3, p. 48). Pin them at the top.

9 Hard-press the pleats if required. Staystitch the top of the pleats in place. The pleats can be basted "shut" along the bottom edge if needed.

VARIATION

This pattern calls for ten pleats, each with a face of 1in (2.5cm) and no spaces between them. Proceed as for spaced knife pleats (see above), but in Step 1 position the second oak tag strip immediately below the first, with no space in between.

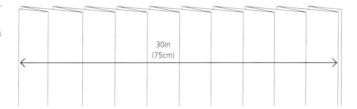

30in (75cm)

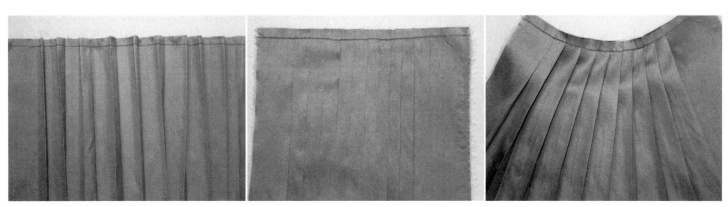

After pressing with the oak tag strips.

Folded flat, hard-pressed, and staystitched.

Spread out to show the pleating.

Box pleats

Box pleats are formed from two knife pleats, one folded from the left and one from the right, with both hidden fold lines meeting underneath the pleat face at the centerline.

Calculating fabric for box pleats

Continuous box pleats that butt up to each other, with no space between them, are measured for fabric width in the same way as knife pleats. The pleat face (C) is twice the width of each fold (A, B). One box pleat = A+B+C+B+A.

In this pattern, A+B+C+B+A = 1+1+2+1+1 = 6in (2.5+2.5+5+2.5+2.5 = 15cm). Each box pleat needs 6in (15cm) of fabric but shows a face of 2in (5cm). The fabric to pleat ratio is 6:2 or 3:1—3 yards (meters) of flat fabric for 1 yard (meter) of pleated fabric.

This pattern has five box pleats (without space between, although the diagram shows a space for clarity), each requiring 6in (15cm) of fabric, so 30in (75cm) of fabric is needed. When pleated, the piece will be 10in (25cm) long.

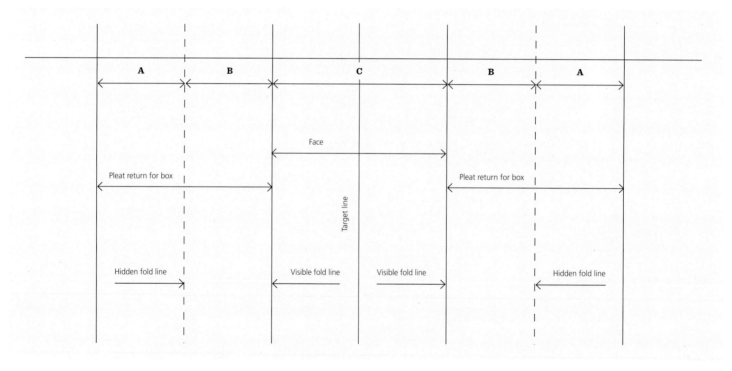

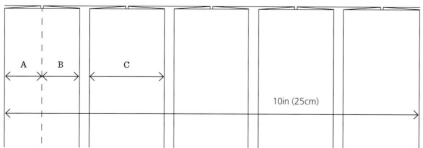

Box pleats with a space between them are measured in the same way as continuous box pleats, with added space (D) between the pleats. One spaced box pleat = A+B+C+B+A+D.

In this pattern, A+B+C+B+A+D = 1+1+2+1+1+2 = 8in (2.5+2.5+5+2.5+2.5+5 = 20cm). Each spaced box pleat needs 8in (20cm) of fabric but shows a face (C) of 2in (5cm) plus a space (D) of 2in (5cm), a total width of C+D = 4in (10cm). The fabric to pleat ratio is 8:4 or 2:1—2 yards (meters) of flat fabric for 1 yard (meter) of pleated fabric.

This pattern has five pleats each requiring 8in (20cm) of fabric, so 40in (100cm) of fabric is needed. When pleated, the piece will be 20in (50cm) long.

CALCULATING PLEATS FOR A SKIRT

To calculate the number of pleats needed for a skirt, divide the hip measurement by the width of one pleat.

If one pleat has a width (A) of 1in (2.5cm), and a space (D) of 1in (2.5cm) between each pleat, the total pleat width is A+D = 2in (5cm).

If the hip measurement is 36in (90cm), then 36÷2in (90÷5cm) = 18 pleats.

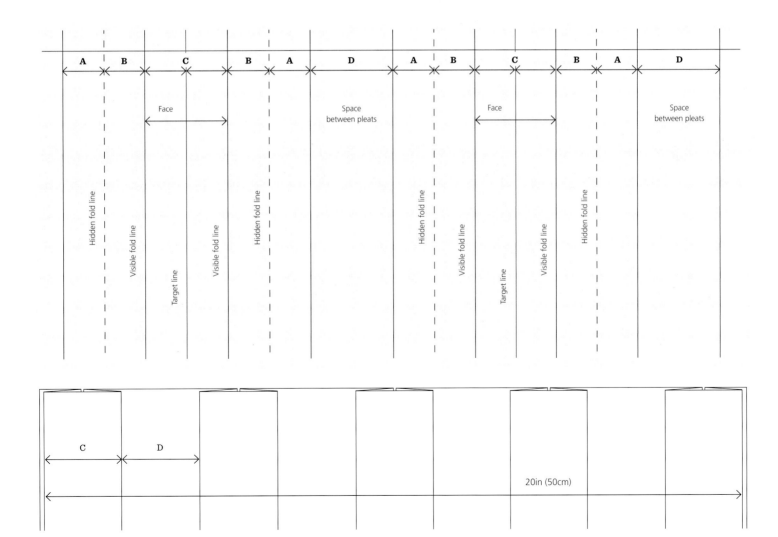

Marking and folding box pleats—Pin method

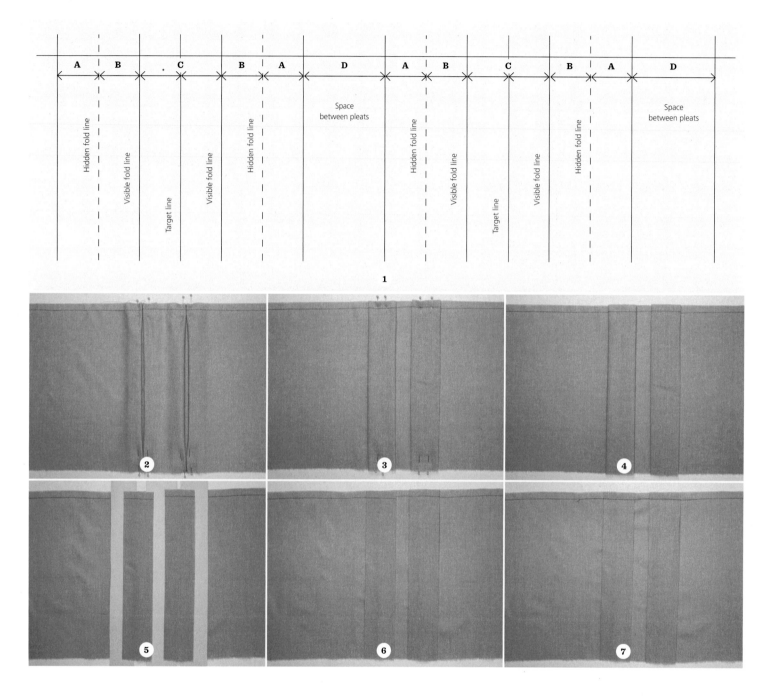

1 Create a paper pattern for the box pleats, labeling the lines for clarity. The horizontal staystitching line is drawn at the top. This pattern shows two box pleats with a space between them. To calculate the fabric required, see p. 66.

2 Transfer the fold lines from the pattern to the fabric. Place pins at the top and bottom of the visible fold lines.

Working on the wrong side of the fabric, fold the hidden fold lines to the center target line. Pin at the top of the pleat and down the fold lines if needed.

3 Turn the fabric over so that the right side faces up.

4 Soft-press the pleats by holding the iron just above the folds and briefly steaming the fabric.

Be sure to remove the pins as you work so that no pin marks are left in the fabric.

5 Place strips of oak tag or brown paper behind the folds before hard-pressing. This will prevent subtle creases or ghost impressions from the under pleats coming through to the right side while pressing. Hard-press the pleats with a damp press cloth (see Marking and Folding Knife Pleats, Step 6, p. 63).

6 The two box pleats after they have been hard-pressed.

7 Staystitch the tops of the pleats in the folded position. They can be basted "shut" along the bottom edge if needed.

Inverted pleats

Inverted pleats are formed from a set of two knife pleats in the same way as a box pleat, except that the pleats now face each other, and the "box" sits behind the two face pleats rather than in front, with the folds meeting at the target line on the right side of the fabric. In other words, an inverted pleat looks exactly the same as a box pleat when viewed from the back.

Calculating fabric for inverted pleats

Inverted pleats that butt up to each other, without space between them, are measured for fabric requirements in the same way as box pleats (see Calculating Fabric for Box Pleats, p. 66).

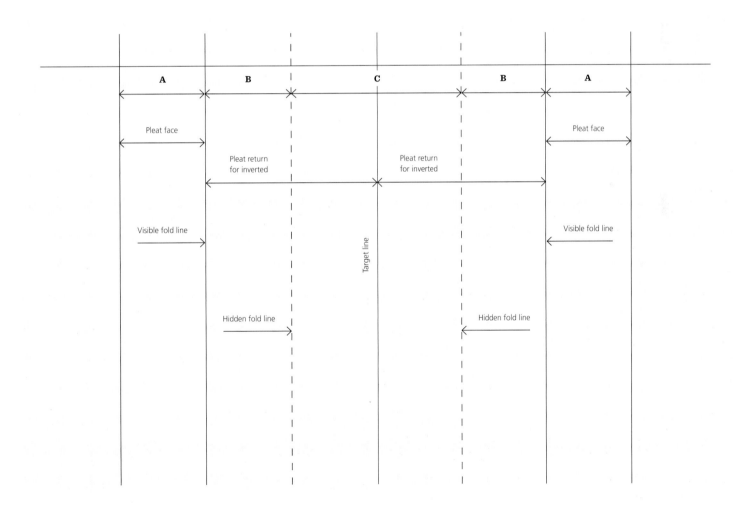

Marking and folding inverted pleats

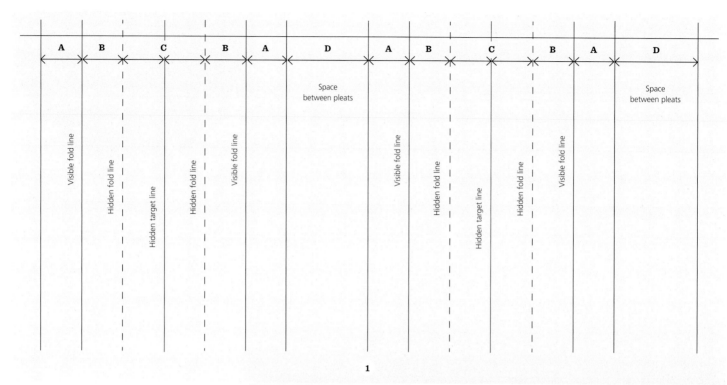

| A | B | | C | | B | A | D | A | B | | C | | B | A | D |

Space between pleats

Space between pleats

Visible fold line

Hidden fold line

Hidden target line

Hidden fold line

Visible fold line

Visible fold line

Hidden fold line

Hidden target line

Hidden fold line

Visible fold line

1

1 Create a paper pattern for the inverted pleats, labeling the lines for clarity. The horizontal staystitching line is drawn at the top. This pattern shows two inverted pleats with a space between them. To calculate the fabric required, see p. 69.

2 Transfer the fold lines from the pattern and place pins at the top and bottom of each line. Pinch the fabric at the pins and bring the pins to meet at the target/centerline.

3 Soft-press the pleats by holding the iron just above the folds and briefly steaming the fabric.

4 Place strips of oak tag or brown paper behind the folds before hard-pressing. This will prevent subtle creases or ghost impressions from the under pleats coming through to the right side while pressing. Hard-press the pleats with a damp press cloth (see Marking and Folding Knife Pleats, Step 6, p. 63).

5 Staystitch across the top of the pleats to hold them in place. They can be basted "shut" along the bottom edge if needed.

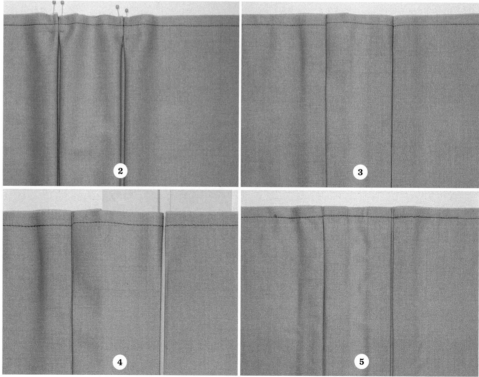

Edgestitched pleats

Edgestitching on pleats makes a very crisp presentation. The edgestitching can be sewn the entire length of the pleats or just partway down to a release point.

1 It is necessary to hem a pleat before it is edgestitched because the edge-stitching makes a permanent crimp on the fold line. The edgestitching should start within the seam allowance at the top of the pleat, so remove any staystitching that holds the top of the pleats in place.

2 Using a little foot (left) or a $1/8$ in (3mm) edgestitching foot (right) will make stitching along the edge of the pleat much easier.

3 Open the hemmed pleat and place the visible fold line at the $1/8$ in (3mm) guide on the sewing machine's throat plate. Sew along the edge of the pleat fold through the hem area. Do not back tack; leave long thread tails. Knot the threads and pull the tails inside the hem fold (see Knotting Thread Ends, pp. 29–30). Repeat on all folds.

4 Press the edgestitching to embed it into the fabric and re-sew the staystitching at the top to hold the pleats in place.

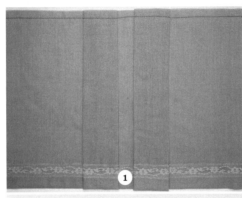

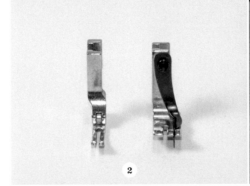

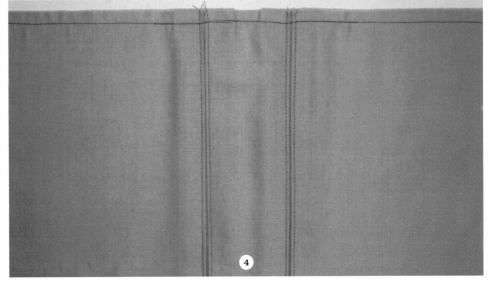

Sewing pleats down to a release point

Sometimes a design calls for the pleated part of a garment to lie flat against the body until it reaches an action point—like a knee—where the garment needs to be free to flare out. The pleat is stitched closed and then edgestitched to keep it flat and neat up to the release point.

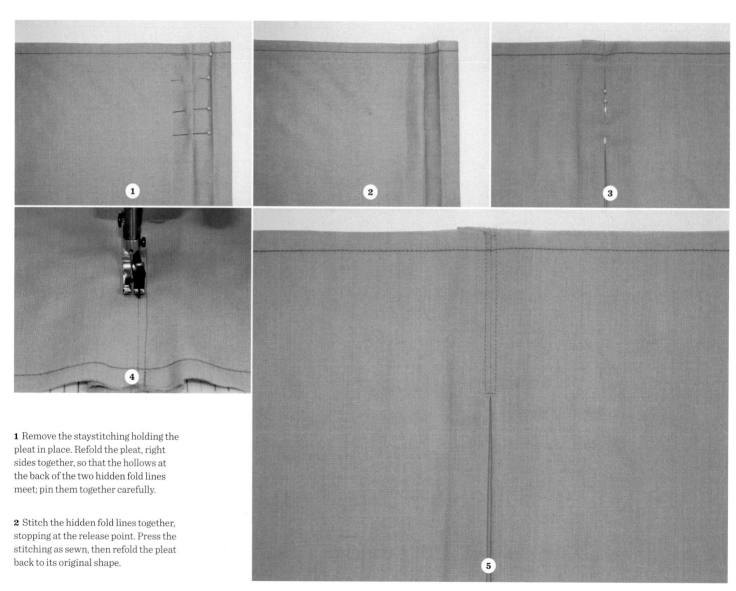

1 Remove the staystitching holding the pleat in place. Refold the pleat, right sides together, so that the hollows at the back of the two hidden fold lines meet; pin them together carefully.

2 Stitch the hidden fold lines together, stopping at the release point. Press the stitching as sewn, then refold the pleat back to its original shape.

3 From the right side, pin down the visible fold stitched line, matching it to the hidden target line. Resew the staystitching at the top to hold the pleat in place.

4 Sewing through all the pleat layers, edgestitch down the side of the visible fold line. If you are stitching an inverted pleat, pivot the fabric with the needle down and sew across the pleat—about three stitches—pivot again and sew up the other side of the visible fold line. Press the stitching to embed it in the fabric.

5 The completed inverted pleat, edgestitched to the release point.

Partial pleat with an underlay

A partial pleat at a hemline, constructed as a kick pleat with an underlay cut from a different fabric, adds an unexpected flash of color with each step.

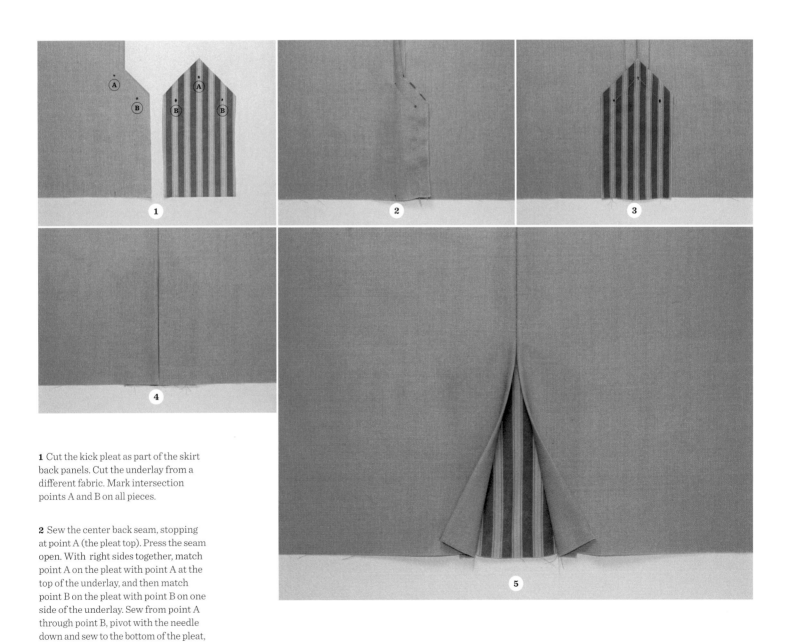

1 Cut the kick pleat as part of the skirt back panels. Cut the underlay from a different fabric. Mark intersection points A and B on all pieces.

2 Sew the center back seam, stopping at point A (the pleat top). Press the seam open. With right sides together, match point A on the pleat with point A at the top of the underlay, and then match point B on the pleat with point B on one side of the underlay. Sew from point A through point B, pivot with the needle down and sew to the bottom of the pleat, matching seam allowances. Repeat along the other side of the pleat and underlay. Press both seams as stitched.

3 Press open the center back seam allowance of the skirt.

4 The closed kick pleat seen from the right side.

5 The underlay peeking out from the kick pleat.

Cartridge pleats

Cartridge pleats are compactly gathered folds of fabric. They are halfway between flat pleats and standing pleats: cartridge pleats only pleat the top of the fabric, while accordion pleats pleat the entire length of the fabric. Cartridge pleats are often used in ecclesiastical robes where the fabric is gathered and then falls in soft, full rolls to the hem. Deep cartridge pleats were used for Elizabethan neck ruffs, with the stiff, starched linen projecting out from the base fabric.

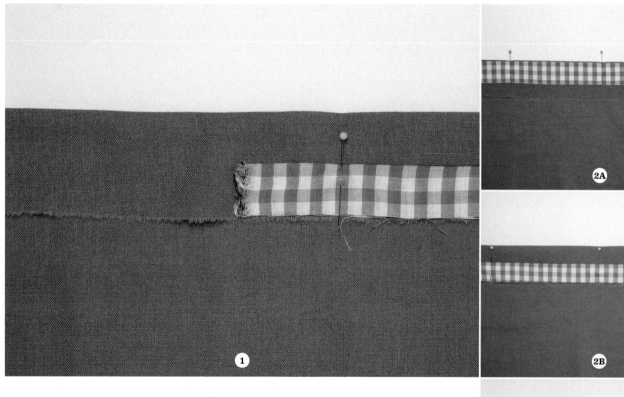

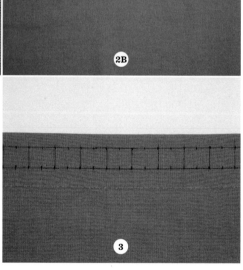

1 Press a hem allowance over at the top of the fabric to create a band equal to the required depth of the pleats. This pleating band will give you a clean finished edge at the top and double the bulk of the pleats, making them robust. Here the pleating band is 2in (5cm). The raw edge of the fabric was torn, not cut, to make a softer transition from two layers to one layer.

2A Cut a piece of gingham the same length as the fabric and pin it to the top edge of the pleating band.

2B The gingham can also be pinned to the bottom edge of the band or made the same width as the band, depending on the effect required.

3 If gingham is not available, the pleating band can be marked as a grid on the fabric for each stitch placement.

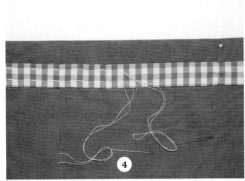

4 Thread two needles with a doubled strand of heavy-duty thread. Sew two parallel rows of gathering stitches, sewing exactly into the corners of the gingham squares to keep each stitch exactly the same length; the stitches of both rows should align. Sew both rows of gathering stitches concurrently.

5 When the threads get short, gather up both rows of stitches. Continue stitching until the fabric is completely gathered.

6 Adjust the width of the pleated fabric as necessary. Tie sturdy knots in the gathering threads.

7 The cartridge pleats seen from the right side. Notice how the pleats flare out at the top, before being tightly compressed in the middle and then releasing all the fabric.

8 Placing the gingham at the top of the band gives a different effect.

9 Turned to the right side, the pleats will now be tightly compressed at the top before releasing into the folds.

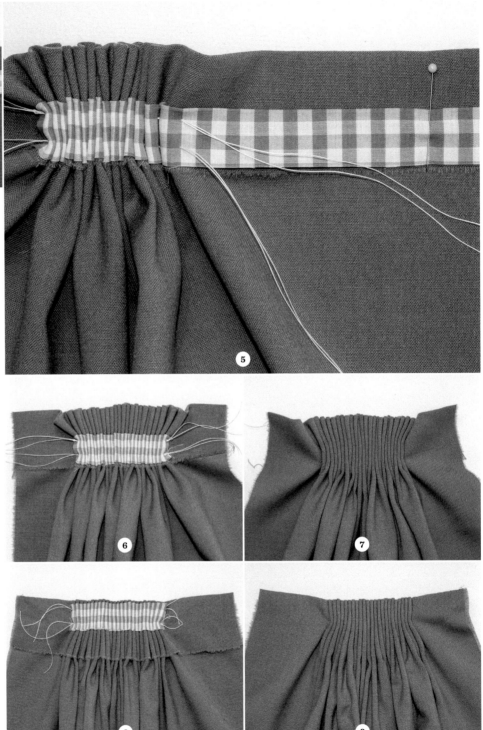

Sewing cartridge pleats onto a garment

You can sew either the front or back edge of a set of cartridge pleats to your garment; sewing the back edge will make the pleating stand proud. If you sew the front edge to a base fabric that is tightly fitted to the body the pleats will jut out slightly before falling in lush rolls. If the base fabric is softly fitted the pleats will pull it away from the body to meet the front folds of the pleats, creating a slope of flat fabric before the densely compacted cartridge pleats.

It is advisable to reinforce the section of the garment to which you are attaching the pleats, because gravity and the sheer weight of the pleated fabric will pull on the surrounding garment. Here the fabric has been underlined with silk organza to give it extra strength. The pleats can also be sewn to a stay, usually Petersham ribbon, which is sewn into the garment.

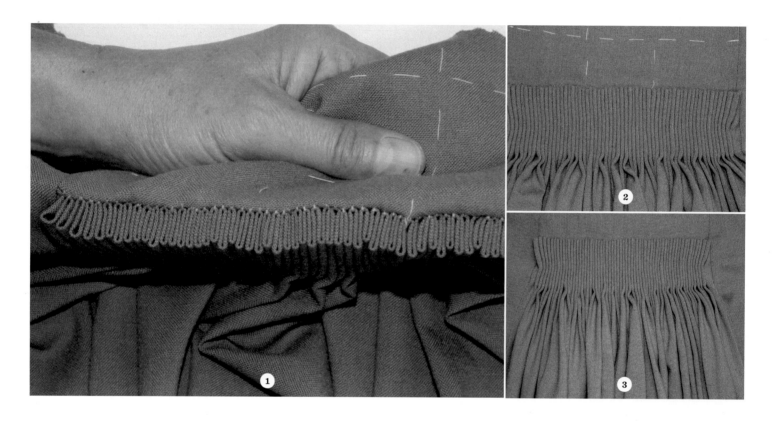

ATTACHING THE BACK OF THE PLEATS TO THE BASE FABRIC

1 Slip-stitch the back of each fold to the base fabric using a double thread.

2 From the right side, 60in (152cm) of wool that has been pleated and sewn into 10in (25cm).

3 When the back edge of the set of cartridge pleats is sewn to the base fabric, the pleats will stand proud.

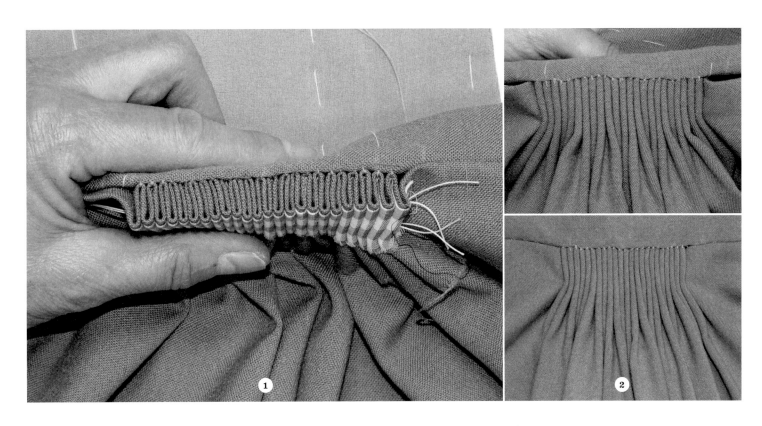

ATTACHING THE FRONT OF THE PLEATS TO THE BASE FABRIC

1 Slip-stitch the front of each fold to the base fabric using a double thread.

2 When the front edge is stitched to the base fabric, the pleats will pull it forward, creating a slope of fabric above the pleats.

Accordion pleats

Accordion pleats are standing pleats; they stand up from the work table. When worn, standing pleats obscure the outline of the wearer's body, adding additional depth to the silhouette. Accordion pleats are named after the straight bellows of an accordion; they are maintained at the same width for their entire length.

Mushroom pleats, which imitate the gills on the underside of a mushroom, are a type of accordion pleat. Fortuny pleats are similar to mushroom pleats but less regular.

One way to make standing pleats is to make a pleat mold in oak tag or other cardboard. Make sure the cardboard will not leach dye when wet, as this process involves sandwiching wet fabric between two pieces of cardboard.

PROFESSIONAL PLEATING SERVICES

Flat pleats, like knife pleats, are pressed flat with an iron so they can be set with relative ease. Standing pleats are more upright and can be more difficult to make.

When standing pleats are needed, the fabric is often sent to a professional pleating company. Depending on the garment and type of pleats, the fabric may be pleated as yardage or as cut pieces. A garment that has been sewn together cannot be pleated because it cannot go through the pleating machinery. Many pleating companies will pleat both small amounts of fabric and entire bolts.

1 Cut two pieces of oak tag slightly larger than your fabric. Draw parallel lines on both pieces of oak tag equal to the width of the pleats. Here the lines are 1¹⁄₄in (3cm) apart.

2 Using an awl or stiletto, punch holes in both ends of the second, fourth, and sixth lines, and in all the even-numbered lines, until the end of the oak tag piece.

Clamp or otherwise secure a metal ruler to the work table, if possible. This will keep the ruler straight as you score the oak tag in the next step.

3 Slide one end of the oak tag under the metal ruler. Line up the first line on the oak tag with the edge of the ruler. Using the awl, score along the first line.

Pull the oak tag through until the third line is along the edge of the ruler. Score the line with the awl. Repeat, scoring every odd-numbered line. Note that the lines with holes punched in them have not yet been scored.

When you reach the end of the oak tag, turn it over and slide the end under the ruler again. On this side the lines will not show. Line up the first set of punched holes along the edge of the ruler and score a line between them. Repeat to score a line between each pair of holes.

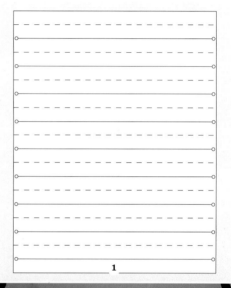

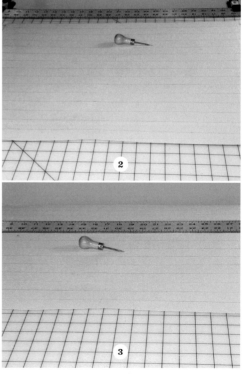

MOUNTAIN AND VALLEY FOLDS

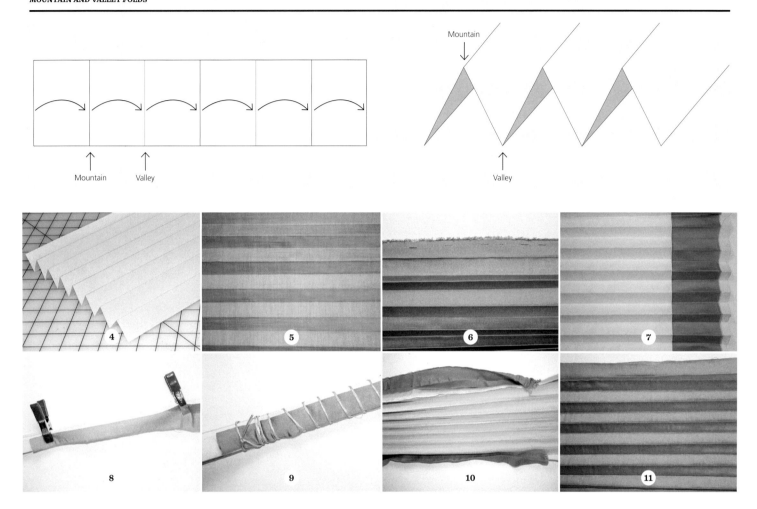

4 Turn the oak tag so that the lined side is facing up. Fold along the first line to make a mountain fold; fold the second line to make a valley fold (see box above). Folding along the edge of the table may be helpful. Continue folding mountains and valleys until the oak tag is all folded.

Repeat Steps 2–4 with the second piece of oak tag. You have now made a set of oak tag molds.

5 Dampen the fabric with a 10:1 solution of water to 5% distilled white vinegar to help set the pleats. Place one oak tag mold on the table with drawn lines facing down. Lay the fabric on top, ensuring that the grainline is parallel to the fold lines. You can staple one edge of the fabric to the edge of the oak tag to keep the fabric on grain and in place. Smooth the fabric over the folds.

6 Lightly fold the oak tag valleys and mountains together.

7 Cover the fabric and oak tag with the other oak tag mold, then firmly fold the molds and fabric together. Rap the folded oak tag sharply on the table to mesh the molds together as tightly as possible.

8 Clamp the molds and fabric together temporarily at either end.

9 Wrap the molds with string to keep them folded together with even tension along their length. Put the molds aside until the fabric is dry, which can take several days.

10 When the fabric is dry, undo the string around the molds.

11 Unfold the molds and remove the top layer of oak tag.

12 The completed accordion pleats with the fabric's right side showing.

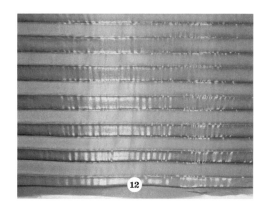

Sunray pleats

Sunray, or sunburst, pleats are based on a circle with a vanishing point, like the rays of the sun. These pleats are often used in circle skirts and sleeve details.

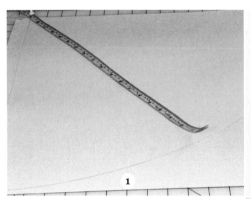

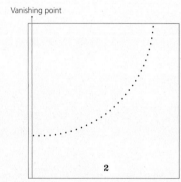

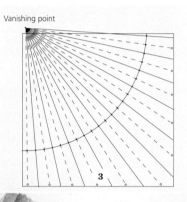

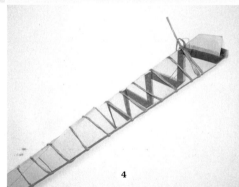

1 Cut two pieces of oak tag slightly larger than your fabric. Anchor a ruler, measuring tape, or string at the vanishing point. Draw one quarter of a circle on each piece of oak tag. The center point of the circle is the vanishing point, which can be located off the oak tag. The circumference of the circle can be the hem, or, as here, it can simply be a guide for measuring the pleats.

2 Mark the width of each pleat along the outer edge, or circumference, of the partial circle. Here the dots are $1\frac{1}{4}$in (3cm) apart.

3 Draw a line from the vanishing point, through the first mark along the circle's circumference, and out to the edge of the oak tag. Repeat with each mark along the circumference.

Create your oak tag molds and begin the pleating process (see Accordion Pleats, Steps 2–9, pp. 78–79).

4 The folded and pleated oak tag and fabric.

5 The completed sunray pleats.

Cutting pattern pieces for a pleated garment

If you are making a garment with many pleats across its length or width, you may find it easier to pleat the fabric before placing the pattern pieces on it and cutting them out. This method works well for large pattern pieces, but for small pattern pieces it may waste fabric, as only smaller sections of pleated fabric are needed.

To establish whether to pleat the fabric before or after cutting, make a paper version of the pleated piece. First pleat a piece of paper with the proper measurements. Lay the pattern piece on top of the pleated paper, then cut it out to create a new pleated pattern piece. When the new pattern piece is unpleated, it will be shaped to accommodate the pleating.

Tracing paper makes a good pleated pattern paper, as the folds are crisp and the transparency reveals any uneven folds.

1 Fold the tracing paper into the desired pleats and pin both ends of each pleat.

2 Lay the pattern piece (here a cuff) onto the pleated tracing paper, straight along the folds.

3 Alternatively, you can lay the pattern piece on the bias.

4 Cut out the pattern piece.

5 Open out the pleated tracing paper to see the actual pattern shape, which will be complex—especially if you have cut the piece on the bias.

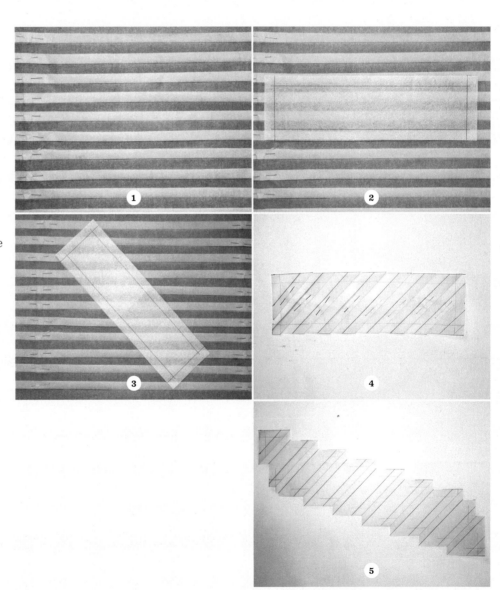

Wrinkled pleating offers a method of adding texture and pattern to a fabric's surface. Entire garments can be made from fabric that has been wrinkle pleated, or smaller sections of wrinkle pleating can be added to create dramatic features within a garment. The choice of fabric can lend different characteristics to the pleating: for example, a piece of Thai silk, with its two-toned weave that changes color when manipulated, becomes a multidimensional fabric that reflects a kaleidoscope of hues when it is wrinkle pleated.

Wrinkled pleating covers several different techniques: some use basic pleating techniques, others are much more intricate. Twist-and-knot, broomstick, and arashi shibori, shown in this section, are just a few examples.

2.4
Wrinkled pleating

These techniques all involve twisting, crimping, or compressing the fabric, securing the compressed shape, and then steaming it to set the pleats. The more complex the technique used, the more control you will have over the intricacies of the pleats.

Many fabrics, both natural and synthetic, pleat well. A lightweight fabric creates delicate crimps when wrinkle pleated, while a heavier fabric creates robust furrows. Always test a sample of the fabric to make sure the dye will not run and that a synthetic fabric will not melt during steaming. To make the pleating more permanent, soak or steam the fabric in a vinegar bath or other acidic solution.

Twist-and-knot pleating

Twist-and-knot pleating is a simple technique. The medium-weight silk shantung shown here was roughly gathered, resulting in deeply furrowed pleats; if a thinner fabric or more controlled gathering were employed, the pleats would be finer and shallower.

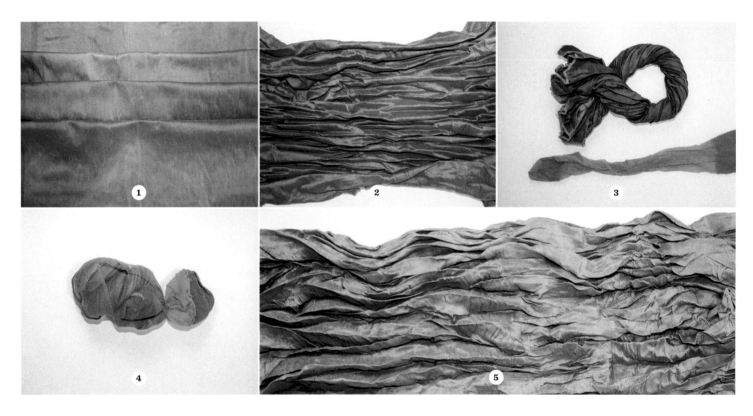

1 Wash the fabric before starting the pleating process to remove any sizing or starch, rinsing it several times to ensure there is no soap residue. For semipermanent pleating, follow the instructions in the tip box opposite.

2 Smooth the largest wrinkles out of the damp fabric with your hands or an iron. If the fabric dries out, re-wet it. Gather the fabric with your hands—the smaller the gathers, the smaller the pleating will be.

3 Holding one end of the fabric in each hand, twist until it coils in on itself.

4 Stuff the coiled fabric into a nylon stocking and knot the stocking at the end. Steam the fabric in a steamer. You can also steam it in a pot by placing it on a wire rack above the water level; cover the pot and steam for 45 minutes.

Remove the stocking with the fabric from the steamer or pot and place in the sink to drain and cool. Do not remove the fabric from the stocking yet. When cool, move to a place where the fabric can dry completely, which can take several days.

Speed up the drying process by putting the stocking with the fabric in a clothes dryer, in a microwave oven for short bursts of time (too long and the fabric might catch alight), or over a hot-air vent.

Remove the dry fabric from the nylon stocking.

5 The dry fabric opened up.

SEMIPERMANENT PLEATING

To make pleating semipermanent, soak the fabric in a vinegar bath or other acidic solution (3–3.5 pH).

1. Mix warm water with distilled white vinegar in a 10:1 ratio.

2. Squeeze the fabric to ensure all layers are wet through. Soak for 20–60 minutes, until all fibers are hydrated—the color will darken from contact with the water.

3. Remove the fabric from the vinegar and water solution and wring it out.

Broomstick pleating

Broomstick pleating is a classic technique of gathering fabric by hand to produce irregular pleats. There are many variations of the technique; the one shown here produces evenly rumpled pleats the entire length of the fabric.

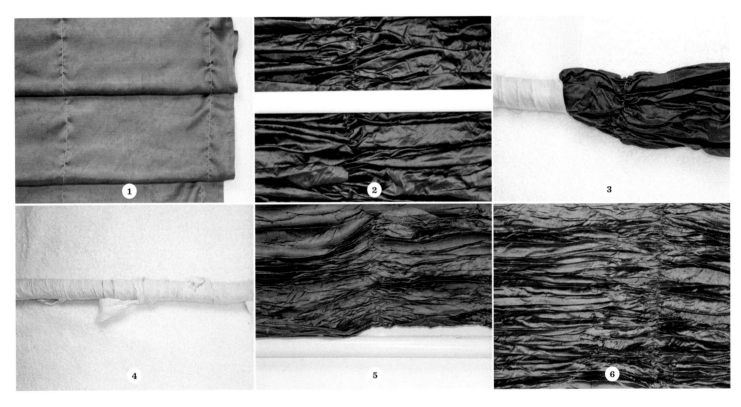

1 Wash the fabric before starting the pleating process to remove any sizing or starch, rinsing it several times to be sure there is no soap residue. When the fabric is dry, iron out any large wrinkles (small wrinkles can be ignored). Sew several lines of gathering stitches the length of the fabric—here the stitching lines are 12in (30cm) apart.

2 Gather the fabric tightly, knotting the threads to hold the gathers in place. Wet the fabric thoroughly, making sure to soak all the creases and folds. Wring out any excess water by rolling up the fabric in a towel. For smaller, shallower pleats, pull the gathering lines apart and stroke the fabric between them to organize the gathers. For fatter, less predictable pleats, push the gathering lines closer together. Lay the broomstick, or in this case a metal mop handle, across the fabric.

3 Roll up the fabric around the broomstick, then tightly wrap the fabric against the broomstick with strips of muslin, compressing the fabric as much as possible.

4 When the entire piece of fabric has been wrapped in muslin, put it aside until it is completely dry, which can take several days.

5 When completely dry, unwrap the muslin strips, saving them for reuse. Unroll the fabric and spread it out. Remove the gathering threads. You can steam-set the pleating with a steam iron; this will hold the pleats until the fabric is washed or dry cleaned. After cleaning, the pleating process will need to be repeated.

6 The finished piece of broom-stick-pleated fabric.

Arashi shibori pleating

Arashi shibori is a Japanese dyeing and pleating technique. *Arashi* means "storm"; fabric dyed and pleated in this way is said to resemble the energy and spirit of a storm. *Shibori* comes from the verb *shiboru*, meaning "to wring," "to squeeze," or "to press."

The following is a simplified version of arashi shibori. True arashi shibori combines dyeing and pleating; here the fabric will only be pleated. Since there is no dye involved, the string wrapping does not need to be as tight as for regular arashi shibori. Traditionally, the string acts as a barrier, preventing the dye from soaking through to the layers of fabric under it; here it is only crimping the fibers to add texture.

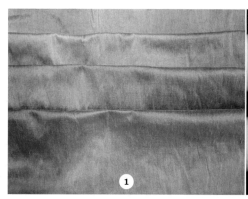

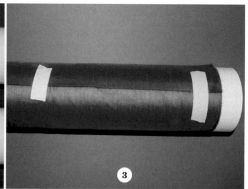

MATERIALS

- PVC plumbing pipe. (Note that the wrapping of the cloth will distort the pipe, so a more durable polypropylene pipe will be needed if you intend to do a lot of arashi shibori.)
- Fine-grit sandpaper or a polypropylene pot scrubber
- Silicone spray for greasing the pipe
- Polypropylene, cotton, nylon, or linen string with low or no twist, which will not stretch but is strong. (If the string is twisted, it will roll along the fabric without taking the fabric with it during the compression steps.)
- White vinegar or other acidic chemical for setting the pleats
- Some spare towels
- A large pot, heavy-duty tinfoil, and a hot plate or stove, or a commercial dyer's steamer
- Low-tack sticky tape

1 Prepare the fabric; here green-gold dupioni silk, 36in (90cm) wide x 54in (137cm) long, is used. Wash the fabric before starting the pleating process to remove any sizing or starch, rinsing it several times to be sure there is no soap residue. When the fabric is dry, iron all the wrinkles from the fabric.

2 Wash the PVC pipe inside and out with a good detergent. Sand the pipe down to make it completely smooth and spray it with the silicone spray, wiping off any excess. Repeat the silicone application. The pipe should be as smooth as glass and very slippery. Take care when moving it; it will be hard to get a good grip. Here the top pipe has been washed and sanded, while the bottom pipe has been washed, sanded, and sprayed with silicone.

3 Carefully wrap the fabric around the pipe. The fabric should be wrinkle free, as any wrinkles will be permanently set in the steaming process. Any wrinkles running at right angles to the pleats will ruin the effect of the pleating.

Tape the ends of the fabric to itself to hold it on the pipe. The tape will be removed once the string is in place.

This piece of dupioni was placed widthwise on the pipe (with the selvages at either end) so the string wrapping and subsequent pleating would follow the striations of the silk.

4 Wrap the string around the end of the pipe twice, avoiding the fabric, and secure it with a knot. Tape the string down so it does not spin on the pipe.

5 Maintaining a firm tension on the string, wrap it around the fabric, keeping the wraps evenly spaced. Wearing gloves may help to pull the string taut. As you wrap, smooth the fabric along the pipe, removing any tape in the way. The smaller the space between string wraps, the smaller the pleats will be.

6 When you have covered a fair portion of the fabric with string, tape the end of the string to the fabric temporarily to maintain the tension. Wrap your hands around the last string wrap and push the string and fabric toward the starting end of the pipe.

7 Compress the wrapped fabric and string as much as possible. It helps to put the end of the pipe against something hard, either the floor or a wall, and push toward it.

8 Repeat the wrapping/compressing process until all fabric is compressed. If you are using a long pipe, you can wrap several pieces of fabric on one piece of pipe.

Fill a bucket or pot with a 10:1 solution of warm water to 5% distilled white vinegar, to make a 3–3.5 pH solution. Insert the pipe and squeeze the fabric with your hands to ensure the water soaks through all layers. Let the fabric soak for 20–60 minutes until all fibers are hydrated—the color will darken from contact with the water.

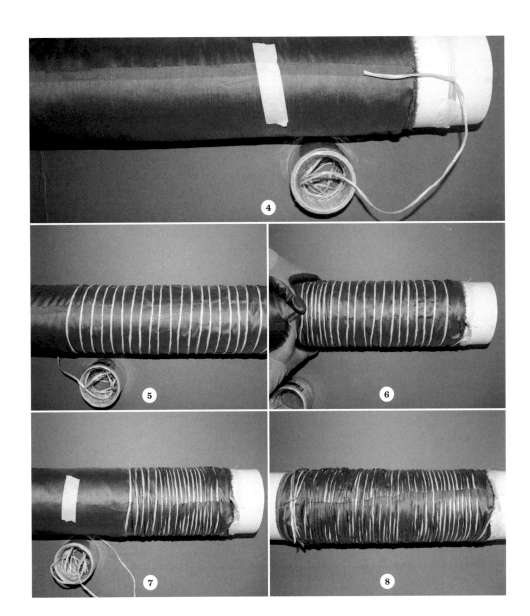

9A To steam on a stove, place a steamer basket at the bottom of a pot and add water. Put the pipe with the fabric into the pot. Make a cone-shaped cover with heavy-duty tinfoil, ensuring the foil does not touch the fabric and does not allow any steam to escape. Add another piece of foil to the top of the pipe if it extends beyond the top of the foil cone. Steam the fabric for 45–60 minutes.

9B If you have access to a commercial dyer's steamer, follow the manufacturer's directions, heating the water and white vinegar solution in the base of the steamer before placing the pipe and compressed fabric inside.

10 Carefully remove the pipe and fabric from the steamer, remembering that the pipe will still be slippery from the silicone spray. Let the fabric dry completely on the pipe, which can take several days. When the fabric is completely dry, you will notice the color has changed back to its original hue.

11 Unwind the string from the pipe and fabric. Save the string for reuse.

12 Unwrap the fabric.

13 The finished, pleated fabric. Note the horizontal folds near the top left of the photo: these were caused by the fabric not being wrapped smoothly around the pipe.

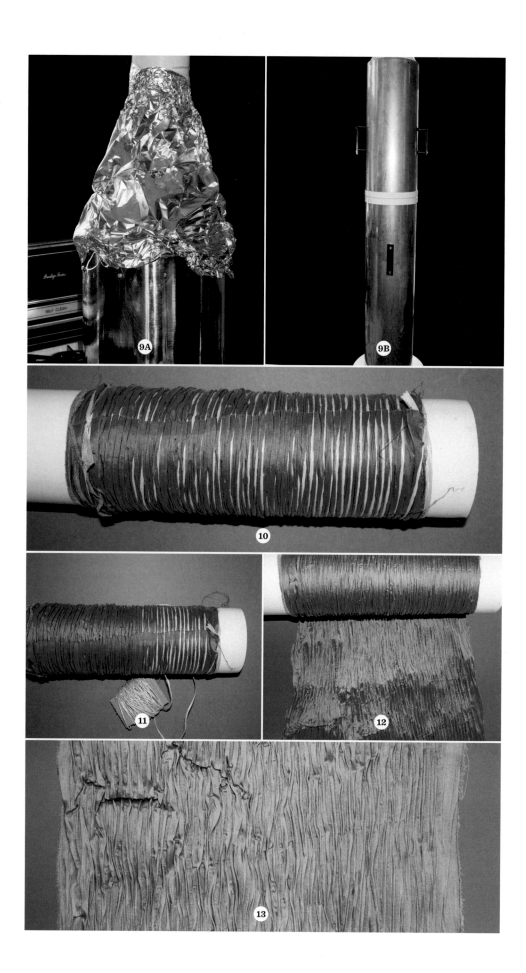

Using arashi shibori to create chevron pleats

Folding the fabric and then wrapping it diagonally around the pipe will create chevron pleats in vertical rows.

1 Here a piece of celadon silk, 58in (147cm) wide x 32in (81cm) long, is used. Wash the fabric and prepare the pipe as directed on p. 86. Fold the fabric into a narrow rectangle: here it was folded into eighths with a finished width of $7^1/_4$in (18.4cm). The folds form the vertical ribs of the chevron pattern; wrapping the fabric in a spiral around the pipe will create the V shape of the chevrons.

2 Place the folded fabric diagonally across the pipe and tape the beginning in place. Wrap the fabric around the pipe. The fabric should be wrinkle free, as any wrinkles will be permanently set in the steaming process. If there are any wrinkles running at right angles to the pleats they will ruin the effect of the pleating. Tape the fabric together across the spiral to help hold it in place. The tape will be removed as the string is wrapped around the pipe.

Wrap the string around the end of the pipe twice and secure it with a knot. Tape the string to the pipe so that it does not spin on the pipe.

3 Maintaining a firm tension on the string, wrap it around the pipe and fabric, keeping wraps evenly spaced. You may find wearing gloves makes it easier to keep the string taut. As you wrap, smooth the fabric along the pipe, removing any tape that is in the way.

If the piece of fabric is short, you will be able to wrap the entire length with string before proceeding to the next step. Knot the string.

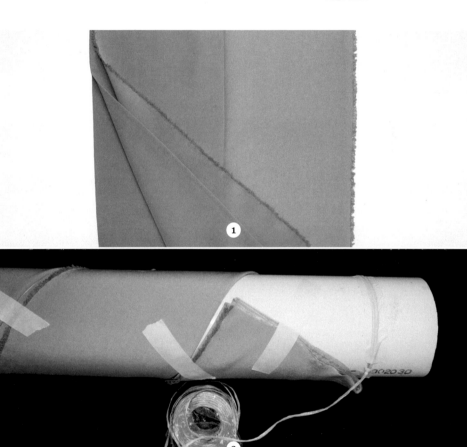

4 Wrap your hands around the last string wrap and push the string and fabric toward the starting end of the pipe, compressing the wrapped fabric and string as much as possible. Steam the fabric as directed on p. 88.

5 Let the fabric dry completely and then unwrap.

6 The celadon silk fabric unwrapped to reveal the chevron pattern pleating.

Sewing with wrinkle-pleated fabric

When sewing with wrinkle-pleated fabric, or any fabric with an unstable texture, you must stabilize the wrinkles or texture along the seam line; if the wrinkle pleating is not stabilized, it will devolve into gathers along the seam line. Stabilize the seam by staystitching along the seam line or by applying a lightweight "ribbon" of organza, stay tape, or twill tape along the seam line.

1 Make your pattern piece. Place it on the fabric and anchor it with weights or pins.

2 Cut out the pattern piece and mark any notches.

3 Make a copy of the pattern on tracing paper or lightweight tear-away interfacing.

4 Pin the tracing-paper pattern to the wrong side of the fabric. Use lots of pins to hold all the wrinkles to the tracing paper pattern in their proper alignment.

5 With the paper lying against the sewing machine bed, sew, $\frac{1}{16}$in (1mm) shy of the seam line, around the perimeter of the pattern piece. Make sure you are looking at the fabric while you sew. Use an awl or other sharp point to prod the wrinkles into place if they start to unfold or gather up. This stitching will anchor the wrinkles' folds to each other and to the paper along the seam line. If further stabilization is needed, a lightweight stay tape can be added; sew organza or nylon stay tape to the wrong side of the fabric along the same stitching line.

6 To keep the wrinkles stabilized, leave the paper attached to the wrong side of the fabric until you are ready to sew the fabric to another garment piece. The paper can be removed before or after the garment pieces are sewn together. Remember to discard the sewing machine needle when you finish, as sewing through the paper will have dulled the needle.

Ruching, shirring, and smocking are three different techniques for integrating sections of gathering into a garment to create surface embellishments.

Ruching can be used to create large areas of gathered fabric, usually between two seams. Panels of fabric, created by gathering the fabric unequally from one side to the other, are said to be "ruched."

Shirring consists of three or more rows of gathered fabric within part of a garment; the initial fabric can range from 1.5 to 3 times the finished gathered width.

2.5
Ruching, shirring, and smocking

Smocking is a combination of decorative embroidery stitches worked on rows of gathered fabric. The fabric is gathered in gridded rows, which form columns called reeds. The embroidery stitched onto the reeds holds them in place, yet allows the fabric to stretch. Originally used to embellish working garments, smocking is now most commonly used on children's garments, but the myriad of patterns that can be created can lend quite contemporary, structured decoration to any garment.

For these techniques, light- to medium-weight fabrics work well. When including areas of ruching, shirring, or smocking, allow for the fabric length to reduce slightly as it is taken up by the gathers; the amount of loss will depend on the number of gathered rows.

Ruching

Ruching is created with a fabric panel that has been gathered along one or more seam lines before being sewn into a garment.

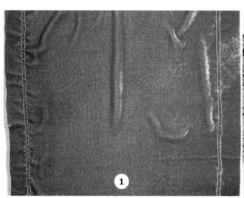

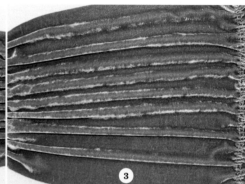

1 Sew two rows of gathering stitches on each side of the fabric (see Basic Ruffles, p. 36). If the fabric panel is very wide, or if you need greater control over the gathering, additional vertical rows of gathering stitches can be sewn throughout the panel.

2 Pull up the gathering threads and adjust the gathers. Here the fabric is gathered by the same amount along both seam lines.

3 The fabric can also be gathered by different amounts on each side.

4 Hand-baste the gathered section into the garment, and then check the final arrangement of the gathers from the right side of the garment before sewing in place. Carefully steam the piece to set the ruching.

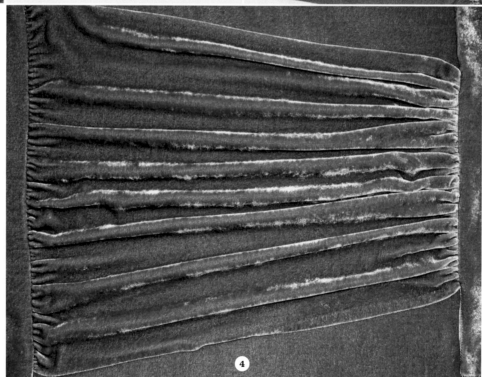

Shirring

In this technique, fabric is gathered in parallel rows using plain or elastic thread. Once the shirring is completed, a fabric stay or backing fabric is sewn to the wrong side to protect the shirring and to create a more comfortable garment.

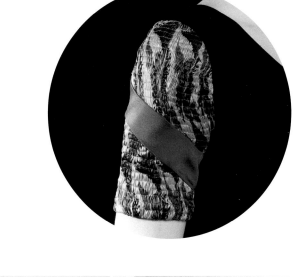

Shirring with plain thread

The advantage and disadvantage of using plain thread is that the shirring is relatively fixed and not stretchy.

1 Make a pattern (see below). Here a piece of medium-weight silk, 18in (45cm) x 24in (61cm), is used. Transfer the lines to be stitched—the "shirring lines"—to the fabric with chalk.

2 With the fabric facing right side up, sew parallel rows of shirring 1in (2.5cm) apart, using the regular gathering method (see Basic Ruffles, p. 36). For clarity, here the needle thread is orange and the bobbin thread is white.

3 Gather all the rows of shirring to the target width, here 11in (27.5cm). Pass the needle threads through to the wrong side of the fabric and knot them at both ends of each row. Do not worry if the fabric is not evenly distributed along the shirring rows; it can be adjusted between rows even after the threads have been knotted.

4 Slide the gathers at the ends of each row slightly toward the middle so the seam allowance area is reasonably flat. Cut a piece of backing fabric to fit the finished piece, here 17in (43cm) x 13in (32.5cm); note the loss in length from the shirring. Pin the shirred fabric to the backing fabric, wrong sides together.

5 Sew the backing fabric to the shirred fabric, being careful to sew over the end of each row of shirring stitches but not catching the gathers of the shirring; this will help to keep the knots secure.

6 Sew the shirred section into the garment. While looking at the right side of the garment, arrange the fabric within each row of shirring. When all the gathers are properly arranged, carefully steam the piece to set the shirring.

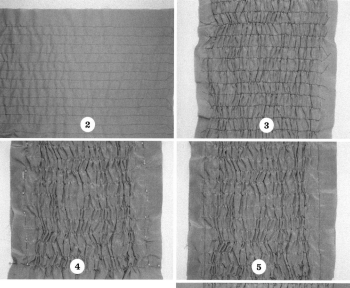

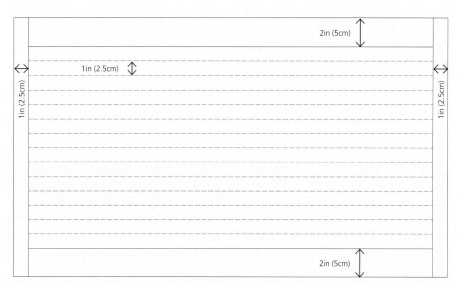

1

SHIRRING ON HEAVYWEIGHT FABRICS

Shirring can also be sewn over a cord (see Gathering Fabric Over a Cord, p. 37), which is ideal for a heavier-weight fabric.

Shirring with elastic thread

Shirring with elastic thread has the advantage of being flexible and form fitting. Unfortunately elastic shirring cannot be covered by a backing cloth because this would restrict the elasticity of the shirring, so the shirring may irritate the wearer slightly.

1 Make a pattern following the diagram on p. 95. Here a piece of medium-weight silk, 18in (45cm) x 24in (61cm), was used. Transfer the lines to be stitched—the "shirring lines"—to the fabric with chalk.

2 Wind the elastic thread onto the bobbin by hand or by machine. Do not thread it through the tension disks and other thread guides leading to the bobbin winder; slowly guide the elastic with your hands, making sure it is wound onto the bobbin in a relaxed state. Since the elastic is much thicker than regular thread, you may need to adjust the tension on the bobbin case (see p. 24).

3 With the fabric facing right side up, sew parallel rows of shirring, 1in (2.5cm) apart. The fabric will gather as you stitch—sew carefully on the marked lines, stretching the fabric flat as necessary. Leave long thread tails.

4 Depending on your sewing machine and fabric choice, you may need to gather the fabric more or stretch it out using the long thread tails. Here the fabric is gathered more to reach the target width of 11in (27.5cm). Pass the needle threads through to the wrong side of the fabric and knot them at both ends of each row. Do not worry if the fabric is not evenly distributed along the shirring rows; it can be adjusted between rows after the threads have been knotted.

5 Slide the gathers at the ends of each row slightly toward the middle so that seam allowance area is reasonably flat. Sew the shirred piece into the garment as required. While looking at the right side of the garment, arrange the fabric within each row of shirring. When all the gathers are properly arrayed, carefully steam the piece to set the shirring.

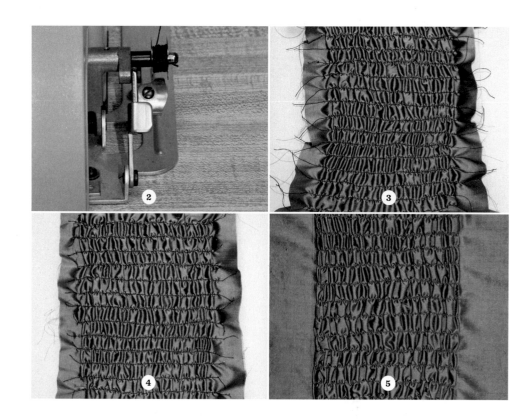

Smocking

When fabric was a precious commodity, many garments were made from uncut rectangular pieces. The fabric was gathered around the neck, at the shoulders, and around the torso and wrist, shaping it to fit the body. In England, labourers' overshirts created in this way became known as smocks. The gathers were embroidered with stitches that helped to hold the gathered fabric close to the body, yet allowed it to stretch as needed. This stretchy embroidery became known as smocking and was later codified into guild symbols: a farmer's smock would be embroidered with wheat grains, for example, while a shepherd's smock would feature shepherd's crooks.

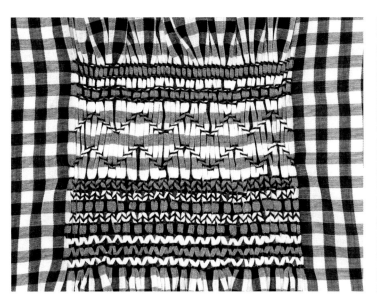

The smocking in its relaxed position measures
4½in (11.5cm) wide x 3¾in (9.5cm) tall.

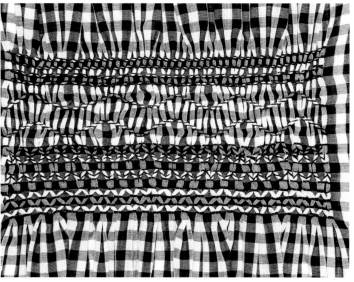

The smocking here is slightly stretched and measures
8in (20cm) wide x 3in (7.5cm) tall.

Choosing the fabric

Any plain weave fabric can be used for smocking: many cottons, lightweight wools, and silks gather well and make good backgrounds for the embroidery. Always start with the grainlines squared up; a piece of fabric that is off-grain will fall unevenly. The columns of deep, even gathers are called "reeds." The embroidery stitches that embellish a smock and provide the elasticity are worked through a third to half the depth of each reed; the stitches must hold the gathers, yet should not be so deep that they flatten the reeds.

If you are using a thick fabric you may need three times the width of the finished piece for your base fabric. If you are using a thinner fabric you may need four to six times the width. Shown above is a lightweight cotton polyester blend gingham, 23in (58.5cm) wide, which was gathered to 4½in (11.5cm), roughly a sixth of the initial width. Remember that all fabrics will loose a little of their length when gathered; here the sample shrank from 3¾in (9.5cm) long to 3in (7.5cm).

Gathering the fabric

Gingham is an ideal fabric for a smocking project—the squares woven into the fabric make their own smocking grid. The gingham can be 100% cotton or a cotton and polyester blend; be sure to preshrink the fabric before you begin.

1 Thread a needle with a long piece of strong thread—long enough to traverse the width of the gingham plus 6in (15cm). Mark the area to be smocked. Make a large knot 3in (7.5cm) from the end of the thread.

Working on the right side, insert the needle and thread into a corner of a gingham square just inside the seam allowance. Bring the needle and thread out at the far corner of the same square. Skip the next square and then sew through the following square. Repeat this sequence right across the fabric, leaving a long thread tail at the end of the row. Continue stitching along each row in the same way.

2 Repeat the same sequence until you have sewn all the rows to be gathered.

3 Slide the fabric across on the gathering threads. Note the depth of gathers formed by the even gathering stitches; these vertical columns are the reeds.

4 Do not gather the fabric as compactly as possible. Leave a little play between the reeds; working the embroidery stitches requires some space, and they will take up some space on their own. When the fabric is gathered to the required width, wrap the thread tails around pins in a figure of eight. You can leave the threads on the pins or knot them together in pairs.

5 Arrange the gathered fabric so all the reeds are straight vertically and horizontally. The reeds do not need to be precisely spaced because you will be shifting them slightly as you work. Steam the reeds lightly to help set their columnar shape.

6 The gathered gingham from the wrong side.

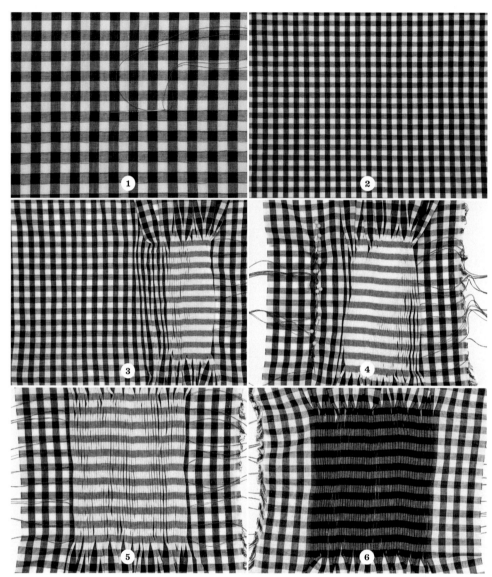

Smocking dots

Gingham provides a ready-made grid for gathering, but if you are smocking a plain piece of fabric you can use wax transfer smocking dots to mark out your grid.

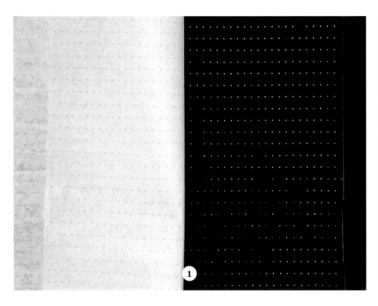

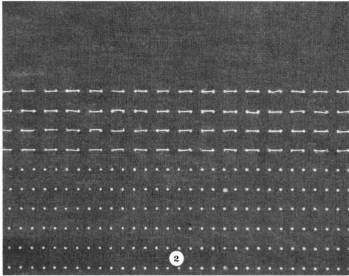

1 First created in the 1870s, iron-on smocking dots are available in yellow and blue wax and should be applied to the back of the fabric following the manufacturer's instructions. Test the dots on a scrap of fabric, as the wax may bleed through to the right side of a lightweight fabric.

2 Use a dressmaker's pencil to fill in any missing dots in the grid. Prepare the fabric for gathering by sewing from dot to dot.

Smocking stitches

The most popular embroidery stitches for smocking are stem, cable, surface honeycomb, honeycomb or spot honeycomb, and wave or chevron. If the embroidery is pictorial, a back-smocking stitch is worked on the wrong side of the gathering to eliminate the stretch in the gathers; cable stitch is good to use for this.

Steaming the smocked fabric

After working all the smocking stitches, remove the gathering threads. Steam the smocked piece, keeping the iron above the fabric. Let the smocking dry completely on the ironing board.

Smocking embroidery—Outline / Edge stitches

Stem stitch and cable stitch are often used for the first or last row in a smocked panel because they provide a straight stitch to butt up against a seam.

STEM STITCH

Stem stitch is a basic outlining stitch with a slanted shape. It can also be worked along a curve for a vine or wave design.

Stem stitch is worked from left to right. Working on the right side of the fabric, bring the needle up through the left side of the first reed, above the gathering stitches, at half to a third of the depth of the reed. Bring the needle and thread to the right and, with the needle pointing left, insert it into the right side of the second reed at the same depth. Bring your needle and thread out on the left side of the second reed, just above the standing thread (the thread coming out of the fabric from the previous stitch). Pull the thread through. Repeat this process across the row, continuing to work from left to right. (See also Hand Embroidery, p. 299.)

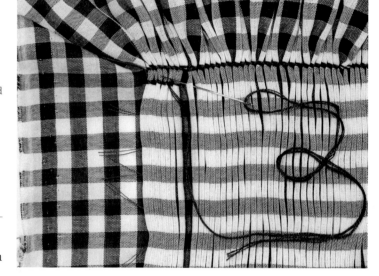

CABLE STITCH

Cable stitch has a stepped shape, as one stitch is worked with the standing thread kept above the needle, and the next stitch with it kept below the needle. Cable stitch can be worked to fill a shape in a pictorial design and as a stabilizing back-smocking stitch on the wrong side to prevent distortion of the pictorial design.

1 Cable stitch is worked from left to right. Working on the right side of the fabric, bring the needle up through the left side of the first reed, above the gathering stitches, at half to a third of the depth of the reed. Bring the needle and thread to the right and, with the needle pointing left, insert it into the right side of the second reed at the same depth. Bring your needle and thread out on the left side of the second reed, just above the standing thread (the thread coming out of the fabric from the previous stitch). Pull the thread through.

2 Repeat Step 1, this time bringing the needle out on the left side of the third reed, just below the standing thread. Pull the needle through. Repeat Steps 1 and 2, continuing to alternate over and under the standing threads.

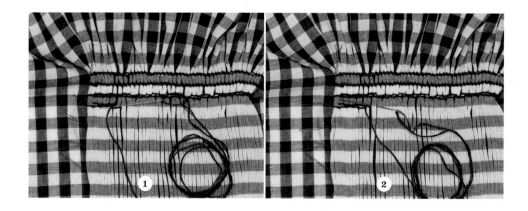

Smocking embroidery— Wave stitch / Chevron stitch

Wave stitch has many variations, depending on how many stitches are created between the top and bottom of the wave. Two sets of wave stitches can be worked in a mirrored pattern to form diamonds. Generally wave stitch is worked between two rows of gathering stitches but here it is worked between three rows.

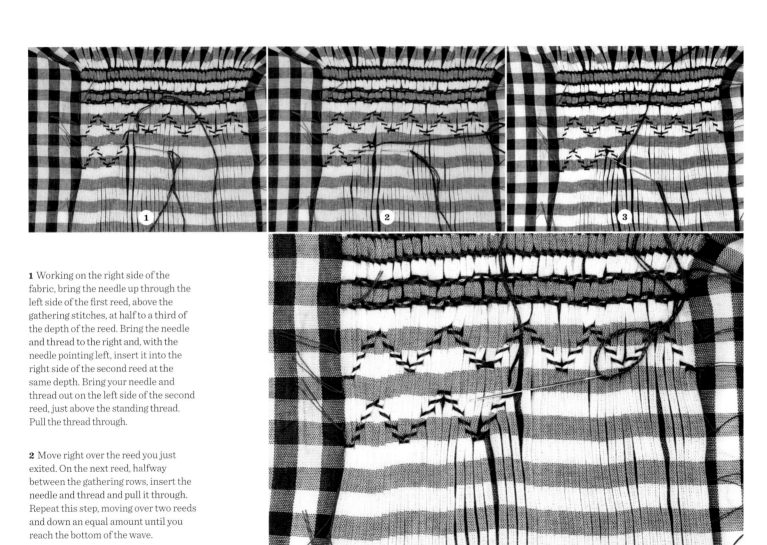

1 Working on the right side of the fabric, bring the needle up through the left side of the first reed, above the gathering stitches, at half to a third of the depth of the reed. Bring the needle and thread to the right and, with the needle pointing left, insert it into the right side of the second reed at the same depth. Bring your needle and thread out on the left side of the second reed, just above the standing thread. Pull the thread through.

2 Move right over the reed you just exited. On the next reed, halfway between the gathering rows, insert the needle and thread and pull it through. Repeat this step, moving over two reeds and down an equal amount until you reach the bottom of the wave.

3 At the bottom of the wave, sew two reeds together with the needle and thread, coming out between the two reeds, as in Step 1.

4 Repeat Step 2, moving over two reeds and up an equal amount until you reach the top of the wave. Repeat Steps 1–4, moving up and down across the row.

Smocking embroidery—
Honeycomb stitch / Spot honeycomb stitch

Honeycomb stitch is surprisingly stretchy, forming straight rows when relaxed and V-shapes when stretched. Honeycomb stitch is surface honeycomb stitch seen from the other side. The name "honeycomb stitch" comes from the pattern created by the stitched fabric when stretched.

1 Working on the right side of the fabric, bring the needle up through the left side of the first reed, above the gathering stitches, at half to a third of the depth of the reed. Bring the needle and thread to the right and insert it into the right side of the second reed at the same depth. Sew left through the first two reeds. Pull the thread through.

2 Insert the needle and thread into the top of the second reed and come out at the next row down of gathering stitches, on the inside of the reed. The stitch will be crossing the reed on the wrong side of the fabric.

3 Move right, skipping one reed. Sew left through two reeds. Pull the thread through.

4 Insert the needle and thread at the bottom of the second reed and come out on the upper row of gathering, on the inside of the reed. Again, the stitch will cross the reed on the wrong side of the fabric. Repeat Steps 1–4 until the row is complete.

Smocking embroidery— Surface honeycomb stitch

Surface honeycomb stitch is the simplest of the diagonal smocking stitches. The diagonal wrapping of this stitch allows the fabric to stretch a lot.

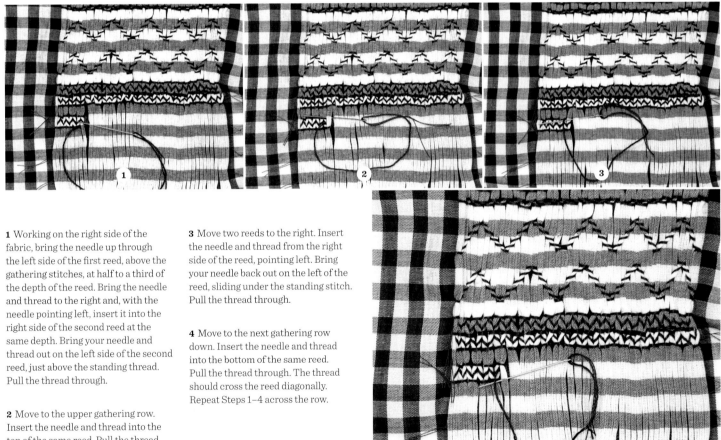

1 Working on the right side of the fabric, bring the needle up through the left side of the first reed, above the gathering stitches, at half to a third of the depth of the reed. Bring the needle and thread to the right and, with the needle pointing left, insert it into the right side of the second reed at the same depth. Bring your needle and thread out on the left side of the second reed, just above the standing thread. Pull the thread through.

2 Move to the upper gathering row. Insert the needle and thread into the top of the same reed. Pull the thread through. The thread should cross the reed diagonally.

3 Move two reeds to the right. Insert the needle and thread from the right side of the reed, pointing left. Bring your needle back out on the left of the reed, sliding under the standing stitch. Pull the thread through.

4 Move to the next gathering row down. Insert the needle and thread into the bottom of the same reed. Pull the thread through. The thread should cross the reed diagonally. Repeat Steps 1–4 across the row.

Quilting is the sewing together of several layers of fabric with lines of stitching. Patchwork, with which it is often associated, involves sewing pieces of fabric together into a larger piece, which is often then quilted. The term "quilt" comes from the old French *cuilte*, which is from the Latin *culcita*, meaning "mattress." Quilting has been used as a technique since at least medieval times: to layer fabrics so as to protect specific areas of hard wear, as a way of recycling precious pieces of fabric, to create garments used for warmth, and for protection under or over armor.

Once the basic utility of quilted garments was established, the needlework became an art form in its own right. Quilting for warmth, for example, evolved into quilting along design lines, which in turn led to corded quilting,

2.6
Quilting

in which cords are incorporated between stitched lines, and trapunto, the practice of stuffing areas between lines of decorative stitching. Patching developed into complex piecing designs like Seminole patchwork. Sashiko began in Japan as a mending technique and has grown into a catalog of complex stitching patterns.

Large pieces of fabric can be quilted and garment pieces then cut from the quilted fabric, or smaller sections of a garment can be quilted to add a three-dimensional, textural quality. While cotton is the traditional fabric used for quilting, the techniques can be used on almost any fabric. Silk and wool have long have been used by couture designers to create sumptuous quilted garments.

Machine quilting

For quilting, you will need both a top fabric and a backing fabric, as well as batting to go between them. Long-arm quilting machines are available, but the directions here are for a regular sewing machine. Since quilting will shrink the surface area, it is best to quilt the fabric and then cut out the pattern pieces. The thickness of the batting and the density of quilting lines will change the drape of the fashion fabric, so make several samples to determine the best stitching plan and batting for your design. Do not use hand-quilting thread in your sewing machine: the coating on the thread will gum up the tension disks.

Preparing your materials

BATTING

Remove the batting from its packaging, lay it on an ironing board, and steam it to remove any creases and restore its inherent loft. Only steam the batting; pressing will diminish the loft.

A layer of cotton flannel works well as a thin batting. Since the nap of the flannel will stick to both backing and top fabric, and the loft it provides is slight, the layers will shift less and the amount of grid basting in Step 5 can be reduced.

1 Iron your fabrics flat. Spread out the backing fabric, wrong side up, so it is taut but not stretched, similar to the tension of fabric in an embroidery hoop. Tape it to the table surface to maintain the tension; here, low-tack blue painter's tape was used to secure lightweight white wool.

2 Lay the batting on top of the backing fabric. If you are using a fabric such as cotton flannel as batting, tape it taut like the backing fabric. If using a matted material, like this wool batting, do not tape it down as this will reduce its loft.

3 Lay the top fabric on top of the batting, right side up, pulling the fabric taut and taping it to the tape holding the backing fabric. The top and backing fabrics should be under the same amount of tension. The two layers of tape will create a sort of quilting frame.

4 Pin the backing fabric, batting, and top fabric together.

5 Grid-baste the quilt sandwich (see Grid Basting, p. 27) to hold the layers together and prevent them slipping out of alignment during quilting. Peeling the bottom layer of tape up from the table should enable you to lift sections of the quilt sandwich without losing the tension aligning the fabrics, which will make grid basting easier.

6 Remove the fabric from the table. Either fold the tape back onto itself to cover the sticky part and keep it as a quilting frame, or remove it and rely on the grid basting to keep the fabric layers aligned.

7 Choose the machine thread tension according to the batting thickness. The thicker the batting, the looser the thread tension; the needle thread needs to travel farther to reach the bobbin thread and a looser tension allows more thread to pass through the tension disks.

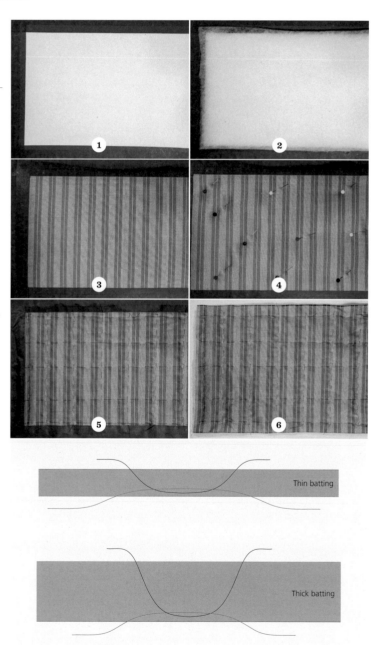

Thin batting

Thick batting

7

8 To quilt in one direction, start sewing in the center. Stitch each line in the same direction, working out to one edge, then start in the center again and work to the other edge.

9 To quilt in two directions, first sew two anchoring lines at the center of your piece, one in each direction. Sew the vertical lines, working from the center to one side. Roll up the quilted portion and work from the center to the other side. After completing the vertical lines, sew the horizontal lines, again working from the center to one side, rotating the work, then sewing the last set of lines.

USING A WALKING FOOT

If the top fabric extends beyond the batting and backing fabric at the end of a row of stitching, the top fabric is being fed too slowly by the presser foot, while the backing fabric and batting are being fed too quickly by the feed dogs. A walking foot will fix this problem. The walking foot replaces a regular presser foot and works with the feed dogs to feed the top fabric through the machine at the same rate as the lower layers.

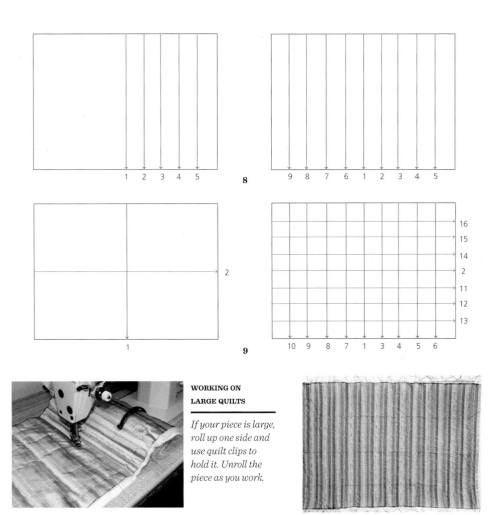

WORKING ON LARGE QUILTS

If your piece is large, roll up one side and use quilt clips to hold it. Unroll the piece as you work.

The piece after quilting.

Using quilted fabric

After quilting, remove the grid basting and press the fabrics.

1 To use the quilted fabric for your garment, pin the pattern pieces to the quilting and trace around the outlines using chalk or another type of marking pen. Here two cuff patterns are pinned to the fabric.

2 Remove the pattern pieces. Hand-baste around each piece within the seam allowances to prevent the quilted layers from coming apart during garment construction.

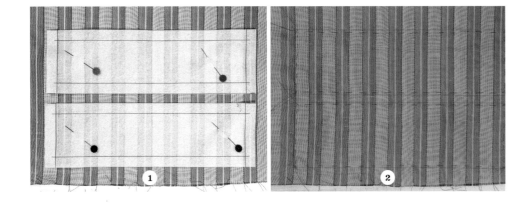

Hand quilting

Hand quilting ranges from sewing straight lines, to outlines of shapes, to intricate motifs. Whatever the design, these stitching patterns all emphasize the three-dimensional quality created by sandwiching a batting material between two layers of fabric. Before you begin, prepare your fabric and batting (see p. 106).

Materials

NEEDLES

Use a very short needle. Betweens or quilting needles make it easier to sew the small stitches that hold the fabric sandwich of top fabric, batting, and backing fabric together.

THREAD

Use beeswax to coat the sewing thread; this strengthens the thread and keeps it from knotting. Hand-quilting threads of various kinds are also available: coated polyester thread, coated and uncoated 100% cotton thread, and silk thread. If you buy coated hand-quilting thread, do not use it in a sewing machine—the coating will gum up the tension disks.

QUILTING FRAMES

Quilting frames are oversized embroidery hoops with stands. They hold the fabric sandwich taut and organized, and leave your hands free to manipulate the needle. A lap quilting frame holds a lap's worth of fabric taut in a frame that stands on the floor; the more traditional quilting frame looks like a loom and holds a bedspread's worth of fabric and batting on two rollers, exposing only a portion of the fabric sandwich at a time. If you are experimenting with hand quilting, you can simply use a large embroidery hoop with a tabletop stand.

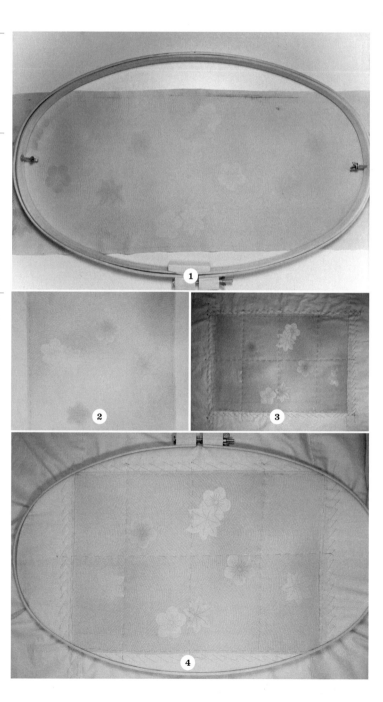

Securing the fabric in the hoop

1 Check the size of your quilting frame against the fabric sandwich.

2 If the hoop is too large, as shown here, hand-baste muslin strips to the sides of the fabric to extend it to fit the frame.

3 Follow Steps 1–5 in Machine Quilting (see p. 106) to sandwich the backing, batting, and top fabric together. Here the three layers were also diagonally basted together at the edge of the muslin for additional security.

4 Place the fabric sandwich in the quilting frame. This version is like a large embroidery hoop, with legs to hold the fabric at table height.

Hand-quilting stitches—Rocking stitch

If you are using thin to medium batting, you can use rocking stitch to quilt your fabric sandwich. If you are using a medium to thick batting, you can use stab stitch (see p. 111).

Rocking stitch is the traditional hand-quilting stitch. Expert hand quilters can sew this stitch nearly as quickly as a sewing machine can.

1 Make a knot in your thread (see Knotting Thread Ends, p. 29) and bring your needle up at the start of the first stitch. Insert the tip of the needle into the fabric $^3/_{16}$in (5mm) away from where you started. Make sure the tip of the needle is absolutely vertical through the fabric sandwich.

2 With your left hand underneath the fabric, feel for the tip of the needle as it pierces the fabric sandwich. As soon as you feel the needle tip, use your right hand to push or rock the eye-end of the needle to the fabric face until the needle is nearly flat against the fabric. Wear a thimble on the finger that does the pushing/rocking motion.

3 Underneath the quilt sandwich, use the tip of your left thumbnail to push the tip of the needle back up to the surface.

4 The rocking of the right hand while deflecting the tip with left thumbnail will return the needle to the right side of the quilt, making a small stitch.

5 Without pulling the needle all the way out of the fabric, make another stitch: rock the tip of the needle back into the fabric face, making sure it goes into the fabric absolutely vertical. This may seem counterintuitive; this is not a sliding stitch and it does stretch the fabric very slightly, as seen in the photo.

6 Rock the needle back up to the fabric surface and complete the second stitch.

7 Push the needle all the way through the fabric to complete these two stitches. Continue making two stitches, or two passes of the needle, at a time. If the batting is very thin you can sew three stitches at a time.

8 When you have finished a line of stitches, after you bring the needle up, and before your final stitch, make a knot on the thread to sit right where the end of the final stitch will be.

9 Insert the needle into the top fabric and the batting where your final stitch will end. Bring the needle up 1in (2.5cm) away from your last stitch. Pull gently until the knot pops down through the fabric.

10 While still pulling gently on the thread, clip the thread at the fabric surface; the tail end of the thread will disappear into the batting.

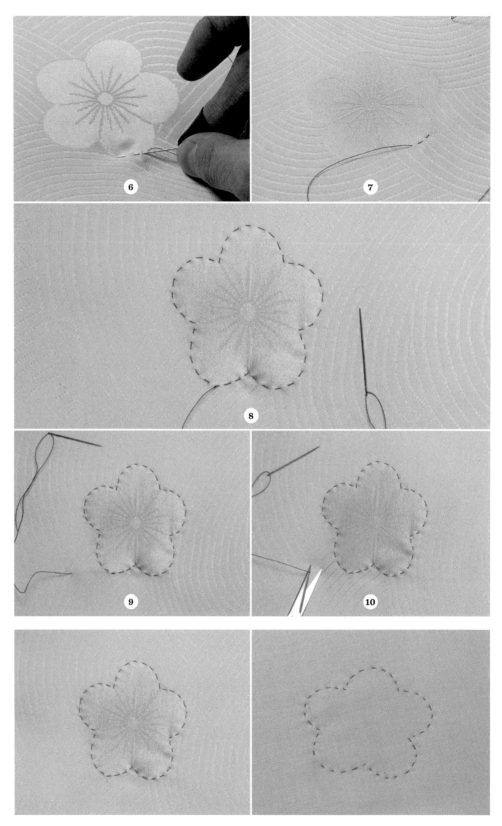

The completed quilted flower, with a layer of cotton flannel fabric as batting.

The quilted flower on the wrong side.

Hand-quilting stitches—Stab stitch

If you are using a thicker batting, you will need to use the stab-stitch method of quilting. The key to stab stitch is to keep the needle vertical in each pass through the quilt sandwich.

1 Make a knot (see Knotting Thread Ends, p. 29) and bring your needle up at the start of the first stitch. Insert the needle $^3/_{16}$in (5mm) away from the start and push it straight down through the fabric sandwich. Here the needle is slightly angled to show the stitch length.

2 Bring the needle up though the quilt sandwich $^3/_{16}$in (5mm) away, keeping the needle vertical.

3 Continue until the line of stitching is complete. When you have finished the line of stitches, knot the end of the thread and pull it through to conceal it under the top layer (see Rocking Stitch, Steps 8–10, opposite).

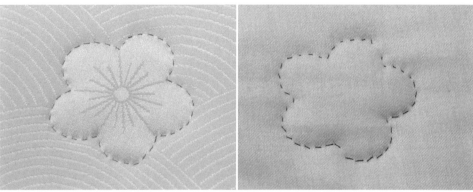

The complete quilted flower with thick wool batting.

The quilted flower on the wrong side.

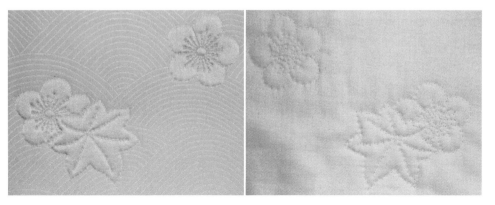

Two flowers and a leaf hand-quilted in cream-colored thread.

The same flowers and leaf on the wrong side.

Seminole patchwork

Perfected by the Seminole Indians of Florida, this style of patchwork looks complex, but the basic technique is simple. It is easy to play with colors, prints, and textures, creating very different designs from just a few small pieces of cloth.

Cotton fabrics make good Seminole patchwork blocks, but silk dupioni and raw silk give the patchwork an elegant finish. Patterned fabrics set against plain fabrics add another dimension to the blocks, especially if the patterns are placed to enhance the patchwork design. Framing a small sample of the patchwork with plain fabric or muslin will help you visualize the completed block.

All seam allowances should be $^1/_4$in (6mm). Seams should be sewn with a small stitch length, 2mm (12 spi), so that when you cut the strips the stitches stay intact. Press the seams as sewn and then press seam allowances to one side or open; do not combine strips until the seam allowances have been pressed.

Checkerboard

MATERIALS

To make a finished block, 3 x 12$^1/_2$in (7.5 x 32cm), you will need:
• A strip of light-colored fabric, 2 x 17in (5 x 43cm)
• A strip of dark-colored fabric, 2 x 17in (5 x 43cm)

1 Sew the strips together lengthwise to make a starter block. Press the seams.

2 Cut the starter block into strips 2in (5cm) wide.

3 Turn every other strip upside down to create the checkerboard.

4 Sew pairs of strips together, matching the center seams very carefully.

5 Sew the newly made squares into a block.

6 Add more squares as needed to complete the design.

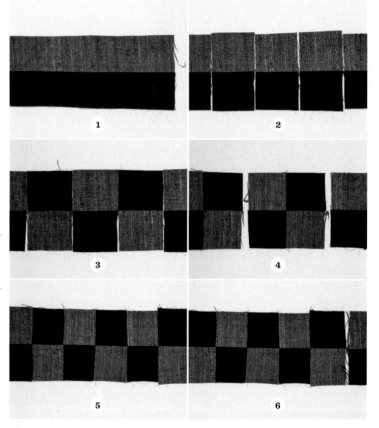

The checkerboard block banded with cream silk.

Offset squares

MATERIALS

• Three strips of different fabrics, each 2 x 12in (5 x 30cm)

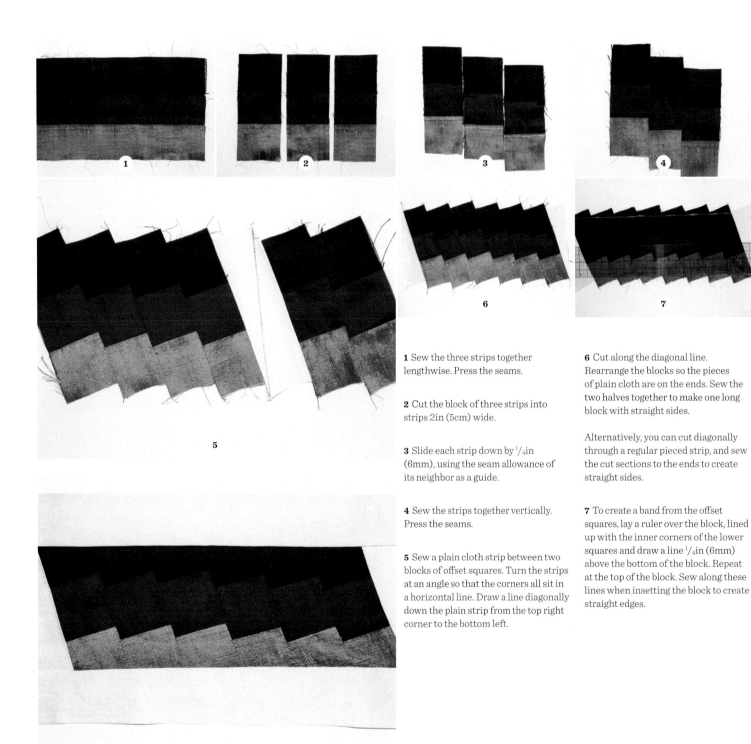

The finished block banded with cream silk.

1 Sew the three strips together lengthwise. Press the seams.

2 Cut the block of three strips into strips 2in (5cm) wide.

3 Slide each strip down by $1/4$in (6mm), using the seam allowance of its neighbor as a guide.

4 Sew the strips together vertically. Press the seams.

5 Sew a plain cloth strip between two blocks of offset squares. Turn the strips at an angle so that the corners all sit in a horizontal line. Draw a line diagonally down the plain strip from the top right corner to the bottom left.

6 Cut along the diagonal line. Rearrange the blocks so the pieces of plain cloth are on the ends. Sew the two halves together to make one long block with straight sides.

Alternatively, you can cut diagonally through a regular pieced strip, and sew the cut sections to the ends to create straight sides.

7 To create a band from the offset squares, lay a ruler over the block, lined up with the inner corners of the lower squares and draw a line $1/4$in (6mm) above the bottom of the block. Repeat at the top of the block. Sew along these lines when insetting the block to create straight edges.

Offset squares—Varying widths

MATERIALS

To make a finished block, 2 x 15in (5 x 38cm), you will need:
• Two strips of different fabrics, each 2 x 17in (5 x 43cm)
• One strip of fabric 1¹/₂ x 17in (3.8 x 43cm)

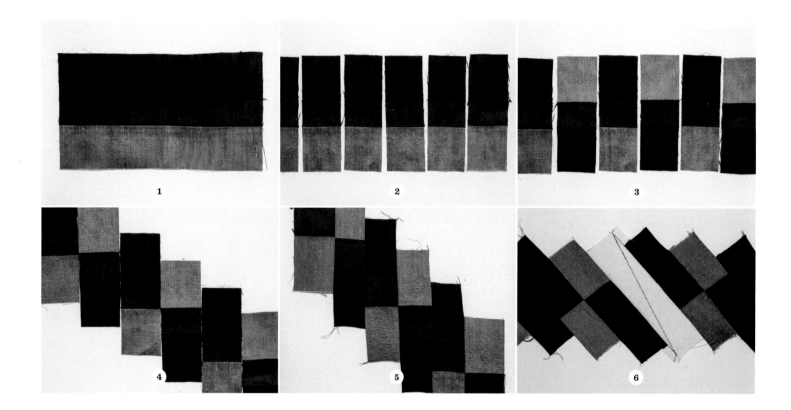

1 Sew the three strips together lengthwise, with the thinner strip in the middle. Press the seams.

2 Cut the block into strips 1¹/₂in (3.8cm) wide.

3 Turn every other strip upside down.

4 Slide each strip down by the height of the middle strip, against its neighbor.

5 Sew the strips together vertically. Press the seams.

6 Reorient and square off the block (see Offset Squares, Steps 5–6, p. 113).

The completed block banded with cream silk.

Diagonals

MATERIALS

- Two strips of dark fabric, each 6¹/₂ x 45in (16.5 x 114.5cm)
- One strip of striped fabric, 2 x 45in (5 x 114.5cm)

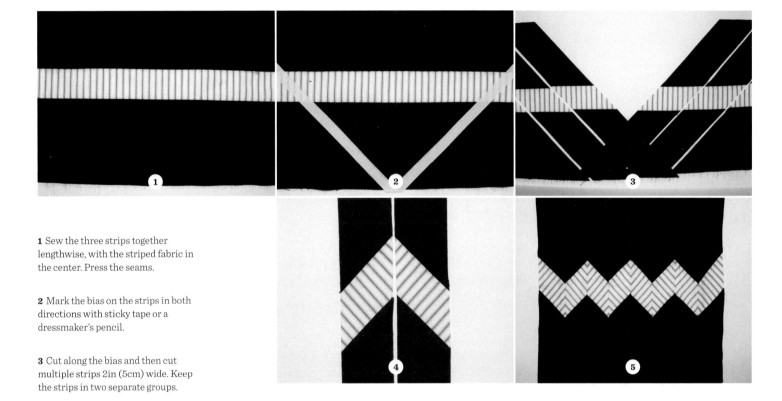

1 Sew the three strips together lengthwise, with the striped fabric in the center. Press the seams.

2 Mark the bias on the strips in both directions with sticky tape or a dressmaker's pencil.

3 Cut along the bias and then cut multiple strips 2in (5cm) wide. Keep the strips in two separate groups.

4 Take one strip from each group. Match the stripes in the center fabrics together, changing strips if needed to get the stripes to match. Sew these strips together.

5 Repeat the matching and sewing until you have used all the strips.

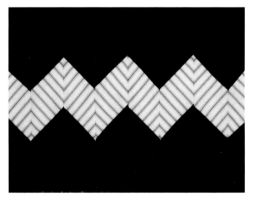

The completed block.

Trapunto

Trapunto is the creation of raised motifs on fabric, using patterns that have been already woven into or printed on the fabric, or ones you have designed yourself. A backing fabric is stitched to the fashion fabric along the pattern lines, creating small pockets. Slits are cut in the pockets and stuffing inserted to create the raised design. After the slits have been sewn shut, a further layer of backing or lining fabric is generally added, as the slits can be abrasive against the skin, and too fragile to stay closed when exposed to regular wear and tear.

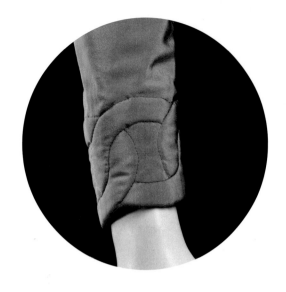

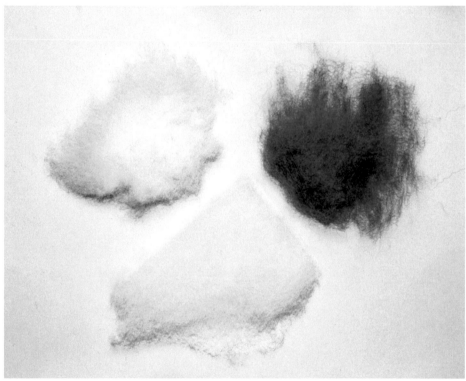

Stuffing fibers commonly used in trapunto include white cotton or polyester pillow stuffing (top left), blue wool roving (top right), and wool quilt batting (bottom).

A number of fibers can be used for the stuffing. The traditional choice is white cotton or polyester pillow stuffing. Quilt batting can also be used. Another good filling is wool roving; this comes in many colors, which can be used to enhance your design.

1 Here a piece of jacquard-woven kimono silk was used as the fashion fabric. The larger design motifs from the jacquard weave were marked using a heat-erasable pen to make them easier to see while stitching.

2 Machine-stitch around each motif leaving long thread tails. Here the outline was sewn in one pass and the interior lines in subsequent passes.

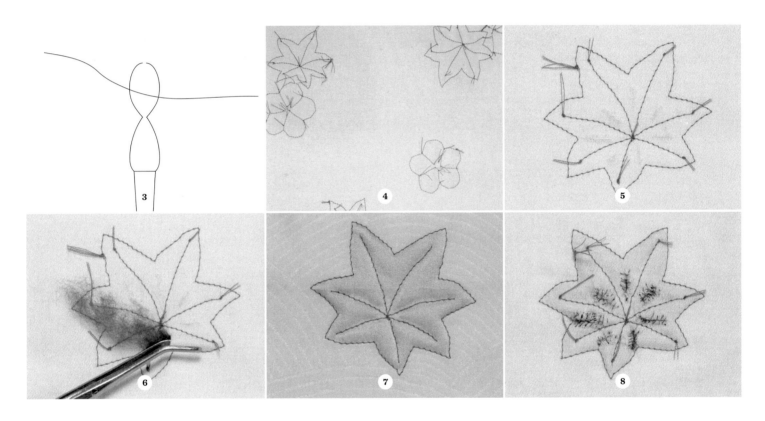

3 Pull the thread tails to the wrong side using an easy-thread needle.

4 Knot the needle and bobbin threads in pairs on the wrong side. Leave the thread tails at least $^1/_2$in (1.3cm) long so that the knots do not unravel. Iron the fabric on the right side to remove the erasable pen marks.

5 Working on the wrong side, make a small slit in the backing fabric of each stitched motif. Depending on the shape, you may need to make more than one slit per motif. Here seven slits were necessary to stuff the leaf.

6 Using tweezers, a blunt needle, or a toothpick, gently poke stuffing into the motif.

7 Check the stuffing distribution from the right side—make sure it is evenly distributed within the motif.

8 Sew the slits closed using whip stitch. If the fabric at the slit frays badly, a small patch of fusible interfacing can be ironed over the slit to close it.

The completed piece. The leaves were stuffed with blue wool roving and the blossoms with maroon wool roving.

Corded quilting / Marseilles quilting / Boutis Provençal

Corded quilting is an old French quilting technique. Two layers of white or light-colored cloth are sewn together in decorative channels and patterns, which are then threaded with yarn to create a textured, quilted cloth. When completed, the wrong side of a corded-quilting piece is almost as beautiful as the right side.

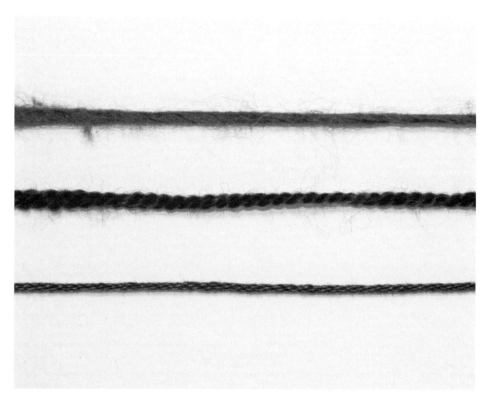

Three different fillers: turquoise blue wool roving with no twist (top), purple wool needlepoint yarn with a double twist (middle), and pink cotton yarn with a round knit twist (bottom).

The channels can be filled with yarn—wool, cotton, and acrylic blends all work well. To be effective, the filler needs to be completely colorfast, highly twisted to facilitate pulling the yarn through the channels, and able to expand to fill the channels.

Roving is difficult to work with because it has no twist to grab when pulling the yarn tails into the channels. Needlepoint yarns work well as they are highly twisted: two wool strands are individually twisted and then the two strands are twisted together to form the yarn. Cotton yarns often have the most complex structure and are thus easiest to pull into the channels, but they are firmer than wool yarns and will not expand to fill the channels.

1 Here a piece of jacquard-woven kimono silk was used as the fashion fabric. The designs from the jacquard weave were marked using a heat-erasable pen to make them easier to see while stitching. Pin a backing fabric to the fashion fabric; here a lightweight wool was used.

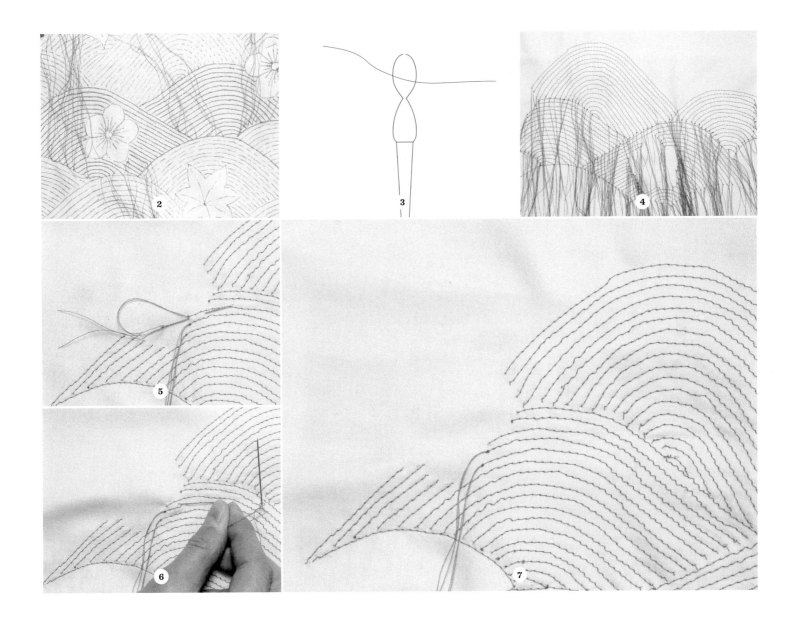

2 The channels can be sewn by hand or machine. Start sewing in the center of the piece, working toward the edges, leaving long thread tails. If you sew the channels by hand, use backstitch, which is stronger than running stitch. Here the channels were sewn by machine using a stitch length of 2mm (12 spi).

3 Pull the thread tails to the wrong side using an easy-thread needle.

4 Knot the needle and bobbin threads in pairs on the wrong side. When looking at the wrong side you can see that some of the stitching lines are unevenly spaced; the minor faults in the sewing will be hidden by the yarn when the channels are stuffed.

5 After the threads are knotted, the knot and thread tails must be buried between the fabric layers. Using an easy-thread needle, insert both threads next to the last stitch, and come out at least $^{1}/_{2}$in (1.3cm) away, being careful to slide the needle between the two layers of fabric.

6 Gently pull the thread until you hear a small pop as the knot slides in between the fabrics.

7 Cut the thread tail where it exits the fabric sandwich.

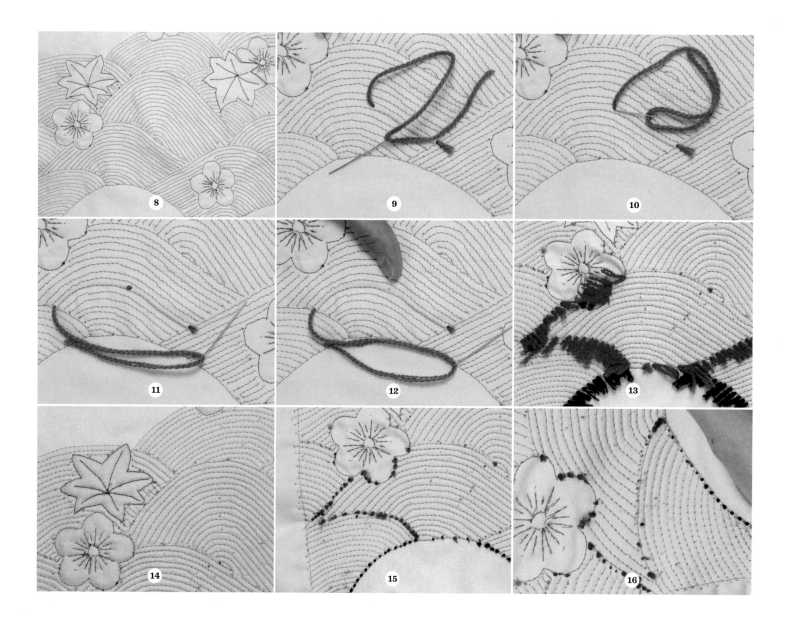

8 Sew the remainder of the pattern. Here the flowers and leaves were sewn in rose and burgundy thread. Note the stretching of the fabric in the densely stitched wave sections; the stretching will be absorbed by the filling later.

9 Thread a chenille or embroidery (or crewel) needle, around size 22, with the yarn. Both needles have large eyes, but a chenille needle has a sharp tip, while an embroidery needle has a blunt tip. Working from the wrong side, insert the needle at the beginning of a channel and slide it through as far as you can. When you can go no further, pull the needle and yarn up to the surface, leaving a yarn tail, $1/2$in (1.3cm) long, at the beginning. Check the right side to make sure the needle and yarn have not pierced through. A needle grabber (a small, flat rubber disk) is very helpful when the needle and yarn are hard to get out of the fabric.

10 To continue working along a channel, carefully insert the needle back into the fabric through the same hole it came out of. Slide it farther along to exit the channel at the end of the stitching.

11 There will be a small opening where the yarn came out and returned to the channel.

12 Rub the opening with a fingernail to realign the fibers, closing the hole. Trim the yarn tail to $1/2$in (1.3cm) long.

13 After a group of channels has been filled, give the fabrics a good stretch with both hands, pulling along the length of the channels. As the fabrics stretch, the yarn will be pulled further into the channels.

14 If the channels are very short, a few stitches through the yarn and the backing fabric will keep the yarn from coming out (here stitched in green thread for clarity).

15 When all the channels have been filled and stretched, trim the yarn tails as close as possible to the fabric, leaving just a small stub visible.

16 Stretch the fabrics again; the yarn tails should now almost disappear into the channels.

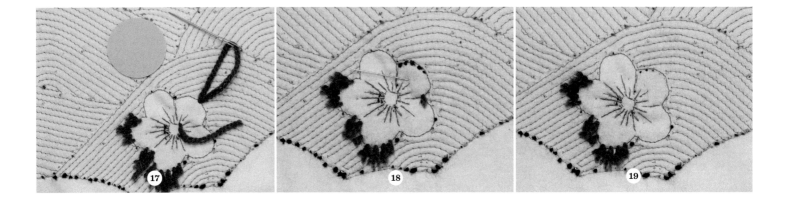

17 Use the same technique to fill the more open shapes, such as the flowers here. The thread tails are left a little longer so they can be pulled into the petal, both by stretching the fabrics and with a sharp needle. Note the tan-colored needle grabber above the flower.

18 Pull the tails back into the shape. Insert a sharp needle into the shape and catch a twist of the yarn on the tip of the needle. Rotate the needle, pulling the yarn tail into the flower.

19 Continue clipping and pulling the yarn ends into the channels until all the yarn is hidden.

Gently wash and shrink the entire piece. Fill a basin with hot water and gently agitate the piece in the water until it is saturated. Let the piece sit in the water until the water has cooled to room temperature. If there are any markings on the fabric, wash them away with soap and rinse the piece well.

Remove the piece from the cool water and gently squeeze out the excess water; do not wring. Roll the piece in a towel and squeeze to extract as much water as possible. Unroll the towel and lay the piece flat on another towel to dry. Drying will take a couple of days, as the yarn and fabric are quite dense.

The finished piece of corded quilting.

Sashiko

Sashiko developed over centuries from a Japanese technique for mending clothes. Striking patterns emerged when the indigo-blue fabric of laborers' clothes were stitched with light-colored thread. Many of these patterns were codified into the art of sashiko. Sashiko patterns are based upon one or two stitching lines, straight or curved, rotated and realigned to create complex designs. The designs were originally created for hand sewing in continuous thread paths, but are easily adapted for machine sewing.

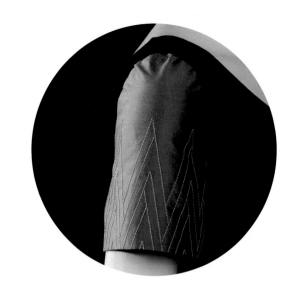

Diamond waves, a straight-line sashiko pattern.

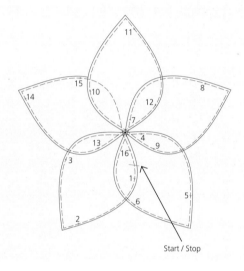

Sashiko patterns can also be composed on curved lines, like this five-petal flower, which is created with a continuous stitching line. All the petals connect at a center point.

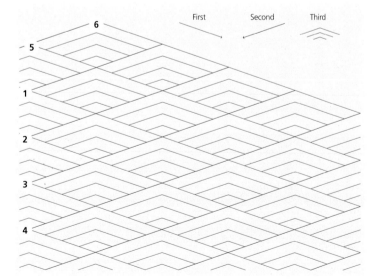

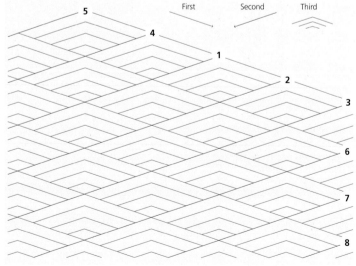

The diamond waves pattern broken into stitching order. First sew the red lines, starting in the center and working toward one edge. Then sew the black lines, again working from the center out. Finally, fill in the diamonds with the brown stitching lines.

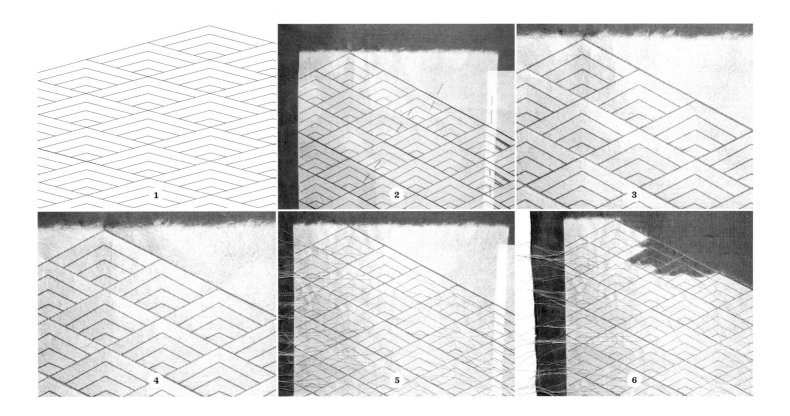

1 These instructions assume heavier thread in the bobbin (see box, right), so you will stitch from the wrong side of the piece. If the design is not symmetrical you will need to reverse it before printing it onto the tear-away interfacing. Here the pattern is shown right side up.

2 Layer two pieces of fabric together to create a fabric sandwich. Print the reversed design onto tear-away interfacing. Place the interfacing on the wrong side of the fabric sandwich and pin in place.

3 Following the stitching-order diagrams opposite, sew the red lines first, starting in the center of the piece and working to one edge, and then from the center toward the other edge.

4 Then sew the black lines, starting in the center of the piece and working to one edge, and then from the center toward the other edge.

5 Stitch the remaining wave shapes.

6 Carefully remove the tear-away interfacing. Knot any needle and bobbin threads together, hiding the knots and threads ends between the two layers of fabric (see Hand Quilting, p. 110). Do this after removing the tear-away interfacing, so that you are sure the knots and thread ends are hidden between the two layers of cloth.

STITCHING LINES

To make the stitching lines stand out more, use a heavier thread such as button or carpet thread. You may find it easier to use heavier thread in the bobbin and regular thread in the needle. Check that the tension on the bobbin casing is set properly for heavier thread; adjust if necessary (see Basic Stitches, p. 24).

The completed sashiko diamond waves pattern.

3
Embellishment and trimmings

A simple fabric strip cut on the bias provides the basis for a wide variety of trims and treatments. The strength of a bias strip is its flexibility, which allows it to conform to curves and angles. Strips can be used to cover raw seam allowances inside and outside of a garment, to add a line of color, or to create piping and cords. Bias strips can also be made into narrow tubes of fabric that can be used to create straps or rouleau loops for button closures. A wide bias trim makes a graphic statement, while a narrow bias trim confers elegance. Bias strips added to a garment can also emphasize seam lines or create decorative surface patterns. Whether used straight or curved, flat or shaped, thick or thin, bias-cut fabric can be manipulated into wonderful embellishments.

3.1
Bias

Bias strips can be cut from lengths of fabric that either match or contrast with fashion fabric. The nature of the strips, which are cut on a 45° angle to the straight grain, means that the pattern of the weave or print—such as a pronounced stripe—can also be employed to add a decorative element to the garment.

The end use of the bias strips will often dictate the best fabric to select. If you are using them as a binding, a light- to medium-weight fabric will avoid adding bulk. Slippery fabrics turn inside out easily for rouleau and cording. Bulky or heavyweight fabrics make flamboyant piping. Bias strips have endless uses; this chapter demonstrates just some of them.

What is bias?

When fabric is woven, the yarns running up and down the length of the fabric, the warp, are threaded through a loom's heddles, and then wound on big rollers or beams; this is called warping a loom. The yarns running across the width of the fabric, the weft, are wound onto shuttles, which are passed from left to right across the fabric and then back again.

When the shuttle with the weft yarn completes a trip across the loom it makes a U-turn and heads back across the loom to form the next row in the fabric. The U-turn creates the selvage.

The lengthwise yarns, the warp, are pulled taut between the beams, which means there will be no stretch along the lengthwise grain of the woven fabric. However the crosswise yarns, the weft, are not pulled as tautly as the warp, so there will be some stretch in the crosswise grain.

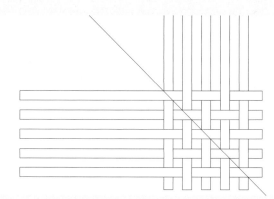

A diagonal line through the intersection of the warp and weft yarns is the bias; this is where the fabric stretches most. When working with fabric on the bias the malleable nature of the bias is exploited; bias can be stretched or shrunk, making it ideal when working with curves and corners.

Making bias strips

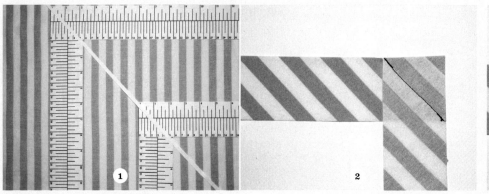

Two bias strips joined together.

1 To make bias strips, start by finding the bias of the fabric. Lay two rulers perpendicular to each other, measuring the same distance from the selvage and straight edge, respectively. Do not include the selvage and the small portion of the edge that is tightly woven in the measurement. Make a mark where the rulers cross each other.

Repeat the same process with the rulers farther into the fabric. Make another mark. When the marks are connected in a straight line, this will indicate the true bias. In the photo above, the true bias is shown with a thin strip of white paper.

Every line that is parallel to the original bias line is also "on the bias." Cutting a strip of fabric of a uniform width following the bias line creates a bias strip.

To join strips of bias to make a longer strip, it is best to place the joining seam on the straight grain. This serves three purposes:

    a It keeps the seam from stretching.

    b It spreads the seam line along the bias strip, creating less bulk when the strip is folded.

    c It makes the seam harder to find, so the strip will look continuous.

2 Lay two bias strips at right angles to each other, right sides together. Pin diagonally across the two strips. Open out the top strip to check your pinning. Sew diagonally across the two strips.

THE CONTINUOUS BINDING (BARREL) METHOD

The continuous binding, or barrel, method is another way to create bias strips. This method involves sewing your piece of fabric into a barrel shape and then cutting the bias strips in one continuous length. The joining seams will be on the straight grain.

Calculating fabric for bias strips

Use these calculations to work out how much fabric you will need to make enough bias trim for a project. The equation is intended to help you find the yardage (meterage) required, but you can also use it to determine how much bias you can get from a particular piece of fabric.

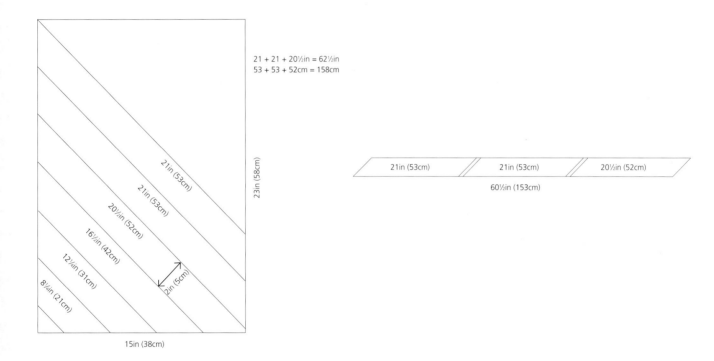

21 + 21 + 20½in = 62½in
53 + 53 + 52cm = 158cm

21in (53cm)   21in (53cm)   20½in (52cm)

60½in (153cm)

21in (53cm)
21in (53cm)
20½in (52cm)
16½in (42cm)
12¼in (31cm)
8¼in (21cm)
2in (5cm)

23in (58cm)

15in (38cm)

Measure the finished length of bias strip needed. You will need to add 6–12in (15–30cm) for seam allowances, depending on how much fabric you are using. The total length is L. Measure the width of bias needed (B) and the width of the fabric you are using (F). A sufficiently generous estimate for the length of fabric you will need (N) can be calculated as follows:

$$N = \frac{(L+6in) \times B}{F} + F \text{ or}$$

$$N = \frac{(L+15cm) \times B}{F} + F$$

If you need 54in (137cm) of bias strip that is 2in (5cm) wide, and the fabric is 15in (38cm) wide:

$$N = \frac{(54+6) \times 2}{15} + 15 \text{ or}$$

$$N = \frac{(137+15) \times 5}{38} + 38$$

$$N = 23in (58cm)$$

The diagram shows that the first two strips are 21in (53cm) long, the third strip is 20½in (52cm), and the remaining strips shorten rapidly. With this method, these shorter strips can be discarded.

Sewn together with ½in (1.25cm) seam allowances on each piece (totaling 2in/5cm loss for two seams), the three longest strips combined will produce a bias strip that is 60½in (153cm) long.

Thus fabric that is 23in (58cm) long x 15in (38cm) wide will provide more than 54in (137cm) of bias strips with minimal piecing.

Measuring bias binding around a curve

The wider a bias binding is, the less flexible it will be around curves. A binding that is wider than $\frac{1}{4}$in (6mm) therefore needs to be cut to the length of the longest side of the curve.

CONVEX CURVE

On this sweetheart neckline, which is an example of a convex curve, the black line is the finished edge and the brown line is the stitching edge. The finished edge is longer than the stitching line, so you will need to cut the bias binding to fit the longer finished edge of the curve.

CONCAVE CURVE

On this armhole, which is an example of a convex curve, the stitching line (brown) is longer than the finished edge (black). Therefore, you will need to cut the bias binding to fit the longer stitching line of the curve.

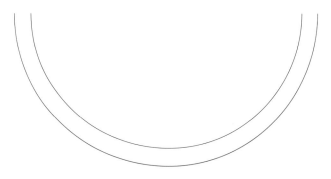

Repositioning seam allowances for bias strips

When adding bias strips to a garment as a binding, the thinner the exposed bias trim, the more elegant it looks. The exercises in this chapter use bias strips 2in (5cm) wide with ½in (1.3cm) seam allowances, unless noted; the finished exposed trims are usually ⅛–¼in (3–6mm) wide.

When using bias strips as a binding, it may be necessary to change the seam allowances and stitching lines on the pattern.

1 To calculate the position of the new stitching line, first label the old stitching line as the finished edge.

2 Measure into the garment the final width of the bias binding plus ⅛in (3mm) to trim away later; here the binding width is ⅛in (3mm) plus ⅛in (3mm) trimming width, giving a total of ¼in (6mm). This will be the new stitching line.

3 Measure from the new stitching line toward the raw edge by the width of the customary seam allowance; here ½in (1.3cm). This will be the new cutting line.

4 Check the math: the new cutting line is ¼in (6mm) above the finished edge. The finished edge is the old stitching line. The new stitching line is ¼in (6mm) below the old stitching line. From the new stitching line to the new cutting line is ½in (1.3cm).

Cut the pattern along your new cutting line to make the seam allowance the correct width.

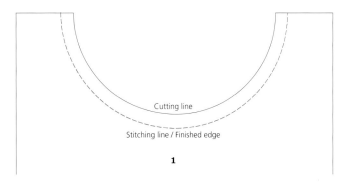

Cutting line

Stitching line / Finished edge

1

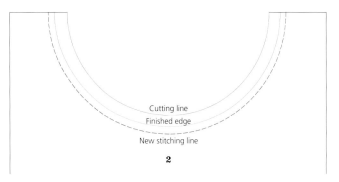

Cutting line

Finished edge

New stitching line

2

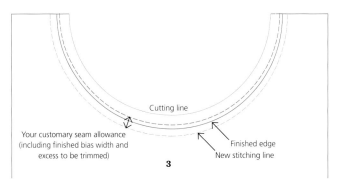

Cutting line

Your customary seam allowance (including finished bias width and excess to be trimmed)

Finished edge

New stitching line

3

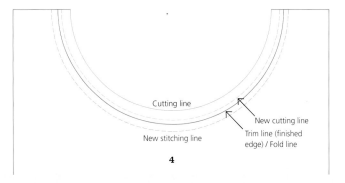

Cutting line

New cutting line

Trim line (finished edge) / Fold line

New stitching line

4

Shaping bias strips

Bias strips are very malleable; they can be stretched, shrunk, and curved with the help of a steam iron. Shaping a strip before it is applied to a curved seam, such as an armhole, makes it easier to work with and produces a neater finish.

STRETCHING

Bias strips can be stretched and the yarns set in a new size using heat and steam from an iron. Here a strip $1^3/4$ x $17^3/4$in (4.5 x 45cm) was stretched until it measured $1^1/4$ x $19^1/4$in (3 x 49cm). Note that as the length increased, the width decreased.

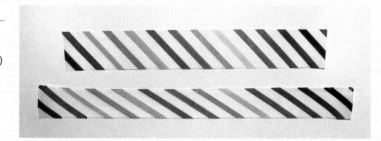

A bias strip before stretching (top) and after stretching (bottom).

SHAPING

Heat and steam from an iron can also be used to curve bias strips by shrinking some yarns and stretching others.

1 Make a bias strip (see pp. 128, 140–41).

2 Place the iron on one end of the bias strip and gently pull the other end of the strip into a curve. While applying steam, move the iron along the curved strip. Ease the curve into existence; do not make it too sharp. It may take several passes with the iron to perfect the curve. If you pull the curve too tightly, the edge of the fabric will fold, making little darts; if this happens, ease up on the tension and let the curve relax.

3 After the bias strip has been worked for a few minutes, stop to let the yarns dry out and relax into their new shape. Here you can see the amount of curve that can be generated on the first pass with an iron.

4 After the second round of shaping, the curve has become much tighter.

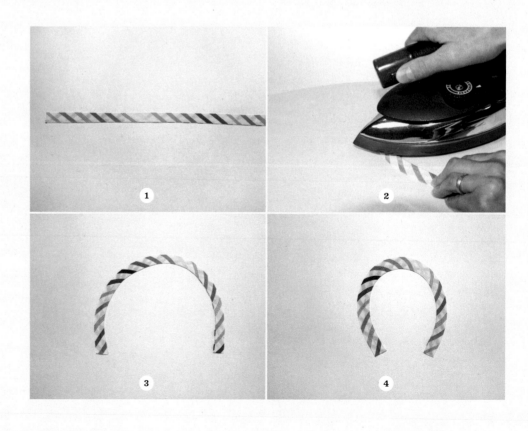

Attaching a narrow bias binding to a curve

When attaching a narrow bias binding—$^1/_4$in (6mm) or less, when finished—to a curve, you can rely on the malleable nature of the bias to help the binding fit along the curve.

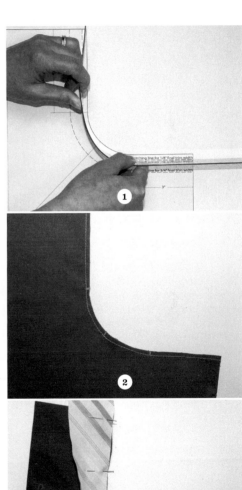

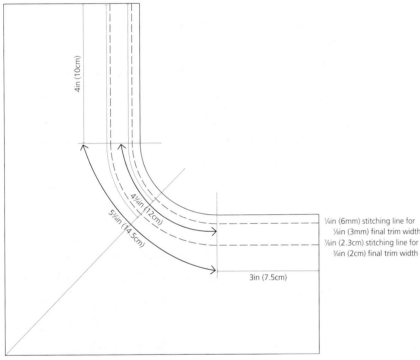

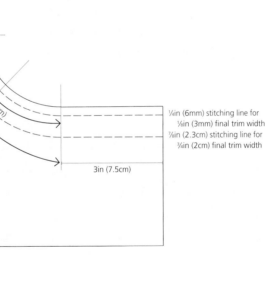

$^1/_4$in (6mm) stitching line for $^1/_8$in (3mm) final trim width
$^7/_8$in (2.3cm) stitching line for $^3/_4$in (2cm) final trim width

3in (7.5cm)

1 Measure the length of the stitching line closest to the edge of the pattern to determine the length of bias strip needed for a narrow trim. This shorter line has a 4in (10cm) straight section, then a 4$^3/_4$in (12cm) curved section, followed by a 3in (7.5cm) straight section. The total length is therefore is 11$^3/_4$in (29.5cm). Cut the bias strip to the same length or longer.

Mark each section of the pattern with a notch. Adding a notch in the middle of the curve will help to ensure the bias strip is evenly distributed around the curve as you work.

2 Marking the notches with small dashes (yellow chalk was used here), rather than small snips in the fabric, works better when the seam allowance is only $^1/_4$in (6mm) wide. Mark the strip with the same measurements and notches. Staystitch just inside the stitching line of the base fabric to prevent the curve from stretching.

3 Pin the bias strip to the base fabric, right sides together, in the straight sections.

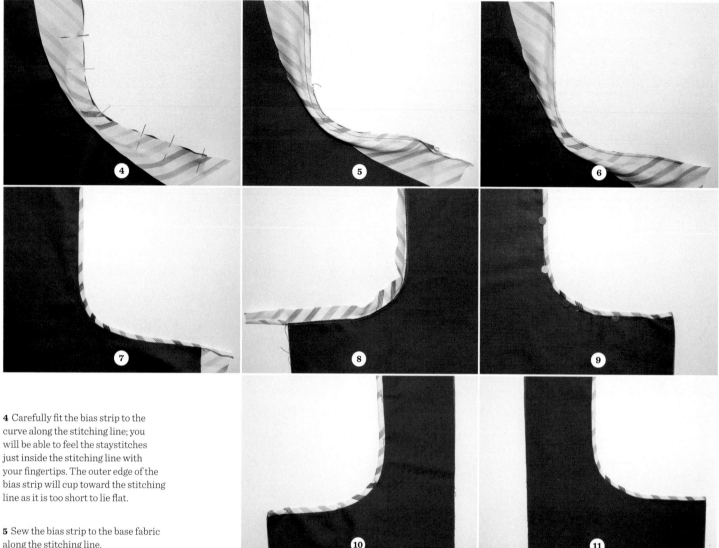

4 Carefully fit the bias strip to the curve along the stitching line; you will be able to feel the staystitches just inside the stitching line with your fingertips. The outer edge of the bias strip will cup toward the stitching line as it is too short to lie flat.

5 Sew the bias strip to the base fabric along the stitching line.

6 Trim the seam allowance to $^1/_8$in (3mm). Press the bias strip just along the stitching line.

7 Wrap the bias strip around the raw edge, carefully measuring the binding width on the right side and keeping it consistent. Press.

8 Working on the wrong side, trim the bias strip to two times the width of the final folded width; here the bias strip is trimmed to $^3/_4$in (2cm) for a final width of $^3/_8$in (1cm), measuring from the raw edge of the base fabric. The bias strip on the wrong side should be slightly wider than on the right side.

9 Fold the raw edge toward the wrong side of the garment, folding the bias strip in half lengthwise. Press, then fold the strip in half lengthwise again and pin it in place on the right side.

10 If the bias has been pinned along the stitching line, the pins will just catch the bias strip on the wrong side, as shown here. Sew the wrong side of the bias binding to the fabric using stitch in the ditch from the right side, or hand-sew the binding on the wrong side.

11 The completed corner, trimmed with a narrow bias binding.

WORKING WITH A CONVEX CURVE

You can attach a narrow bias binding to a convex curve with the same technique, noting that, in this case, the binding outer edge will ripple as it is too long to lie flat.

Attaching a wide bias binding to a curve

A binding that is wider than ¼in (6mm) when finished needs careful easing around a curve so that it does not develop pulls and gathers.

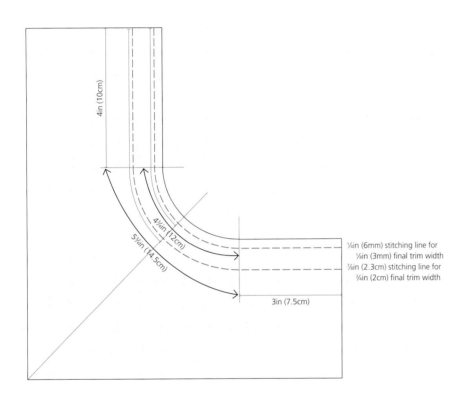

4in (10cm)

4¾in (12cm)

5¾in (14.5cm)

3in (7.5cm)

¼in (6mm) stitching line for
⅛in (3mm) final trim width
⅞in (2.3cm) stitching line for
¾in (2cm) final trim width

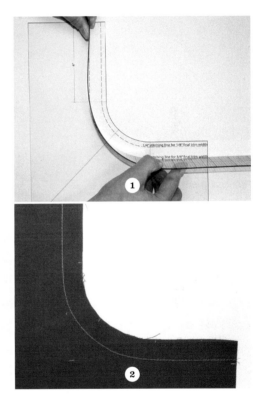

1 Following the same pattern as for previous exercise, measure the longer stitching line on the pattern—in other words, the line farther from the curved edge. This line has a 4in (10cm) straight section, then a 5¾in (14.5cm) curved section, followed by a 3in (7.5cm) straight section. The total length of the stitching line is 12¾in (32cm).

Cut a length of bias strip corresponding to the length of the stitching line. When working with a wide bias curve, however, shorten the length of the bias strip by ⅜–½in (1–1.3cm). Later you will stretch the bias slightly along the stitching line to compensate;

this will avoid there being too much fabric gathered along the finished edge of the curve.

2 Mark each section of the pattern with a notch. Adding a notch in the middle of the curve and at the same point on the bias strip will help to ensure the bias strip is evenly distributed around the curve. Transfer these marks to the fabric and the bias strip with dashes (yellow chalk was used here). Staystitch just inside the stitching line to prevent the curve from stretching.

THE FINISHED EDGE OF THE BINDING

The finished edge is where the bias folds to the wrong side. It is usually the raw edge less the amount trimmed off from the seam allowance once the seam is sewn.

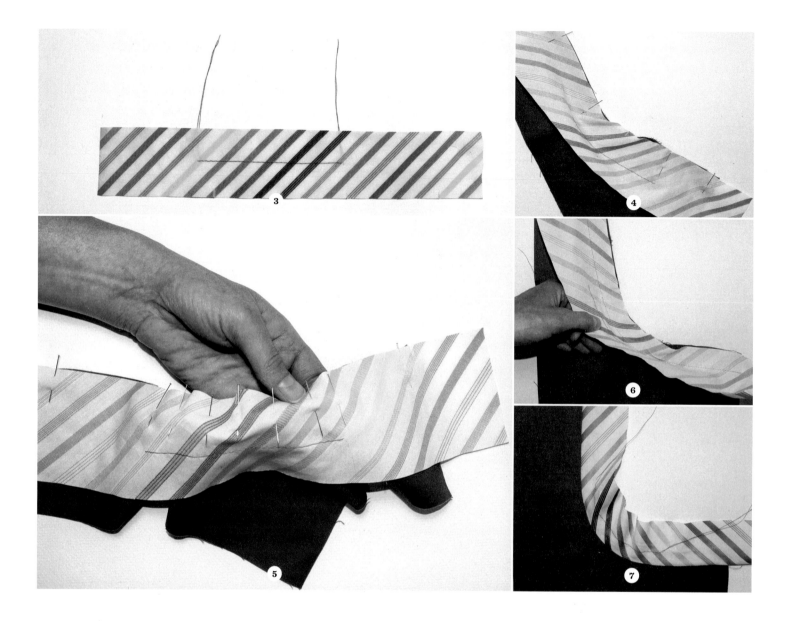

3 In what will be the curved section on the bias strip, sew a line of gathering stitches where the finished edge will be, here 1¼in (3cm) from the notched edge. This will help with the shrinking of the bias in Step 8.

4 Pin the bias strip in place along the straight sections.

5 Carefully fit the bias strip to the curve along the stitching line; you will be able to feel the staystitches with your fingertips. Pushing the base fabric up into the bias strip, over your fingertips, will help match the stitching lines.

6 Sew along the stitching line, just inside the line of gathering stitches. With a concave curve, the outer edge of the bias strip will cup toward you as it is too short to lie flat.

7 Trim the seam allowance to ¾in (2cm). Press the bias strip along the seam line, leaving the strip beyond the base fabric untouched by the iron.

WORKING WITH A CONVEX CURVE

If the curve is convex, the binding outer edge will be a little too long. Adding some gathering stitches along the stitching line will help ease the bias strip to the base fabric along the curve.

Right side, after stitching.

Wrong side, after stitching.

8 Wrap the bias binding around the finished edge, carefully measuring the width of the binding on the right side. Press the straight sections of the bias strip flat. Now lightly gather the bias strip until it just fits the curve; the gathering stitches should fall just at the finished edge.

9 Steam the gathered bias in the curve until all the fullness has been shrunken out and the bias strip lies flat.

10 Turn the fabric to the wrong side. The bias binding will cup toward you at the raw edge.

11 Fold the raw edge under so that the bias binding on the wrong side is slightly wider than on the right side. Press.

12 Pin the bias binding from the right side along the stitching line.

13 You should just catch the bias on the wrong side, as shown here.

Sew the wrong side of the bias binding to the fabric using stitch in the ditch from the right side, or hand-sew the binding on the wrong side.

14 The completed corner, trimmed with a wide bias binding.

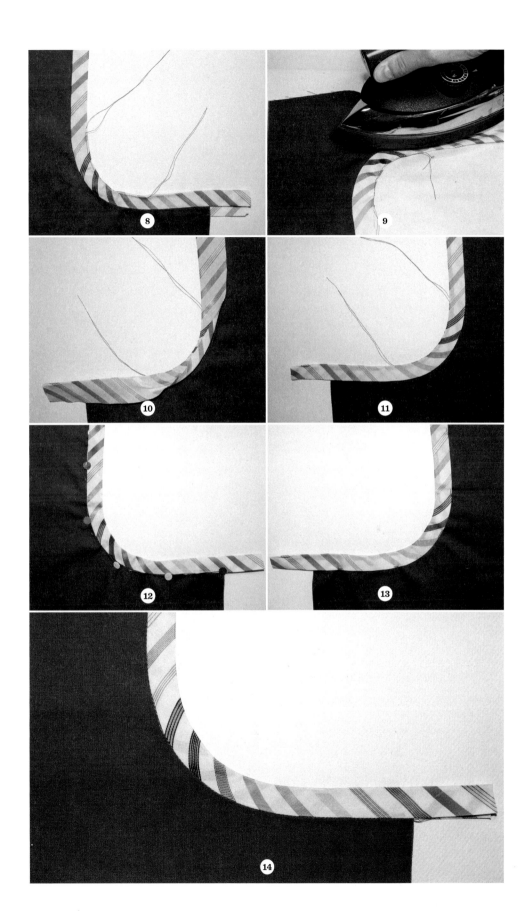

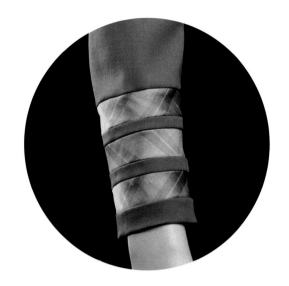

Inset bias strips

Bias strips can be used to add a decorative feature along the style lines of a garment. Choosing a fabric for inset strips that emphasizes the bias can be particularly dynamic.

1 To insert bias strips, first cut apart the pattern along the style lines you wish to create—in this case, the front side seams on a bodice. Add a seam allowance to each cut edge (see box opposite). Add notches along the new style lines to help realign the pattern pieces correctly.

2 If you wish to line the garment, cut an underlining on the same grain as the fashion fabric and hand-baste it to the wrong side of the fabric.

3 To give the bias strips some stability, line them with the same underlining fabric, but cut the underlining on the straight grain to prevent the strips from stretching. Mark the notches on both the bias strips and the fashion fabric.

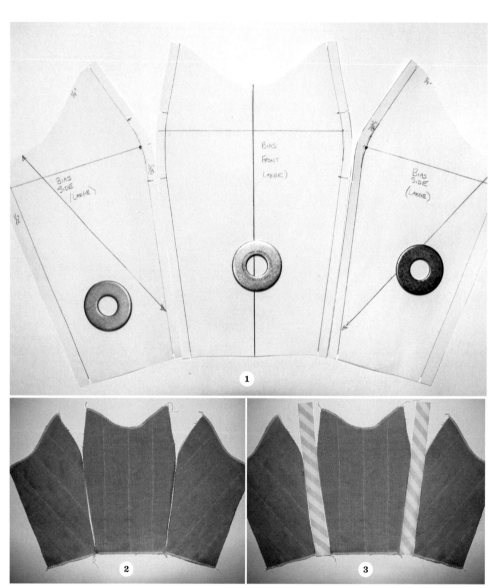

**CALCULATING THE STRIPS AND
ALTERING THE SEAM ALLOWANCE**

*To create bias strips ¼in (6mm)
wide when finished, cut strips 1¼in
(3.2cm) wide: the finished strip of
¼in (6mm) plus ½in (1.3cm) seam
allowance on each side.*

*To compensate for the insertion of
the bias, add ⅜in (1cm) along the
style line of each pattern piece.*

1. *Remove the width of the finished
   bias strip from each style line: ¼in
   (6mm), or ⅛in (3mm) from the
   side of each pattern piece.*

2. *Then add seam allowances of ½in
   (1.3cm) to each pattern piece.*

4 Sew the bias strips to either side
of the central pattern piece, with
a ½in (1.3cm) seam allowance,
matching notches.

5 Now sew the bias strips to the
side pattern pieces, with the same
seam allowance.

6 Grade the seam allowances and
finish the seams; here the seam
allowances were pinked.

7 The right side of the bodice front,
with the bias strips sewn in place.

Rouleau

Rouleau, or thin bias tubing, can be used to make appliqués, spaghetti straps, button loops, or cording. There are many ways to make rouleau; shown here are three different versions: stitched and folded, stitched and turned, and serged and turned. The Fasturn tube-turning set will also turn bias strips very quickly.

Stitched and folded

This technique makes good fabric tubes for appliqués, Celtic knot appliqués, and passementerie swirls.

1 With wrong sides together, sew a long bias strip into a tube. Trim the seam allowance to $1/8$ in (3mm).

2 Fold the seam to one side and press it so that the seam runs down the back of the tube. The raw edges remain unfinished but are covered by the bias.

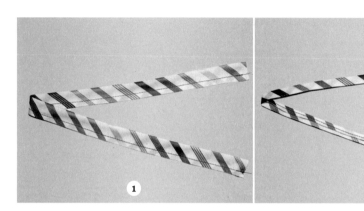

Stitched and turned

This technique works well for very narrow tubes.

1 With right sides together, sew a long bias strip of fabric into a tube. Thread a blunt tapestry needle with a double strand of thread, slightly longer than the tube length. Heavyweight threads such as pearl cotton or button thread work well, as does regular thread that has been doubled for strength. Sew the ends of the thread to one end of the fabric tube with a few quick stitches.

2 Drop the needle through the fabric tube, starting at the end where the thread is attached. If you have used a long enough piece of thread the needle will drop all the way through the tube.

3 Gently pull the needle and thread, turning the tube right side out.

4 The completed fabric tube turned right side out, with the seam inside.

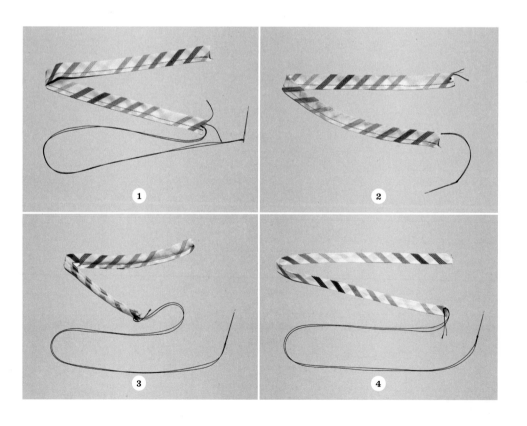

Serged and turned

This technique works well with fabrics that fray easily because the completed tube is clean finished before turning.

FITTING SHOULDER STRAPS

Adding lightweight elastic inside rouleau tubes will keep a shoulder strap on the shoulder. The elastic should be just snug enough to keep the strap in place, but not so snug that it gathers the fabric.

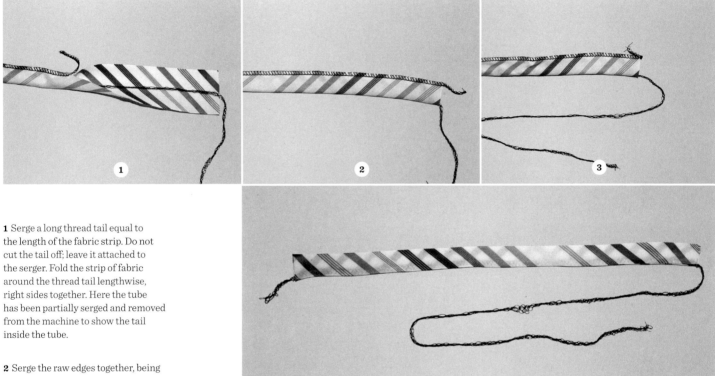

1 Serge a long thread tail equal to the length of the fabric strip. Do not cut the tail off; leave it attached to the serger. Fold the strip of fabric around the thread tail lengthwise, right sides together. Here the tube has been partially serged and removed from the machine to show the tail inside the tube.

2 Serge the raw edges together, being careful not to catch the inner thread tail in the serging.

3 Gently pull on the thread tail at the bottom of the tube, turning the tube right side out.

4 The completed fabric tube turned right side out, with the serged seam on the inside.

VARIATION

The fabric tubes shown above are fairly wide and will stretch when used. To make a narrower, prestretched tube, you can use any of the methods above, following these slight modifications.

1 Cut a bias strip 1in (2.5cm) wide.

2 Sew the tube using your preferred method, pulling on the fabric strip to stretch it as you sew. Trim the extra seam allowance.

3 While applying heat and steam with an iron, stretch the bias tube.

4 Turn the tube right side out and press again. The final tube should be thinner and much longer. The sample shown here was made from a 13in (33cm) bias strip and was stretched to 16in (40.5cm).

The terms "piping" and "cording" are often used interchangeably. In the following pages, piping is used to describe a filled bias strip of fabric with the seam allowance forming a flange for sewing into a seam. Cording has no flange; it is a filler wrapped in a bias strip with the seam allowance turned inside.

The round lines of piping can be used to emphasize seams within a garment, or to define edges such as a neckline or jacket collar and revers. Cording can be hand sewn in sinuous shapes that snake across the surface of a garment. Custom-made piping and cording can vary from dainty to corpulent, depending on the thickness of the filler.

3.2
Piping and cording

Cording can also be used to create custom-made braids or Chinese knots, which are made by weaving and twisting cords or strands into stylized patterns. While the Chinese knots shown in this section are generally used for closures, the fanciful intertwining of the cords that create the button and loop pair can also be used as embellishments.

Other decorative trims, such as beaded fringe sewn to a strip of fabric, can be added to seams and garment edges using the same techniques shown for adding piping.

Piping

Piping adds a line of graphic detail to any seam. The thickness of the filler and the fabric used to cover it will determine the effect it has on the finished garment.

Cutting the filler

Some fillers unravel or puff out when they are cut. To avoid this, wrap two pieces of tape around the filler, $\frac{1}{8}$in (3mm) apart, then cut between the two.

Remove the tape before enclosing the ends of the filler inside the bias strip—the tape will be a different texture inside the piping, and the glue may seep through the bias fabric at a later stage.

If the filler does not lie flat on the work table, give it a good steaming and, while it is still damp, roll it under your palms as you would roll a sausage-shaped piece of dough.

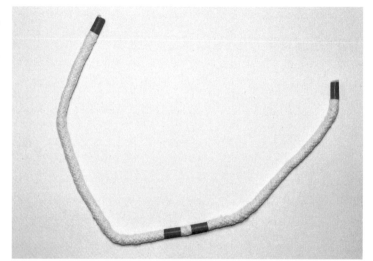

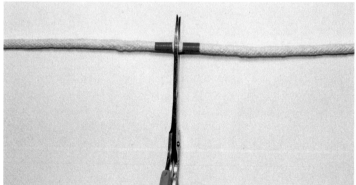

Measuring the circumference of the filler

Wrap a slip of paper tightly around the filler and pin the ends together. When you unpin the paper, mark the pinholes. Draw a line to connect the marks; the distance between the lines is the circumference of the filler. Add a seam allowance to each side— here it is $\frac{1}{2}$in (1.3cm)—and this will give you the required width of bias strip.

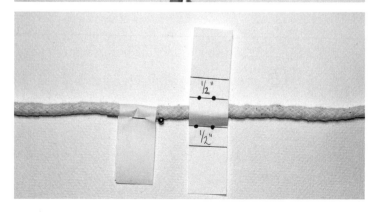

Making piping

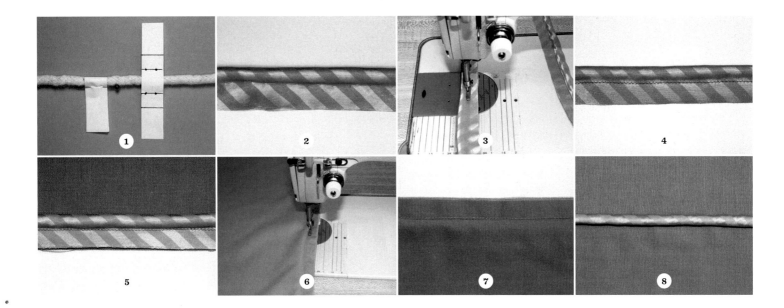

1 To make a fabric flange (the seam allowance) so that you can sew the piping into a seam, first measure the circumference of the filler and add seam allowance to both sides (see opposite). The filler used here is $^7/_8$in (2.3cm) in circumference. Adding 1in (2.5cm) of seam allowance makes the bias strip needed 1$^7/_8$in (4.8cm) wide. Cut the bias strip (see Making Bias Strips, p. 128).

2 Wrap the bias strip around the filler, right sides facing out, wrong sides together. Take the time to hand-baste the bias around the filler because it is easy for the bias to wriggle out of alignment while stitching with the sewing machine. If the bias strip twists, the seam allowances will be inaccurate, which will cause trouble when you sew the piping into the garment.

3 Using a zipper foot or little foot, stitch the filler into the bias, leaving $^1/_{16}$in (1mm) between the filler and the seam line. When the piping is sewn to the fashion fabric you will stitch in this $^1/_{16}$in (1mm) gap so that this first line of stitching is hidden.

4 Here the bias strip has been stitched around the filler in orange thread. The basting stitches, in green thread, can now be removed.

5 Place the piping on the fashion fabric, matching raw edges. Note that the filled bias is inside the seam line. Using a zipper foot, sew the bias in place, stitching very close to the filler. This line of stitches, shown in green thread, anchors the piping in place and provides a guideline for the next line of stitches.

6 Pin the second piece of fashion fabric in place, right sides together, forming a sandwich, with the piping in the middle. Place the fabric sandwich in the sewing machine with the first piece of fashion fabric on top so that you can see the stitching line created in Step 5 (shown here in green)

7 Stitch just to the inside of the previous stitching line, close to the piping. This second seam here is sewn with orange thread.

8 Open the fabric sandwich. The piping will stand proud of the base fabric.

Piping a corner

The key to adding piping to a corner or a curve is in clipping the piping's flange. The finished corner will always be slightly curved due to the round filler in the piping.

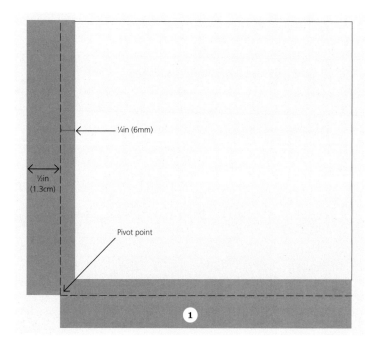

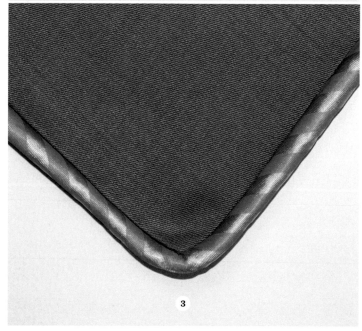

1 Mark the pivot point on the fashion fabric and piping. Slash the flange of the piping up to the stitching that holds the filler in place.

2 Sew the piping to the base fabric (here sewn with green thread). About 1in (2.5cm) before the pivot point, change to a short stitch length of 1.5mm (15 spi) for better control. Stitch to the point, stopping with the needle down; lift the presser foot, pivot the fabric and piping, lower the foot, and continue stitching. Remember to return the stitch length to normal once you are 1in (2.5cm) beyond the pivot point.

If you are backing the fashion fabric, see Making Piping, Steps 6–7 (p. 145).

3 The completed piped corner.

Piping a curve

1 Baste the piping in place on the right side of the garment—here, around the neckline. Ignore the slight gathering of the piping seam allowance; concentrate on fitting the piping to match the neckline seam line. Sew the piping to the neckline (shown here sewn with green thread). Clip the seam allowance of the piping only, to lie flat within the curved area.

2 Turn the seam allowance of the garment and piping to the wrong side; the clipped seam allowance now splays out. Carefully staggering the clips, clip the seam allowance of the garment itself around the neckline to allow it to lie flat; if the clips on the piping and the garment align they will create a lumpy neckline.

3 The piped neckline seen from the right side.

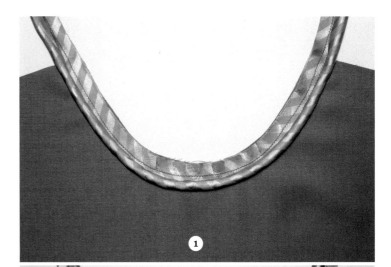

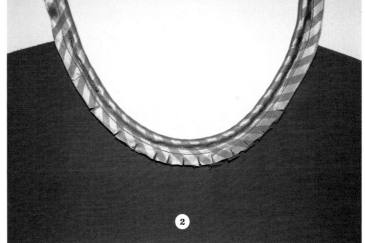

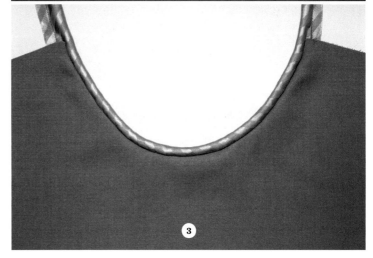

Joining two pieces of piping

To complete piping all the way around an object you need to overlap the beginning and ending of the piping and reduce the bulk where the two pieces meet. There are two methods for this: butting the filler within the bias and overlapping the bias.

BUTTING THE FILLER

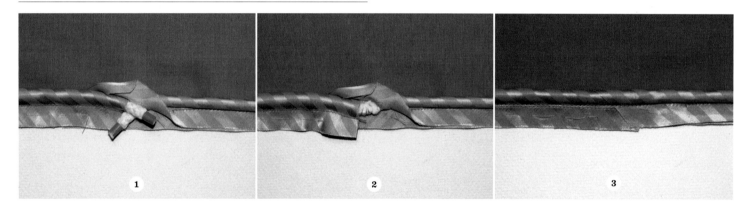

1 Sew the piping to the fashion fabric on one side of the piping intersection (here the right-hand piece), leaving a 2in (5cm) tail. Open the right end of the bias strip, exposing the filler. Cut the bias strip on a 45° angle. Fold the raw edge of the bias strip to the inside.

2 Cut both ends of the filler so that they butt together. Sew the two filler ends together by hand (sewn here in pink thread).

3 Wrap the angle-cut bias strip around the joined fillers. Continue to sew the piping in place across the intersection (here stitched in green thread). Here the two bias stripes join at the double silver stripe.

OVERLAPPING THE PIPING

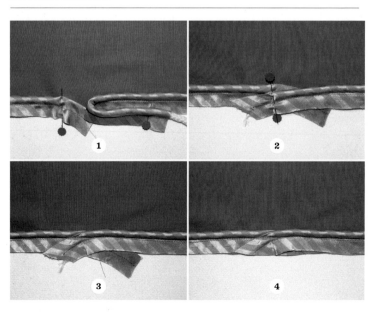

1 Baste the piping to the fashion fabric, matching raw edges. Sew the piping to the fabric on one side of the piping intersection (here the right-hand piece), leaving a 2in (5cm) tail. Using pins, mark where the piping overlaps. On the left side, push back the bias strip to expose the filler and trim the filler back to the overlap point. Angle the empty end of the bias strip into the seam allowance.

2 Place the right-hand piece of piping over the left-hand piece, butting the right-hand tail snugly against the trimmed end of the left-hand piece. Place a pin in the filled tail to mark the intersection of the two pieces, then trim the filler in the right-hand piping back to the pin.

3 Lay the trimmed piping back down, butting the filler ends together. Angle the empty ends into the seam allowance. Stitch both ends of the piping to the fashion fabric (shown here in green thread).

4 Trim away the excess fabric.

Piping with fringe

Many trims can be sewn into a garment using the same method as for piping.

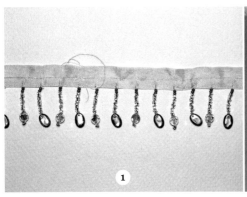

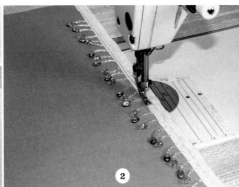

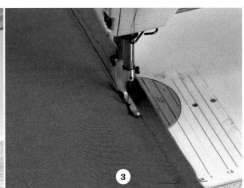

1 Buy or make some beaded fringe. Here, beads and crystals were sewn onto rayon hem tape. Break off the spacer beads (here the red beads). (See Beaded Fringe, p. 237.)

2 Hand-baste the ribbon to the fashion fabric (sewn here in yellow thread). Machine-sew the ribbon to the fashion fabric using a little foot, stitching exactly $\frac{1}{8}$in (3mm) from the inner edge of the ribbon, the edge closest to the fringe. This line of stitches will anchor the ribbon in place and provide a guideline for the next line of stitches.

3 Pin the second piece of fashion fabric in place, right sides together, forming a fabric sandwich, with the beaded fringe in the middle. Measure $\frac{1}{4}$in (6mm) into the fabric from the first line of stitching (here sewn in orange): this is the seam line. The seam line should be $\frac{1}{8}$in (3mm) from the inner edge of the ribbon, plus the width of the spacer beads. Using a zipper foot to get the needle as close to the beaded fringe as possible, stitch the two fabrics together, sandwiching the beaded fringe in the middle (here sewn in black thread); the goal is to hide the ribbon in the seam, without catching any beads in the seam.

The completed beaded fringe in the garment seam.

STITCHING LINES

The three lines of stitching, from the top:

1. Yellow hand basting

2. Orange machine stitching, holding the ribbon to the base fabric

3. Black machine stitching, completing the fabric sandwich around the beaded fringe.

Cording

Cording is made by wrapping a bias tube around filler. The bias strip is sewn onto the filler with wrong sides out and then turned right side out, over the filler, to hide the seam allowances. This technique works best with smooth or slippery fabric.

MATERIALS

• Bias strips the width of the circumference of the filler (see Measuring the Circumference of the Filler, p. 144) plus 1in (2.5cm) seam allowance. The length of each piece of bias should be equal to the length of the finished cord plus 1in (2.5cm).
• Cotton or cotton polyester filler.

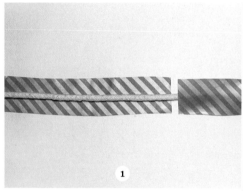

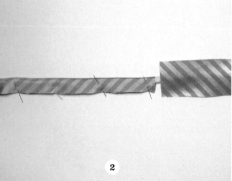

1

2

3

LONG VS. SHORT LENGTHS

If you are making multiple pieces of cording, it is easier to make several pieces in a row than to make one long piece of cording and then cut it up; turning long pieces of bias strip over the filler is difficult.

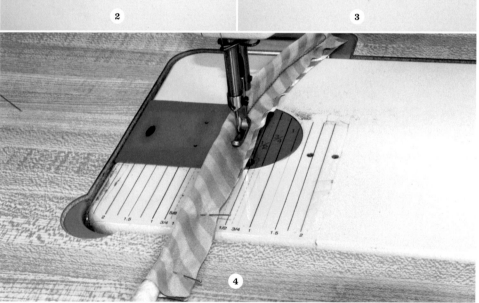

4

1 Place two bias strips of equal length along the filler. The first strip, on the right, is a place marker.

2 Wrap the left bias strip around the filler, right sides together, and pin the fabric in place.

3 Move the first bias strip (the place marker) to the left, beyond the second strip, and pin it around the filler. The two bias strips wrapped around the filler are shown here with the now empty section of filler at the top.

4 Using a zipper foot or a little foot, on the right-hand side sew across the top of one bias strip and filler with small stitches to anchor the filler in place. Pivot with the needle down, and sew down the length of the bias strip.

Do not stitch too close to the filler; you need to leave some room for the seam allowance to sit inside the strip when you turn it right side out. Repeat Step 4 for each bias strip.

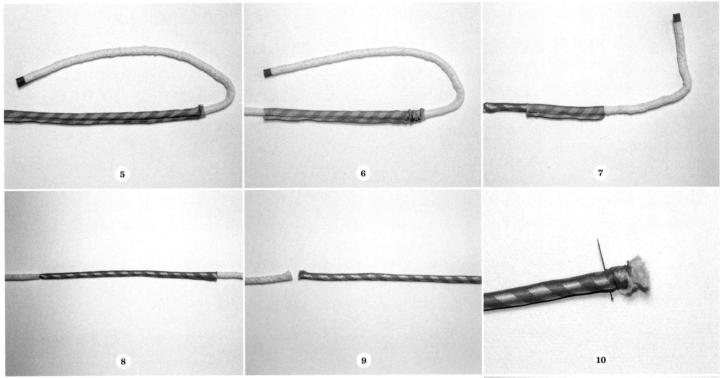

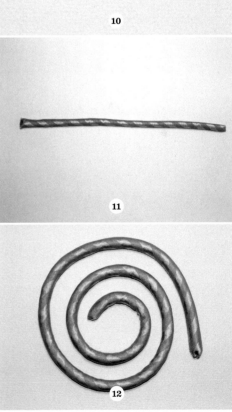

5 Trim the seam allowance to $^1/_8$in (3mm), including the corner around the pivot point and across the filler.

6 Starting where the stitching crosses the filler, ease the bias strip over the stitching, turning the fabric to the right side.

7 The beginning is always tricky, but once started, the fabric should roll over itself easily.

8 The fabric will cover the piece of filler you left empty in Step 3.

9 Cut each section at the turning point, snipping away as much excess filler as you can without cutting into the bias strip.

10 At the open end of the cord, pin through the bias fabric and filler. The pin will keep the filler from bunching up inside the bias strip. Slide the bias strip back slightly to expose the filler. Trim the filler to the correct length. When the bias strip is smoothed out the fabric should extend beyond the filler; this will reduce the bulk at the end of the cord. Fold the raw end of the bias strip over the end of the filler and stitch closed.

11 The finished piece of cording.

12 A long, completed cord.

Chinese knots

Chinese knots, sometimes called frogs or frog closures, have been used on Chinese clothing for many centuries. Whether made in rat-tail cord or custom-made cording, they add an oriental flavor to any garment. Pairs of knots can be used to make button-and-loop fastenings, where one knot is made as a button and the other is finished as a loop.

The length needed to tie each knot will vary, depending on the thickness of the cord. The knots shown in this chapter were made with $^7/_8$in (2.3cm) filled cording (see pp. 150–51); this is quite thick for Chinese knots, so a length of 36in (91.5cm) was required. Always start with a cord that is too long; you can always move the knot along the cord once the knot is tied.

Use a gridded board to help keep the knots even from side to side and top to bottom. Cover a cork bulletin board with fabric, then draw a grid of lines, $^1/_2$in (1.3cm) apart.

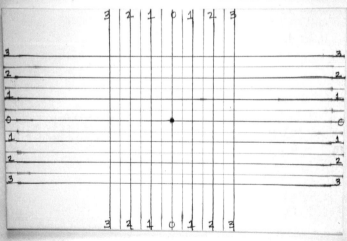

Simplified good luck knot

This simplified version of the good luck knot can be used as the loop for a button-and-loop fastening. If you have made your own cord, work this knot with the seam in the cord facing up.

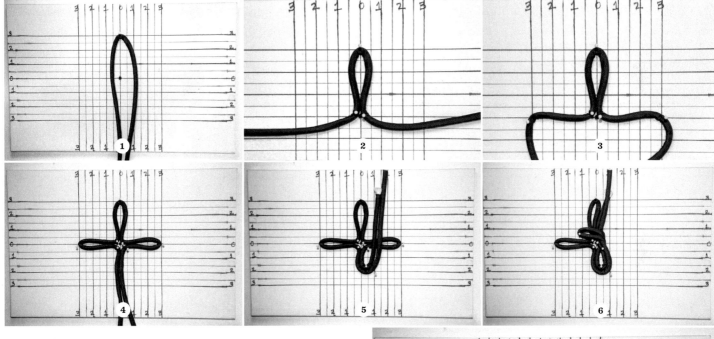

1 Fold the cord in half and pin the midpoint at the top of the board.

2 Pin the cord ends at the center of the board, forming the first loop. Pull both ends out to the sides.

3 Pin the ends, making them equal in length to the top loop.

4 Bring the ends back to the center point and pin them. Make sure the seam is facing up throughout.

5 Lift the cord ends over the right loop. Place pins in the curve. The seam in the cord ends should be facing down as the they cross over the loop.

6 Unpin the right loop and bring it over to the left, crossing over four cords: the two cord ends and the two cords of the top loop pointing up. Pin the end of the loop in its new position.

7 Unpin the top loop and bring it down toward the bottom, crossing over four cords: the loop that you just brought over and the two cords of the left loop. Pin the end of the loop in its new position.

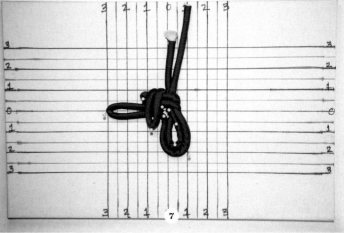

8 Unpin the left loop and bring it over to the right. Cross over the top of the loop you just brought down and then over the first two cords of the bottom loop. Then slide under the second two cords of the bottom loop. Pin the end of the loop in its new position.

9 Remove the four pins from the center of the knot.

10 Remove the pins from the loop sitting below the knot. Pull the cord ends until they start to draw the bottom loop into the knot.

11 Remove the pin holding the lower left loop. Pull the loop until it starts to tighten. Make sure the seams in the cords are not visible as you pull the cords tighter; twist the cords to hide the seam if needed.

12 Remove the remaining pins. Pull the right and left loops, and the top and bottom loops, until the knot is tight.

13 To finish the knot, working with one cord tail, slide the fabric up, exposing the filler inside. Cut off the excess filler. Straighten out the fabric tube and trim it to ½in (1.3cm).

14 Work with the other cord tail to make a button loop: loosen the small loop closest to the long cord tail very slightly. Slide the tail end of the cord into the loosened loop. Pull the cord tail until you have created a loop of the correct size for a button. Tighten the small loop around the cord tail end. In the photo the button loop is on the right, the unfilled cording is just below it, and the tail from the button loop is hanging down.

Turn the knot over and remove any extra filler from the cord tail as explained in Step 13. Shorten the fabric tube to ½in (1.3cm). Fold under the raw ends of both fabric tubes and sew to the wrong side of the knot. Secure each loop with a few stitches on the wrong side.

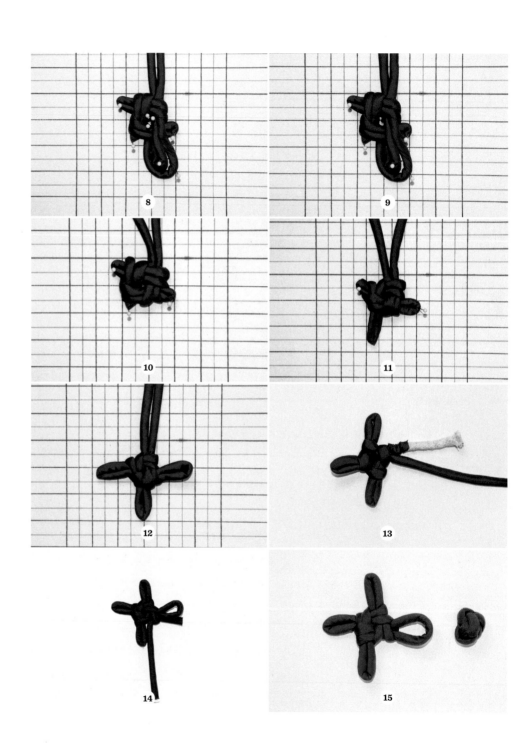

15 A fastening consisting of a good luck knot loop and double coin knot button (see opposite).

Double coin knot

A double coin knot can be used to create the loop or the button of a fastening. If you have made your own cord, work this knot with the seam in the cord facing down.

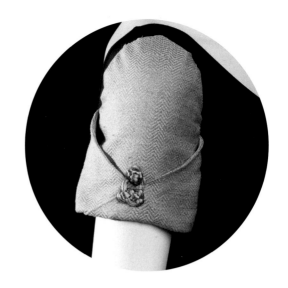

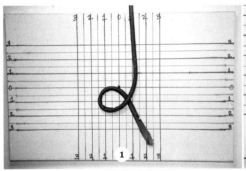

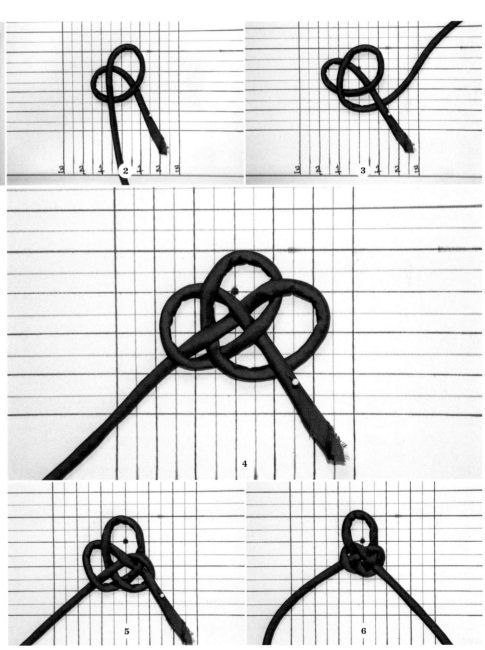

1 Near the end of the cord, make a loop, pointing left, with the long end passing over the short tail. Pin the short tail to the board.

2 Take the cord end over to the left then down to make another loop, pointing up. Pass the end over both cords of the first loop.

3 Working toward the right, slide the cord end under the cord tail near the pin.

4 Loop the cord end back toward the center of the knot. Pass it over the right-hand edge of the top loop, under the next cord, over the third cord, and under the fourth and outside edge of the lower loop.

5 Pull the cord end to begin to tighten the knot.

6 Unpin the short cord tail and pull it to tighten the knot from the other side. The top loop becomes a button loop. To make the button loop larger, push more cord from the cord tail into the knot and work the excess through the knot to the loop. To make the loop smaller, reverse the process.

Double coin knot button-and-loop fastening

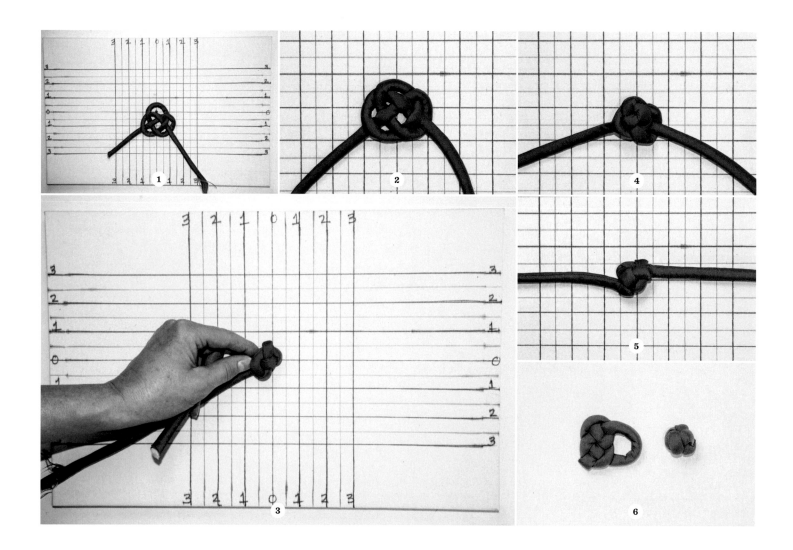

1 Make a double coin knot (see p. 155), but rather than leaving a button loop at the top, draw this loop into the knot. Pull the two cord ends to tighten the knot.

2 Shorten the cord within the knot further by pulling both cord ends and working the excess cord within the knot through the knot to the ends.

3 As the knot begins to tighten and get smaller, mold it around the tip of your finger to form a mound.

4 Keep sliding the extra cord through the knot and out.

5 Tighten the knot.

Finish the button by removing excess filler from the cording and sewing the ends to the back (see Simplified Good Luck Knot, pp. 153–54).

6 The finished double coin knot button-and-loop fastening.

Figure-of-eight knot

This knot consists of three interlocking figures of eight; a pair of figure-of-eight knots can be used to make a button-and-loop fastening. If you have made your own cord, work this knot with the seam in the cord facing down.

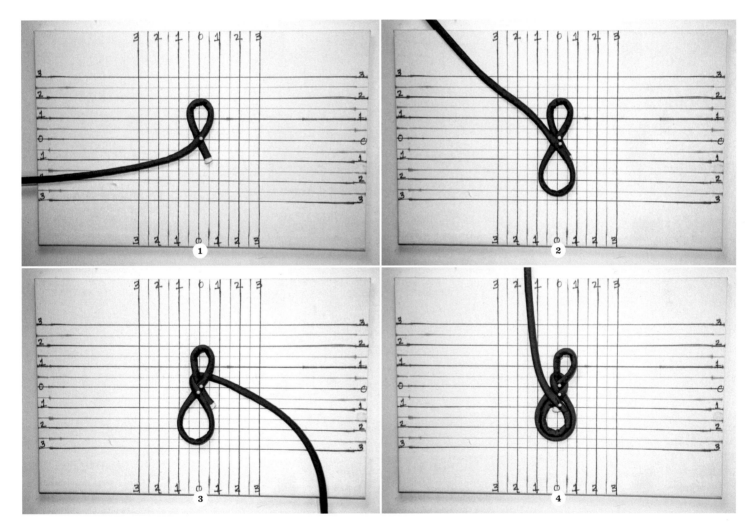

1 Make a loop pointing up, with the cord end crossing over the cord tail, pointing to the left. Place a pin at the cord intersection.

2 Make a second, larger loop pointing down, with the cord end crossing over itself at the center intersection.

The cord end should now point up and left. Place a pin in the intersection of the lower loop.

3 Wrap the cord end around and behind the upper loop and pull it so that it fits snugly. This completes the first figure of eight.

4 Make another loop with the cord end inside the lower loop; the cord end should finish pointing up and left again. Place a pin in the intersection of the new lower loop.

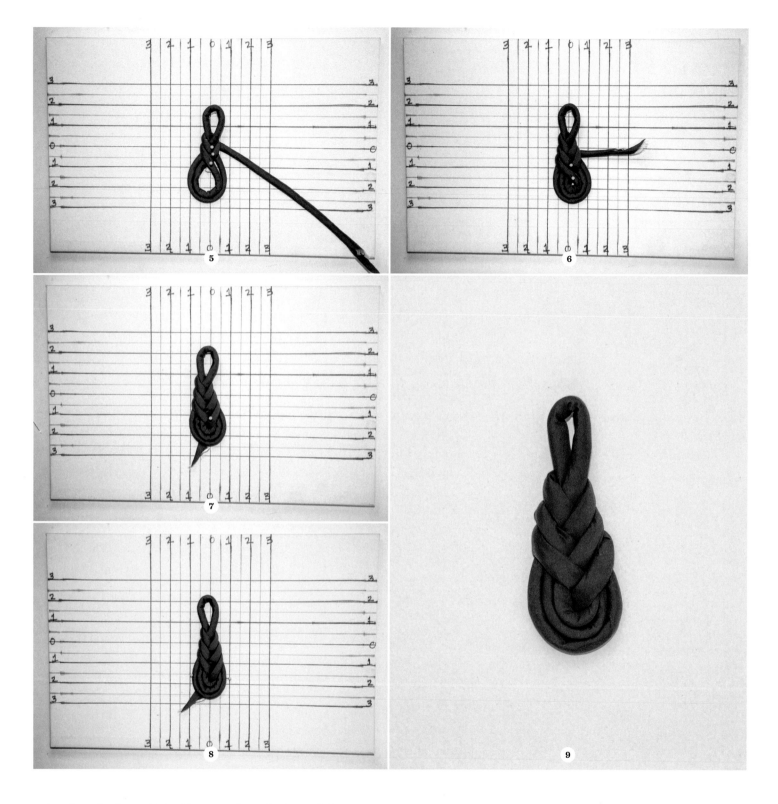

5 Wrap the cord end around behind the upper loop, below the previous wrap, and pull it snug. You may need to remove the top pins to pull it into place. This completes the second figure of eight.

6 Make another loop with the cord end inside the lower loop. The cord end should finish pointing up and left again. Remove the pin from the first intersection and place it in the intersection of the lowest loop. Wrap the cord end around the neck and pull it snug.

7 Slide the cord end into the center of the lower loop and pull it to the wrong side—using a pair of tweezers can help. Remove pins as needed.

8 Slide a pin into the lower loops from each side to hold the figure of eight together. The length of the loop above

the neck can be adjusted to fit a button by sliding the cord tail left in place in Step 1 in or out. Sew the knot together with a few stitches on the wrong side. A shot of steam from the iron will help settle the cord into place.

9 The completed figure-of-eight knot.

Figure-of-eight button-and-loop fastening

1 Make a double coin knot button near one end of the cord (see p. 155). Pin the knot to the board.

2 Start the figure-of-eight knot (see p. 157) just below the button knot, bringing the cord over itself and the tail below the knot, around and behind the neck of the knot, and finally crossing over both cords, pointing to the right.

3 Sew the figure-of-eight knot together with a few stitches on the wrong side.

4 Make a second figure-of-eight knot with a loop the same size as the button on the previous figure-of-eight knot. Adjust the loop to fit over the button knot by sliding the right-hand cord tighter or looser. A shot of steam from the iron will help to settle the cord into place.

5 The completed figure-of-eight button-and-loop fastening.

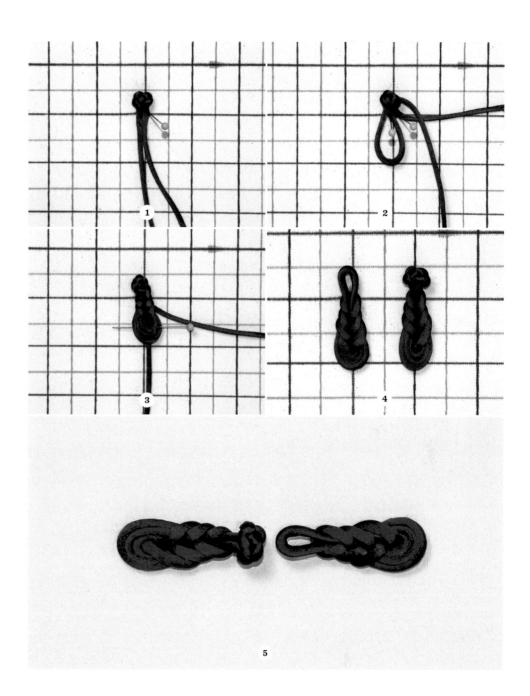

Passementerie, from the French *passement*, or "braid," refers to trims and braids that are sewn onto a garment. Historically, creating intricate patterns of scrolls, paisleys, and waves and sewing them onto garments was a time-consuming and costly process that only the wealthy could afford. Nowadays many trims are mass-produced and can be sewn on with a sewing machine, making passementerie a more affordable and approachable technique. Whether as an accent for a simple curve or as part of a complex design element, passementerie can transform an ordinary garment into something stylish and unique.

Many different kinds of trim are available—cord, braid, lace, beaded edging, rickrack, and ribbon, to name a few—made in a wide selection of materials.

3.3
Passementerie

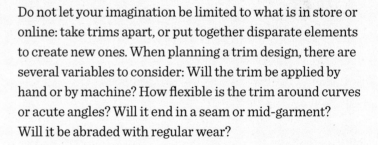

Do not let your imagination be limited to what is in store or online: take trims apart, or put together disparate elements to create new ones. When planning a trim design, there are several variables to consider: Will the trim be applied by hand or by machine? How flexible is the trim around curves or acute angles? Will it end in a seam or mid-garment? Will it be abraded with regular wear?

Trims come in many shapes and sizes, with different application methods. Flat trims are quickly sewn on with a sewing machine. Flexible trims can be manipulated into serpentine shapes or angular motifs. Narrow trims can be sewn on with zigzag stitch; heavier trims may need strong monofilament thread. Some trims have a high profile that won't fit through a sewing machine, and must be sewn on by hand. Additionally, heavy trims may require extra interfacing (see p. 17) for support. Passementerie is usually applied following a design transferred to the base fabric (see Transferring Patterns, pp. 18–23).

Customizing trim

Sometimes finding trim in the correct color or at the correct scale is not possible. It is possible, however, to make your own trim or to alter an existing trim to suit your design.

DISMANTLING A PURCHASED TRIM

Most trim is made up of different yarns sewn together with a machine stitch similar to a blind hem stitch; taking these yarns apart will reveal several different patterned trims. The joining stitch makes it easy for the trim come apart very quickly; be careful that the trims do not disintegrate into a pile of frizzy yarns on your work table.

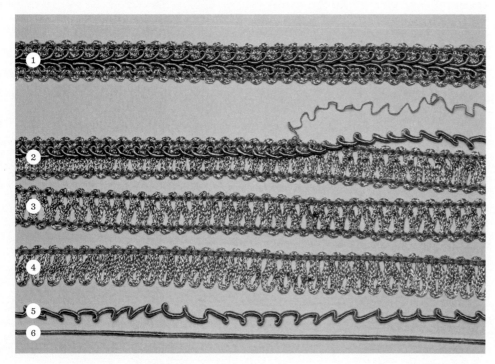

1. The complete trim.

2. The trim with the top scrollwork being removed. The very thin yarn is the thread that holds the scrollwork in place; the fatter yarn is the scrollwork yarn.

3. The base trim, with the top and bottom anchoring threads in place.

4. The anchoring thread removed from the bottom, leaving loops anchored at the top only.

5. The scrollwork yarn as it came off the trim.

6. The scrollwork yarn after being ironed flat.

METALLIC FRINGE

Metallic fringe is fairly delicate and malleable; it comes with the bottom of the fringe anchored together with a temporary stitch to help maintain the fringe's integrity until it is sewn in place. It is a simple matter to undo the anchoring stitches—gently pull on the thread holding the fringe together at the bottom.

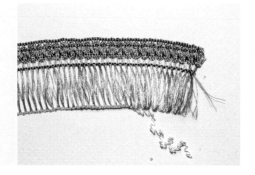

ASSEMBLING LENGTHS OF PURCHASED TRIM

You can also put pieces of trim together to make your own trim. Here, two pieces of the same trim are joined back to back to create a more substantial decoration.

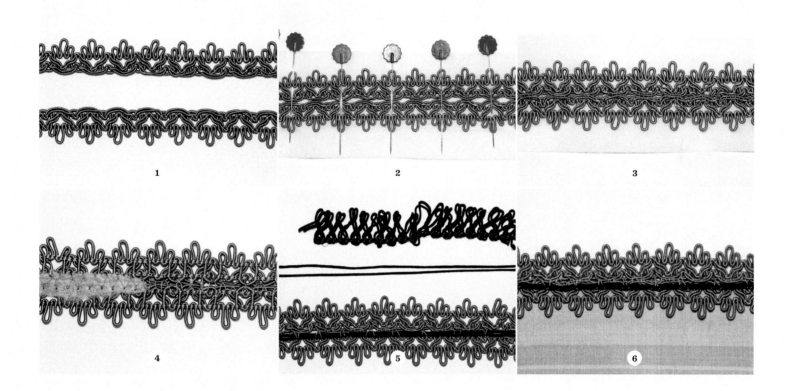

1 Assemble the lengths of trim on a strip of tear-away interfacing or tissue paper. This backing serves two purposes: it provides a stable background to anchor the trims; it also keeps the trims from being sucked down into the throat plate and jamming the sewing machine.

2 Pin the trims to the interfacing. Note that these pins are very long and, when pinned through both layers of trim, they securely anchor it to the interfacing. The large flower heads help keep the pin heads from disappearing into the trim.

3 Sew a zigzag stitch across the backbone of the two trims to anchor both trims in one pass (here stitched in orange for clarity). Experiment with the width of your zigzag stitching to catch both pieces of trim. A denser zigzag stitching could also be used, creating a satin stitch down the center of the trim.

4 Working on the wrong side, gently remove the interfacing; the little pieces stuck between the stitches can be teased out with tweezers or a pin.

5 To complete this trim, you can take two pieces of black yarn from another trim (shown at the top of the photo), iron them flat (center), and then thread them through the zigzag stitches (bottom).

6 The completed trim.

Finishing trim ends

Many trims unravel when you cut the ends. In stores, tape is wrapped around the trim end at the cutting point; cutting through the center of the tape leaves both cut ends wrapped in tape. Do not sew tape into your garment, though—it can be bulky and the glue may seep through and stain the fabric. Before attaching trim to a garment you must stabilize the ends. When trim ends meet in a seam they must match precisely.

STABILIZING THE END OF A TRIM

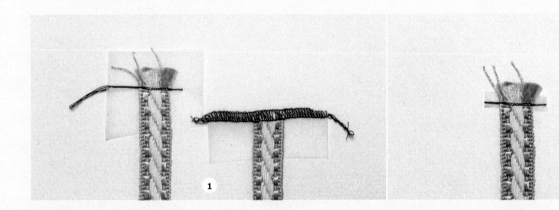

1 Place a piece of tear-away interfacing or tissue paper under the trim. Sew very small, straight stitches of 0.5mm (50 spi) across the backing and trim (left in the photo) or serge (right). The interfacing should allow the trim to feed through the machine without jamming.

2 Using paper scissors, carefully trim away the interfacing: cut through the stitching on both sides of the trim, leaving 1/8in (3mm) stitching behind to prevent unraveling. Finally, cut away the interfacing along the stitching line on the wrong side.

FOLDING TRIM ENDS OVER

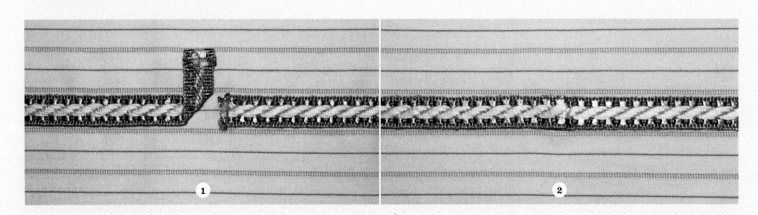

1 Sew the trim to the garment, starting with a raw end (see Flat Trim, p. 169). When you get back to the start, fold over the finishing end by 1/2in (1.3cm). Sew down the folded end, making sure the two raw ends finish at different places, forming steps.

If both raw ends finish at the same place, there will be a big hump under the trim—the aim is to have two smaller humps. Hand-sew the two trims together at the center if needed.

2 The finished overlapped trim.

HIDING TRIM ENDS IN A SEAM

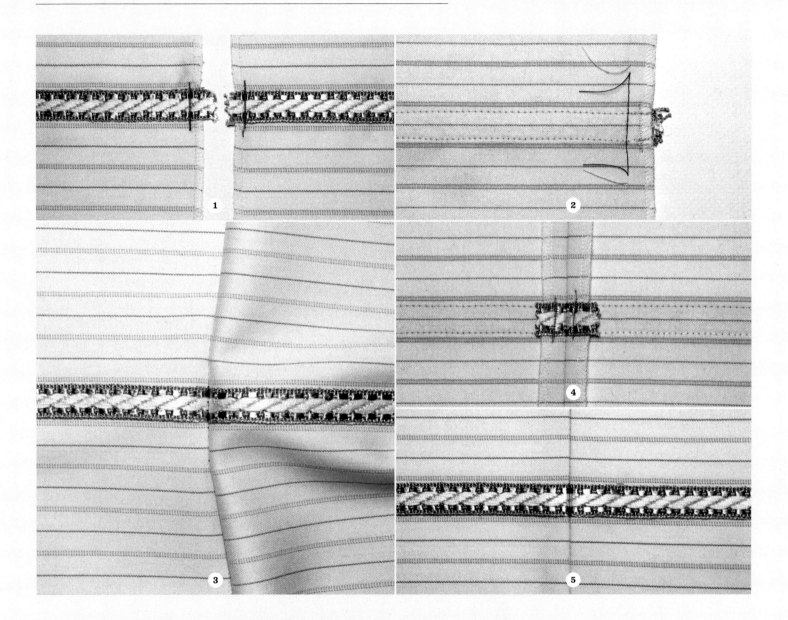

1 Cut the ends of the trim slightly longer than the seam allowance of the garment to prevent a large lump forming at the edge of the seam allowance. Using pinking shears will diffuse the edges even further. If the bulk of the trim ends in the seam allowance is troublesome, grade the ends after sewing the seam.

2 After sewing the trim to the fabric (see Flat Trim, p. 169), match the ends of the trim together. Pin and machine-baste the trim and 1in (2.5cm) of the seam on either side of the trim.

3 Check that the trim matches exactly, then sew the entire seam using a regular stitch length.

4 The completed seam from the wrong side.

5 The completed seam from the right side.

Pushing trim ends through the fabric

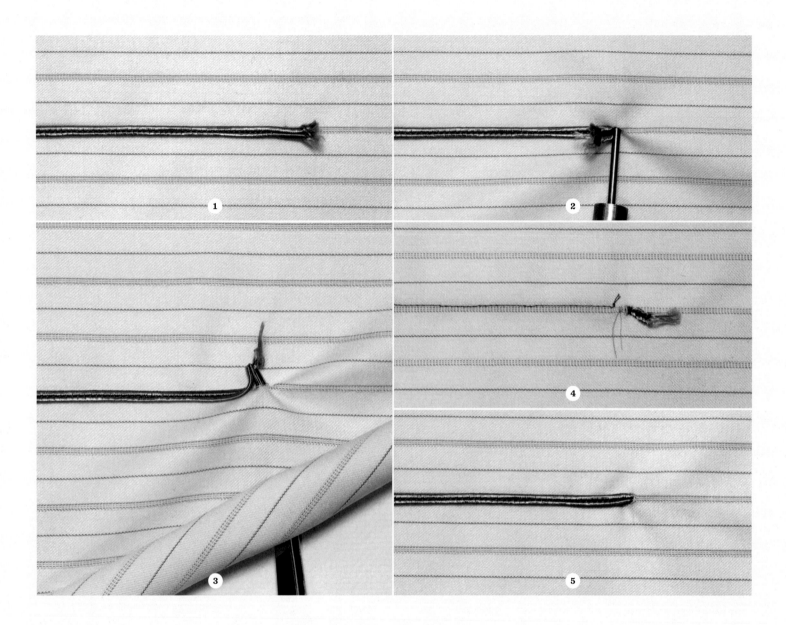

1 Sew the trim to the fabric, stopping 1in (2.5cm) before the end of the trim. Pull the threads to the wrong side and knot them.

2 Using a large needle and then an awl, create a small hole in the fabric by separating the yarns. Be careful not to break the yarns while making the hole; you do not want to weaken the cloth.

3 Working from the wrong side, insert a pair of tweezers through the hole in the fabric and grab the loose end of the trim. Gently pull the trim end through the fabric.

4 Sew the end of the trim to the wrong side of the fabric with a few stitches to keep the trim from being pulled back to the right side.

5 The completed trim.

Attaching trim with machine stitches

When a trim is too narrow to be sewn on with a straight machine stitch, a zigzag stitch can be used. You may need to use an interfacing backing—either tear-away interfacing or an iron-on/sew-in interfacing—to prevent a ridge or tunnel from forming around the trim.

STITCH LENGTH AND TENSION

Make several samples to test the zigzag stitch width and density (or length), and the balance between the needle and bobbin threads (see Balanced Zigzag Stitch, p. 25). Use brightly colored threads so you can see what the needle and bobbin threads are doing in each stitch. When the stitch width is correct, the stitches will fall on either side of the trim without catching it. When the stitch length is correct, the stitches will create a cage that protects the trim from snagging and being pulled out. You may choose to make the stitch width slightly narrower so the stitches pierce the trim to hold it in place, in which case you can make the stitch length longer (less frequent), as you will not be relying on the zigzag cage to hold the trim. In the samples shown here, interfacing was used as a backing and as a fronting, representing the pattern-transfer medium.

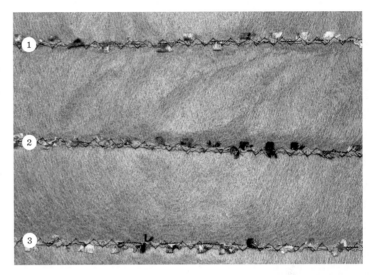

Right side

1. The needle tension is too tight, causing the interfacing to ripple.

2. The needle thread disappears to the wrong side at stitch points. This is good, but check the wrong side to make sure it is not too loose.

3. The needle thread disappears to the wrong side at stitch points, without causing puckering. Check the wrong side, but this might be the right tension setting.

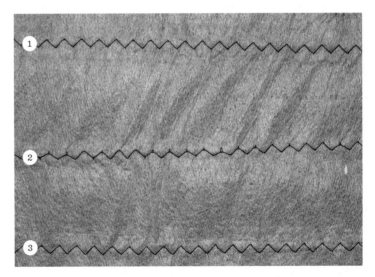

Wrong side

1. The needle tension is too tight, causing the interfacing to ripple.

2. The needle thread (orange) is showing too much; the needle tension is too loose.

3. The threads are well balanced; there are small dots of needle thread (orange) just coming through.

ATTACHING TRIM WITH A ZIGZAG MACHINE STITCH

1 Draw or print the pattern for the trim design on tear-away interfacing (see Transferring Patterns, pp 18–23).

2 Place the interfacing with the pattern on the right side of the fabric. Place another piece of tear-away interfacing on the wrong side to act as a stabilizer and prevent the zigzag stitches from creating tunnels around the trim.

Machine-baste all three layers together—pattern, fabric, and stabilizer—before the trim is pinned in place (here stitched in orange thread).

3 If the trim needs to be pinned to the fabric and interfacing sandwich to follow the pattern, the pins are anchored into the fabric, skimmed over the trim, and then are anchored into the fabric again.

4 Sew the trim to the fabric and interfacing sandwich with a zigzag stitch. A medium-width stitch is used here.

5 Feeding the trim through the top of presser foot may help you guide it into the zigzag stitches. Here the trim is pulled up to show the threading of the trim through the presser foot toes.

6 Remove the basting stitches holding the fabric and interfacing together. Gently tear off the interfacing from both back and front of the fabric. Use tweezers or a pin to help remove small pieces of interfacing caught in the zigzag stitches.

Finish the trim ends using one of the methods given on pp. 164–65.

7 The completed trim sewn on with matching threads. The top two rows were sewn with cream thread in the needle to match the trim. The bottom two rows were sewn with tan thread in the needle to match the base fabric.

8 The completed trim sewn with clear monofilament in the needle and regular thread in the bobbin (see Sewing with Monofilament Thread, p. 26).

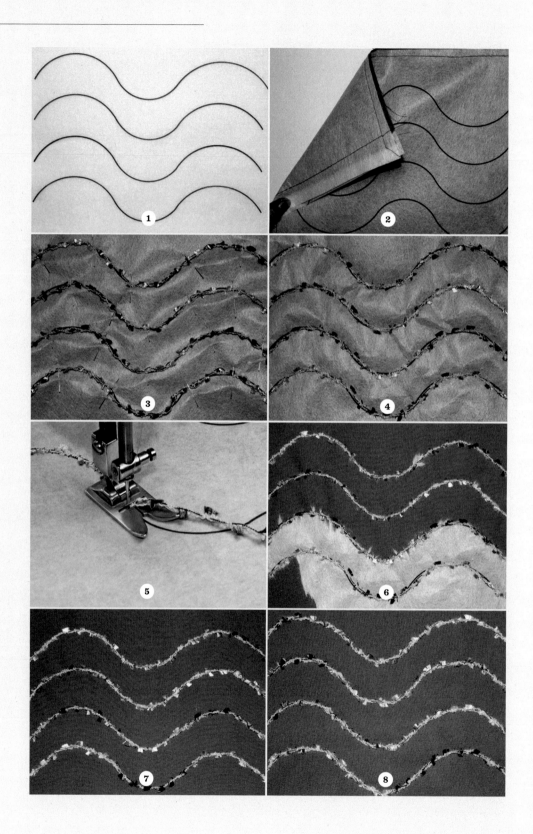

Flat trim

A flat gimp braid is an easy trim to add to fabric with machine stitching. Here it is used to cover the stitching on the hem of a garment.

1

2

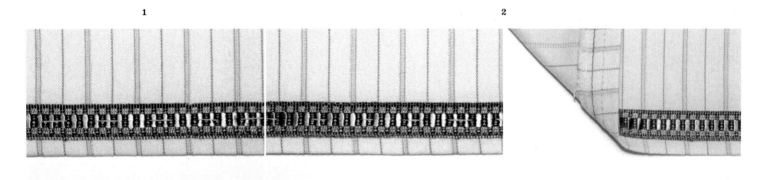

3

4

5

1 Sew the hem (here stitched in orange for clarity).

2 Pin the trim so that it covers the hem stitching. The ripples in the fabric are from the pins.

3 Hand-baste the trim in place. Note that the ripples in the fabric have disappeared with the removal of the pins. Machine-sew one side of the trim to the fashion fabric (here the lower edge is sewn in orange thread). Press.

4 Sew the other side of the trim down, sewing in the same direction as the previous pass. The pressure of the sewing machine foot will push the trim slightly; you want to be sure to push the trim in the same direction on both sides. In this example, if the second side had been sewn from the other direction, the center blocks of the trim would lie on an angle instead of straight up and down. Finish the trim ends using one of the methods given on pp. 164–65.

5 The finished hem and the wrong side.

USING STICKY TAPE TO POSITION THE TRIM

There are several double-sided sticky tapes suitable for fabric on the market, as well as double-sided iron-on tapes. These can be used instead of basting, or even in place of machine sewing, but ask the following questions:

- *Will the glue on the tape gum up the machine needle when stitching?*

- *If the tape is water soluble, can the trim and fabric be immersed in water to dissolve the tape without harming the fabric or trim?*

- *If the tape is left in place and sometime later the glue dissolves, will the tape be bulky under the trim?*

Soutache (Russian braid)

Soutache is a braid used as a decorative trim. (The French *soutache* comes from the Hungarian *sujtás*, meaning "trimming.") It is made from two or more cotton filler cords wrapped in rayon yarn in a herringbone pattern, creating a flat trim. The valley down the middle of the trim is perfect for hiding stitches. Soutache can be applied in numerous ways, from straight lines to complicated, curling scrollwork.

Soutache works best with curved designs; it does not make sharp corners, which are better made with middy braid (see p. 172). For a small design, you can shape soutache by pulling on the filler cords to create curves; some cords curl nicely, others not as well. All soutache braids can be finger-pressed and steamed into curves; use the warmth of your fingers to create the initial curves and then steam them with an iron to set the shape permanently. Always test the base fabric to make sure it has enough heft to support the trim and stitching involved in scrollwork. Adding interfacing may be necessary to support the trim.

RESIZING A DESIGN

Tracing a design by hand onto tear-away interfacing works well. But creating a design digitally has several benefits: you can enlarge or reduce its size easily, and rotate or flip it; you can also print the design directly onto interfacing (see p. 19).

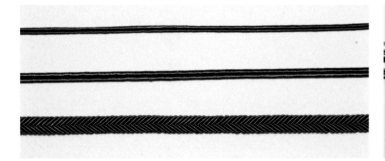

Soutache is available in several sizes.

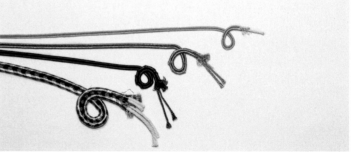

The moss green soutache (top) and silver and black (bottom) curl easily when the filler is pulled. The blue braids (center) do not curl quite as smoothly.

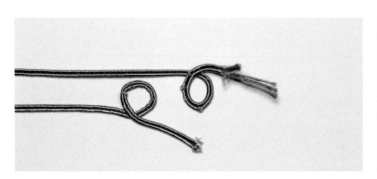

The top soutache was curved by pulling the cotton cord filler, while the lower soutache was curved by finger pressing and steaming.

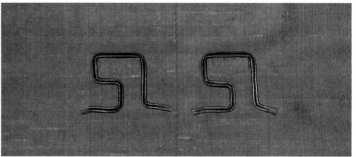

The scroll on the left was stitched to silk dupioni supported by lightweight knit fusible interfacing; the base fabric is absolutely flat. The sample on the right was stitched to the dupioni with no backing and shows some subtle wrinkles, which would cause problems with a lot of scrollwork.

1 Create a design either on the computer or by hand. Here a wavelike pattern has been manipulated until it fills a cuff pattern piece. Print or trace the design onto a piece of tear-away interfacing.

You can add registration marks to the pattern before printing. In this pattern, the red lines indicate the $^{1}/_{2}$in (1.3cm) seam allowance and the blue lines represent the cutting and folding lines.

2 Working just with the soutache and the interfacing, pin the soutache to the interfacing. With your fingers, stretch and pat the soutache around the first curve. There will be some small lumps on the inside of the curve; try to distribute them evenly around the curve.

3 Once you have 1–2in (2.5–5cm) of the soutache shaped, steam the curve with your iron. Keep the iron 1–2in (2.5–5cm) above the soutache—do not press the curve with the iron. You want to shrink the cotton cord filler on the inner curve and stretch the filler on the outside curve. The steam will help you do this. While the soutache is still warm and damp from the steam, reform the same curve, easing the lumps with your fingertips until they are no longer visible. Steam the soutache again to set it.

4 When the curve is dry, pin the soutache into place and move on to the next section. Continue working in small portions until you complete the design.

5 Place the pinned trim and interfacing onto the fabric. Machine-baste the fabric and interfacing together (here the basting is shown on the seam lines in red thread for clarity, and the placement line was stitched on the fabric in blue).

6 Using a little foot for increased visibility, and a short stitch length of 2mm (12 spi) for increased control, sew along the middle of the trim. Depending on the complexity of your design, this can be slow and painstaking sewing. Here, the inner corners were sewn by manually turning the hand-wheel to place each stitch accurately.

As you work your way around the design, remember to keep the needle down when lifting the presser foot to pivot the work. An awl or small scissors can be used to help poke the trim into place under the foot (but be careful not to stitch over either as they will break the needle).

7 Do not press the piece immediately after you have finished sewing. Remove the basting stitches that hold the interfacing in place and gently tear it away. Tweezers can be used to remove little pieces of interfacing caught in the corners.

8 Once all the interfacing is removed, smooth the piece and reshape the fabric, and trim it if it has become distorted. Press the piece very carefully; too much pressing can make the trim shiny. Finish the trim ends (see pp. 164–65).

9 The finished soutache piece sewn into a cuff, ready to add to a sleeve.

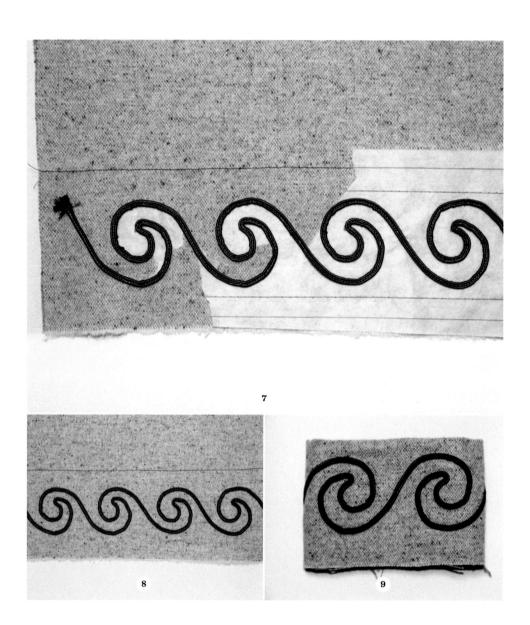

7

8

9

VARIATION

Middy braid is a flat trim commonly seen on the yoke of a sailor's shirt— it is very good for making sharp, angular designs. It can be attached in the same way as soutache, but the corners are mitered.

1 To create a miter at a corner, fold the middy braid back down on top of itself. Press.

2 Holding the top tip of the crease, refold the middy braid to the side. Carefully move the braid until you have an exact 45° angle at the corner. Press. Continue placing the middy braid on the pattern and making mitered corners until the design is complete. Sew as for soutache (see Step 6, p. 171).

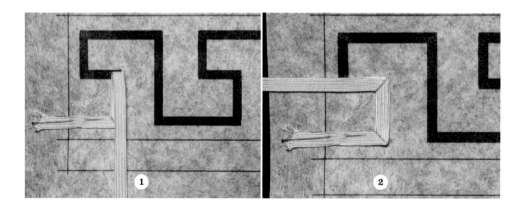

1

2

Rickrack

Rickrack comes in cotton or polyester, and a variety of sizes. It can be sewn on in several ways, but the most common methods are to use a straight stitch along the middle, or a zigzag stitch that follows the shape of the rickrack; the latter requires samples to perfect stitch length and width. If the rickrack is sewn in the middle of a garment, follow the directions for flat trim (p. 169) or soutache (pp. 170–72). Rickrack can also be used to edge a hem, as explained below.

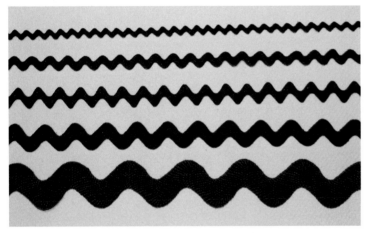

Different sizes of rickrack.

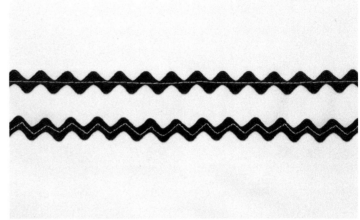

Rickrack sewn straight along the middle (top) and using a zigzag stitch to follow the shape (bottom).

1 Machine-baste the hemline (shown here in white thread), then machine-baste a placement line for the bottom of the rickrack. Here the rickrack is $\frac{1}{2}$in (1.3cm) wide; sew a placement line (here shown in orange) half the width of the rickrack—$\frac{1}{4}$in (6.5mm)—below the hemline.

2 Working on the right side, hand-baste the rickrack so the bottom just touches the placement line.

3 Sew just below the horizontal center of the rickrack.

4 On the wrong side, fold the hem allowance up on the rickrack stitching line; this will be fractionally below the hemline, but the turn of the cloth should put the hemline right on the fold. Press lightly.

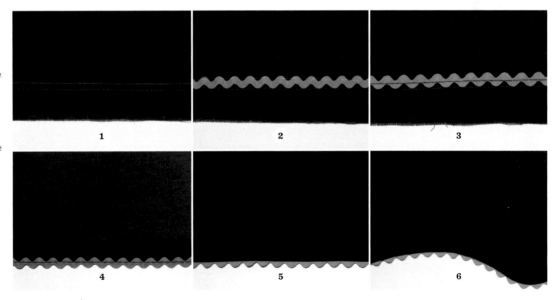

5 Turn the fabric to the right side. Press the rickrack and hem, making sure an even amount of rickrack shows along the hemline. Finish the trim ends (see pp. 164–65).

6 Rickrack can also be applied to a curved hem.

Hand-sewn trim

Some trims are too bulky to sew on using a sewing machine and must be sewn on by hand. You can use a large embroidery hoop to hold the fabric taut. The hoop used here has a stand to raise it off the table and allow you to rotate the fabric from right side to wrong side. Here a heavyweight wool was used as the base fabric, so interfacing was not required on the wrong side of the fabric.

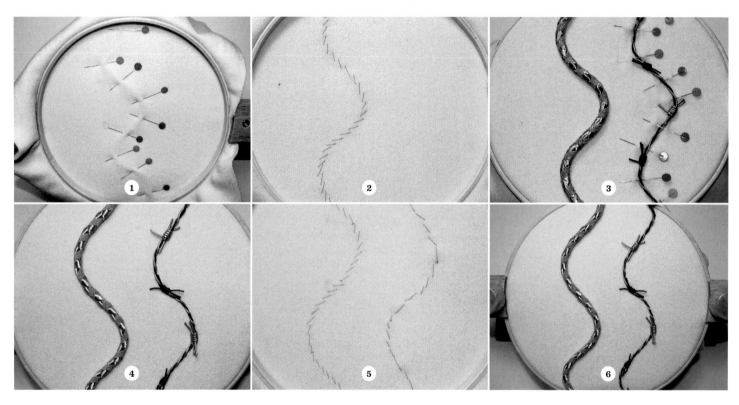

1 Pin the trim in place from the wrong side, catching just a few strands of the trim with the pins.

2 Working on the right side, sew the trim in place using diagonal or pad stitch (see Diagonal Basting, p. 28). Catch a few strands of the trim with each pass of the needle. Knot the thread every few inches and then continue sewing with the same thread. Since the trim stands proud of the fabric, it will be subject to snagging; with a knot every few inches, only a short length will need to be resewn if the stitching breaks. The wrong side is pictured here to show the stitch pattern.

3 Some trims are more easily pinned from the right side. Here the barbed-wire trim is secured with the pins anchored into the fabric, skimmed over the trim, and then anchored into the fabric again.

4 Working on the right side, sew the trim in place using diagonal or pad stitch, or similar; if sewn carefully, the thread should be barely visible.

5 The two different stitching lines from the wrong side: the blue thread on the left anchors the round gray trim; the orange thread on the right anchors the black and gray barbed-wire trim. Note the frequent knotting along both stitching paths.

6 The two finished lines of trim, sewn on white wool.

Ribbon zigzag appliqué

This is a traditional method used to sew ribbon, or any other trim, by hand. The ribbon is folded back and forth to create a sinuous design.

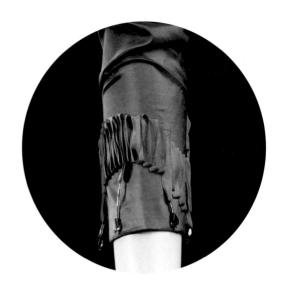

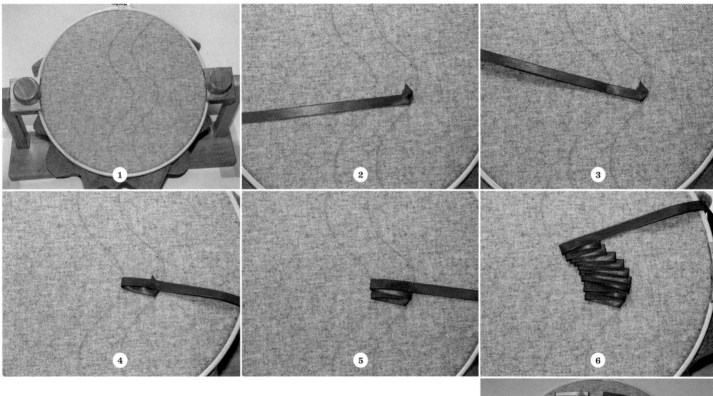

1 Transfer the pattern to the fabric. Place the fabric in a hoop to hold the fabric taut.

2 Fold under the raw end of the ribbon and secure it to the fabric with a few stitches, with the fold of the ribbon at the edge of the design line. At the completion of this stitch, the needle and thread should be on the wrong side of the fabric. Here the ribbon is positioned in the middle of the design for clarity; usually it is placed at the bottom of the design.

3 Lay the ribbon across the design. At the left-hand side bring the needle up through the center of the ribbon, just inside the design line, then down to the wrong side at the top edge of the ribbon, again inside the design line.

4 Fold the ribbon to hide the stitch just made, slightly askew so the ribbon travels upward. Make another stitch on the right-hand side of the design, catching the underneath ribbon and the new layer of ribbon, as in Step 3.

5 Repeat Steps 3–4.

6 Follow the design lines as you work.

7 The completed designs.

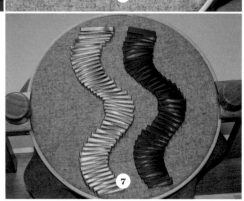

Appliqué, a French word meaning "applied," started as a way to patch a torn or well-worn garment. The practice quickly evolved into a decorative technique, with the patches themselves becoming works of art. While appliqué is often associated with cotton quilting fabric, it can be a glorious embellishment when created in silk, wool, or Ultrasuede®.

Appliqués can be made from a single layer of fabric sewn to a base fabric, or from multiple layers, stitched to add dimension. When choosing fabrics for appliqué, remember that the edges of each piece are usually turned under with a very narrow hem and that, therefore, slippery fabrics like chiffons and polyesters will be difficult to work with, as will crepes and loosely woven fabrics like wool bouclé.

3.4
Appliqué

Cottons, rayons, and many wools and silks, however, will fold under crisply, making beautiful appliqués. There are also many fabrics that do not require the raw edge to be turned under but can be sewn straight onto the base fabric after being cut out: Melton wool, felt, Ultrasuede®, and leather. In this chapter, all but one of the appliqués were created with solid colored fabrics, but multicolored wovens and printed fabrics can alter your garments in unexpected ways, adding depth and texture with a single piece of fabric.

Appliqués can be small or large, a multiple pieced image that is complete only when all the elements are sewn together, or a simple, solo shape. In the Decorative Application Techniques exercise (p. 187), sewing machine stitches are added to the centers of flowers, but embroidery stitches, beads, buttons, and other trims can be added as well to create an unexpectedly modern garment.

Basic appliqué stitches

There are several special sewing techniques used in appliqué: slip stitch,
roll-under stitch, and a method of stitching into an acute-angled corner. Here
the stitches are sewn with a doubled white thread for clarity; when sewn with
a single, matching thread the stitches will disappear.

SLIP STITCH

Slip stitch can be used to attach appliqué pieces to the base fabric.
It should be invisible from the right side.

1 Lightly press the seam allowance to
the wrong side. Bring the needle up
from the wrong side, through both the
base fabric and the appliqué.

2 Insert the needle into the base fabric
catching two or three threads to make
a tiny stitch at the edge of the appliqué.

3 Insert the needle into the folded edge
of the appliqué. Slide the needle inside
the fold for $^1/_8$–$^1/_4$in (3–6mm) before
coming out of the appliqué fabric.
Repeat Steps 2–3 until the appliqué
is sewn to the base fabric.

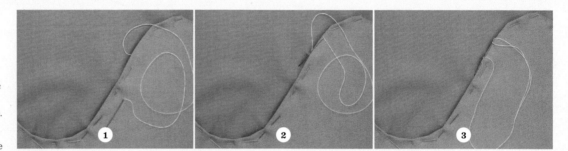

ROLL-UNDER STITCH

This stitch catches the raw edge of the appliqué and rolls it under
before securing the appliqué to the base fabric.

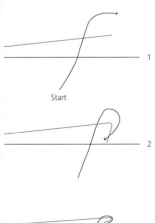

Start

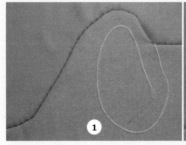

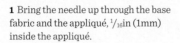

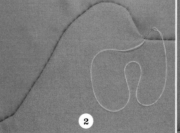

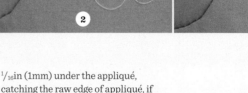

1 Bring the needle up through the base
fabric and the appliqué, $^1/_{16}$in (1mm)
inside the appliqué.

2 Turn the raw edge of the appliqué under
with the point of your needle and then
insert the needle into the base fabric,

$^1/_{16}$in (1mm) under the appliqué,
catching the raw edge of appliqué, if
possible. Pull the needle and thread to
the back of the work. The stitch will
pull the raw edge of the appliqué under.

3 The completed corner.

Sewing acute-angled corners

Roll the raw edge of a slashed corner under to tame any seam allowances that jut out too far.

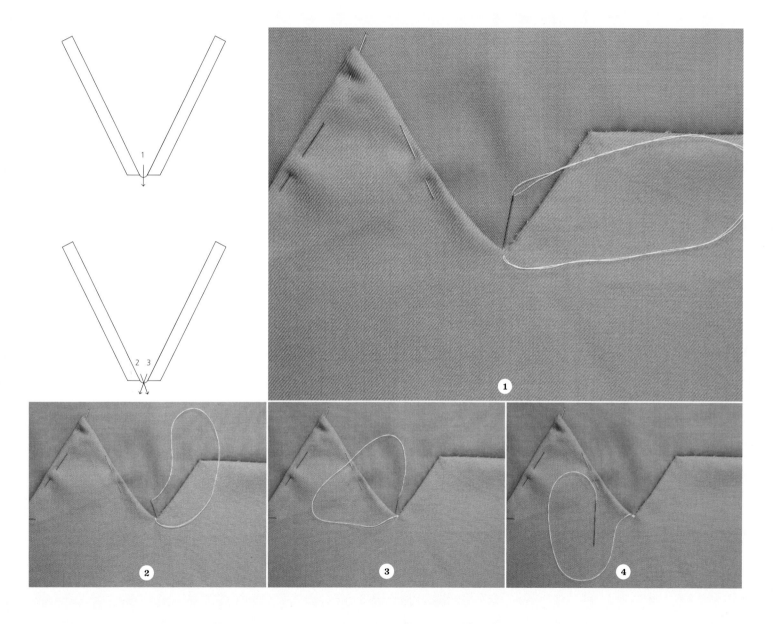

1 Clip the seam allowance to within $^1/_{16}$in (1mm) of the seam line. Using a slip stitch sew to within $^1/_4$in (6mm) of the V. Using a roll-under stitch (see opposite), place the first stitch in the center of the V, rolling the raw edge under without distorting the fabric.

2 Place the second stitch to the right of the first stitch.

3 Place the third stitch to the left of the first stitch.

4 Once you have secured the V with three stitches, add more small stitches to keep the fabric from unraveling in the V, if needed.

Folding sharp corners

If your appliqué piece has a pointed corner, you will need to fold the fabric and trim it to reduce the bulk.

1 Press both side seam allowances.

2 Fold back the fabric that extends beyond the triangle, folding it just shy of the seam allowance fold.

3 Insert a pin along the fold line created in Step 2 to mark the fold.

4 Remove the pin and cut along the folded line.

5 Refold the seam allowances so that the newly cut raw edge of the tip is tucked under the seam allowance of the adjacent side. If properly folded, no raw edges will be visible along the outer edges of the triangle.

6 The finished, folded corner.

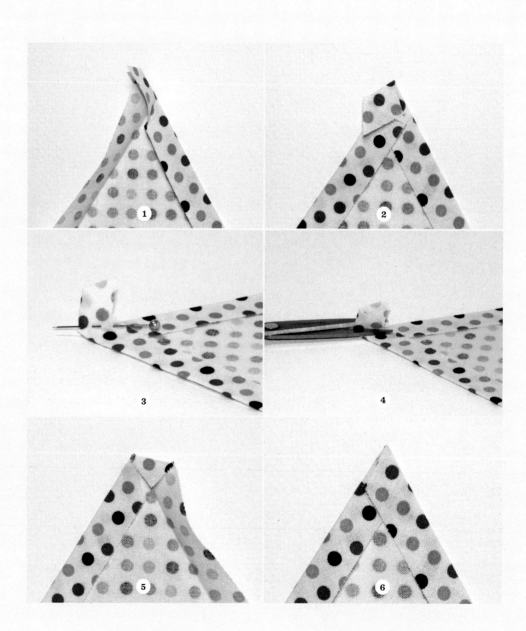

Hand appliqué

There are many ways to mark the placement of an appliqué. Here oak tag is used for placing the petals of a flower (for other methods, see Transferring Patterns, pp. 18–23). The petals are sewn in place using slip stitch.

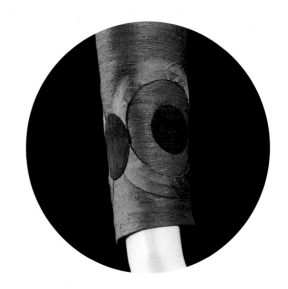

1 Draw the design on oak tag.

2 Cut around the outline of the design.

3 Place the outline on the base fabric; use either the piece of oak tag from which you cut the design (the negative shape) or the cutout piece (the positive shape). Here, the negative shape is used. Trace around the outline onto the base fabric.

4 Cut out the individual petals from a second fabric, adding a seam allowance. Turn under the seam allowance, press, then position the petals on the base fabric, arranging them within the design outline. Pin in place.

5 Remove the oak tag. Baste the petals in place, or use a small piece of double-sided fusible interfacing in the center of each petal to hold it in place.

6 Use slip stitch (see p. 178) to sew each petal in place. Tuck in any corners of fabric with your needle as you work.

7 The finished appliquéd flower.

Machine appliqué

Different machine stitches and techniques can be used to attach appliqué pieces to fabric, each giving a different effect.

Straight stitch

A straight stitch is the most basic method of attaching appliqué pieces by machine. Work out stitching paths before you start sewing. Here the simplest path is around the perimeter of each petal.

1 Transfer your pattern to freezer paper and prepare your fabric pieces (see Transferring Patterns, p. 23). Position and pin the pieces following Hand Appliqué, Steps 1–5 (p. 181).

2 Lift one overlapping petal and begin machine-stitching the petal underneath at this point so that your stitches start and end underneath the overlapping petal. Stitch around each petal in turn.

3 On the last petal, sew from the edge of the previous petal, around the tip of the petal, down the side, over the bottom of the first petal, and to this petal's ending point, stopping exactly at the edge of the previous petal with no overlapping stitches. Pull the needle threads to the wrong side and knot together with the bobbin threads.

4 The completed appliqué, sewn with a straight stitch.

Zigzag stitch

Zigzag stitch is another method of applying appliqué pieces by machine. A zigzag stitch has three parts to control: the stitch length, the stitch width, and the thread tension.

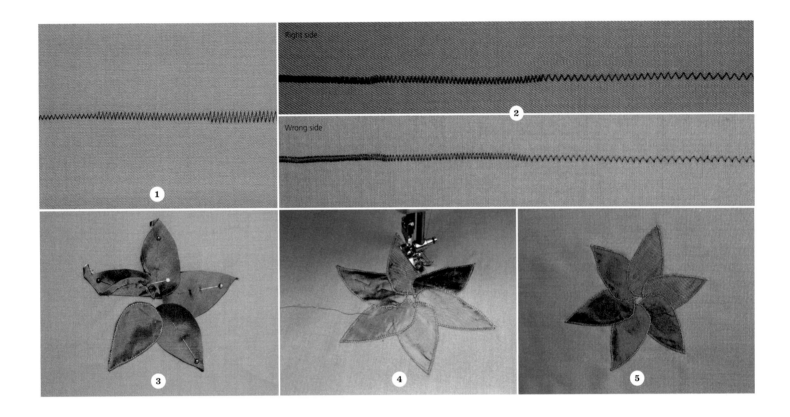

1 First select the stitch width, which dictates how far the needle travels from side to side. In this sample, from left to right, the stitch width increases from 2, to 4, to 8mm. Each machine will produce slightly different stitches from another machine set at the same numbers.

2 Next select the stitch length, which dictates the distance between stitches. From left to right, the stitch length increases from 0.5, to 1, to 2mm (50, to 25, to 12 spi). Needle tension dictates where the needle and bobbin stitches intertwine to make the stitch. For appliqué, the intertwining should fall on the wrong side. (See Balanced Zigzag Stitch, p. 25.)

3 Pin or baste the petals in place. Lift one overlapping petal and begin stitching the petal underneath at this point so that your stitches start and end underneath the overlapping petal.

4 With zigzag stitch you can position the needle to enter the fabric along the outer edge of the petal, or have the stitch fall equally, with half on the petal and half on the base fabric. Stitch around each petal in turn. Pull the thread tails to the wrong side and knot.

5 The completed appliqué, sewn with a zigzag stitch.

USING INTERFACING TO BACK APPLIQUÉ PIECES

Consider applying interfacing to the back of the appliqué to support the satin stitching.

Here tunneling, or gathering of too much fabric into the stitches, especially around the bottom of the petal, causes the base fabric to pucker. Adding interfacing to the base fabric will help eliminate tunneling.

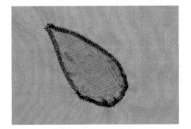

Corded satin stitch

A satin stitch sewn over both the raw edge of an appliqué and a rayon cord provides a way to create a decoratively detailed appliqué with just a single layer of fabric.

The addition of the cord can also change the appearance of the satin stitch itself. Here, on the left, the rayon thread is matte when stitched in a plain satin stitch, but is much brighter with the additional depth from the rayon cord on the right.

Test the fabric layers: is your fabric sturdy enough, or do you need interfacing? You can interface the base fabric or the appliqué. Interfacing the appliqué will help prevent the raw edges from unraveling before they are covered by satin stitches.

1 Create a stitching pattern.

2 The stitching line is worked continuously as numbered.

3 Draw the stitching lines on the fabric; here a heat-erasable pen was used. Cut out the appliqué. Pin or hand-baste the appliqué in place on the base fabric.

4 When stitching over a cord, it is important to loosen the tension on the needle thread because it must travel farther from one side of the cord to the other. Loosening the needle tension lets more thread slip through the tension disks for each stitch.

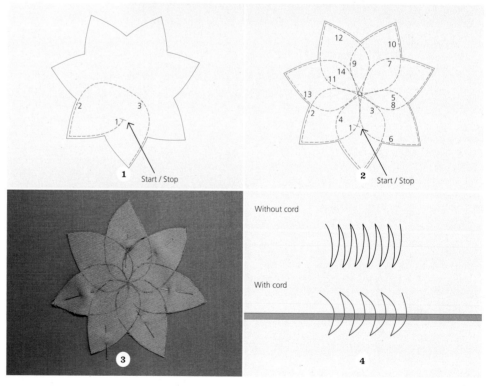

5 Make several samples before you start in order to adjust the zigzag stitch to the right width, length, and thread tension to cover the cord and the appliqué's raw edge.

Place the cord under the foot, centered between the toes, with a couple of inches of cording behind the foot. Sew along the edge of the appliqué, keeping the cord centered between the toes. You also need to decide if the cording should show through the zigzag stitch or just add height to the stitching. Here the cording shows through the zigzag stitch for a more colorful effect.

6 Once you have adjusted the thread tensions, follow your stitching pattern to sew the appliqué to the base fabric. Press the appliqué with lots of steam to meld the stitches and the fabrics, but be sure to let the appliqué dry on the ironing board before moving it.

7 Pull the needle threads to the wrong side and knot them with their bobbin thread mates. Thread a large-eyed needle with the cord end and pull the end through to the wrong side.

8 Do not knot the cord, but thread the end through the back of some of the zigzag stitches (shown here in red for clarity).

9 The completed appliqué, sewn with a corded satin stitch.

Sew then cut

This technique is another way to appliqué a single layer
of decorative fabric to base fabric. Make samples before you
start to adjust the zigzag stitch to the right width, length, and
thread tension. Test the fabric layers: is your fabric sturdy enough,
or do you need interfacing? If you interface the appliqué fabric,
will it show when you cut away excess fabric?

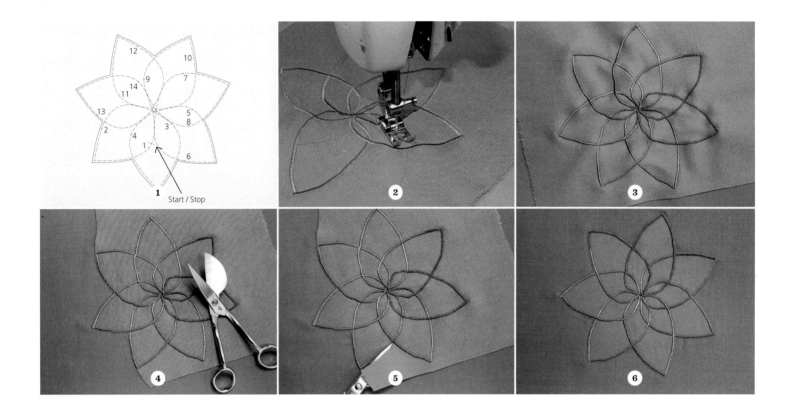

1 Create a stitching pattern. Here, the
base fabric was interfaced with a knit
fusible interfacing.

2 Satin-stitch along the design lines.

3 The entire piece may be puckered
after the stitching; press the appliqué
well. Use lots of steam but be sure to let
the appliqué dry completely on the
ironing board before moving it.

4 After the piece is pressed and dry,
use appliqué scissors to cut away
excess fabric. These scissors have a
blade shaped like a duckbill or a paddle,
which slides under the extra cloth,
snuggling up to the stitching line. The
bent handles help to minimize the
movement of the fabric as you cut.

5 With a little practice, you can
position the scissors right next to the
stitching line and move just the top
blade, getting a very close cut.

6 The completed appliqué. Note the
thin border of pink fabric outside of
the gray satin stitching.

Decorative application techniques

Using a fabric that does not fray—like Ultrasuede®, leather, or felt—allows design elements to be attached to base fabric in unusual ways.

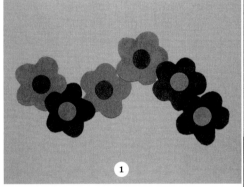

1 Cut out your design elements (here, flowers) and place them on the base fabric. The elements can be pinned, basted, or fused in place with small pieces of double-sided fusible interfacing placed on the wrong side.

2 Sew through the center of each flower four times in a contrasting thread, starting and stopping one stitch outside of the flower center. This design leaves the outer petal section of the flower loose so the arrangement of the overlapping petals can be changed.

VARIATION

Experiment with other techniques. These Ultrasuede® flowers were sewn to the base fabric with three concentric circles, with a bead in the center.

Reverse appliqué

Reverse appliqué is created by layering several different fabrics together and then cutting away selected areas of fabric to reveal a multilayered design. The Kuna Indians of Panama's San Blas Islands are well known for using this technique to produce colorful geometric designs called "molas," which they traditionally used to decorate women's blouses. Here, a flower design, in wool and silk, has three layers of petals, with a net appliqué at the center.

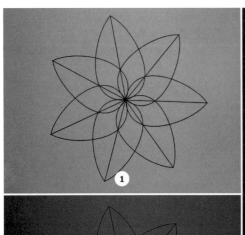

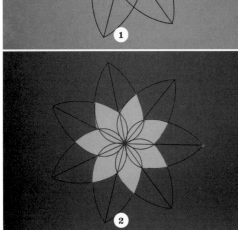

1 Create a full-size mock-up using colored paper or colored pencils to get a good sense of the complete design. First, draw or print the whole flower on paper. This will provide the bottom layer of the design.

2 Next, draw or print the design on a second sheet of paper, which will become the middle layer. Cut out the central flower to reveal the bottom layer.

3 Now draw the outline of the whole flower on a third sheet of paper to create the top layer. Cut out this shape to reveal the middle and bottom layers.

4 Take apart the paper version and use the paper layers as patterns to mark the sewing line on each fabric layer. Machine-baste the seam line on each layer; the stitched line will provide a precise guide for turning under the seam allowance. Here you can see the top layer after the outline has been machine-basted.

5 Layer the fabrics together, matching key design points through the layers. Grid-baste the layers together (see Grid Basting, p. 27).

6 Mark the seam allowance inside of the seam line, here $^1/_4$in (6mm). Cut away the center of the top layer, leaving the seam allowance.

7 Mark the seam allowance on the next layer and cut away the center. Continue marking and cutting until you reach the base layer. In this design, the petal tip on each layer will meet the layer above, so the bottom layer must be carefully marked. Print the bottom-layer petals on tear-away interfacing and sew in place. Stitch over this petal design, then carefully remove the interfacing to leave the stitched design in place.

8 Using hand-appliqué stitching techniques (see p. 178), turn under the seam allowance of the top layer, folding the fabric under to the machine-basting line and clipping where necessary. Pin and finger-press. Remove the machine-basting stitches on the seam line. Sew the folded edge to the next layer down with very small slip stitches. Repeat the turning and sewing of the seam allowances on each layer until complete.

9 To add the net appliqué to the center of the design, remove the inner petals previously stitched. Print the central flower on tear-away interfacing. Place a layer of net over the center of the flower and place the interfacing on top.

10 Machine-stitch around the central flower with small stitches. Tear away the interfacing. Trim the net to the machine stitching line, leaving $^1/_{16}$in (1mm) of net outside of the stitching line. Remove all the grid basting and press the entire piece.

11 The finished reverse appliqué piece.

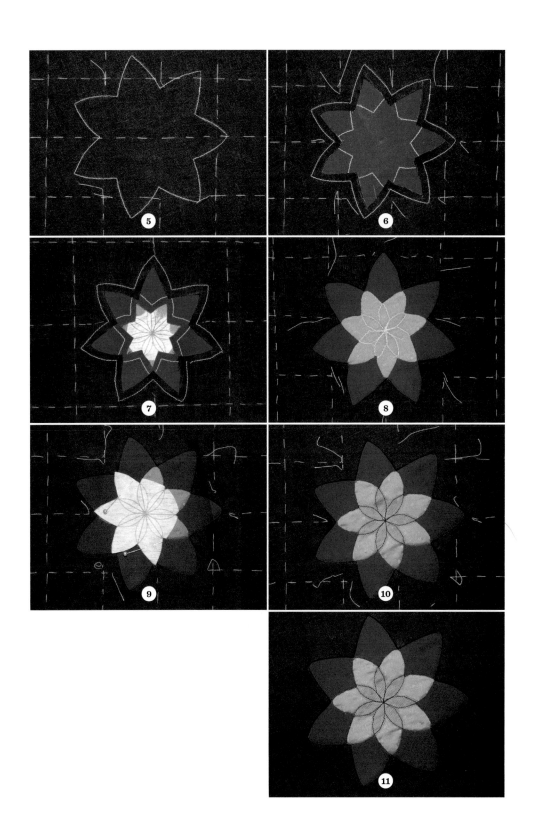

Braiding, or plaiting, is a technique that weaves strands of yarn together to add strength, or to create width for straps, belts, and ties. Many regions and countries have unique braiding techniques and their braids are often incorporated into their traditional costumes. This chapter focuses on the technique sometimes called "plaiting," as opposed to loop, card, or lucet braiding, Japanese kumihimo, Peruvian woven braids, or any of the many other braiding techniques.

There are numerous design possibilities within each braid pattern, depending on the number of strands, colors, and layout order you choose. This chapter gives patterns for three-, four-, five-, and ten-strand round and flat braids; these are shown in a limited color palette to demonstrate clearly how small changes in technique will alter the braids.

3.5
Braids

A wider color palette will offer more options, and including a strand in a different texture or material will also add interest.

Braids can be made out of rat-tail cord, yarn, shoelaces, store-bought cording, custom-made cording (see Cording, pp. 150–51), leather, cloth, yarns pulled from fabric, or any other fiber that suits your garment. In this chapter, all the yarns, cords, and fibers will be referred to as strands.

Calculating the length for each strand

Wrapping strands over and under each other shortens their length. The number of strands in a braid and the thickness of filler will affect how long each strand needs to be for the completed braid, but a good rule of thumb is $1\frac{1}{2}$ times the finished length. For example, 24in (61cm) of $\frac{3}{32}$in (2mm) rat-tail cord in a four-strand round braid results in a finished piece 17in (43cm) long, while 24in (61cm) of $\frac{3}{32}$in (2mm) rat-tail cord in a ten-strand round braid results in a finished piece 15in (38cm) long.

Securing the ends

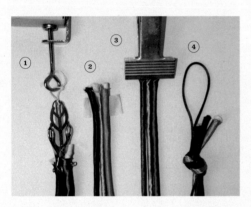

1. A single strand held by a third hand or sewing clamp.

2. Three strands on some sticky tape.

3. Three strands held in a clamp.

4. Strands knotted together with an extra strand to hook onto a doorknob.

To start a braid, join the strand ends and anchor them to something secure so you can pull them taut. There are various methods: holding the knotted strand ends between your knees, knotting the strands and attaching a loop to a doorknob, and using improvised or custom tools.

If the braid ends will be sewn into a seam, sew the ends together and stabilize them (see Stabilizing the End of a Trim, p. 164). If the braid ends mid-garment, you will need to bind the ends. Often manufactured cording has two parts: covering and filler. Slide back the covering to expose the filler. Trim the filler to the correct length, then slide the covering back over the filler end; this reduces bulk. Fold the covering under the braid and sew.

You can also wrap the braid end with cord, similar to the way the neck of a tassel is wrapped (see Tassels, Steps 7–12, p. 211).

1. A three-strand rat-tail braid, bound with natural pearl crown rayon thread.

2. The other end of the braid, bound in navy pearl crown rayon thread.

Working with the strands

While learning each braiding sequence, it helps to say each step out loud as you work. For example, for a four-strand standard braid: "Left over 1, under 1; Right over 1. Organize strands (before continuing). Left over 1, under 1; Right over 1," and so on.

The directions for making braids have been abbreviated:
R = Right-most strand   L = Left-most strand
O = Over   U = Under
# = number of strands to pass over or under

If you get lost, undo to a place you recognize and begin again.

Finishing and steaming

When a braid is complete it may be distorted, and not lie flat or straight. Steaming will fix many problems, but do not let the iron touch the braid. While the braid is warm and damp, manipulate it to lie flat and orderly. Steam it again and let it dry in the perfected shape. Braids can also be shaped into curves and set using steam.

Finished braid can be sewn to fabric (see Hand-Sewn Trim, p. 174).

A bound end.

Steaming a braid with an iron.

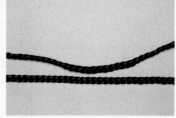

Before steaming (top) and after steaming (bottom).

Three-strand round braid

A three-strand round braid is among the simplest forms of braiding.

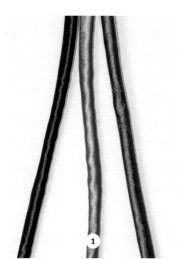 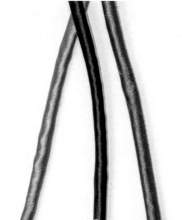 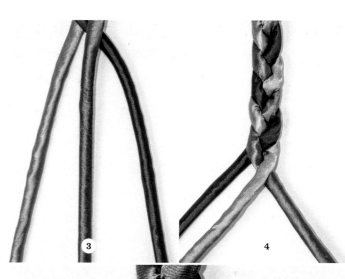

1 Secure three strands.

2 LO1 = Left-most strand over 1.

3 RO1 = Right-most strand over 1.

4 Continue repeating Steps 2–3 until the braid is complete.

5 The completed three-strand braid in three colors.

Four-strand round braid

Plaiting four-strand round braids with four different colors creates a thick, colorful cord, while using two different colors creates a simpler oscillating effect.

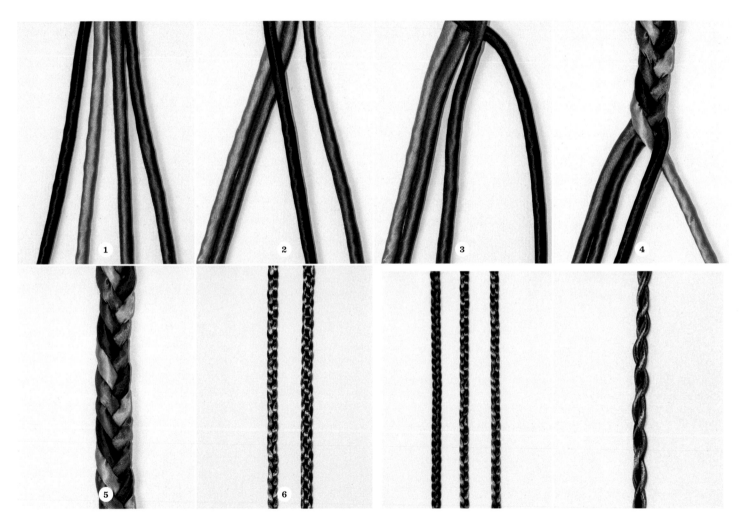

1 Secure the four strands, here in four different colors.

2 LO2 = Left-most strand over 2.

3 RO1 = Right-most strand over 1.

4 Repeat Steps 2–3 until the braid is complete.

5 Complete four-strand round braid.

6 A four-strand round braid and four-strand flat braid (see opposite) in $^3/_{32}$ in (2mm) rat-tail cord.

VARIATION

Try four-strand braids in different colorways and braiding orders. Shown here (left to right) are braids in all blue; blue, gray, blue, gray; and gray, blue, blue, gray.

You can also create a four-strand round braid by twisting two strands of cord together, such as $^3/_{32}$ in (2mm) rat-tail cord, until they fold back upon themselves (see Fringe, p. 202, and Twists and Braids, pp. 203–5).

Four-strand flat braid

A four-strand flat braid plaited in four colors features a repeating diagonal bar, which becomes a diagonal stripe in a two-color rendering.

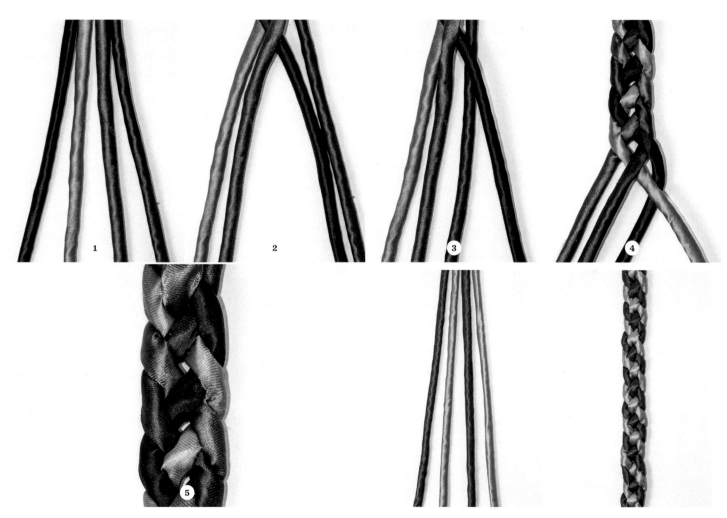

1 Secure the four strands, here in four different colors.

2 LO1, U1 = Left-most strand over 1, under 1.

3 RU1 = Right-most strand under 1.

4 Repeat Steps 2–3 until the braid is complete.

5 Completed four-strand flat braid.

VARIATION

Use two colors and alternate them for a braid striped with a barber's pole pattern.

Five-strand round braid

A five-strand round braid has a denser pattern than a four-strand flat braid. When plaited in five colors, each color is featured two times in the repeating sequence: at the edge and at the center.

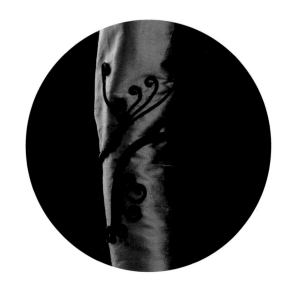

1 Secure the five strands, here in five different colors.

2 LO2 = Left-most strand over 2.

3 RO2 = Right-most strand over 2.

4 Repeat Steps 2–3 until the braid is complete.

5 Completed five-strand round braid.

6 A five-strand round braid and five-strand flat braid (see opposite) in $^3/_{32}$ in (2mm) rat-tail cord.

Five-strand flat braid

A five-strand flat braid has a more tightly woven appearance than a four-strand flat braid.

1 Secure the five strands, here in five different colors.

2 LO1, U1 = Left-most strand over 1, under 1.

3 RO1, U1 = Right-most strand over 1, under 1.

4 Repeat Steps 2–3 until the braid is complete.

5 Completed five-strand flat braid.

Ten-strand round braid

A ten-strand round braid has a raised, inverted V shape in the center. This is essentially a five-strand round braid made with double strands.

1 Secure the ten strands. Separate the strands into a group of six on the left and a group of four on the right before you start. As you work, the groupings of six strands and four strands will shift from left to right, and vice versa.

2 2LO1, U3 = Two left-most strands over 1, under 3. Note that the group of six strands is now on the right.

3 2RO1, U3 = Two right-most strands over 1, under 3. Note that the group of six strands is now on the left.

4 2LO1, U3 = Repeat Step 2—two left-most strands over 1, under 3.

5 2LO1, U3 = Repeat Step 3—two right-most strands over 1, under 3.

6 Repeat Steps 2–3 until the braid is complete.

7 The wrong side of the ten-strand round braid.

8 The right side of the ten-strand round braid.

9 A ten-strand round braid and ten-strand flat braid (see opposite) in ³/₃₂ in (2mm) rat-tail cord.

CORRECTING MISTAKES

If you get lost, undo the braid until the pattern makes sense and you have the groups of six and four re-established.

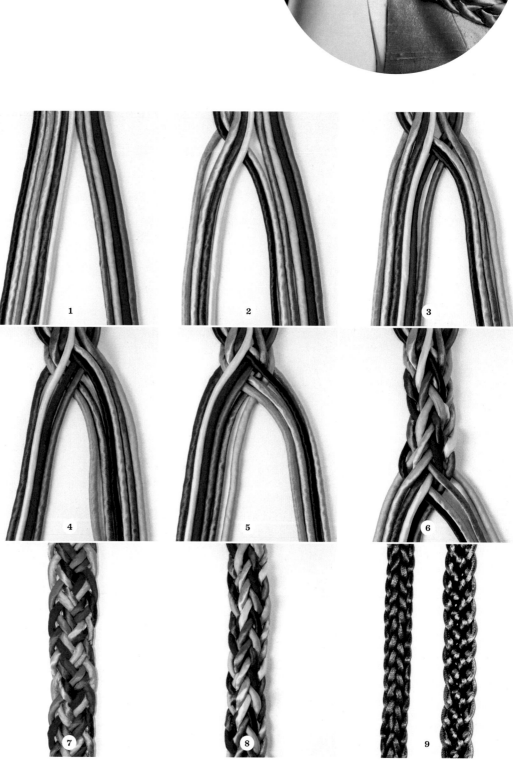

Ten-strand flat braid

A ten-strand flat braid is created by making a five-strand flat braid with double strands.

1 Secure the ten strands, here arranged with two of each color grouped together. Separate the strands into a group of six on the left and a group of four on the right. As you work, the groupings of six strands and four strands will shift from left to right, and vice versa.

2 2LO2, U2 = Two left-most strands over 2, under 2.

3 2RO2, U2 = Two-right most strands over 2, under 2.

4 Repeat Steps 2–3 until the braid is complete.

5 Completed ten-strand flat braid.

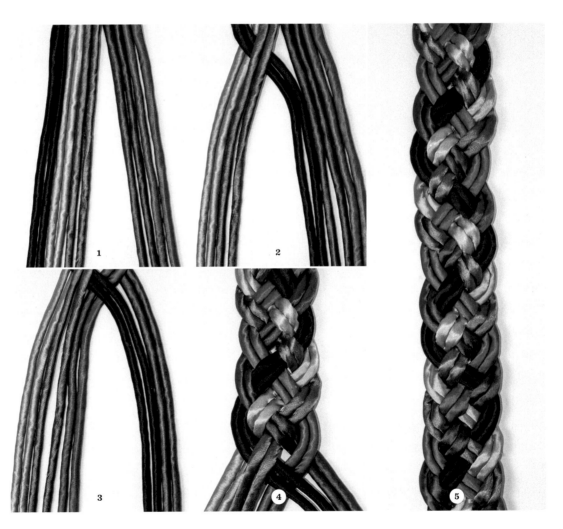

Fringe, pompoms, and tassels are often used on very specific garments, or areas of garments—a fringe around the edge of a shawl, a pompom on the top of a hat, or a tassel on the end of a zipper pull, for instance—and yet each can also be used in many other creative ways.

Long, elegant silk fringe evokes the flapper style of the 1920s, while short woolen fringe was often used by Chanel to trim jackets. An internally fringed garment can provide glimpses of midriff, pompoms can be massed to form a ruff, and tassels can be used to weight a handkerchief hem.

3.6
Fringe, pompoms, and tassels

All of these trims can be made from a variety of yarns, from rat-tail to metallic threads, which can be knotted, twisted, or banded together before being sewn onto a garment.

Fringe can also be created as an integral part of a garment, at the hemline or cuff. Similarly, a garment's fibers can be used to create pompoms and tassels that exactly match the rest of the garment.

Fringe

Fringe is easily made with a loosely woven fabric, and harder to make, but not impossible, with a tightly woven fabric. Fabrics used in the following exercises include a loosely woven basket-weave cotton and silk blend, a tightly woven silk shantung, and a wool bouclé.

When choosing a fabric to fringe, look at the warp and weft threads: if they are of different colors, the fringe will be a different color from the base fabric.

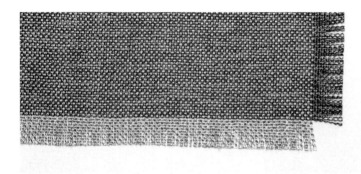

In this fabric, the warp is beige/gold and the weft is blue.

Basic fringe

This technique is for making a fringe at the hem of a garment or on a shawl's edge.

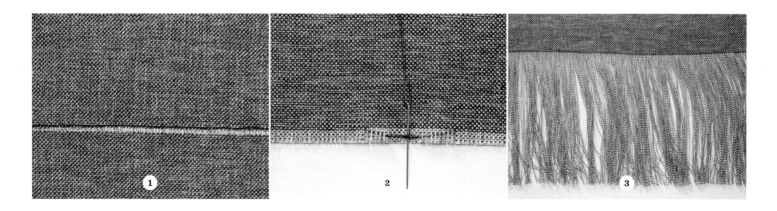

1 Cut the end of the fabric exactly straight across: any irregularities in the cut edge will show at the bottom of the fringe. One way to get a very straight edge is to pull a thread out all the way across the fabric, and then cut in the space left by the missing thread.

Measure to the top of the proposed fringe. Pull a thread out across the fabric to mark this height. Sew with a small zigzag stitch just above the removed thread to secure the top line of the fringe (here sewn in orange thread).

2 Using a blunt needle (here threaded with orange thread for clarity), separate each weft (or warp) thread from the weave and pull it out. Do not try to pull multiple threads at once as they will bind together and distort the fabric's weave. Keep pulling threads until you have reached the zigzag stitching.

3 The finished fringe.

Twists and braids

There are many kinds of knots and twists that can be used to decorate a fringe. Shown here are three popular versions of twists, folded twists, and braids. Rat-tail cord is used for clarity.

Twists

These twists are made from a basic fringe with exposed ends.

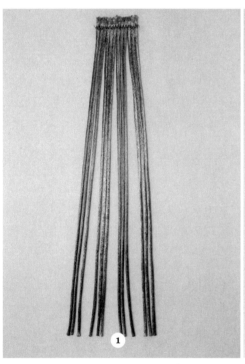

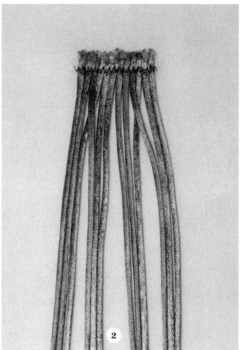

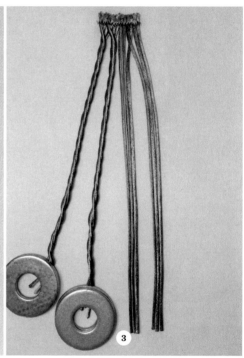

1 Fringe the edge of your fabric to a length 1½ times longer than the desired finished length: a 6in (15cm) fringe will make a 4in (10cm) twist.

Separate the fringe into bundles, either counting the strands or measuring across the top of the fringe. Shown here are bundles of three strands each.

2 Take a least one strand from each bundle and swap it with one from the adjoining bundle. This will keep the top of the fringe from rippling.

3 Twist two bundles of strands. It does not matter whether you twist clockwise or counterclockwise, but you must twist both bundles in the same direction. You can use weights to hold the twists in place as you work.

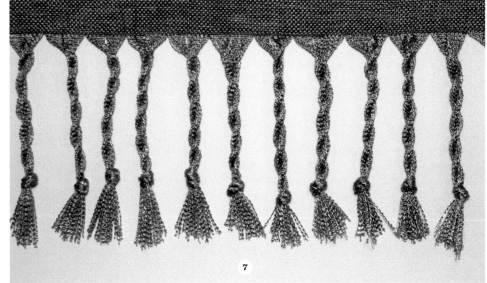

4 While maintaining the twist in each, knot two bundles together at the bottom of the fringe.

5 Let go of the knot: the two bundles will partially untwist and then twist together. Note that the double-bundle twists in the opposite direction to the original twists.

6 The completed double twists.

7 Twists made from a basic fringe.

Folded twists

With this technique, the ends of the twists are hidden in the base fabric.

1 Create the fringe, separate the yarns into bundles, and twist each bundle, as described in Twists, Steps 1–3 (p. 203). Using a pin, hold down the center of a twisted bundle.

2 While keeping the pin stationary, fold the end back toward the fabric. The bundle will twist back onto itself. Remove the pin.

3 Sew across the top of the fringe with a small zigzag stitch to anchor the yarn ends to the base fabric. You can do this on the right or wrong side of the fabric, depending on whether you wish to feature the tape or ribbon (see Step 4) that will cover the raw ends as part of your design.

4 Trim the yarn ends. Cover the ends and the zigzag stitching with another piece of fabric or ribbon (see Flat Trim, p. 169).

5 The finished folded twists viewed from the other side.

Braids

Braids provide another decorative finish for a fringe.

Follow Twists, Steps 1–3 (see p. 203), to create the fringing and bundles of yarn, and then choose a braiding pattern from the Braids chapter (see pp. 190–99).

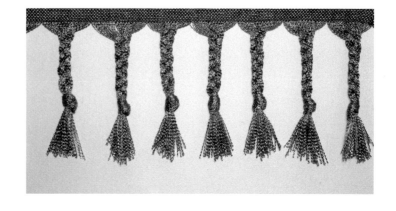

Internal fringing

Internal fringing is a creative way to introduce a pattern or texture into a flat fabric, or to change a pattern within the weave by pulling a few yarns.

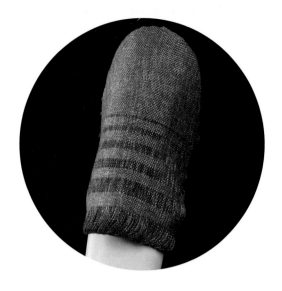

1 Make a small snip to expose the end of the yarn you want to pull.

2 Gently pull on the yarn all the way across the fabric and extract it. With the weft yarn removed, the warp yarns are more exposed.

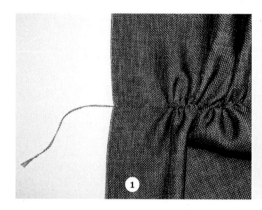

REMOVING A FINE YARN

If you are working with a tightly woven fabric, you may need to use a needle to grab the thin yarn to pull it out.

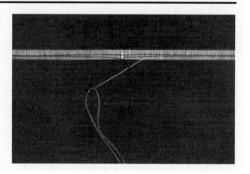

IDENTIFYING THE YARNS

If you have trouble seeing the yarns, place the fabric on a light table or against a day-lit window; the yarns will be easier to see when backlit.

VARIATION

Remove the yarns in bands of different widths to create a pattern.

If you remove yarns from both the warp and weft directions, the intersections will have no yarns in them and will add to the patterning.

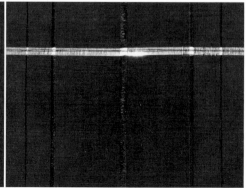

Chanel-like sew-on fringe

Inspired by the fringe on Chanel jackets, this fringe can be made from any fabric but works particularly well with a wool bouclé because the nubby texture of the bouclé adds extra depth to the fringe.

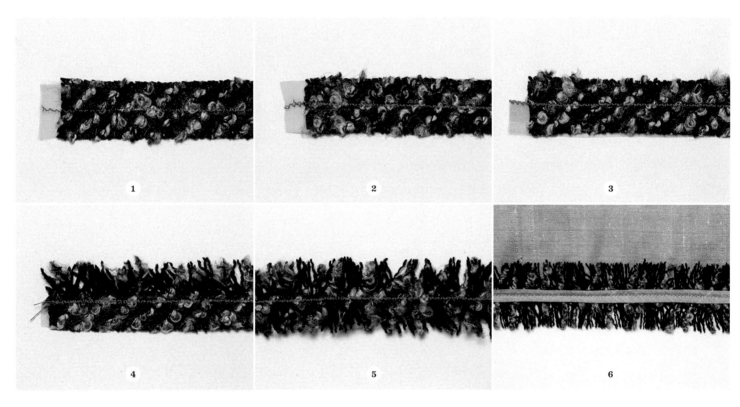

1 Lay a bias strip of wool, 1in (2.5cm) wide, on a strip of organza, 1in (2.5cm) wide, cut on the straight grain. Sew down the middle of both strips with a narrow zigzag or small 1.5mm (15 spi) straight stitch. The organza serves as a flange for attaching the fringe to the garment (see Piping with Fringe, p. 149).

2 If the wool is loosely woven, sew a second row of zigzag stitching to doubly secure the wool fibers to the organza.

3 Fold the organza in half and press it to one side.

4 Use a blunt needle to pull apart the yarns from the weave, one at a time. Leave a small solid section near the stitching to prevent the fibers from pulling out completely. Note that the fringed side is wider than the unfringed side; the fibers have been pulled out of their angled bias orientation and now come straight out from the center stitching, which makes them slightly longer.

5 Once both sides have been fringed, trim the fringe if it is too long or uneven.

6 Trim the organza flange, if necessary, then use it to sew the fringe to the fashion fabric. Cover the zigzag stitching with a bias strip or other trim.

Chanel-like fringe, with decorative trim, around the edge of a jacket.

Pompoms

There are several ways to make pompoms: one version is shown here; another involves winding the yarn around two pieces of donut-shaped oak tag. Pompoms can be big, small, and anywhere in between; they can be tight balls of yarn or floppy puffs with a tactile fuzziness.

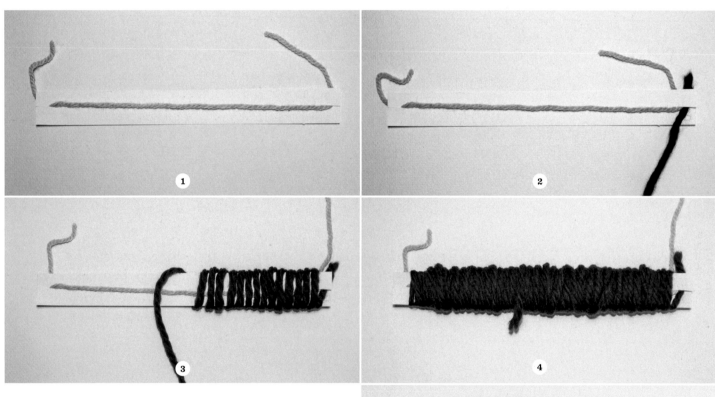

1

2

3

4

1 Cut a piece of oak tag 1 x 10in (2.5 x 25cm). Cut a slit in each end. Place the ends of a 12in (30cm) length of yarn into the slits to keep the yarn running down the length; this will be the pompom's hanging string.

2 Place one end of a 20yd (18m) length of yarn into one of the slits; this will be the body of the pompom.

3 Wrap the long yarn around the oak tag. You don't need to be particularly neat with this.

4 Continue wrapping the yarn around the oak tag until you have wound the entire 20yd (18m) length. Finish with the end of the yarn in the middle of the bundle.

5 Tie the ends of the short piece of yarn together in a bow as tightly as possible; here, for clarity, it is loosely tied. Do not tie a knot as you will be retying the hanging yarn in Step 9.

5

6 Cut through the pompom yarn down the middle of the oak tag. You may need to tighten the hanging yarn as you cut to keep the yarn from slipping out.

7 When you have cut through all the yarn, the oak tag will spring open, revealing the hanging yarn.

8 Carefully turn the bundle of yarn so the bow of the hanging yarn faces up.

9 Untie the bow and pull the hanging yarn as tight as possible. The tighter the yarn is pulled, the rounder the bundle will become.

10 When you have created a ball, knot the hanging yarn; you will now have a lumpy pompom.

11 Carefully tug out any short yarns until they are even with the other yarns. Trim any long yarns until the pompom is nicely rounded.

Completed pompoms of different sizes, all made with 20yd (18m) of yarn. From left to right: a pompom made using 1in (2.5cm) oak tag; 2in (5cm) oak tag; 3in (7.5cm) oak tag.

Tassels

Tassels can be made from a variety of yarns—even ribbon—but be aware that they require a lot of material.

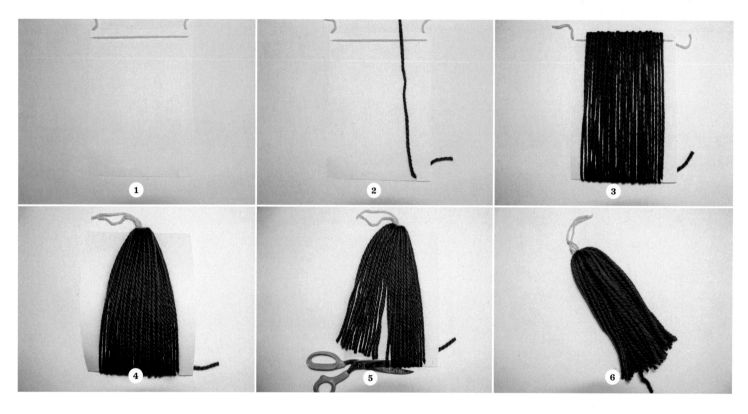

1 Cut a piece of oak tag 5 x 10in (12.5 x 25cm) long. Cut a slit in each side of the longer sides of the oak tag near the top. Place the ends of a 12in (30cm) piece of yarn into the slits to keep the yarn running across the top of the oak tag; this will be the tassel's hanging string.

2 Cut a slit in the bottom of the oak tag. Place one end of a 20yd (18m) length of yarn in the slit.

3 Wrap the long yarn around the oak tag until you have wound the entire 20yd (18m) length.

4 Tie the ends of the short hanging string together in a bow as tightly as possible. Do not tie a knot as you will be retying the hanging yarn in Step 6. Pulling the yarns together at the top may cause the oak tag to bow.

5 Flatten the oak tag with your hand or a weight if it bowed in Step 4. Cut the yarn at the bottom of the oak tag.

6 Untie the bow of the hanging string, pull it as tight as possible, and knot it.

7 Using a new 30in (75cm) length of yarn, make a loop 2in (5cm) long. Place it on the top of the tassel, with the loop pointing down.

8 Working with the long tail, cross the yarn over the loop and wrap it around the body of the tassel.

9 Wrap the yarn around the body of the tassel, keeping the wraps tight and orderly, and the loop sticking out below the neck wraps, until the neck suits your design.

10 Thread the tail of the yarn through the loop.

11 Pull on the top end of the loop, at the top of the neck; this will pull the loop and tail up into the neck. If your neck wraps are tight, the loop and the tail will be held securely in place.

12 Bury the short end of the loop in the head of the tassel. Trim the long tail end of the neck wrap to the same length as the tassel strands.

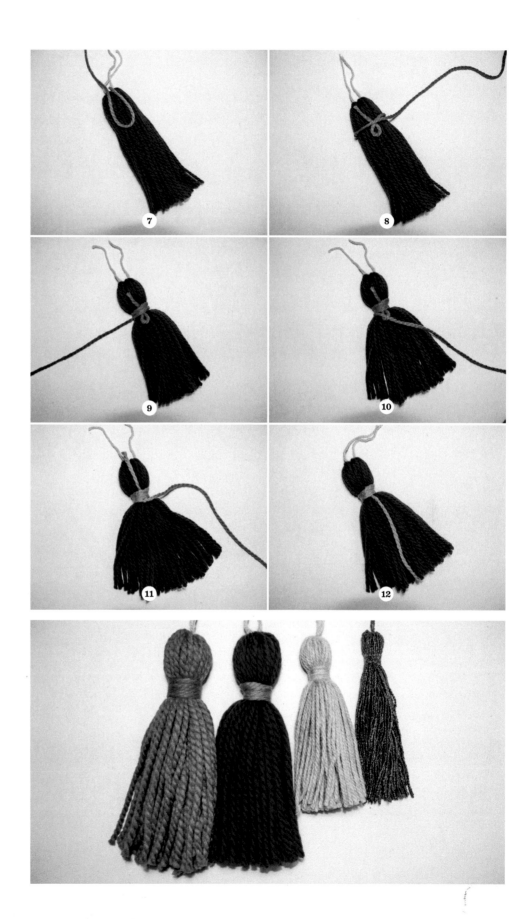

The orange and blue tassels on the left were made with a bulky woolen yarn, the beige tassel was made with a medium-weight woolen yarn, and the brown tassel was made with a thinner rayon yarn.

From goose to peacock, feathers add an exotic touch to any garment. Feathers are commonly used to trim millinery, but they can also be used to adorn a glamorous gown, to trim a neckline, or emphasize a shoulder. Their myriad uses stem from the wide variety of feathers available. All birds have several different kinds of feather, each with different characteristics and different purposes: some are downy; others, like the tail and flight feathers, are less pliable. Today many feathers are dyed and shaped, creating even more choices for the designer. Whether modified or in their natural state, feathers add movement, elegance, and sophistication to a garment.

3.7
Feathers

All bird feathers—found or bought—can be used to embellish clothing. If you hope to use "found" feathers, there are several caveats to consider: Some wild birds are protected and it is illegal to use their feathers, even if you find them on the ground. Many birds have feather lice and mites; possible sanitizing processes include boiling the feathers for 20 minutes or freezing them for several days in a sealed plastic bag. Found feathers need to be stored in mothballs; commercially sanitized feathers are unlikely to attract bugs.

When purchasing feathers, it helps to be acquainted with retail feather terminology, which is based on the species of bird, which part of the body the feathers come from, and how they are packaged.

Feather terminology

All feathers have the same parts. The shaft, or rachis, is the spine. Branching off the spine are the barbs, and branching off the barbs are the barbules. Together the barbs and barbules make up what we think of as the feathery part. At the bottom of the feather are fluffy flues. Collectively, the barbules, barbs, and flues form the vane. The hollow part of the rachis, where no flues or barbs grow, and where the feather attaches to the bird, is the quill.

Parts of a feather

All birds have four groups of feathers:

1. Down feathers to trap air for insulation.
2. Body feathers that cover the down feathers, for waterproofing, coloration, and contouring.
3. Wing feathers for flying.
4. Tail feathers for balance, steering in flight, and mating displays.

Birds are shaped differently and move in different ways, and so their feathers vary, too: long, sleek, and stiff, or short, fuzzy, and soft. Generally you will be using feathers from more common birds, so many of the feathers will be similar.

ROOSTER AND TURKEY FEATHERS

- Marabou feathers are small, downy fluffs, named for their original source, the marabou stork, which is now protected. Today marabou feathers come from roosters and turkeys.
- Hackle feathers from roosters are long and slender, changing from fluffy flues to thin, wispy barbs halfway along the shaft. Saddle hackle feathers have rounder, fuller flues than neck hackle feathers.
- Schlappen feathers are larger than hackle feathers and the barbs remain wide and full along the vane. They are the most luxurious of the rooster feathers.
- Coque, coq, or tail feathers are long and stiff, usually with even barbs on both sides, and often with uneven or irregular textures and edges. The quill may arc to right or left, depending on whether it comes from the right or left side of the tail.
- Turkey plumage starts as fluffy flues and changes to flatter barbs. Turkey flats are the same shape as plumage but larger.
- Turkey round feathers have round tips and are often bleached, then artistically dyed and painted as imitation eagle feathers.

Rooster and turkey feathers

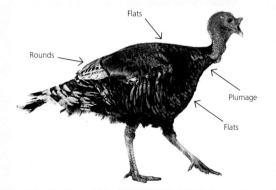

Turkey

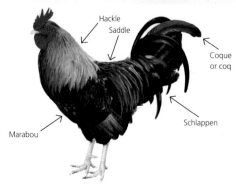

Rooster

Goose

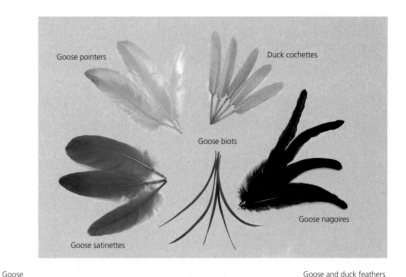

Goose and duck feathers

GOOSE AND DUCK FEATHERS

- Goose feathers have a noticeable sheen, even when dyed.
- Goose and duck pointers have uneven barbs.
- Goose nagoires are 4–8in (10–20cm) long, with a blunt tip and even barbs.
- Goose biots are made from the leading edge of a primary flight feather. The quill is quite stiff and the barbs are trimmed to $\frac{1}{8}$–$\frac{1}{4}$in (3–6mm) long.
- Goose satinettes are straight, stiff feathers, $4\frac{1}{2}$–6in (11.5–15cm) long—the quintessential "craft feathers."
- Duck cochettes are straight, stiff feathers with a hard quill. They are similar to goose satinettes but smaller.

OSTRICH FEATHERS

- Plumes have long, drapey flues.
- Drab flues are shorter and less floaty, and therefore cheaper. Plumes and drabs come in many lengths.
- Spadonas (or spads) have flues that are shorter than drabs.
- Nandus are spadonas trimmed into a spear shape.

Ostrich feathers

PEACOCK FEATHERS

Peacock feathers make a bold addition to any garment, regardless of which portion is used: the flues, eyes, or coronas from the peacock's crest.

OTHER TYPES OF FEATHERS

Feathers from pheasants, parrots, macaws, and other exotic birds can also be used to make embellishments.

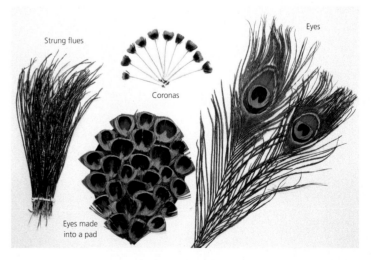

Peacock feathers

Packaging

Feathers may be packaged loose, or they can come as pads, strung together, as pinwheels or fans, or as feather boas. Feathers can also be stripped and reshaped, changing their character according to the needs of the garment design.

LOOSE

Loose feathers are sold in a bag, by weight: a few ounces (grams), a half-pound (225g), or a full pound (450g).

PADS

Feathers may also be sold glued to a piece of buckram, felt, or leather in decorative patterns and colors; these are called pads.

Left: A pad of pheasant feathers.
Right: A pad of peacock eyes.

STRUNG FEATHERS

Strung feathers are carefully sorted and sized, and then strung together into one yard (meter) strips, with all the feathers neatly lined up, gradually increasing in size over the length of the strip.

Feathers are also sold as premade trims. Sorted and sized, the feathers are sewn onto a rayon or cotton tape with all the feathers neatly lined up, again increasing in size over the length of the strip. Feather trim is sold by the yard (meter).

STRIPPED FEATHERS

The flues and the lower barbs can be stripped off the quill, leaving a shaped feather tip. Both coque and hackle rooster feathers are stripped. Stripped hackle feathers are wispy and ethereal, while stripped coque feathers have a more formal shape. Goose feathers, which can also be stripped, have the stiffest spine and most solid shape of the three. Stripped feathers are sold by the dozen or by the yard, sewn to rayon tape.

PINWHEELS OR FANS

Stripped feathers can be glued into a fan-shaped fabric base (also known as a pinwheel); the feathers can be used in the fan shape or removed from the fan and used individually. Fans are available in half or full circles and also with beads or crystals threaded onto the spines and glued into place.

Top: Strung natural rooster hackle feathers.
Bottom: Strung dyed rooster hackle feathers.

Stripped and dyed rooster hackle feather trim.

A fan of stripped feathers with beaded spines.

Boas are made from many different kinds of feathers.
Top: 3-ply rooster marabou, center: 4-ply ostrich, bottom: turkey chandelle.

BOAS

To make a boa, feathers are sewn or glued onto a cotton or nylon cord, making a fluffy scarf. When selecting a boa there are many qualities to consider: the kind of feathers, their quality, the quantity of feathers used (indicated by the number of plies), the diameter and/or weight of the boa, and the finished length. A 6ft (1.8m) ostrich boa, for example, can cost up to 100 times as much as a rooster marabou boa of the same length.

Quality of feathers:
Inexpensive boas often have small, bent or half-stripped feathers, while more expensive boas have long, full feathers.

Plies:
Some boas are sold according to ply. The feathers are sewn and/or glued onto a cotton cord called a ply. Several plies may be twisted together. Standard ostrich boas have from one to three plies twisted together, but up to 18-ply ostrich boas are available.

Weight/diameter:
An inexpensive turkey chandelle boa weighing 1³/₄oz (50g) with a 6in (15cm) diameter is available, but a chandelle boa weighing 3oz (85g) with an 8in (20cm) diameter costs four times as much. Rooster hackle, saddle, and schlappen boas are often sold in diameters of 3 to 10in (7.5 to 25cm).

The end of a fuchsia half-bronze coque feather boa, 6in (15cm) in diameter. This end is 10in (25cm) long.

"Swan boas" are made of turkey marabou feathers that are trimmed to look like fur. They are sold by diameter or by the ply; a very good 6-ply swan boa will be about 10in (25cm) in diameter.

Curled feathers

There are two easy ways to curl feathers: with a butter knife and with a curling iron.

RESHAPE THE FEATHER

Before you begin working with a feather, always steam it to reshape any barbs that have been crushed in shipping and to return the barbs to their fluffiest and shiniest state. If the barbs have separated, you can massage them back together with your fingers.

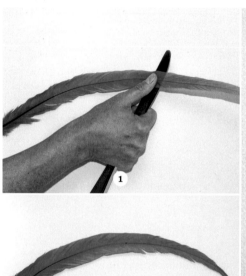

Curling feathers with a butter knife

Curling a feather with a butter knife, or any blunt-edged knife, is just like curling ribbon with scissors, except that you need to curl with the arc of the feather and use the blunt edge of a knife, instead of scissors, so that you do not damage the shaft.

1 Steam a feather (here, a rooster coque feather) to restore its fluff and shine. Starting at the quill end, pull the blunt edge of the knife along the shaft of the feather, applying gentle pressure to the feather with your thumb.

2 The coque feather will curl a little after the first pass with the knife.

3 The coque feather curls more after a second pass with the knife.

4 Three knife-curled feathers.

Curling feathers with a curling iron

A curling iron can also be used to shape feathers.

1 Remove the bottom 3in (7.5cm) of flues and barbs from a feather (here, a rooster coque feather) and steam it to restore its fluff and shine.

2 With the curling iron preheated to high, clamp the base of the feather.

3 Slowly pull the feather through the curling iron. Repeat if necessary until the feather has enough curl. Working with or against the natural curl of the spine will produce different results.

4 Four feathers curled with a curling iron several times in order to achieve different shapes.

Trimmed feathers

Feathers can be trimmed to create different shapes—geometric or fanciful. Trimming is also a good technique to use with damaged feathers; trimming away the damaged parts to make the most of what remains. There are two ways to trim feathers: pulling the barbs away from the shaft, or cutting the barbs away.

Pulling the barbs

You can pull the barbs from many types of feather.

1 Grab a few barbs and gently pull down and away from the shaft. A thin layer of the shaft will peel away with the barbs.

2 Remove the barbs from the other side of the shaft.

3 You can create numerous designs by removing the barbs from selected areas of the shaft.

RESHAPE THE FEATHER

Before you begin working with a feather, always steam it to reshape any barbs that have been crushed in shipping and to return the barbs to their fluffiest and shiniest state. If the barbs have separated, you can massage them back together with your fingers.

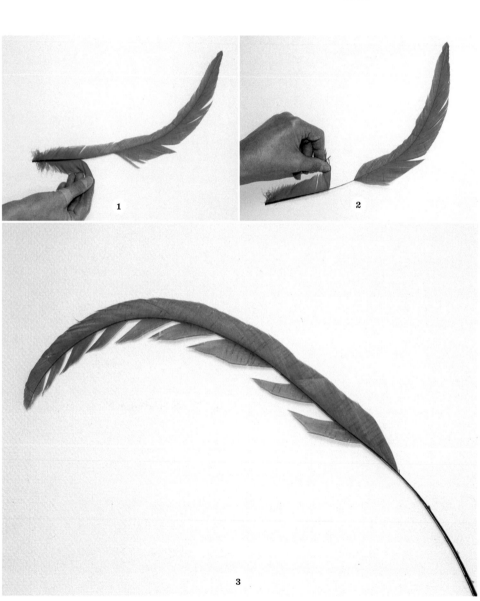

Cutting the barbs

Cutting the barbs away offers two benefits: the shaft remains intact and strong, and the cutting may be more precise. Try both methods to see which suits you better.

1

2

3

4

1 Place the feather wrong side up so that you can hold it with a fingernail in the slot on the back of the quill. Using a rotary cutter or craft knife, cut as close to the shaft as possible. Here, another pass with the knife is still needed on the lower side of the shaft.

2 The exposed white inner shaft can be colored in with a permanent marker.

3 Trimming away the barbs near the top of the feather and blunting the tips creates an antenna-like look.

4 Trimming away the barbs in sections along the shaft creates an arrow-like look.

Feather fringe

Feathers can be made into a fringe to simplify the process of sewing them into a seam or a hem.

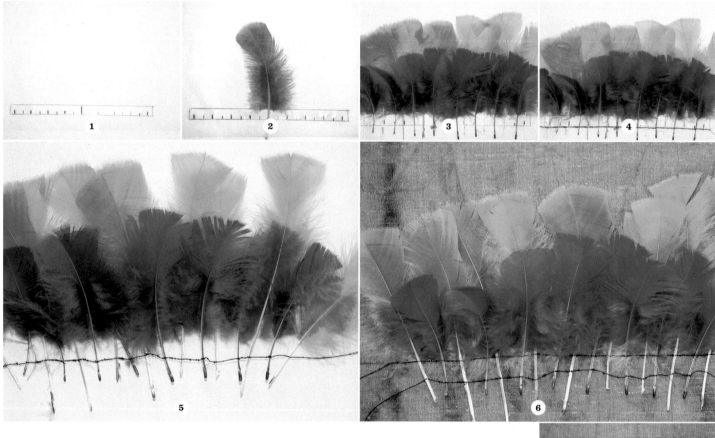

1 Draw a line the length of the desired fringe on a piece of tear-away interfacing or tracing paper. Mark $1/4$in (6mm) increments along the line. (These increments can be made bigger or smaller, depending on the density of fringe you are creating.) The marks will help you place the feathers evenly along the line. Place a strip of double-sided sticky tape on the line; here the sticky tape is outlined in purple.

2 Place the shaft of a feather on the tape, with $1/8$–$1/4$in (3–6mm) of shaft extending below the tape. The tape will hold the feathers in place but allow you to move them if needed.

3 Continue placing feathers on the sticky tape. Add a second layer of feathers to increase the density, if needed.

4 With very small machine stitches, sew $1/8$in (3mm) below the sticky tape. Do not sew through the sticky tape as it will gum up the needle.

5 Gently pull the interfacing or tracing paper and sticky tape away from the stitching.

6 Sew the feathers to the fashion fabric with very small machine stitches, $1/8$in (3mm) below the seam line. Continue sewing the fringe in place (for instructions, see Piping with Fringe, p. 149).

7 The completed turkey marabou feather fringe.

Feather fringe with added beads

Adding beads to stripped feathers provides another layer of ornamentation. Beads can be glued on the shaft in a pattern or randomly. Use store-bought stripped feathers, or strip them yourself (see pp. 220–21). Small beads, pearls, or crystals work well; the hole needs to be large enough for the quill, but not so large that a lot of glue is needed to hold the bead in place.

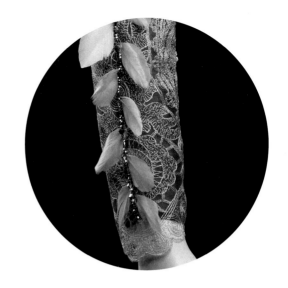

1 Draw a line the length of the desired beaded feather trim on a piece of tear-away interfacing or tracing paper. Mark ¼in (6mm) increments, depending on the density of fringe you are creating. The marks will help you place feathers evenly along the line. The ends of the shafts need to extend into this section. Place a strip of double-sided sticky tape ¼in (6mm) above the line; here the sticky tape is outlined in purple.

2 Cut the bottom of the quill at an angle and slide a bead onto it and up onto the stripped shaft. Using a pin or toothpick, place a small amount of good craft glue onto the shaft just above the bead. Slide the bead into the glue and hold in place until the glue hardens enough to hold the bead.

3 Place the beaded feather on the sticky tape with the end of the quill touching the bottom line. The sticky tape will hold the feathers in place but allow you to move them if needed. Continue adding the beaded feathers.

4 Slide a length of rayon hem tape, or other lightweight ribbon, under the ends of the feathers. Place another length of hem tape of top of the quills.

5 With very small stitches, sew through the two layers of hem tape, the feather shafts, and the tear-away interfacing or tracing paper, stitching very close to the top edge of the tape. Sew another line of very small stitches at the bottom of the tape. Add a further line of stitches near the top of the tape if any feathers can be pulled out. Gently remove the tear-away interfacing or tracing paper and sticky tape. Sew the trim in place (see Piping with Fringe, p. 149).

6 The finished trim, ready to sew into a garment.

Burned feathers

Feathers can be burned in bleach to alter their character and make them wispy. The barbules are made of keratin and submerging the feather in bleach will dissolve them, leaving the skeletal remains of the barbs and spine behind. Here two ostrich feathers and two goose satinettes were subjected to a bleach bath.

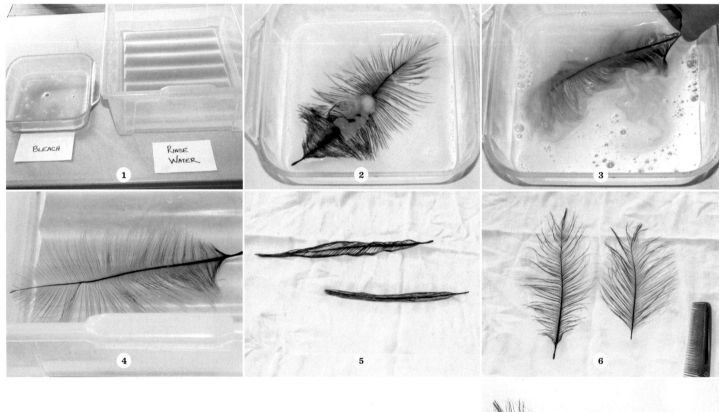

1 Lay out all supplies before you start; the barbules dissolve very quickly. You will need feathers, a pan of straight bleach, a container of rinse water, and blotting rags or paper towels. Wear old clothes in case the bleach splashes.

2 Submerge an ostrich feather in the bleach.

3 The dissolving keratin barbules will create foam in the bleach.

4 After half a minute, move the feather to the rinse water. If the barbules are not quite dissolved, you can return the feather to the bleach.

5 Blot the feathers dry.

6 Use a fine-toothed comb or your fingers to separate the barbs. Steam the feathers after they have dried. If they remain stiff, there is still bleach on the barbs; rinse the feathers again in clean water, then dry and fluff them again.

7 The finished ostrich feathers (left) and goose satinettes (right). Goose satinette barbules take longer to dissolve than ostrich barbules because they are thicker.

Sewing on single feathers

When sewing on single feathers, it is important to prevent the fabric from bunching around the shaft of the quill. Using an embroidery hoop will hold the fabric taut, ensuring that the fabric size and shape remain unchanged.

RESHAPE THE FEATHER

Before you begin working with a feather, always steam it to reshape any barbs that have been crushed in shipping and to return the barbs to their fluffiest and shiniest state. If the barbs have separated, you can massage them back together with your fingers.

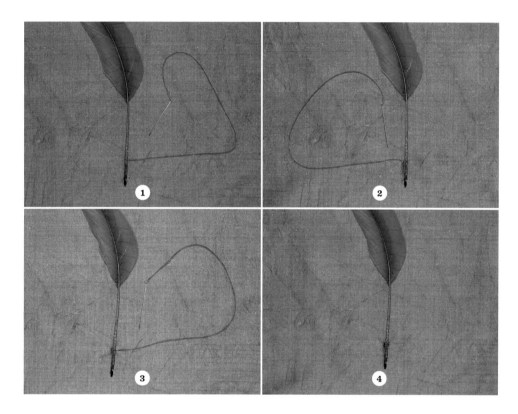

1 Remove the bottom 3in (7.5cm) of flues and barbs from a rooster coque feather. Sew a small stitch on the fabric where the feather will be placed to anchor the thread. Place the feather over the stitch.

2 Insert the needle and thread in the middle of the quill and push the needle through the quill and through to the wrong side of the fabric. Bring the needle up to the right side of the fabric on the other side of the quill.

3 Insert the needle and thread in the middle of the quill, and push the needle through the quill and through to the wrong side of the fabric. The quill is now held in place by two stitches, each one passing through the center of the quill. Make two more stitches over the entire quill and then knot the thread on the wrong side.

4 The single feather sewn in place.

KEEPING THE THREAD CLEAR OF THE FLUES

Sew an anchoring stitch through the quill. The rest of the stitches can be sewn over the quill, amid the flues. Slide the needle through the fabric to the right side, over the quill, and then back to the wrong side of the fabric in a single motion, without pulling up the thread. Then pull the needle and thread through to the wrong side to complete the stitch. Any flues that do get tangled in the thread can be teased out from the stitches with a pin.

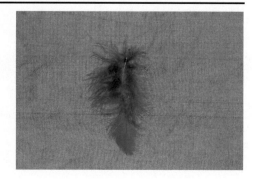

Sewing on rows of feathers by hand

The technique of sewing on feathers in rows is the same as for sewing on single feathers (see p. 225). The art is to place the feathers so that they form a dense pattern.

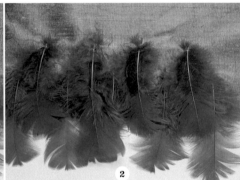

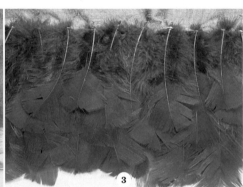

1 Sort and plan the feather layout, choosing the longest feathers for the bottom row and the shortest for the top row, or vice versa, depending on the design. Sew the first row of feathers in place (see Sewing on Single Feathers, p. 225). If the base fabric starts to bunch up under the feathers, place it in an embroidery hoop to hold it taut.

2 Sew on the next row of feathers, placing the feathers in between the quills of the first row and covering the flues of the first row of feathers. Trimming the flues from the shafts is an option, but the flues provide color saturation and loft beneath the upper rows of feathers.

3 Continue placing feathers in rows. To hide the flues, you can sew a final row of feathers on top with the flues cut off so that just their barbs remain.

4 The finished rows of feathers with the final row of barbs on top.

Sewing a feather boa to a garment

Sewing a boa to a garment adds an exotic touch. If the boa is large you may need to add an interfacing to the fashion fabric to help support the weight of the feathers. Silk organza is a good choice for interfacing under feathers because it provides strength without bulk.

1 If you are using an inexpensive boa, like this purple chandelle boa, part the feathers to find the cotton cord at the center of the boa.

2 Using doubled thread, sew the boa cord to the fashion fabric by hand. Guide the needle and thread through the feathers, sewing through or around the cord of the boa. Match the thread to the feather color so it does not show (orange thread is used here for clarity).

3 Continue to expose the cord and sew it to the fashion fabric. When it is sewn, move the feathers to cover the cord.

4 The finished boa sewn in place with feathers rearranged.

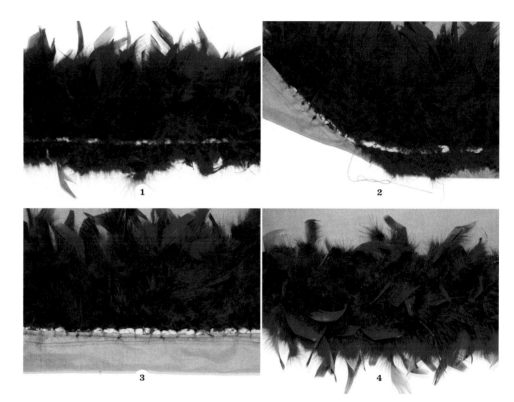

SHORTENING A BOA

If the boa is longer than needed, place a piece of tear-away interfacing or tissue paper under the boa where you want to cut, to prevent the feathers from getting sucked down into the sewing machine. Sew two parallel rows of small machine stitches across the cords (here in orange thread for clarity). Cut between the two rows of stitches.

VARIATION

If the boa is better quality, the plies will be tightly twisted together, so finding the center cord will be difficult, as with this light blue ostrich-flue boa. Here the feathers have been teased away from the cords as much as possible and held down with weights, but the cords are still well hidden. Do not untwist the boa to expose the cord. Carefully use a long needle to guide the thread as close to the spine as possible, pulling each stitch tight. After the boa is sewn to the fashion fabric, use a long pin to tease out any feather tips that are caught in the thread.

Using weights to hold down the feathers can help you access the cord at the center of the boa.

The finished boa sewn in place with feathers fluffed out.

Beads and sequins add sparkle, color, texture, depth, and dimension to any garment. A scattering of beads, sewn on with a running stitch (see p. 234), can suggest raindrops or the rays of the sun. A deluge of beads sewn on with a double-needle couching stitch (see p. 235) can be an exuberant display of color and sparkle, or even a complete painting. Whether you choose and strategically place a few beads or sequins, or amass them in larger groups, they can take a garment from plain to sublime.

Beads add another dimension to a garment, both literally and figuratively, providing both a physical density and a counterpoint to the softness of textiles that many other embellishments, such as embroidery and ribbon, cannot.

3.8
Beads and sequins

Beads come in a variety of shapes and finishes: seed, bugle, oval, round, teardrop, donut, faceted, translucent, opaque, matte, polished, shiny, silver lined, and more. While many beads are glass, they can also be made of many other materials: ceramic, wood, stone, metal (precious, semiprecious, and common), plastic, pearl, crystal, bone, shell, and even real seeds.

When choosing your beads remember that they are going onto a wearable garment and will stand proud of the fabric's surface. Larger beads may be heavy, requiring extra interfacing for support. Consider, too, where you will place your bead embellishments with respect to the function of the finished garment—for example, beads are hard to sit on.

Bead sizes and types

Seed beads, the smallest and most common beads, are made from a long glass cane or tube that is cut into beads. The beads are further processed to fashion them into rounder shapes with smooth holes. Seed beads are sized in "aughts"; an 11-aught bead would be marked as 11° or 11/0. Like needles, the larger the number, the smaller the size of the bead, thus an 11/0 seed bead is smaller than an 8/0 seed bead.

There are several ways to determine the size of your beads or how many beads you will need for a project: you can measure the bead using a bead caliper (see Beading Tools, p. 233), you can lay 10 beads flat on the diagram below, or you can count how many beads there are in a line 1in (2.5cm) long. Bead sizes vary slightly from one manufacturer to the next, so the tables and diagrams given here are only guidelines.

Within the seed bead family are several types of special beads: rocaille, which are silver-lined beads; delicas, which are Japanese 11/0 seed beads that have slightly squared-off ends; two-cut or hex-cut beads (the cuts or facets make the beads sparkle); and tilas, which are square with two parallel holes.

Bugle beads are also cut from canes of glass but are not further processed, which can leave them with sharp edges. Bugle beads have their own sizing system (see right).

In addition to seed and bugle beads, there are many other kinds of glass beads: lamp-worked beads often have more glass or colors added to the surface; fire-polished beads are glass beads, faceted by machine and then placed in hot ovens to soften and polish the facets; pressed-glass beads are made by pressing a glass cane into a mold to create a myriad of shapes. There are also many kinds of beads made out of other materials.

SEED BEAD SIZES

Size	Diameter (mm)	Diameter (in)	Beads per 3cm	Beads per 1in
15/0	1.4	$^1/_{16}$	27	23
11/0	1.8	$^5/_{64}$	20	18
10/0	2.4	$^3/_{32}$	16	14
8/0	3	$^7/_{64}$	14	12
6/0	4	$^5/_{32}$	10	8

BUGLE BEAD SIZES

Size	Length (mm)	Length (in)	Beads per 3cm	Beads per 1in
1	2.5	$^1/_8$	12	8
2	5	$^3/_{16}$	6	5
3	7	$^1/_4$	4	4
4	9	$^3/_8$	3	2+(silvers)
5	12	$^1/_2$	2+	2
20	20	$^3/_4$	1+	1+

BEAD SIZE PER 10 BEADS

Bead size	Bead length	Threaded beads per 1in	10 beads flat (actual size)	Length of 10 beads (mm)	Length of 10 beads (in)
15/0	1.4mm	23	○○○○○○○○○○	14	$^5/_8$
11/0	1.8mm	18	○○○○○○○○○○	18	$^{25}/_{32}$
10/0	2.4mm	14	○○○○○○○○○○	24	$^{15}/_{16}$
8/0	3mm	12	○○○○○○○○○○	30	$1^3/_{32}$
6/0	4mm	8	○○○○○○○○○○	40	$1^9/_{16}$

BEAD SIZES MEASURED ACROSS THE HOLE

⊖	2mm ($^5/_{64}$in)	◯	6mm ($^{15}/_{64}$in)
⊖	3mm ($^7/_{64}$in)	◯	7mm ($^9/_{32}$in)
⊖	4mm ($^5/_{32}$in)	◯	8mm ($^5/_{16}$in)
⊖	5mm ($^{13}/_{64}$in)	◯	9mm ($^{11}/_{32}$in)

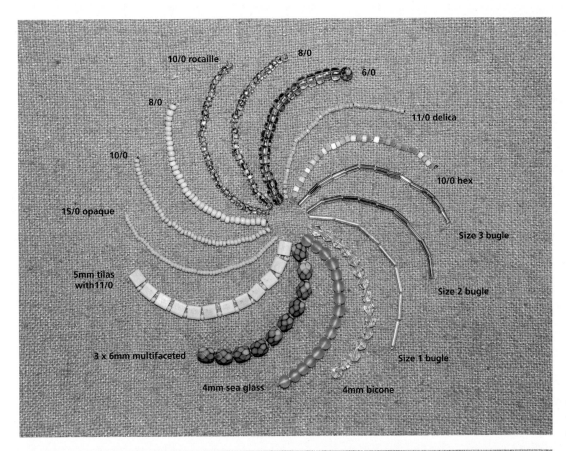

10/0 rocaille

8/0

6/0

8/0

11/0 delica

10/0

10/0 hex

15/0 opaque

Size 3 bugle

5mm tilas
with 11/0

Size 2 bugle

3 x 6mm multifaceted

Size 1 bugle

4mm sea glass

4mm bicone

The seed and bugle bead
families contains many types
of beads.

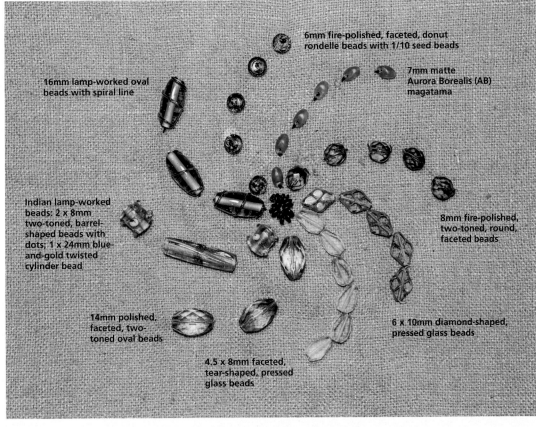

6mm fire-polished, faceted, donut
rondelle beads with 1/10 seed beads

16mm lamp-worked oval
beads with spiral line

7mm matte
Aurora Borealis (AB)
magatama

Indian lamp-worked
beads: 2 x 8mm
two-toned, barrel-
shaped beads with
dots; 1 x 24mm blue-
and-gold twisted
cylinder bead

8mm fire-polished,
two-toned, round,
faceted beads

14mm polished,
faceted, two-
toned oval beads

6 x 10mm diamond-shaped,
pressed glass beads

4.5 x 8mm faceted,
tear-shaped, pressed
glass beads

Glass is also used to make
other kinds of beads.

Beading thread

There is a bewildering array of beading threads available and each manufacturer has their own name and sizing conventions. Beading threads break down into two basic groups: parallel-filament nylon and parallel-filament gel-spun polyethelene.

Parallel-filament nylon threads—Nymo, Superlon (S-Lon), C-Lon, Silamide, K.O., and SoNo—are extruded nylon fibers that are bonded together into a single thread, often just called nylon threads. Nylon threads will fray, so before using them run the thread through some beeswax or a microcrystalline lubricant; this will also help a double strand of thread stick together and lessen fraying as the beads rub against the thread. Nymo is the oldest of these threads; many newer brands compare their threads to Nymo in their descriptions.

Parallel-filament gel-spun polyethelene threads—FireLine and WildFire—are polyethelene fibers that are spun and bonded into a single thread. They are very thin and strong, don't stretch, and resist fraying. The Smoke (gray) and Crystal (clear) colors allow the threads to nearly disappear on fabric.

K.O., Nymo D, Silamide, WildFire 0.15mm, and FireLine B are all about the same thickness as regular Gütermann and Mettler 100% polyester threads. All of these threads work well when sewing beads to fabric, especially if you use a double thread and beeswax for strength.

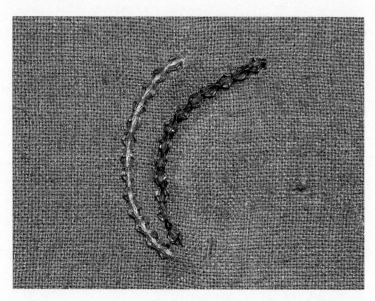

Changing the thread color can change the color of the beads. The 4mm crystal bicone beads on the left were sewn on with white S-Lon #18 thread and the same bicone beads on the right were sewn on with turquoise S-Lon #18 thread. Choose thread to match either the fabric or the beads.

BEADING THREAD AND BEADING CORD

Beads sewn on fabric stand proud of the garment and are subject to rubbing, so beading threads must be especially strong yet thin enough to slide through the center of the smallest seed beads.

Beading cords, used for stringing beads into necklaces, are much thicker and sturdier than threads used for sewing on beads.

BEAD THREAD CHART

Name	Size	Comments
Coats & Clark Dual Duty	0.3mm diameter	Regular sewing machine threads.
Gütermann, Mettler	0.3mm diameter	While it is tempting to use sewing thread you already own—don't. Beading thread is specially designed to withstand the abrasive wear and tear that beadwork is subject to.
Nymo	00: 0.08mm diameter for #15 needles 0: 0.45mm diameter for #13 needles B: 0.2mm diameter for 12/0 beads, #11 needles D: 0.3mm diameter, similar to regular polyester thread in thickness	Prone to fraying and stretching; precondition with beeswax or microcrystalline lubricant before use.
Superlon (S-Lon) by BeadSmith	AA: for 15/0 beads Micro or #18: 0.5mm diameter for 11/0 beads	S-Lon is a little more wiry than C-Lon.
C-Lon	AA: 0.45mm diameter, similar to Nymo 0, with a 4lb test rating D: similar to Nymo D, with a 7lb test rating	C-Lon is a little bit softer than S-Lon.
Silamide	A: similar to Nymo D	Has a flat profile that makes it easier to thread onto a needle.
K.O. thread (from Japan)	1 size only: similar to Nymo B	Thin, strong, and easy to thread onto a needle.
FireLine by BeadSmith	0.006in (0.15mm) diameter: similar to Nymo B, with a 4lb test rating 0.008in (0.20mm) diameter: similar to Nymo D, with a 6lb test rating	Originally made as a fishing line, FireLine is very thin and strong, and won't fray, making it easy to thread onto a needle. Now also available dyed in other colors.
WildFire by Beadalon	0.006in (0.15mm) diameter, with a 10lb test rating 0.008in (0.20mm) diameter, with a 15lb test rating	Very similar to FireLine. Very thin and strong; these threads appear wiry but are quite malleable.

Beading tools

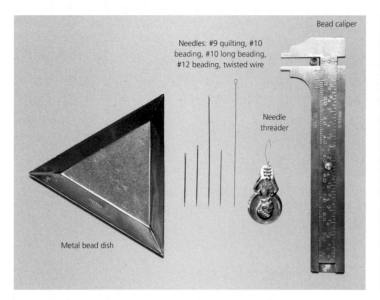

Metal bead dish, needles, needle threader, and bead caliper.

An embroidery hoop on a stand.

BEAD DISHES

Bead dishes with sides are helpful for scooping and corralling beads, but metal dishes, as pictured above, can be slippery when you are trying to grab the beads with a needle. To hold beads while you are working, plastic container lids work well, or a bead board covered with a spongy, napped polyester. A flannel- or cotton-velveteen-covered board works well, too.

NEEDLES

The tiny hole of seed beads requires tiny needles. Pictured here are several needles all suitable for beading, from left: #9 quilting, #10 beading, #10 long beading, and #12 beading. As you may remember, the larger the number, the thinner the needle. The thinner the needle, the harder it is to thread, so a needle threader may come in handy. A twisted wire needle can be used, but will not be sharp enough to penetrate most fabric and is usually used for bead weaving on a loom.

BEAD CALIPER

A bead caliper is used for measuring beads and can be helpful when trying to size beads that have become inadvertently mixed up.

EMBROIDERY HOOP

A standing embroidery hoop is invaluable for holding the fabric taut when sewing on beads so they will lay flat on the garment. The stand elevates the fabric off the work table and holds it steady, allowing you to work without constantly flipping the fabric over. When you do need to see the reverse side just loosen the side knobs and turn the work. If the fabric piece that you are beading is too small to fit into the hoop, you can baste muslin around the edges of the piece to increase its size.

SPILLED BEADS

Spilled beads can be picked up with sticky tape or, for bigger jobs, you can use a sticky lint roller. If the beads have gone all over the floor, place a piece of nylon stocking or lightweight fabric over the nozzle of your vacuum cleaner to keep the beads from being sucked up into the bag, and turn the vacuum cleaner on—hold the nozzle over a bead container when you turn it off.

Basic stitches for beading

There are many ways to attach beads to fabric. The four basic stitches are running stitch, backstitch, double-needle couching stitch, and single-needle couching stitch. Running stitch is good to use when you want to sprinkle beads across an area. Backstitch is good for sewing several beads in a group. Double- and single-needle couching stitches are best used when sewing a line of beads to fabric.

HOLDING THE NEEDLE

Always insert the needle straight up and down for each stitch. If the needle is inserted at an angle, it will skew the bead sideways.

RUNNING STITCH

Running stitch is the most basic beading stitch; it can be used to apply a single bead, or thousands of them. Beads are sewn on one at a time, which offers great flexibility, but is quite painstaking.

1 Transfer the design to tear-away interfacing and pin it to the fabric (see Transferring Patterns, p. 19).

2 Knot the thread on the wrong side of the base fabric to anchor the end.

3 Keeping the needle at right angles to the base fabric, bring the needle and thread up to the right side of the fabric.

4 Slide a bead onto the needle and thread and all the way down to the fabric. Place the bead in its position.

5 Insert the needle directly next to the bead and, keeping the needle at right angles to the fabric, pull the needle and thread through the fabric. Repeat with the next bead.

BACKSTITCH

Backstitch provides a quick and secure way to sew a line of beads onto a base fabric. It also allows the beads to sit close together.

1 Transfer the design to tear-away interfacing and pin it to the fabric (see Transferring Patterns, p. 19).

2 Knot the thread on the wrong side of the base fabric to anchor the end.

3 Keeping the needle at right angles to the base fabric, bring the needle and thread up to the right side of the fabric.

4 Slide four beads onto the needle and thread and all the way down to the fabric. Place them in position.

5 Insert the needle directly next to the fourth bead and, keeping the needle at right angles to the fabric, pull needle and thread through the fabric.

6 Count backward two beads and bring the needle up between the second and third beads.

7 Thread the needle through the third and fourth beads. Repeat Steps 4–7.

You can vary the number of beads you work back and forth: for example, three back and six forward, or any combination.

SEWING ON SPACED BEADS

If the beads are widely spaced, knot the thread before moving on to the next bead.

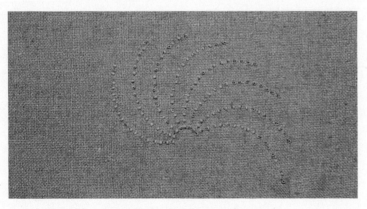

Beads sewn on with running stitch, after the interfacing has been torn away.

DOUBLE-NEEDLE COUCHING STITCH

Single- and double-needle couching look exactly the same on the right side of the fabric. In both stitches, the beads are strung on a strong thread, and then a second thread anchors the first thread and the beads in place. These stitches work well if you have long strands of beads to sew onto fabric. Double-needle couching stitch is easier to do than single-needle. You need two separate needles and threads; for clarity, these will be called the beading thread and the couching thread.

SINGLE-NEEDLE COUCHING STITCH

Single-needle couching stitch works in the same fashion as double-needle couching stitch, but the beading thread and couching thread are the same piece of thread.

1 Transfer the design to tear-away interfacing and pin it to the fabric (see Transferring Patterns, p. 19).

2 Knot the beading thread on the wrong side of the base fabric to anchor the end.

3 Keeping the needle at right angles to the base fabric, bring the needle and thread up to the right side of the fabric.

4 Slide as many beads as needed onto the beading thread to complete the run.

5 Position the first bead in place on the fabric.

6 Knot the couching thread on the wrong side of the base fabric to anchor the end.

7 Bring the needle and couching thread up to the right side of the fabric.

8 Loop the couching thread over the beading thread between two to four beads from the start of the run, then return needle and couching thread to the wrong side of the fabric.

9 Slide between two and four beads down the beading thread and place in position on the fabric. Repeat Steps 7–9 until complete. Bring the beading thread to the wrong side and knot.

1 Transfer the design to tear-away interfacing and pin to the fabric (see Transferring Patterns, p. 19).

2 Knot the thread on the wrong side of the base fabric to anchor the end.

3 Keeping the needle perpendicular to the base fabric, bring the needle and thread up to the right side of the fabric.

4 Slide as many beads onto the thread as needed to complete the run.

5 Insert the needle and thread at the end of the design line, laying all the beads on the fabric.

6 Do not pull the thread taut; leave a small bubble of thread that can be pulled down to the surface of the fabric between the beads by the couching stitches.

7 Bring the needle and thread up to the right side of the fabric, two beads from the end of the run.

8 Loop the thread over between two beads and then return needle and thread to the wrong side of the fabric.

9 Slide between two and four beads down the thread and place in position. Repeat Steps 7–9 until complete.

Beads sewn on with double-needle couching stitch.

Picot stitch

Picot stitch is an easy stitch that adds texture within a garment or along an edge.

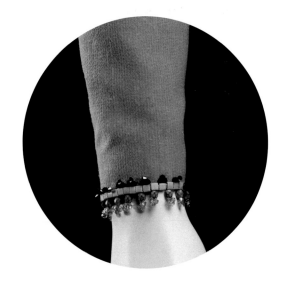

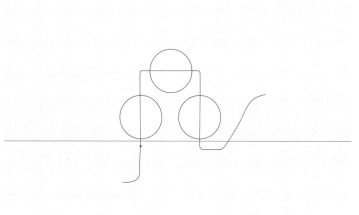

Picot stitch sewn with two styles of beads alternating: smaller shiny rocailles and tear-shaped magatama beads.

1 Knot the thread on the wrong side of the base fabric to anchor the end.

2 Keeping the needle perpendicular to the base fabric, bring the needle and thread up to the right side of the fabric.

3 Slide three beads onto the needle and thread and all the way down to the fabric. Place the beads into position.

4 Insert the needle directly beneath the third bead and, keeping the needle perpendicular to the fabric, pull the needle and thread through the fabric. Repeat Steps 3–4 until complete.

Beaded fringe

Beads can be sewn directly to a garment or to a ribbon to make a beaded fringe. If adding fringe to a neckline seam, the beading thread between fringe strands can be hidden by the garment and facing seam allowances. If adding fringe to a hem, do so after the hem is pressed up but before it is sewn, so you can hide the beading thread. With beads sewn to ribbon, you need a seam to hide the ribbon (see Piping with Fringe, p. 149).

When you sew in the ribbon of a fringe you want to be sure the ribbon is placed within the seam allowance and the beads hang down from the seam. There should be ⅛in (3mm) of space at the top of the fringe to allow for the fabric taken up when turning the seam; use an expendable, cheap seed bead as a spacer at the top of each line of beads and remove it later (see Step 7).

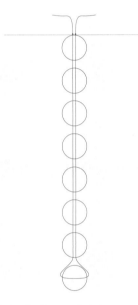

The bottom bead is perpendicular to the others in a fringe; it is called a turning bead, as it allows the thread to turn to the top again.

Larger ending beads tend to have different drillings: the spotted teardrop bead used here is top drilled, allowing it to hang from one end; the silver-edged oval bead is drilled lengthwise, requiring a turning bead at the very bottom. When using a top-drilled bead, many beaders hide the thread by adding a bead on either side of the drilled hole.

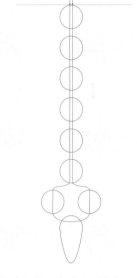

Add beads to either side of a top-drilled ending bead to hide the thread.

1 Mark the garment or a piece of ribbon at regular intervals to help with spacing each strand of the fringe. Knot the thread or make a small stitch in the fabric or ribbon to anchor the end.

2 Keeping the needle perpendicular to the fabric, bring the needle and thread up to the right side of the fabric.

3 Slide two cheap seed beads (here shown in red) onto the needle and thread, followed by nine beads; move the beads all the way down the thread to the fabric. Note: when sewing the fringe directly to the garment, skip the spacer seed beads.

4 Return the needle and thread up through the beads, from the eighth to the first.

5 Insert the needle directly beneath the first bead and, keeping the needle perpendicular to the fabric, pull the needle and thread through the fabric. Make a small stitch or knot in the fabric to anchor the thread.

6 Repeat Steps 2–5 until the fringe is complete.

7 Carefully break the top glass seed beads with pliers; this will create the ease at the top of the fringe strand. To insert the fringe into a seam, see Piping with Fringe, p. 149.

A finished beaded fringe sewn into the hem of a garment.

Beaded net fringe

Beaded net fringe can be sewn directly onto a garment or sewn onto a ribbon.

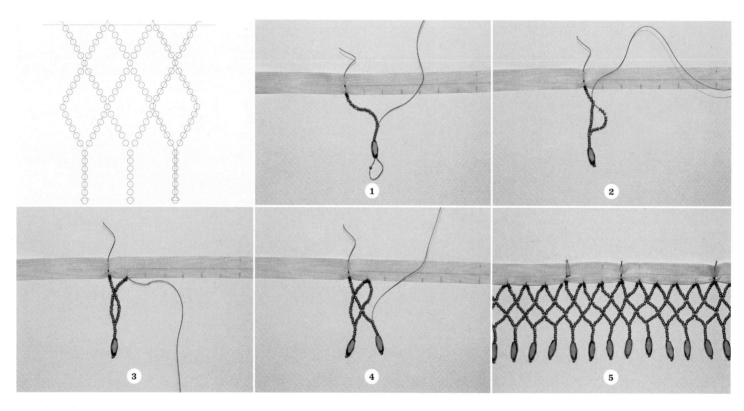

The thread paths here have been color-coded for clarity, but just one continuous piece of thread has been used throughout the netted fringe.

1 Make a small stitch or knot on the wrong side of the fabric or ribbon to anchor the thread. Start the stringing with two red spacer beads. String six gray #11 seed beads, one #10 turquoise bead, six gray #11 seed beads, one #10 turquoise, six gray #11 seed beads, one large oval silver-edged bead, and one gray #11. The last bead is a turning bead. Return the needle and thread up through the large oval bead, the bottom-most group of gray beads and the turquoise bead.

2 String on another six gray beads, one turquoise bead, and six gray beads. Slide the needle and thread through the first turquoise bead on the first line of beads.

3 String on another six gray beads, which will return you to the top of the fringe. Add two spacer beads, sew a couple of small stitches in the ribbon and knot the thread before proceeding to the next downward strand.

4 String on another two red spacer beads, six gray beads, one turquoise bead, and six gray beads. Slide the needle through the second turquoise bead on the second line of beads. Add another six gray beads, one turquoise bead, and six gray beads. Add a large oval bead and a turning bead. Return the needle up through the large oval bead, the bottom most group of gray beads and the third turquoise bead. Repeat Steps 2–4.

5 The finished fringe.

SHAPING BEADED FRINGE

When the fringe is complete, it may need to be steamed with an iron and pinned to a board to even out the diamond shapes. Beading threads respond well to this process.

Beaded cabochon / Cabuchon / Cab

A cabochon is a stone, glass, or porcelain piece that is flat on the back and slightly rounded on the front. You can also use any found object with blunt edges in place of a cabochon. The cabochon is glued to the fabric and then a beaded cage is constructed around it so that the beads appear to be holding the cabochon in place.

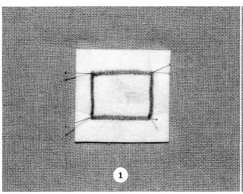

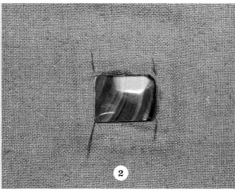

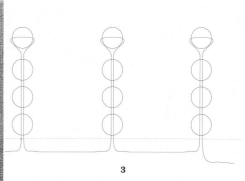

1 Draw the outline of the cabochon on a piece of beading foundation, such as Lacy's Stiff Stuff™ (see box below), and cut out a piece slightly larger than the outline. Glue the foundation to the wrong side of the fabric, centered where the cabochon will go, gluing only within the drawn outline; it is very hard to sew through the glue. Push a pin through the fabric at each corner of the cabochon placement.

2 Turn the fabric to the right side and glue the cabochon to your fabric within the area marked by the pins, being careful to keep the glue only on the cabochon. Let the glue dry for an hour or more.

3 Match beads and thread so that the thread can pass through the beads multiple times; here 3mm beads were matched with K.O. thread, doubled. Knot the thread on the wrong side. Keeping the needle perpendicular, bring the needle and thread to the right side.

Slide a stack of beads onto the needle and thread and all the way down to the fabric and cabochon. Create a stack of beads tall enough to bend over the cabochon, but not obscure it. After passing through the top turning bead on the stack, slide the needle back down the stack and back through the fabric. Continue creating stacks in the same way along the edge of the cabochon.

SUPPORTING THE CABOCHON

The cabochon is large and heavy and will drag the fabric down, so it is wise to put interfacing behind the cabochon and fabric as support. Lacy's Stiff Stuff™ is sturdy yet lightweight interfacing specifically designed for cabochon beading. The manufacturer of Lacy's Stiff Stuff recommends E6000™ glue, which is very potent, so be sure to work in a well-ventilated space.

If Lacy's Stiff Stuff is not available, you can add a heavyweight interfacing after the cabochon is in place to support it and cover the stitching.

4 Repeat until you have sewn all the stacks. The stacks can be placed with space between them, or they can butt up tightly to each other. Here, half the stacks are folded over the cabochon to show their height.

5 Starting with the thread anchored on the wrong side, thread the needle up through a stack of beads. Go through the turning bead, add a "linking" bead, go through the next turning bead, and add another linking bead.

6 Repeat to encircle the cabochon.

7 Pull the thread tight, causing the bead cage to collapse over the cabochon. Slide the needle and thread down through a stack of beads and knot the thread on the wrong side.

On the wrong side, trim the Lacy's Stiff Stuff as close to the stitches as possible to eliminate unnecessary bulk around the cabochon.

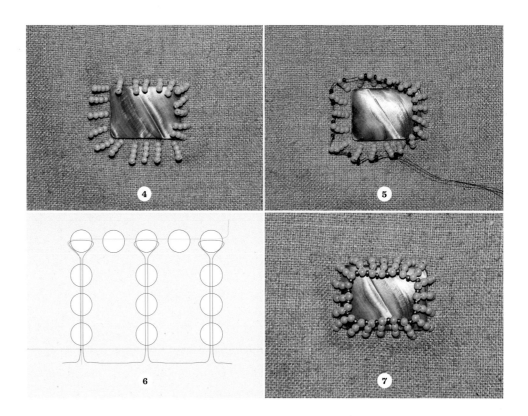

VARIATION

In this example, eight equally spaced stacks of 8/0 black seed beads were sewn around the cabochon and linked together with size 1 black bugle beads across the top. Finally, a turquoise faceted bead bracketed by four 8/0 black seed beads was sewn between the stacks, around the cabochon base.

Sequins

Sequins are small disk-shaped beads with a hole in the center that are sewn onto fabric. The sequin was originally a gold coin, produced in Venice and known in Italian as a *zecchino*; it took its name from the Zecca, or mint (which, in turn, got its name from the Arabic *sikka*, a mold or die used to make coins). These coins were sewn onto garments for safekeeping, a practice that led to the later use of coin-shaped beads as ornamentation.

Sequins are available in many sizes, ranging from $^3/_{32}$in (2mm) to $^5/_8$in (1.5cm) in diameter. They can be flat, cupped, or faceted, and come in many shapes. Sequins also come in a variety of finishes: matte, satin, metallic, transparent, moonshine (clear with a silvery finish), iridescent, iris (with heavier iridescence than plain iridescent), glossy, silky, ultra glossy, opaque, and printed.

Sequins can be purchased loose or prestrung on thread (a "worm"). Loose sequins may be sold by the quantity (35–1,000 pieces in a bag) or by weight.

You can also purchase sequin trim, in which sequins are already attached to a thread chain. As you work with this trim, some of the sequins will fall off the ends; save them to fill in any odd spaces.

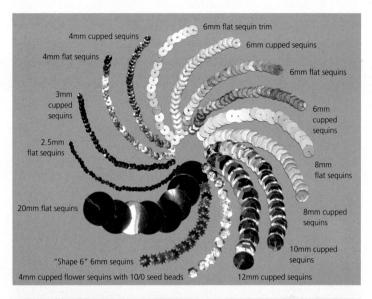

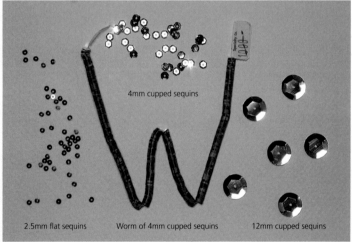

TESTING SEQUINS BEFORE PRESSING

Sequins may melt when ironed. Always test a couple of sequins with an iron before pressing any sequins on a garment.

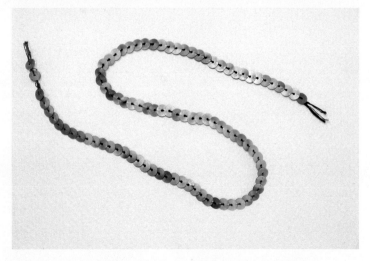

Sequin trim, with sequins already fastened to threads, ready for stitching onto fabric.

Sewing loose sequins

Sequins may be sewn as single, reflective points scattered across the fabric, or sewn in lines to create glittering patterns. A bead can also be added to the center of a plain sequin for more color, sparkle, or texture.

1 Anchor the thread by making a small stitch on the wrong side of the fabric. Bring the needle and thread up through the center of the first sequin; this sequin should be cup side up—the cup side is the "right" side. Bring the needle and thread down just at the edge of the sequin. Then bring the needle and thread up half a sequin's width away from the edge of the first sequin.

2 Thread a second sequin onto the needle, cup side down. Here the wrong side of the sequin is colored purple for clarity. Bring the needle and thread down at the edge of the first sequin.

3 When you pull the thread taut the sequin should flip onto its back so the cup faces up and the sequin covers the previous stitch.

4 Repeat Steps 2–3. When you are comfortable judging the width of each sequin you will be able to sew them on very quickly.

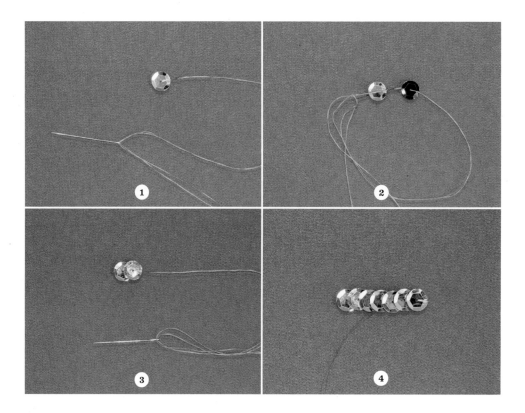

VARIATION

1 Anchor the thread by making a small stitch on the wrong side of the fabric. Bring the needle and thread up through the center of the first sequin, with the sequin cup side up. Add a bead, and bring the needle and thread back down through the sequin to the wrong side of the fabric. Repeat for the next sequin.

2 Alternate rows of plain sequins with rows that have a different type of bead added in the center of each sequin.

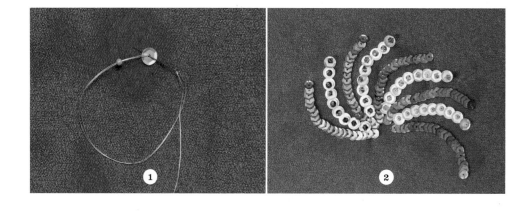

Sewing sequin trim

There are a number of ways to sew sequin trim to fabric. If you are attaching it by hand, you can couch it in place as if it were a string of beads (see Single-Needle and Double-Needle Couching Stitch, p. 235). If you want to attach it by machine, you can use either a straight stitch or zigzag stitch on a regular sewing machine, or you can use a serger.

Straight stitch

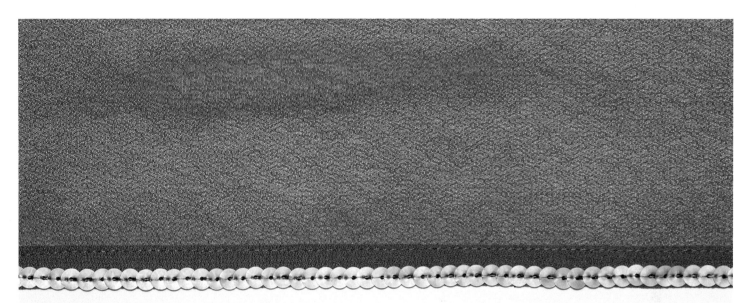

With a straight machine stitch, you can stitch down the middle of the sequin trim. While this method firmly attaches the trim, it has some drawbacks: the sewing line is visible, and if you make a mistake the trim is ruined—the sewing machine needle leaves holes in the sequins—so you must start with a new piece of trim. If you need the security of the straight-stitch method, use a needle/thread lubricant to help the needle repeatedly pierce the plastic sequins. Finally, be sure to change the needle after completing the project.

SEWING SEQUINS WITH A MACHINE

For all machine applications, place the sequin trim so that the overlapping edges of the sequins are facing you. If the trim is going the wrong way, the sequins will snag on the presser foot.

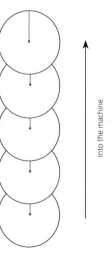

Into the machine

Zigzag stitch

1 Before purchasing the trim, check the width of the widest zigzag stitch on your sewing machine. Lay the sequin trim on the fabric and adjust the zigzag-stitch width so that it is just wider than the sequins. Stitch over the sequin trim, being careful not to let the needle pierce the sequins. You can add a layer of lightweight tear-away interfacing on top of the sequin trim if the sewing machine stitches are skipping. Here, part of the interfacing is removed to show the stitches.

2 Remove the interfacing. Pull the sequin trim toward the end of the seam and then back toward the start of the seam. The stitches should slide under the sequins. There will be several sequins that will not slide over the thread; move these sequins around by hand until the thread is hidden.

3 The finished sequin trim sewn with a zigzag stitch using thread that matches the fabric.

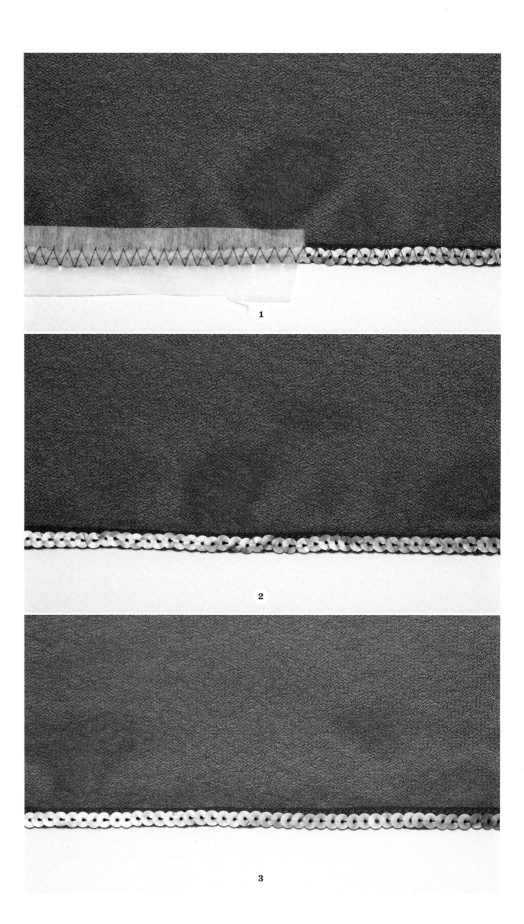

Using a serger

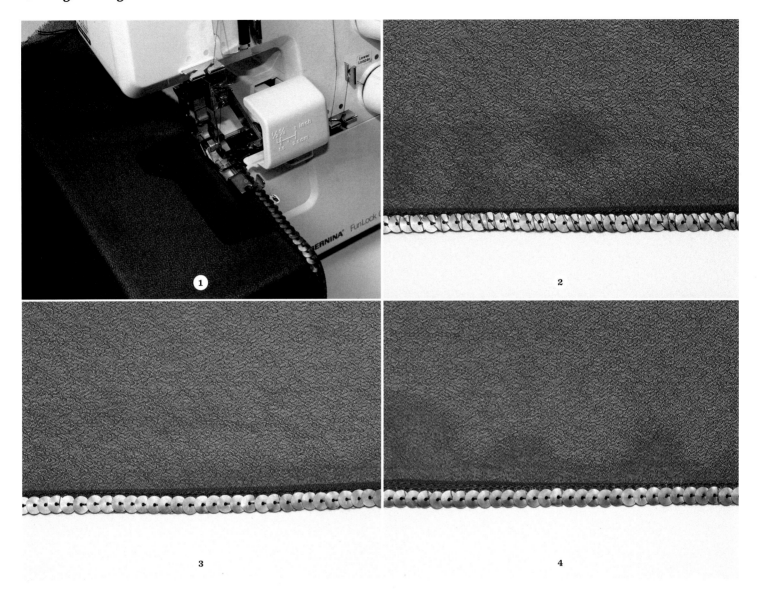

1 Remove the knife from the thread path. Change the presser foot to a multipurpose or bead and sequin foot if possible; these feet have a slot that guides the trim into the stitch path. With the serger needle down, lay the sequin trim into the trim slot, making sure to place it so that the overlapping edges of the sequins are feeding into the serger.

2 Serge over the trim.

3 Pull the sequin trim toward the end of the seam and then back toward the start. The stitches should slide under the sequins. There will be several sequins that will not slide over the thread; move these around until the thread is hidden.

4 The sequin trim serged with thread that matches the fabric.

Sewing a seam through sequined fabric

When using fabric that is embellished with sequins, it is necessary to remove any sequins from the seam allowance and along the seam line. If the sequins are left in the seam line, they will prevent the seam from lying flat; if they are left in the seam allowance, they will add bulk and be uncomfortable against the skin.

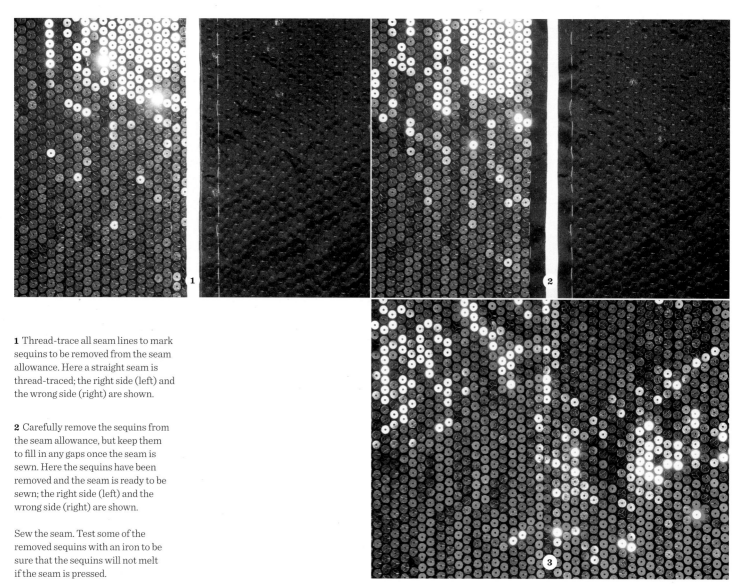

1 Thread-trace all seam lines to mark sequins to be removed from the seam allowance. Here a straight seam is thread-traced; the right side (left) and the wrong side (right) are shown.

2 Carefully remove the sequins from the seam allowance, but keep them to fill in any gaps once the seam is sewn. Here the sequins have been removed and the seam is ready to be sewn; the right side (left) and the wrong side (right) are shown.

Sew the seam. Test some of the removed sequins with an iron to be sure that the sequins will not melt if the seam is pressed.

3 The completed seam.

Paillettes

Paillettes, from the French meaning "speck" or "flake," are large disk-shaped beads that have a hole near the top for sewing them onto fabric; they are also called spangles or diamantes. Paillettes are available in many colors and finishes: metallic, transparent, holographic, iridescent, opaque, and printed. They range in size from ⅝ in (15mm) to 1¼ in (30mm) in diameter. The hole can be small or large. Paillettes can be sewn on in basic patterns: straight rows and columns, or staggered rows. The staggered pattern produces a fish-scale effect.

SEWING ON PAILLETTES

Sew paillettes on loosely; the glittery shimmer they are known for comes from their free movement as the fabric moves.

After sewing one to three paillettes onto the fabric, knot the thread on the wrong side. The looseness of the thread that allows paillettes to move freely also increases the chance of pulling them off by accident. With knots in place, only a few paillettes will be lost, rather than a whole row.

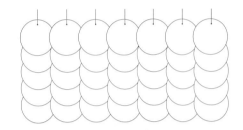
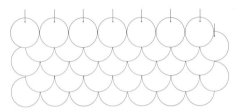

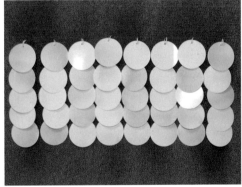
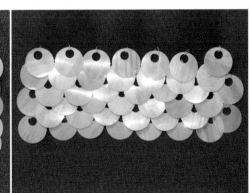

Small-holed paillettes sewn in straight rows and columns.

Large-holed paillettes sewn in a staggered pattern.

1 Decide whether you want small-holed or large-holed paillettes.

2 Draw a pattern on tear-away interfacing to use as a guide to space the paillettes evenly. A bamboo skewer sanded down to the diameter of a toothpick will help you keep your stitches loose (a thin, double-ended knitting needle would also work well). Sew on each paillette with two stitches around the skewer and through the paillette hole. After sewing one to three paillettes onto the fabric, knot the thread on the wrong side. When the skewer is removed, the paillettes will move freely.

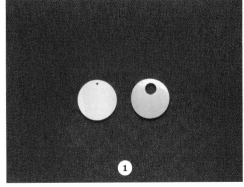
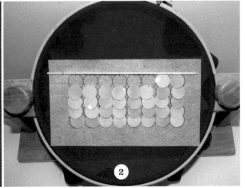

Nothing says "red carpet" like a crystal-embellished gown. The Rhine River was the original source of the rock crystals known as rhinestones, used as imitation diamonds. In the eighteenth century, jeweler J. G. Strauss began to manufacture imitation crystals by coating the underside of glass with a metallic powder. The terms "rhinestones," "rhinestone crystals," and "crystals" are interchangeable. Rhinestone crystals use their own measuring system, uniform across the industry, in which SS stands for "stone size." Today Swarovski in Austria and Preciosa in the Czech Republic are the major manufacturers of high-quality crystals.

Crystals can be affixed to fabric in many ways: this chapter covers sew-on, Hotfix, glue-on, and prong-set crystals. Nailheads have similar settings and fixing methods.

3.9
Crystals and nailheads

The easiest methods for attaching crystals are sewing and Hotfixing. Swarovski Hotfix crystals are particularly robust, withstanding many performances and laundering on theatrical costumes; inexpensive crystals can fall off, leaving the foil backing glued to the fabric.

Keep in mind the limitations of your fabric: Hotfix crystals require a hot iron/applicator that may melt acetate fabric; the glue in glue-on crystals may also melt acetate. Any garment with Hotfix elements can be hand-washed, but should not be put in a dryer or ironed; the glue is sensitive to steam and heat, and may release the crystals. Prong settings work best on thicker fabrics—denim, heavyweight wool, or Ultrasuede®, for example—because the prongs can cause lighter fabrics to pucker.

Crystals

Crystals and rhinestones come in many sizes, and with a variety of backs and settings. They can be attached to fabric in several different ways.

Sew-on crystals

Rhinestone rystals are available in premade trim that can be sewn on.

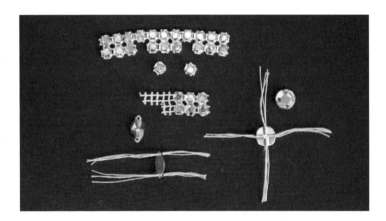

The small crystals at the top (above) are enmeshed in a net fabric. Individual crystals can be cut out to allow the trim to bend around a curve. The stones on the right have a metal backing with tunnels or thread guides. At the bottom is a crystal with holes in the ends. All of these crystals are easily sewn onto fabric.

To attach the crystals, transfer the design to the right side of the fabric. Sew on the crystals with several stitches, sewing through the mesh, through the holes in the end of the crystals, or through the thread guides, depending on the setting of the crystals.

RHINESTONE SIZES		
Stone size	Stone diameter	Actual size
SS 5	0.9mm	
SS 7	2.0mm	
SS 9	2.8mm	
SS 10	2.8mm	
SS 12	3.0mm	
SS 16	4.0mm	
SS 20	4.8mm	
SS 30	6.0mm	
SS 34	7.0mm	
SS 40	8.5mm	
SS 48	11.0mm	

Hotfix crystals

Hotfix crystals have glue on the back. After positioning the crystals, the glue is melted with an iron or an applicator.

Hotfix transfer paper, or Mylar paper, is a two-layer product: one layer is clear and sticky; the other, a backing sheet, is white and not sticky. Using this paper allows you to check that the crystals are positioned correctly when using an iron, and to make multiple versions of the same pattern.

PLACING CRYSTALS DIRECTLY ON THE FABRIC

If you can place the crystals directly on the fashion fabric, right side up, then you do not need to use transfer paper. You should, however, place a Teflon ironing sheet on top of the crystals and the fabric before ironing to prevent the fabric from becoming shiny or scorched.

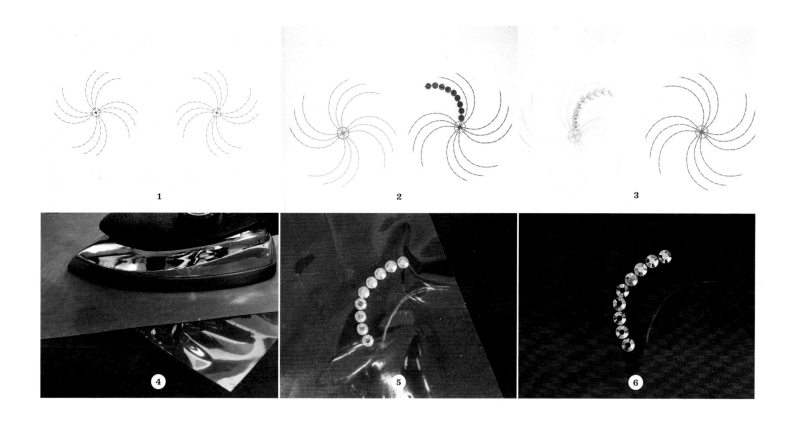

1 Draw your design (shown here in black). You need to work on the reverse side—that is, with the right side of the crystals facing down—so invert the design (shown here in red).

2 Tape a piece of transfer paper over the reversed design, with the sticky side up and backing sheet removed. Place the crystals, right side down, over the design lines on the sticky transfer paper.

3 Place the backing sheet over the crystals. Lift up both layers of the transfer paper and lay them down, crystals right side up, on the original design. Correct any misplaced crystals.

4 Remove the backing sheet and place the transfer paper with the crystals on the fabric. Cover with a Teflon ironing sheet and then place the hot iron on top. The iron temperature should be set as high as the fabric will tolerate.

Leave the iron in place for 30 seconds; the timing is approximate and will change with the wattage of your iron. Lift the iron and place it on the next section to be fixed. Do not slide the iron as this may cause the crystals to slide on the fabric.

5 Peel away the transfer paper, which can be reused.

6 One line of fixed crystals.

USING A HOTFIX APPLICATOR

Using a Hotfix applicator is an easy way to attach Hotfix crystals one by one: the design is on the right side of the fabric and you can see exactly where you are putting each crystal. The biggest drawback to the Hotfix applicator is that you have to leave a small space around each crystal due to the metal applicator tip.

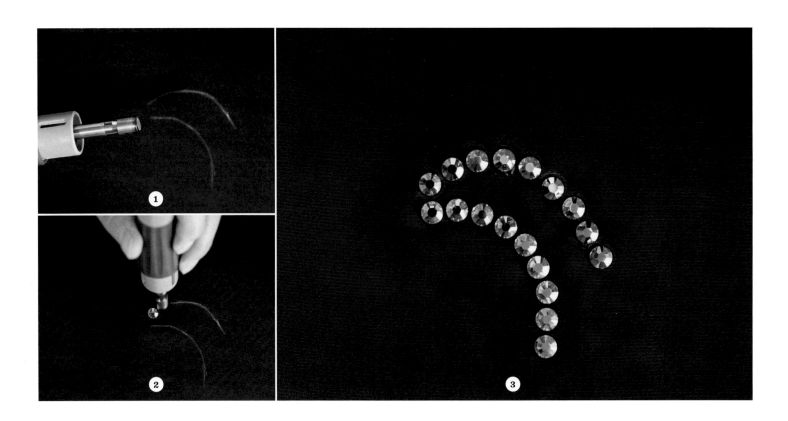

PLUGGING IN THE APPLICATOR

Do not plug the applicator into a surge-protected extension cord, as the surge protector will not let the applicator get hot enough.

1 Transfer your design to the right side of the fabric. Select and install the correct Hotfix applicator tip to fit the crystals. Plug in the applicator and let it heat up. Pick up a crystal with the applicator, with the flat/glue side facing out.

2 When the glue becomes shiny, place the crystal on the fabric. Hold the Hotfix applicator on the fabric for ten seconds. Lift away the applicator, leaving the crystal affixed to the fabric. If the crystal does not separate from the applicator, insert a pin through the slot in the tip to hold the crystal down. If the glue has not melted enough, place the applicator on top of the crystal for a bit longer.

3 Two rows of fixed crystals.

Glue-on crystals

Glue-on crystals can be affixed to fabric individually or in
a group. A good glue for adhering flat-back crystals to fabric
is 9001™ adhesive or E6000™; they are both very potent, so be sure
to work in a well-ventilated area. Swarovski makes a glue pen that
has a small tip and works well, but it is not widely available.

SINGLE CRYSTALS

When positioning individual crystals on fabric, you must be
precise; any sliding crystals will smear the glue on the fabric.

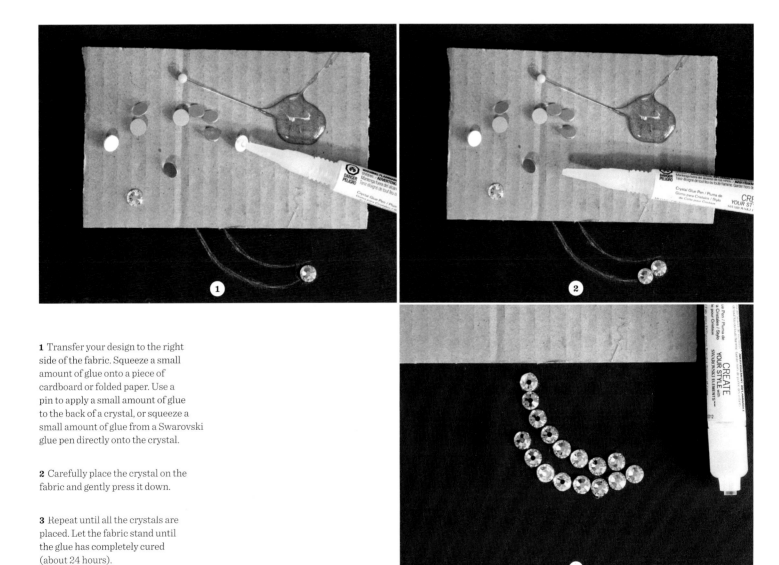

1 Transfer your design to the right
side of the fabric. Squeeze a small
amount of glue onto a piece of
cardboard or folded paper. Use a
pin to apply a small amount of glue
to the back of a crystal, or squeeze a
small amount of glue from a Swarovski
glue pen directly onto the crystal.

2 Carefully place the crystal on the
fabric and gently press it down.

3 Repeat until all the crystals are
placed. Let the fabric stand until
the glue has completely cured
(about 24 hours).

GROUPS OF CRYSTALS

Glue-on crystals can also be positioned on Hotfix transfer (Mylar) paper (see p. 251) and then glued onto fabric as a group. Using transfer paper allows you to check that the crystals are positioned correctly before fixing them to the fabric, and to make multiple versions of the same pattern.

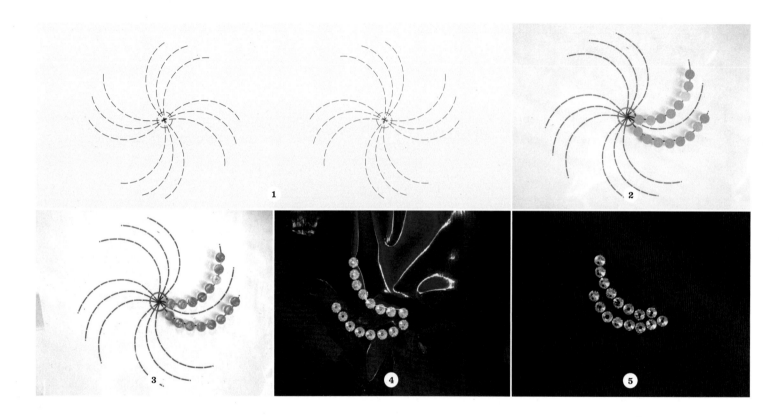

1 Draw your design (shown here in black). You need to work on the reverse side—that is, with the crystals right side facing down—so invert the design (shown here in red).

2 Tape a piece of transfer paper over the reversed design, with the sticky side up and backing sheet removed. Place the crystals, right side down, over the design lines on the sticky transfer paper.

3 Put a small dot of glue on the back of each crystal. Be careful not to put on too much, as the extra glue will ooze out and mar the fabric.

4 Place the crystals and transfer paper on the fabric. You must be precise in your placement; the glue cannot be removed from the fabric if it is smeared. Gently press the crystals onto the fabric. Carefully peel off the paper, leaving the crystals affixed to the fabric. Let the fabric stand until the glue has completely cured (about 24 hours).

5 Two rows of crystals glued in place.

Crystals with a flat-back prong setting

Flat-back crystals can be affixed to heavyweight fabrics using "Tiffany setting" prongs (first created by Tiffany & Co. in 1886 to showcase diamonds). Prongs are sized to match stone size (SS), and are available with regular or long legs. Use long-leg prongs with thick fabrics, such as a Melton wool or several thicknesses of fabric. Regular-leg prongs work well with denim, wool, and leather. Prong settings may cause your fabric to ripple; they are best used when glue will not bond to the fabric, or when you want to feature the settings themselves.

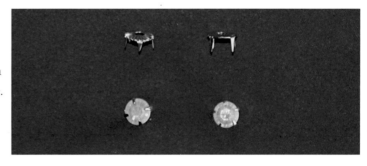

The setting, or flat-back prong, on the left has shorter legs than the setting on the right.

1 Draw your design (shown here in black). You need to work on the wrong side of the fabric, so invert the design (shown here in red) and transfer it to the wrong side of the fabric.

2 Working on the wrong side of the fabric, place the first setting on the design line and push the prongs by hand through the fabric to the right side. The setting does not need to grip the fabric tightly.

3 The Brisk-Set rhinestone-setting tool can be used to apply prong settings. Rhinestone setters are widely available; all work in a similar fashion.

4 Place the crystal in the lower cup, crystal face down, flat-back up. Position the fabric, wrong side up, with the setting over the crystal in the cup. Press the lever arm to push the top portion of the setter down onto the prong setting. When the prong setting is forced into the lower cup the prongs will curl around the crystal, holding it against the fabric.

5 Two rows of set crystals. The top row consists of jet hematite crystals, while the bottom row is black diamond crystals; both use Tiffany setting prongs. "Hematite" is a satin finish applied to jet (black) crystals for a soft sheen.

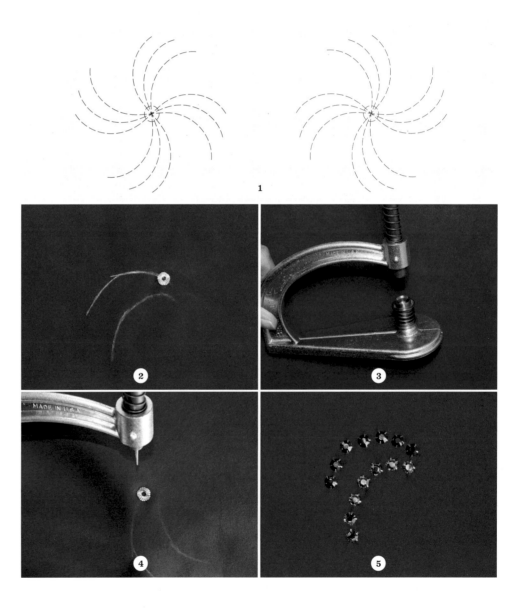

Nailheads / Studs

Nailheads or studs can be affixed to fabric in the same ways as rhinestones and crystals: by ironing on, with glue, or with prongs. Nailheads are sized in the same way as crystals: by stone size (SS) or in millimeters.

Iron-on nailheads

The iron-on nailheads used for the design here are shown right side up on the top row and glue side up on the bottom row. Note that the pyramid and the gold half-circle on the right have more depth to them than the other nailheads. The whole interior of the shape is filled with glue; when large elements are overheated, the glue oozes out onto the fabric. To prevent this, apply the smallest elements first and the largest elements last. Heat all elements just until the glue melts enough to adhere them to the fabric; how long this takes will vary on the elements and your iron.

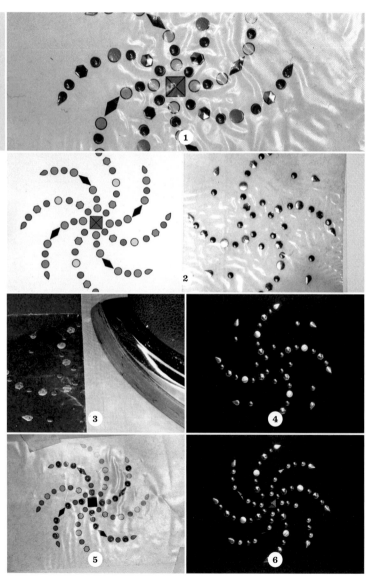

1 Place the smaller nailheads of the design on the sticky side of a transfer sheet, right side down, remembering to reverse the design (see Hotfix Crystals, p. 251).

2 Place the backing sheet over the nailheads and smooth the layers of the transfer paper together. Lift up both layers and turn them over, showing the nailheads right side up. Correct any misplaced elements. Here the reversed design is shown next to the nailheads.

3 Remove the backing sheet and place the nailheads and transfer paper on the fabric. Cover with a Teflon ironing sheet and iron the nailheads onto the fabric. Do not slide the iron as this may cause the nailheads to slide on the fabric.

4 Peel away the transfer paper.

5 The transfer paper and backing sheet are reusable. Place the remaining elements on it and iron them in place on the fabric.

6 The final design, with all the elements in place.

Nailheads with a prong setting

Nailheads with a prong setting can be affixed in a similar way to crystals with a prong setting (see p. 255). You can use a Brisk-Set rhinestone setter adapted for nailheads, or a small screwdriver and mallet.

From the left: SS 40 Dutch copper antique flat nailhead, SS 40 woven canvas nickel-domed nailhead, and 12 x 7mm wave ribbon frosted nickel nailhead, each shown from the top and the side.

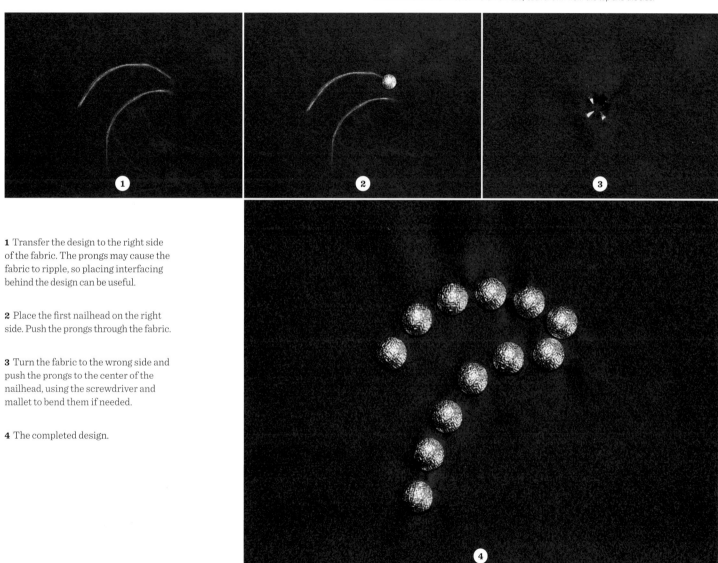

1 Transfer the design to the right side of the fabric. The prongs may cause the fabric to ripple, so placing interfacing behind the design can be useful.

2 Place the first nailhead on the right side. Push the prongs through the fabric.

3 Turn the fabric to the wrong side and push the prongs to the center of the nailhead, using the screwdriver and mallet to bend them if needed.

4 The completed design.

Lace can be seductive or chaste, ephemeral or substantial, with motifs and patterns created from twisted and twined fibers. The word comes from the old French *lassis* or *lacis* and the early English *lacez*, meaning "noose" or "string." Emerging in the sixteenth century, lace was made with either a single thread and needle (needle lace) or multiple bobbins filled with thread (bobbin lace). This luxury fabric was produced by master lace makers at the rate of an inch a week in damp, dark rooms that kept the fibers pliable.

Although designs were copied worldwide, each lace was named for the area where it was originally created: Chantilly, Alençon, and Valenciennes from France; Milanese, point de Venise, and Genoese from Italy; Binche and Bruges from Belgium; Bedfordshire, Honiton, and Northamptonshire from England.

3.10
Lace

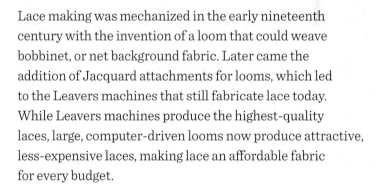

Lace making was mechanized in the early nineteenth century with the invention of a loom that could weave bobbinet, or net background fabric. Later came the addition of Jacquard attachments for looms, which led to the Leavers machines that still fabricate lace today. While Leavers machines produce the highest-quality laces, large, computer-driven looms now produce attractive, less-expensive laces, making lace an affordable fabric for every budget.

The structure of lace

It is important to understand the structure of lace so that you can recognize different types. Knowing how lace is structured will also help you to choose the lace that best suits the design of your garment.

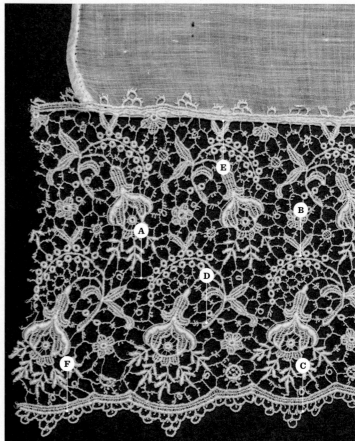

A. Bobbinet/net ground: The base of the lace, here made using a hexagonal pattern.

B. Clothwork/mat/plain work: The background is completely filled in to look like cloth.

C. Half stitch/gauze stitch/satin stitch: The net ground is half filled in to suggest depth.

D. Filling: Decorative, netlike stitches between sections of clothwork.

E. Cordette: A yarn used to outline the clothwork motifs. It can be a fine yarn, as on this piece of Chantilly lace, or heavier, as on Alençon lace.

F. Picots: The twisted threads along the edge of the lace. One of the hallmarks of a quality lace are fine picots, so they should not be trimmed off.

A. Brides/bars: The bars linking the design motifs together. The simplest bars or brides are made with a pair of twisted threads.

B. Brides ornées: Bars made with a buttonhole stitch, often in a round shape.

C. Picots: Small loops made with the threads.

D. Brides picotées: Bars with picot loops along their length.

E. Footside: The sturdy edge of the trim, designed to be sewn to fabric.

F. Headside: The decorative edge of the trim.

Types of lace

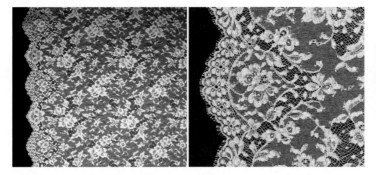

Chantilly lace: Originally made with bobbins in Chantilly, France, this is one of the most popular laces. Chantilly lace is lightweight and has a delicate appearance, with a fine net ground, filling stitches, half stitches, and precise clothwork. A feature of this lace is the fine, thin yarn, called cordonnet, that outlines the clothwork motifs. Design motifs feature flowers, leaves, bows, and swags of ribbons with scalloped weft edges. The even length of picot edging, the filling work linking the leaves, and the straightness of the net ground are some of the indicators of a quality Chantilly lace. This piece is 35in (89cm) wide.

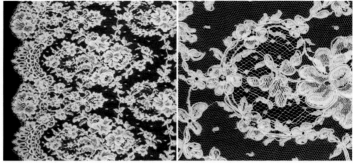

Alençon lace: Originally made in Alençon, France, as a needle lace, Alençon lace has many of the characteristics of Chantilly lace: a fine net ground, filling stitches, half stitches, and clothwork. The major design motifs, however, are outlined with a heavier cord than in Chantilly lace, creating a more three-dimensional result. Flowers, leaves, and swags are common design motifs for Alençon lace. This piece is 33in (84cm) wide. Alençon laces often have coordinating trims up to 8in (20cm) wide that can be used to create short sleeves or to edge hems.

Chantilly lace on point d'esprit net: Chantilly lace can also be made on a point d'esprit net (a background with woven dots) with or without the cordonnet. In this particular piece, the design motifs decrease in size and frequency from left to right. This piece is 53in (135cm) wide.

Guipure lace/Swiss chemical lace/burnt lace: Guipure lace is recognizable by design motifs connected to each other only by brides, rather than a net base fabric. This lace, which can be made of cotton, silk, or metallic threads, has a density and heft unlike many of the more delicate laces. Sometimes a lace is woven on a net fabric that is later burned away with a chemical, leaving behind the brides and design motifs characteristic of guipure lace. These laces, often called burnt or chemical laces, are guipure laces too. This piece is 18$\frac{1}{2}$in (47cm) wide.

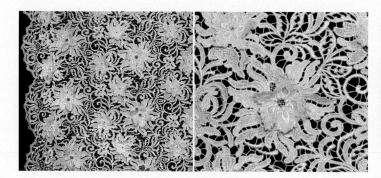

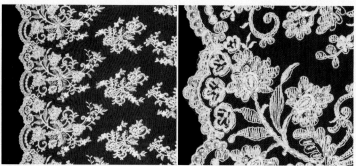

Re-embroidered guipure lace: This lace has an extra layer of lace flower petals anchored to the center of each blossom, creating a three-dimensional effect. This piece is 43in (109cm) wide.

Embellished lace: Lace can be embellished with beads, sequins, crystals, or ribbons. This is Schiffli lace that has been embellished with pearls, seed beads, and bugle beads. The embellishments can be sewn on with chain stitch, which, when cut, unravels easily, allowing the embellishments to be removed. Keep in mind that sequins and some beads have a very low melting point and may be damaged if ironed. This piece is 56in (142cm) wide.

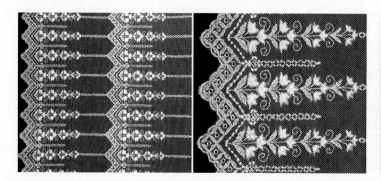

Schiffli lace: The Schiffli machine for making lace was developed in the late 1880s. Schiffli lace is usually made on an English net background and features embroidered motifs that are sewn with a satin stitch, imitating hand embroidery. (English and French nets are fine and soft, and quite strong.) This piece is 23in (58cm) wide.

Metallic lace: Metallic lace is made with metallic thread or a combination of metallic and polyester threads. This lace was made with silver and gold threads, but metallic laces are also available in a variety of colors. This piece is 50in (127cm) wide.

Cluny lace: Originating in the nineteenth century, this is said to be based on the designs of old laces held in Paris's Musée de Cluny. A feature of Cluny lace is the wheatear, which forms the spokes of wagon wheel motifs. Made with a stout cotton or linen thread, Cluny lace is often used to trim nightgowns, camisoles, and slips as it can withstand repeated washing in hot water.

Filet lace/lacis/net work/ darned netting: Originally a needlepoint lace, filet lace was embroidered on a knotted mesh or ground called réseau. When made by hand the design motifs were embroidered using stitches called point de reprise and point de toile, similar to darning stitch. Since the motifs are based on square mesh, filet lace often has a blocky feel to it. This piece is 5in (12.5cm) wide.

Cotton lace: This particular piece of lace was made with a soft cotton cord and designed to look as if it had been crocheted, but the cotton cords are actually held in place by very thin threads on the wrong side. The fabric is quite soft and spongy, with a three-dimensional quality. This piece is 36in (91.5cm) wide.

  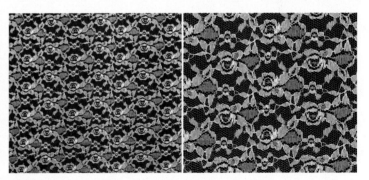

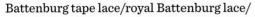

Battenburg tape lace/royal Battenburg lace/ Milanese tape lace/modern lace: Tape laces are made with flat fabric tapes that are sewn together with needlepoint lace stitches. Manipulated into varying shapes, the pieces are eventually all sewn together to create inserts or edgings for clothing and household goods.

Allover lace: Allover lace is the least expensive lace available. Made with plain selvages and no embellishments, allover lace often features a one-way design and frequent pattern repeats. This piece is 45in (114cm) wide.

Selecting lace

When you begin to choose the lace for your design, lay the pattern under the lace to ensure that the motifs work well with the shape. You can choose to use specific areas of a piece of lace, or several different types of lace to create different effects: some pieces of lace have areas that are densely covered with motifs, others have a scalloped edge that can be placed along a hemline. You can also select individual motifs from a lace to be cut out and appliquéd onto the garment.

A densely woven Chantilly lace spread over a bodice pattern.

A less densely woven section of the same Chantilly lace spread over the pattern.

A guipure lace spread over the pattern. This lace has a definite horizontal pattern, which could be used to draw attention to a small waist.

A re-embroidered guipure lace spread over the pattern.

An embellished lace spread over the pattern. Here a lace motif is placed at center front line on the bodice pattern.

The same embellished lace turned sideways and spread over the bodice pattern.

The scalloped edge of the Chantilly lace placed along a hemline.

The scalloped edge of the guipure lace placed along a hemline.

The scalloped edge of the re-embroidered guipure lace placed along a hemline.

The scalloped edge of the embellished lace placed along a hemline.

Combining lace with fashion fabric

If you are placing lace on top of a fashion fabric, consider the effect of the colors. A contrasting fashion fabric can be used to enhance the effect of the lace design, while fashion fabric in a similar color can be used to create a textured effect.

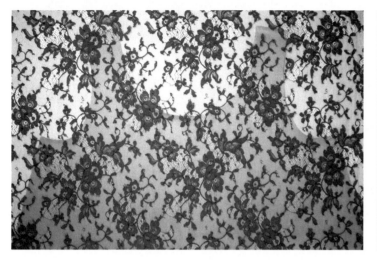

With a cream fashion fabric underlining, all design details of the lace are visible. If the color of the underlining fabric is very close to skin color the garment may appear to be made purely from lace.

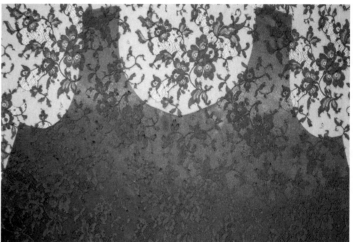

With a gray fashion fabric underlining, the details of the lace are just visible as a textured effect.

Identifying the elements of the pattern

Lace designs consist of several motifs working together to form a larger picture, or a single design motif repeated through the fabric. Identifying the design motifs in your lace can help clarify how best to place the motifs on your garment. Basting around a few of the motifs will help you identify the design elements

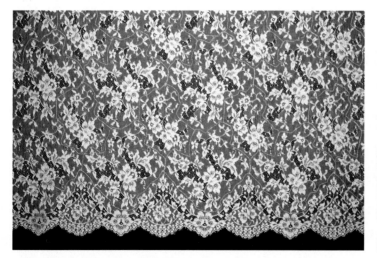

Here, the motifs have been outlined with white basting stitches. Note that there are two distinct interlocking motifs: a large motif and a smaller motif.

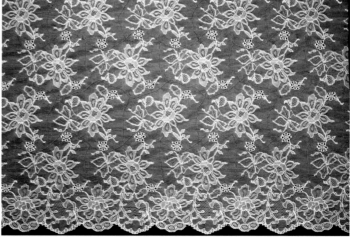

Here, the motifs have been outlined with orange basting stitches. Note that there is single repeated motif in a horizontal pattern, offset like a bricklaying pattern. This is a less expensive lace, with a coarser net ground, less opaque filling stitches, and less dense clothwork.

Placing lace motifs

Rarely will lace motifs fit onto a pattern piece exactly as you want them to; often some adjustments need to be made to make the motifs fit properly within the boundaries of the pattern. The malleability of lace means that the net ground and brides can be shrunk with steam and heat from an iron to ease the motifs into place.

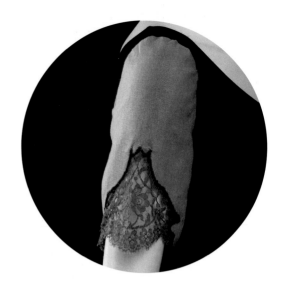

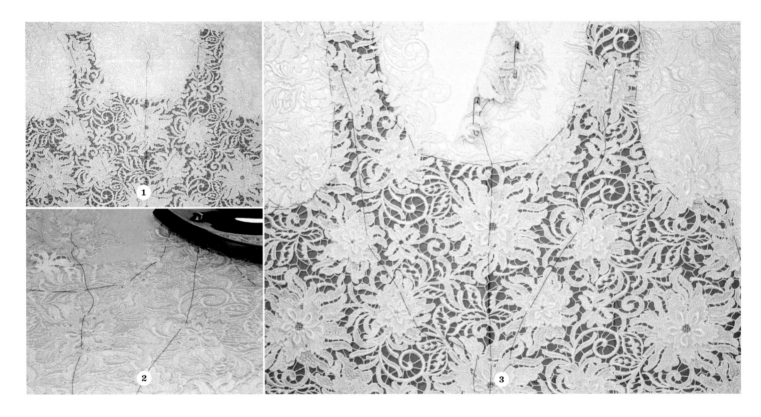

1 Here, a bodice pattern piece has been used. Place the lace over the pattern piece. Baste the centerline of the lace. Identify how the lace should fit around the neckline of the pattern and baste. In this case, the lace around the shoulders needs to be shifted to the right to balance the motifs.

2 Cut into the lace above the neckline to release some of the fabric. Cut in small increments until you are able to reposition the relevant motifs. There may be a few wrinkles in the net ground fabric or brides near the armhole; steam these wrinkles away and set the new motif placement by holding the iron over the lace. Do not put the iron down on the lace as that may flatten some elements.

3 Baste the seam lines around the outside of the pattern.

Sewing seams in lace

Lace seams can be sewn in two different ways. The lace can be treated as a fashion fabric and simply sewn together with the underlining in the usual way. Or, for a more couture finish, an appliqué seam can be used to arrange motifs so that the finished garment has no obvious seam lines. Appliqué seams can be done by machine or by hand.

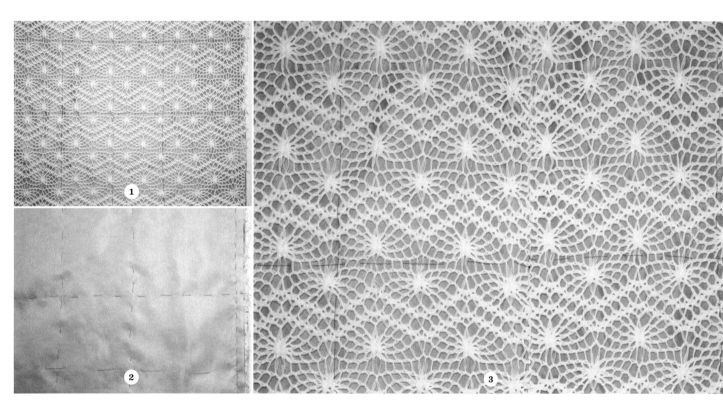

Treating lace as a fashion fabric

This is a good technique to use when the lace is being sewn directly into the seam. Here a thick cotton–polyester blend lace is used and the underlining is a slippery polyester taffeta.

1 Grid-baste the lace and underlining together with a white or matching thread. Here the basting was sewn with orange thread for clarity.

2 Hand-baste the seams together with small stitches (here sewn in green thread for clarity). When several layers of different fabric, such as thick lace and slippery taffeta, are sewn together by machine, the sewing machine presser foot and feed dogs will feed the fabrics through at slightly different speeds. Hand-basting the seams will ensure that the fabrics travel though the machine together.

3 Sew the seam. Press as sewn, then press the seam allowance open.

Lace appliqué seam—Matched motifs

One way to produce an appliqué seam is by matching motifs where possible in the lace at the seam. The seam line will then look like part of the cordonnet (the thread or cord used to outline the motifs) within the lace. Cut the seam allowance of the lace extra wide (2–4in/5–10cm) to allow for the finessing of the seam with this technique.

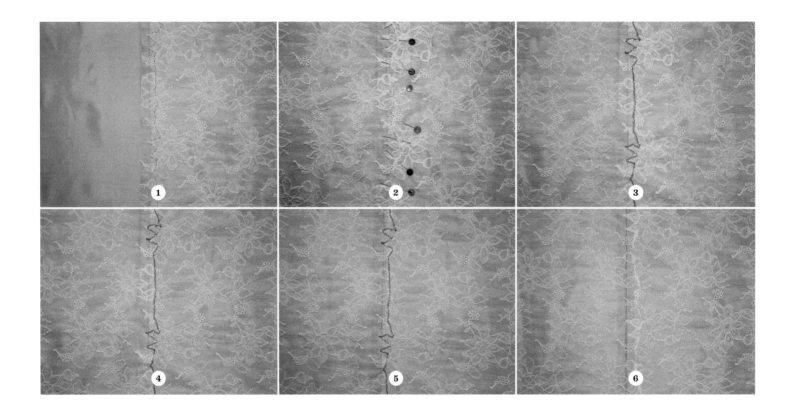

1 Sew the seam of the underlining. Lay one lace piece right side up on the right side of the underlining, matching all notches and seam allowances. If sewing a side seam, for example, the front piece of lace should lie on top of the back piece of lace—just as a side zipper overlap smooths to the back—so lay the back lace piece down first.

Look for a straight path through the lace motifs, while still following the cordonnet outline. Thread-trace the path in a matching color thread in case it gets trapped in the appliqué stitching. Here it is sewn in orange for clarity.

2 Lay the other piece of lace on the underlining, matching all notches and seam allowances. Match the lace motifs, if possible, and pin the two pieces of the lace together along the thread-traced line.

3 Using a narrow zigzag stitch, sew over the thread-trace line in a color to match the lace. (Here it is sewn in orange thread for clarity.) You will be sewing the lace to the underlining, so make sure the layers are carefully matched. Steam the seam with an iron and pat the lace flat with your hands; if the lace is unembellished, place a press cloth over it and press gently.

4 Carefully trim away the excess lace from the top layer, cutting as close to the zigzag stitching as possible. Be very careful not to cut the main piece of lace below.

5 Lift the top layer of lace up, exposing the under layer. Carefully trim away the excess lace from the under layer, cutting as close to the zigzag stitching as possible. Lay the lace back on the underlining and check the seam. In some places you may not be able to cut close to the stitching; it is best to leave such areas to avoid accidentally cutting the main lace fabric.

6 The lace appliqué seam, sewn in a white thread.

Lace appliqué seam—Interwoven motifs

When the lace motifs do not match at a seam allowance, interweave the motifs, using one motif from the right-hand side of the seam and another from the left-hand side and so on, letting the seam travel back and forth between the two pieces. Cut the seam allowance of the lace extra wide (2–4in/5–10cm) to allow for the finessing of the seam with this technique.

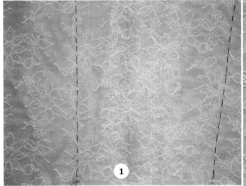

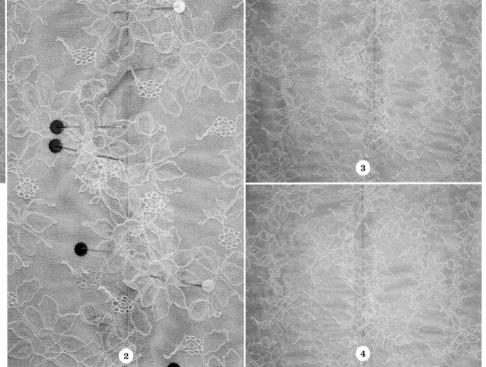

1 Sew the seam of the underlining. Lay one lace piece right side up on the right side of the underlining, matching all notches and seam allowances. Lay the other lace piece on the underlining, matching all notches and seam allowances. Here the grainlines are basted in red thread on both lace pieces to show that the grainlines and the lace motifs will not match at the side seam. The two pieces of lace should overlap along the the seam of the underlining. (If working on a side seam, lay the back lace piece underneath and the front on top.) The two pieces of lace overlap along the seam of the underlining.

2 Look at the lace motifs to identify the dominant motifs in the seam area. (Here, it is the flowers.) Carefully trim around these motifs only, leaving large seam allowances between them. Interweave the motifs, lifting the lace on one side of the seam and then the other in turn. Pin in place. Here the motifs from the right are secured with yellow pins and the motifs from the left are secured with blue pins.

3 Carefully trim away the fabric between motifs, making sure that there is always $1/4$in (6mm) underlap or overlap in the lace. A lack of underlap/overlap can lead to exposed "bald spots" of underlining. Thread-trace the path in the lace in a matching thread color in case the thread gets trapped in the appliqué stitching. (Here it is sewn in orange thread for clarity.) You will be sewing the lace to the underlining, so make sure the layers are carefully matched.

Sew the seam following the directions for Lace Appliqué Seam—Matched Motifs (Steps 4–6, opposite).

4 The interwoven lace appliqué seam, sewn in a white thread.

Lace appliqué seam—Hand sewn

Lace appliqué seams can also be sewn by hand using
blanket stitch. Cut the seam allowance of the lace extra wide
(2–4in/5–10cm) to allow for the finessing of the seam with
this technique.

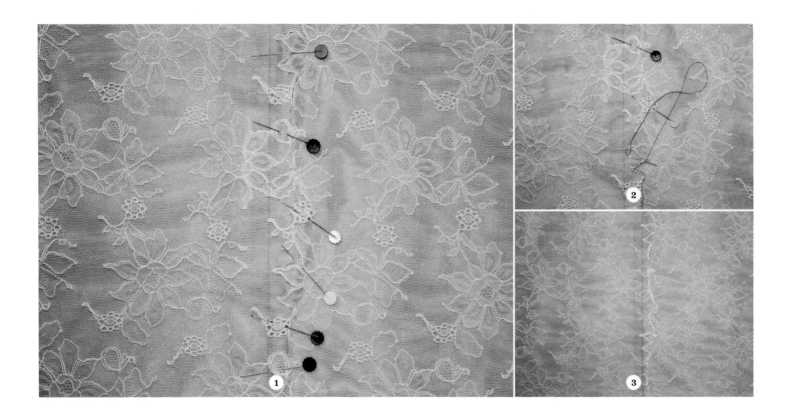

1 Prepare the seam following the
directions for Lace Appliqué Seam—
Matched Motifs (Steps 1–2, p. 268).

2 Using blanket stitch (see p. 306),
sew the lace pieces together. The
stitches should be very small and
quite close together. A ruler placed
between the lace and the underlining,
along the seam line, will prevent the
stitches from piercing the underlining;
this will also result in a lace layer that
floats on top of the underlining.

3 The hand-appliquéd lace seam sewn
with blanket stitch in a white thread.

Appliqué and cutaway

A piece of lace can be used to create a decorative border or a cutaway section in a piece of fabric, by first appliquéing the lace to the fabric and then cutting away the fabric behind the lace to reveal the pattern.

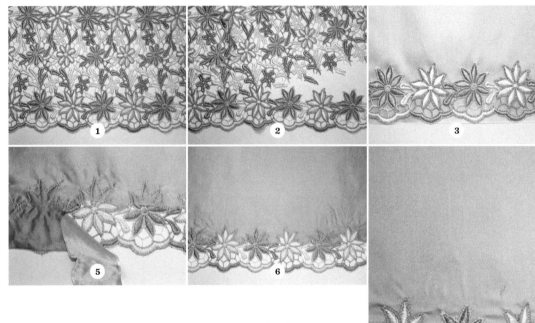

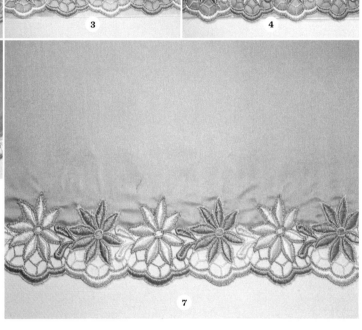

1 Thread-trace the path in the lace around the motifs you want to use with a matching thread. (Here it is sewn in orange thread for clarity.)

2 Carefully cut the motifs from the main piece of lace. Trim the brides or bars close to motifs, but be careful not to cut into the motifs themselves. Any stray brides and threads can be trimmed away after the appliqué process. Remove the thread tracing.

3 Lightly press the lace with a press cloth, making sure all the motifs are the same size and shape. Lay the lace on the backing fabric and hand-baste in place with a neutral-colored thread. (Here the basting is sewn in orange thread for clarity.)

4 Using a narrow but dense zigzag stitch, sew over the outline of the motifs. The zigzag stitch serves two purposes: to attach the lace to the base fabric and to prevent the base fabric from fraying after it is trimmed away in Step 5. Lightly press the lace with a press cloth to embed the stitches into the fabrics.

5 Working on the wrong side, trim away the backing fabric behind the lace. Turn the lace over and decide if you need to trim more; depending on the openwork of the lace, you can stop trimming at this point or continue, as shown in the next step.

6 To expose more of the lace appliqué, use very sharp scissors to carefully trim the base fabric from behind any fine details.

7 The completed lace appliqué border.

If you do not want to use a large panel of lace, or if your design calls for multiple styles of lace, then you can use lace trim. Usually sold on a reel or card, lace trim is available in many designs, sizes, colors, and fibers, from fine metallic threads, to subtle nylon or polyester threads, to heavy cotton yarns, and ranging from simple to sophisticated to flamboyant. All can be used as a single line of simple ornamentation anywhere on a garment—often to emphasize a design line or a feature, such as a seam, hemline, or collar edge—or combined in endless ways to produce unique decorative features: perhaps laid side by side down the front panels of a blouse to add texture and interest, or trailed across a dress to create a whimsical pattern.

3.11
Lace trim

Lace trims can be divided into categories based on their function—for example, appliqués, galloons, edgings, beadings, and insertions or entredeux—and then into families based on their design. This chapter provides an introduction to some of these, alongside some techniques used to incorporate them in a garment, but these are just a starting point; lace trims can used in so many ways that it is worth experimenting to create your own unique designs.

Types of lace trim

Lace trim families have common design elements. These cotton machine-made trims all feature a similar triangular edging detail.

From the top:

- Cotton beading, 1⅜in (3.4cm) wide.
- Cotton beading, ½in (1.3cm) wide.
- Cotton trim, ⅜in (1cm) wide.
- Triangular pointed trim, ⅜in (1cm) wide, including net edging.

Lace appliqué trims can be created on a very fine net or organza fabric and are designed to be overlaid on a fashion fabric.

From the top:

- Scalloped appliqué, 2in (5cm) wide.
- Schiffli appliqué, 6¾in (17cm) wide.

Galloons are scalloped on both edges. They often coordinate with a lace fabric and can be used to create short sleeves and for edging hems. This Chantilly galloon is 8in (20cm) wide.

Many galloons can be divided lengthwise, halfway between the scalloped edges, to create two appliqué pieces.

Edgings have one straight side (footside), which is sturdy and designed to be sewn to fashion fabric, and one decorative side (headside). Edgings range from ¼in to 6in (6mm to 15cm) wide. Wider edgings are called flounce laces.

From the top:

- Rayon machine-made trim, ¾in (2cm) wide, with overlapping half circles.
- Cotton machine-made trim, ⅞in (2.3cm) wide, with overlapping circles.
- Hand-crocheted trim, 1½in (3.8cm) wide, with clothwork stitches in a scallop design.
- Cotton machine-made trim, 1in (2.5cm) wide, with fine threads holding the flowers.
- Rayon machine-made trim, 2⅛in (5.3cm) wide, with delicate brides holding the motifs together.
- Venise lace trim, 3⅛in (7.8cm) wide, made from thick rayon or polyester yarns to create a three-dimensional lace without a net or organza background.

Beading lace trims are designed to have a ribbon or yarn threaded through their eyelets. Fabric-based beading is stronger than lace-based beading.

From the top:

- Nylon beading, 1½in (3.8cm) wide, with and without ¼in (6mm) ribbon. Often used on lingerie as the nylon's slim fabrication adds little bulk to garments.
- Insertion lace beading, 1⅜in (3.4cm) wide, with and without ¼in (6mm) ribbon.
- Cotton fabric beading, 1in (2.5cm) wide, without and with ⅜in (1cm) ribbon.
- Cotton fabric beading, 1in (2.5cm) wide, with and without ⅛in (3mm) ribbon.
- Polyester beading, ¾in (2cm) wide, with and without ³⁄₃₂in (2mm) rat-tail cord.

Insertion or entredeux laces are designed to be sewn between two pieces of fabric. Both sides are straight and edged with strong threads or excess fabric, meant to be hidden in the seams.

From the top:

- Crocheted trim, 2in (5cm) wide; sew on fabric surface.
- Cotton trim, 2in (5cm) wide; sew on fabric surface.
- Polyester and rayon insertion, 1½in (3.8cm) wide; finishes to ½in (1.3cm) of soutache braid when sewn into the fabric.
- Polyester insertion, ¾in (2cm) wide; sew on fabric surface.
- Polyester insertion, ⅝in (1.5cm) wide; sew on fabric surface.

- Cotton insertion, 1¼in (3cm) wide; finishes with ladder-bordered flowers, ⅞in (2.3cm) wide, exposed.
- Cotton fabric insertion beading, ⅞in (2.3cm) wide; finishes with ladder, ⅛in (3mm) wide, exposed.

Lace beading

Lace beading is available as a plain trim, an ornamented trim, and as a cotton trim called eyelet beading. It can be threaded with ribbon, or left unadorned. It can also be inserted between two pieces of fabric.

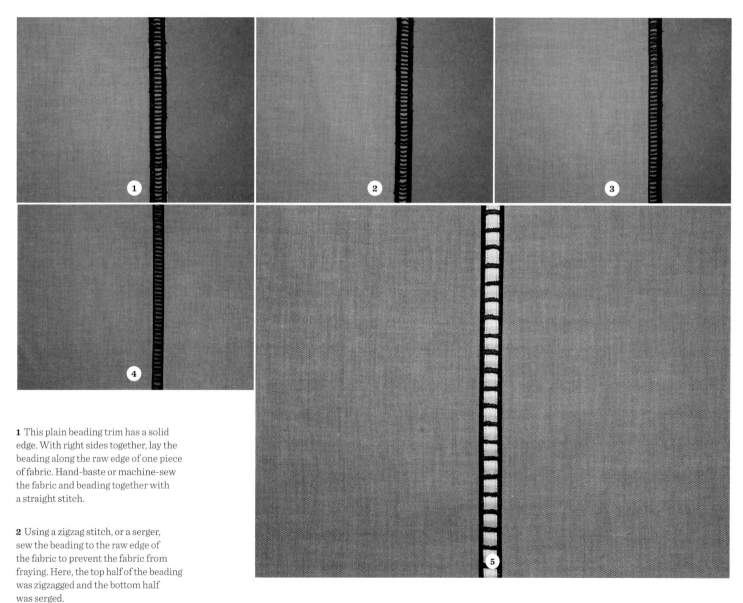

1 This plain beading trim has a solid edge. With right sides together, lay the beading along the raw edge of one piece of fabric. Hand-baste or machine-sew the fabric and beading together with a straight stitch.

2 Using a zigzag stitch, or a serger, sew the beading to the raw edge of the fabric to prevent the fabric from fraying. Here, the top half of the beading was zigzagged and the bottom half was serged.

3 Press the beading as stitched and then press again with the beading opened out from the fabric.

4 Repeat Steps 1–3 to sew a piece of fabric to the other side of the beading.

5 The beading can be left open or filled with a ribbon, as above.

Eyelet lace insertion

Lace insertion trim can be added to fabric using either a zigzag stitch or a serger.

Using a zigzag stitch

This lace trim has small eyelets along both sides. A zigzag stitch will overlock the raw edge of the fabric to keep it from fraying, so the trim can be added to fabric pieces with no seam allowances.

1 Test the zigzag stitch length on a scrap of fabric until the needle enters each eyelet of the trim on the "zig." Here, above the marked line, the stitches are too far apart, or too long; below the line, the stitches match the holes. Adjust the width of the stitches to extend just slightly beyond the width of the solid edge of the trim.

2 Lay the trim just overlapping the raw edge of one piece of fabric. The solid edge of the trim should lie on the fabric and the holes should be off the fabric. Join the trim and the fabric with the zigzag stitch.

3 Repeat Step 2 with the other piece of fabric on the other side of the trim, shown here stitched with white thread.

Using a serger

This eyelet lace insertion trim is embroidered on cotton fabric. Often there is a fabric flange on both sides of the eyelets; using a serger to attach the eyelet lace allows the portion of the fabric flange that is not needed to be trimmed away as the lace trim is sewn to the fabric.

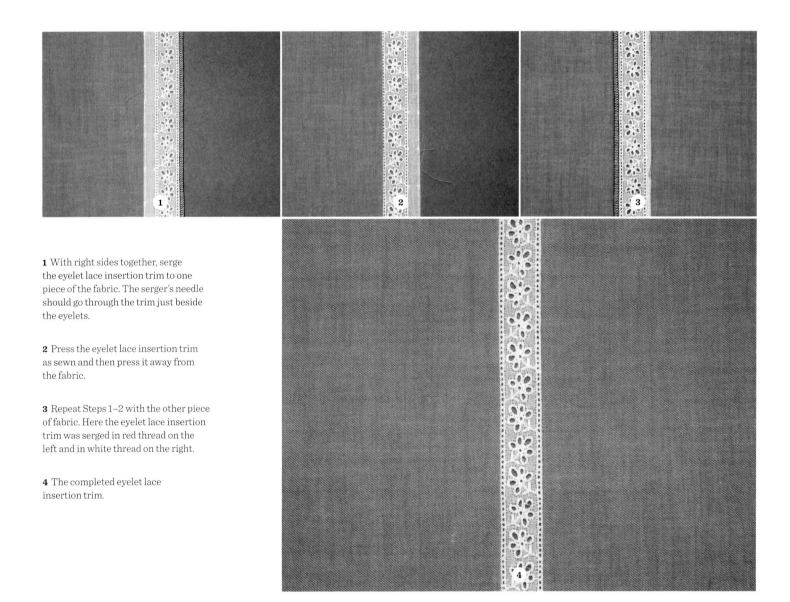

1 With right sides together, serge the eyelet lace insertion trim to one piece of the fabric. The serger's needle should go through the trim just beside the eyelets.

2 Press the eyelet lace insertion trim as sewn and then press it away from the fabric.

3 Repeat Steps 1–2 with the other piece of fabric. Here the eyelet lace insertion trim was serged in red thread on the left and in white thread on the right.

4 The completed eyelet lace insertion trim.

Adding lace to beading

Lace trim can be sewn to beading to create a larger customized trim. The trim can be sewn to the beading by hand, or by machine using a straight stitch or a zigzag stitch. Here a straight machine stitch is used. The beading has a fabric flange that is trimmed away in Step 5.

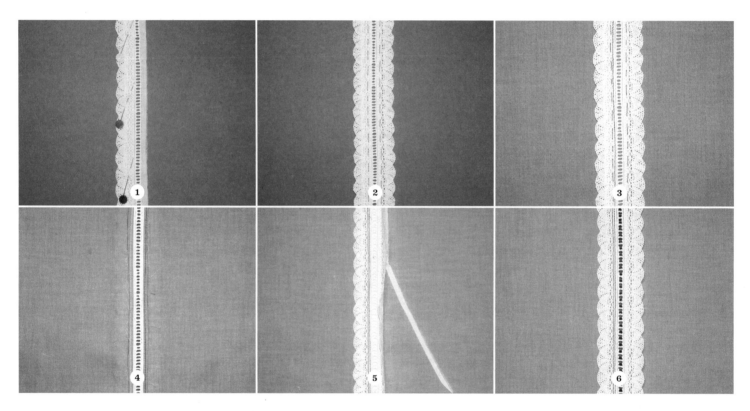

1 Lay the beading on a table. Pin a piece of lace trim to the fabric portion of the beading, butting it up to the thread of the beading.

2 Pin another piece of lace trim to the other side of the beading, matching the trims from one side to the other. Hand-baste both rows of lace trim to the beading. Pin the basted trim to the fashion fabric, centering the beading on the design's lace trim placement guideline.

3 Sew the trim and beading, right side up, to the right side of the fabric. Here the left side is stitched in orange thread for clarity and the right side is stitched in white thread.

4 Working on the wrong side, cut through the fashion fabric only, along the centerline of the beading. Press the fabric open to expose the beading.

5 Working on the right side, sew another line of stitches $1/16$in (1mm) out from the first line of stitches to hold the flaps of the fabric window in place. Fold the lace trim toward the beading and trim away the cotton fabric flange from the edge of the beading.

6 The completed lace and beading insertion, sewn in orange thread on the left and white thread on the right.

Mitering a corner with lace trim

When turning a corner trimmed with lace, miter the lace for a neat finish.

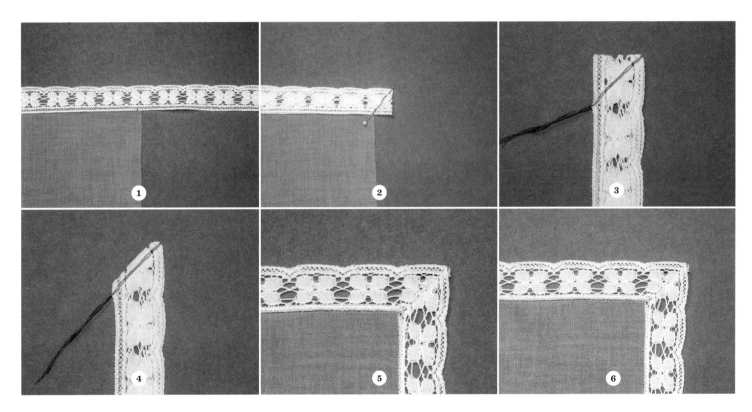

1 Mark the lace at the corner along the footside (straight edge).

2 Fold the lace and, from the footside, place a pin across the lace at an angle. Here a 45° angle was marked along the pin for a 90° corner.

3 Starting at the footside edge, sew along the pin-marked line using a small stitch of 1.5mm (15 spi). At the headside (decorative edge), with the needle down, pivot the lace and sew back to the footside. Here, the lace has been sewn in orange thread for clarity.

4 Trim the excess lace. Open the lace and press the seam allowance either to one side or open.

5 Sew the lace to the fabric.

6 The completed mitered corner.

Fitting lace around a curve

When sewing lace trim, or any other trim, to a corner, you must gather the footside (straight edge) as you sew it to the fabric, leaving sufficient length of trim at the headside (decorative edge) to go around the corner without straining. Here the measurement along the footside of the final lace trim is 10in (25cm); the measurement along the headside of the lace is $10\frac{1}{2}$in (26.5cm).

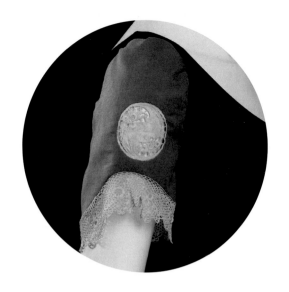

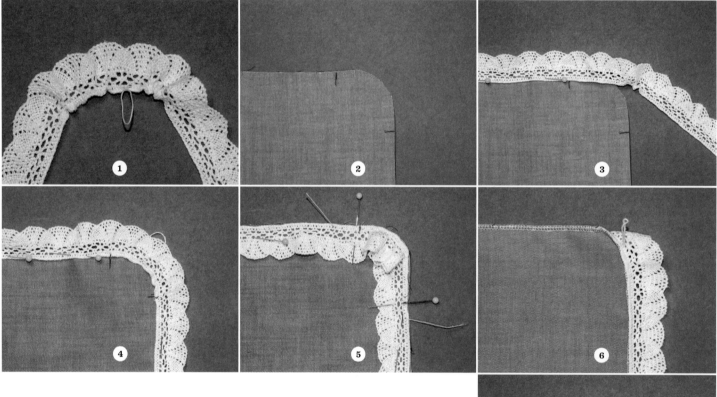

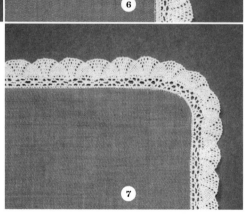

1 Many lace trims have gathering thread along the footside. On the wrong side of the trim, look for a protruding stitch with a thread running through it. If your trim does not have this, hand-sew a gathering stitch in the area where the trim will go around the corner.

2 Mark the start and end of the curve on the fabric.

3 Pin the lace trim in place up to the start mark. Gently pull the gathering thread until the trim curls around the corner, with the headside lying flat on the table.

4 Mark the lace trim at the start and end of the curve with a pin, matching the marks on the fabric.

5 Remove the lace trim and pin to the fabric with right sides together, matching the marks and pins around the curves. Note that the gathered lace in the corner is very dense. Hand-baste the trim around the corner.

6 Sew the trim to the fabric. (Here, the trim was serged.) Thread the loop of gathering thread into a tapestry needle. Slide the needle between the serger stitches, hiding the gathering thread.

7 The completed lace-trimmed corner.

Scallops

Rounded fabric scallops and triangular Vandykes can be made to lie behind a lace trim or to stand alone as decorative features. Here the scalloped edge partially backs a lace trim. Experiment with different sized circles and ellipses to find the best decorative effect for your design.

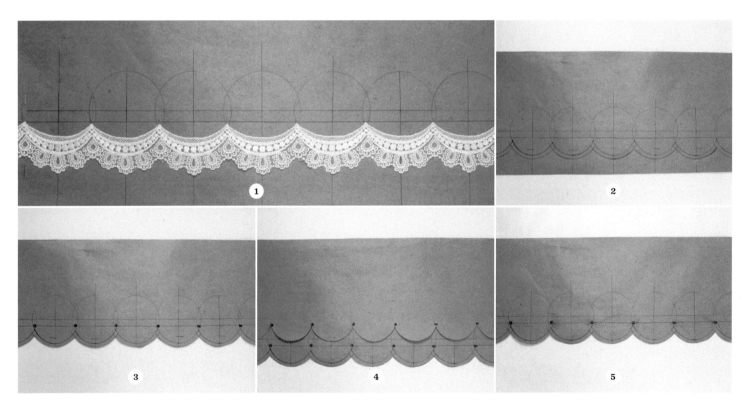

1 Staple together two pieces of pattern paper so that you can make two copies of the pattern. If you are creating a backing, measure the scallops of the trim, or create your own design. Scallops can be made from a section of a circle, or as part of an ellipse. Try to place the circles so that the intersection between them allows for two short stitches.

The trim here is placed so that the denser embroidered edge will sit on the bottom of the scalloped fabric backing, while the lower scalloped edge of the lace will hang freely.

2 Once the scallops have been drawn, staple each scallop in the pattern to prevent the two paper layers from shifting when you cut them out. Add a $1/4$in (6mm) seam allowance to the bottom of the scallops.

3 Cut out the paper patterns. At the intersections between two scallops, poke a hole in the paper patterns with an awl or stiletto. The holes will provide a reference point when you transfer the pattern to the fabric.

4 Separate the paper patterns. Remove the $1/4$in (6mm) seam allowance from the second paper pattern, which has fewer pencil or pen marks on it. This pattern will be used for the pressing pattern in Step 7.

5 Place the paper pattern with the seam allowance on the fabric. Cut out the scallops. Sew tailor's tacks at each hole. Repeat with the lining fabric. Here silk organza was used as a lining fabric and the tailor's tacks sewn in orange thread for clarity.

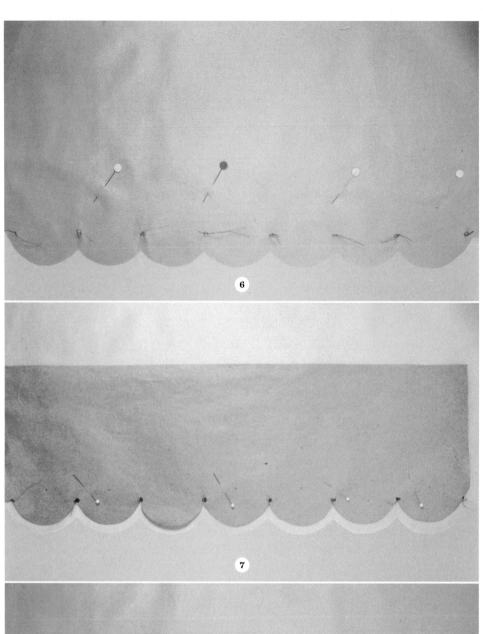

6 Place the lining fabric on the fashion fabric, right sides together. Pin the layers together.

7 Pin the pressing pattern to the lining fabric, using the tailor's tacks to help with positioning.

8 Draw the seam line on the lining with chalk or a heat-erasable pen.

BACKING LACE OR A TRIM WITH AN IRREGULAR EDGE

When backing lace or a trim with an irregular edge, the same techniques used for symmetrical scallops are helpful.

1 *Pin the pressing pattern onto the lining fabric, using tailor's tacks to help with positioning.*

2 *Draw the seam line onto the lining with chalk or a heat-erasable pen.*

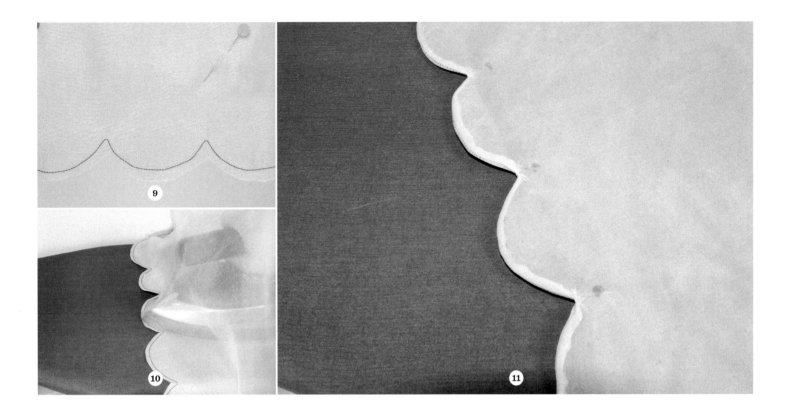

9 Sew the scallops using a stitch length of 1.5–2mm (12–15 spi); the short stitch length will give you better control around the curves. At the intersection of the scallops, sew two horizontal stitches, rather than pivoting; this will help the intersection lie flatter.

10 Trim the seam allowance to $^1/_8$in (3mm). Press the scallops flat, as sewn, to embed the stitches. Keeping the scallops flat on the ironing board, lift the lining fabric and gently slide the tip of the iron into a scallop. Move the tip of the iron over and along the stitching line, letting the lining fabric move as

needed but keeping the fashion fabric flat. This will press the seam open along the stitching line.

11 Clip the seam allowance around the curves and directly into the intersection. Turn the fabrics right

side out. Slide the pressing pattern in between the fashion fabric and the lining. Use the curved edge of the pattern to help press the scallops, rolling the seam line slightly to the back.

Adding lace trim to scallops

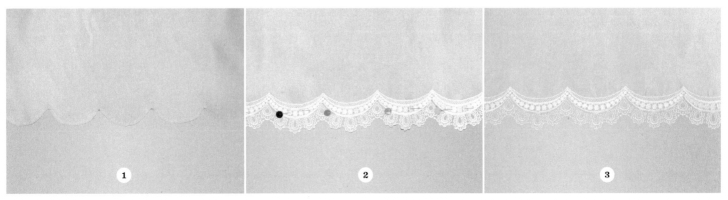

1 The completed scallops.

2 Pin the lace trim to the scalloped fabric. Sew the trim to the fabric by hand or machine.

3 The completed scallops with the added lace trim.

Lacing is the oldest known form of sewing; early garments were made from animal skins laced together to form body coverings. As sewing became more sophisticated, the holes made for lacing were reinforced with thread to protect them from wear and tear; these bound holes eventually became known as eyelets.

In modern dress, eyelets are sewn, or are made from a single piece of metal inserted into a small hole in the fabric and then hammered or crimped flat. The barrel of some eyelets is scored, so when they are pressed or hammered onto the fabric, the sections split open and curl into the fabric like claws.

3.12
Eyelets, grommets, and lacing

Grommets protect a larger hole from abrasion. They are made from two pieces: a barrel and a flat washer. When the grommet is pounded or pressed flat, the barrel collapses onto the washer to cover the fabric edge in metal. The barrel of a grommet is not scored.

There are many different lacing patterns to use with eyelets or grommets, including the criss-cross, over-and-under, and single-helix styles shown in this chapter.

Tools

The tools needed for "setting," or inserting, eyelets and grommets are often sold with them as kits. Plastic eyelets, like those found on sneakers, require special plastic setting equipment. You can also purchase eyelets and tools separately. The most common eyelet used in corset construction is the #00 size. The inside diameter of the eyelet corresponds to the size of hole required, the length under the flange corresponds to the thickness of the fabric, and the flange diameter corresponds to the diameter of the circle of fabric covered by metal. You can also purchase eyelets in the form of ready-made tapes: lacing tape is a twill tape with the eyelets preset, and eyelet tape is a heavy-duty cotton tape with the eyelets preset next to a casing for boning.

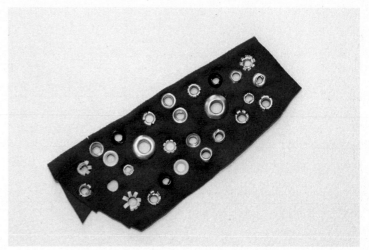

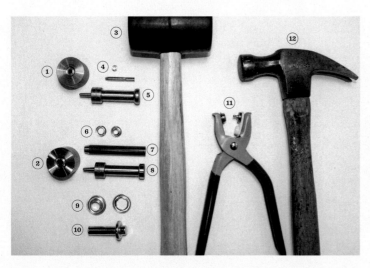

1. Eyelet anvil
2. Grommet anvil
3. Rubber mallet
4. #00 eyelet and hole punch
5. Eyelet setter
6. #0 grommet and washer
7. #0 hole punch
8. Grommet setter
9. #2 self-piercing grommet and washer
10. Self-piercing grommet setter
11. Eyelet pliers (these can be used with the anvil holding the right side of the eyelet and with the male setter on top, or vice versa)
12. Hammer

Before you work on your garment, test your eyelet pliers or setter and mallet on fabric scraps. You will need to test the thickness of the fabrics against the height of the eyelet's barrel, and judge whether eyelet pliers or a mallet and setter will work better with your eyelet-and-fabric combination.

EYELET SIZES			
Eyelet size	Hole diameter (decimal inch)	Hole diameter (fraction inch)	Hole diameter (cm)
#0	0.275	$9/32$	0.70
#00	0.215	$7/32$	0.55
$1/8$in	0.125	$1/8$	0.32
$3/32$in	0.094	$3/32$	0.24

GROMMET SIZES			
Grommet size	Hole diameter (decimal inch)	Hole diameter (fraction inch)	Hole diameter (cm)
#00	0.188	$3/16$	0.48
#0	0.25	$1/4$	0.64
#1	0.281	$9/32$	0.71
#2	0.375	$3/8$	0.95
#3	0.438	$7/16$	1.11
#4	0.5	$1/2$	1.27
#5	0.625	$5/8$	1.59
#6	0.813	$13/16$	2.07

Eyelets

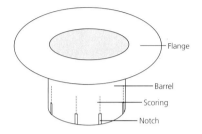

Flange

Barrel

Scoring

Notch

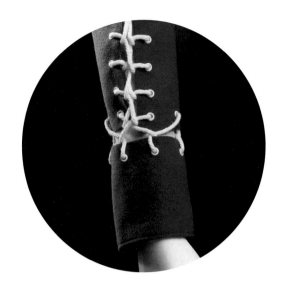

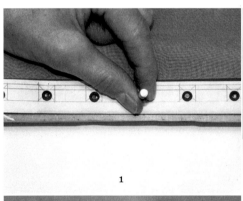

1

2

3

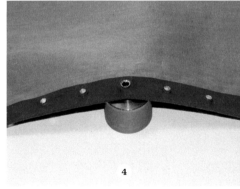

4

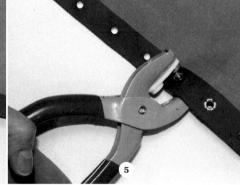

5

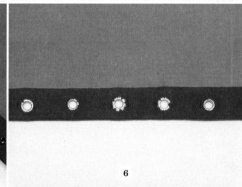

6

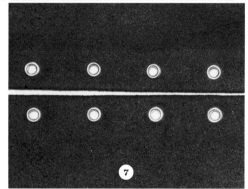

7

1 Make a paper pattern showing the eyelet placement. Prepare the fabric—here underlining was fused to the facings running down the center back opening of a bodice. The facings were then folded to the wrong side of the fabric. Place the fabric on a wooden board and position the paper pattern over the facing. Create the holes by hammering the punch through the fabric. The holes should be slightly smaller than the eyelet opening.

2 Place an eyelet in each hole from the right side. Position each eyelet in turn over the anvil beneath.

3 Insert the setter into the eyelet hole.

4 Lightly strike the setter with a rubber or wooden mallet to spread the barrel evenly. Increase the strength of blows until the barrel is crimped all the way around the hole.

5 Alternatively, use eyelet pliers, squeezing them to crimp the barrel.

6 The completed eyelets from the wrong side.

7 The two back panels with completed rows of eyelets.

Grommets

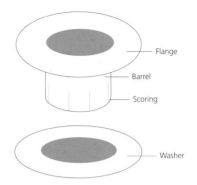

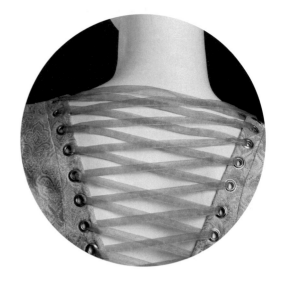

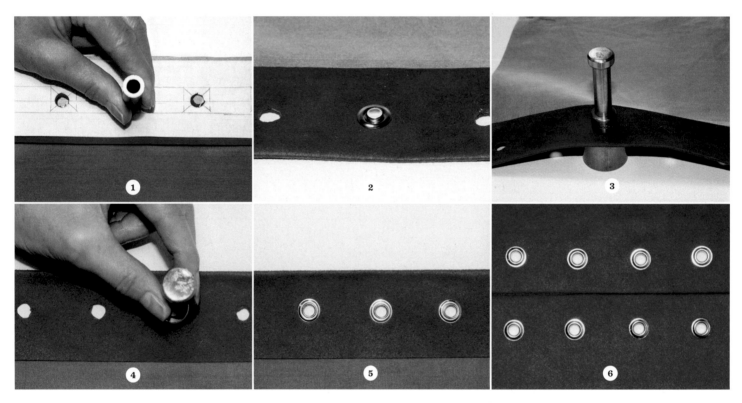

1 Prepare a pattern and create the holes in the same way as for eyelets (see Step 1, p. 287).

2 Insert a grommet through a hole from the right side. The hole should fit snugly around the barrel. Lay the washer on the barrel, on the wrong side of the fabric.

3 Place the anvil under the grommet. Insert the tapered end of the setter through the grommet and into the anvil center.

4 Hit the setter firmly with the mallet several times. This should flatten the barrel over the washer edge, making a firm, uniform circle of metal around the fabric hole.

5 The grommets on the wrong side.

6 The two back panels with completed rows of grommets.

Lacing

For hundreds of years, various parts of clothing were attached using lacing: hose were laced to pants, sleeves were laced to vests. The zipper was invented in 1851, and by the 1930s its use was widespread, but prior to this, pants, shirts, and dresses were either buttoned or laced up the front or back. There are thousands of lacing patterns; shown here are three of the most popular: criss-cross, over and under, and single helix.

Criss-cross

Criss-cross lacing from the right side.   Criss-cross lacing from the wrong side.

Over and under

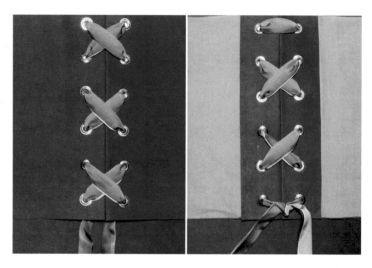

Over-and-under lacing from the right side.   Over-and-under lacing from the wrong side.

Single helix

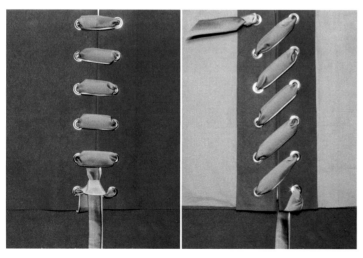

Single-helix lacing from the right side.   Single-helix lacing from the wrong side. Note the end of the ribbon at top left.

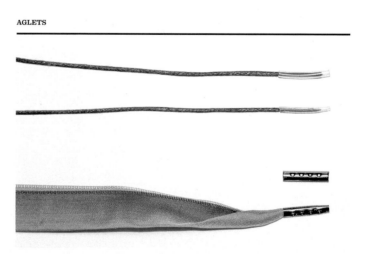

AGLETS

Aglets, or tips, can be added to lacing to make it easier to grasp and lace, and to keep the ends from fraying. For rat-tail cord, put a piece of plastic tipping on the end and then heat-shrink it with an iron or hair dryer to fit. For a thicker cord or ribbon, crimp a metal aglet onto the end.

Chain stitch, cross stitch, satin stitch, stem stitch, feather stitch, French knot—the names of ancient and modern-day embroidery stitches. Whether sewn in traditional patterns or contemporary designs, embroidery can adorn any garment. It can be sewn with cotton, rayon, metallic, shiny or matte threads—and with many other fibers, including ribbon. The embroiderer's skill is in controlling the entrances, pathways, and exits of the embroidery threads.

Embroidery, like sashiko and other forms of quilting, evolved from stitching originally used to mend, patch, and pad precious pieces of cloth. New cloth was not readily available, so clothes were patched when torn, padded in areas of heavy wear, and retailored for smaller bodies and according to changing fashions.

3.13
Hand embroidery

Once the basic work was completed, sewers began to view the stitching as decoration. Most ancient articles of clothing have rotted away, leaving us few physical examples of ancient needlework. When very old pieces of embroidery are found, the stitches are very similar to those we use today.

As decorative stitching evolved into embroidery, it also became an art form; around the world, people began decorating cloth with beautiful stitching. Embroidery today covers many decorative hand- and machine-sewing techniques: surface decoration, Chinese embroidery (in which the wrong side is as beautiful as the right side), counted-thread stitching, crewelwork, needlepoint, bargello, gold work, black work, and white work, to name just a few. Machine embroidery has become popular and accessible to many sewers. This chapter will only examine hand surface-work: stitches that sit on top of the cloth and do not change the weave of the base fabric.

Embroidery stitches

There are hundreds of embroidery stitches, many of which have multiple names. Often the name derives from an animal or plant that the stitch resembles, or the place where it may have been invented. For example, coral stitch, resembling a coral branch, is also known as German knot, beaded stitch, knotted stitch, and snail-tail stitch. All embroidery stitches are created from a few simple actions: for example, passing the needle over or under the thread, and looping to the left or to the right. These actions combine in various ways to form five basic stitch groups:

Flat or straight stitch: back, running, wrapped back, stem, satin, long and short, couching stitch, rosebud.
Cross stitch: cross, herringbone.
Looped stitch: blanket, buttonhole, feather, ribbon, spider rose.
Linked stitch: chain, twisted chain, lazy daisy.
Knotted stitch: Chinese knot, French knot, bullion, coral.

The same embroidery stitches can be classified into families, although many fall into several families: for example, chain stitch can be an outline or a filling stitch.

Outline, for outlining an object: running, back, stem, chain.
Border, for securing edges or highlighting an area: blanket, buttonhole, coral.
Independent (detached), for creating independent motifs: chain, lazy daisy, feather, Chinese knot, French knot, coral, spider rose, rosebud.
Filling, for filling an area: chain, satin, long and short, Chinese knot, French knot, coral.

Thread

WOOL

Wool embroidery thread (crewel wool), is a two-strand, twisted, fine thread. Needlepoint and tapestry yarns are heavier cotton and wool yarns that require a looser-woven base fabric so the needle and yarn can pass through the fabric without distorting it.

SILK, RAYON, AND METALLIC

Silk, rayon, and metallic threads are glossy, shiny, and lovely to use, but often are rubbed thin in the eye of the needle, requiring extra care while sewing.

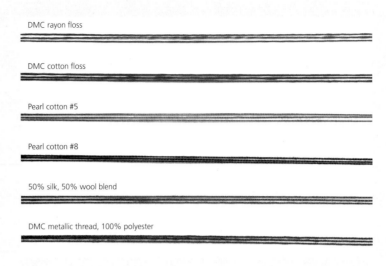

DMC rayon floss

DMC cotton floss

Pearl cotton #5

Pearl cotton #8

50% silk, 50% wool blend

DMC metallic thread, 100% polyester

A selection of popular embroidery threads.

COTTON

Six-stranded embroidery floss is often made from cotton. It is soft, glossy, and available in many colors. Depending on the design, the floss can be separated into fewer strands: three strands is the most popular, but any number of strands can be used to achieve the desired thickness and density. Mixing different color strands to achieve a different shade is also possible.

Cotton is also available as pearl cotton, which is heavier and more tightly twisted than floss, and will stand proud of the fabric surface. Pearl cotton comes in several weights and is sold in skeins or balls, but has a more limited color palette than floss. Floche is very fine cotton thread used for monograms and "heirloom sewing" work.

BLENDED THREADS

Blended threads come in many varieties, such as silk and wool blend.

Fabric

Embroidery can be sewn on any fabric. Sections of embroidery can even be sewn onto dissolvable interfacing to be placed on another fabric. The only limitation is that the fabric must physically support the embroidery: a dense garden of flowers on wispy 16-momme silk will fold in on itself, hiding all your work. Interfacing, organza, or voile can be placed under the base fabric before it is embroidered to help support fabric and embellishment.

Hoops

A standard embroidery hoop is circular, but any shape of frame can be used to hold fabric taut while you are sewing. Embroidery hoops all work the same way: one hoop is slightly smaller to fit inside the other and hold the fabric taut as you sew. The screw closure on the larger hoop allows it to expand or contract to fit the heft of the fabric.

An embroidery hoop stand holds the hoop off the table, leaving both hands free to guide the needle and thread. It will adjust the fabric surface to sit at any angle, including upside down. Note that stands come with a hoop of a particular size, and will only hold hoops of that size.

If a new hoop has rough edges, sand them with fine-grade sandpaper. When using delicate or impressionable fabric, like velvet, wrap the smaller hoop in strips of washed cotton to pad it; this will lessen any marring of the fabric. If the hoop is too large for your fabric piece, baste muslin to the edges until it fits the hoop (see Hand Quilting, p. 108).

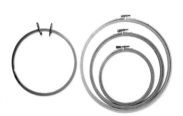

Hoops come in many sizes and are made from wood, plastic, or metal.

An embroidery hoop on a stand.

USING EMBROIDERY HOOPS

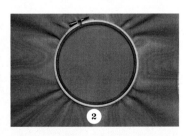

1 Place the smaller hoop under the fabric.

2 Place the larger hoop over the fabric and smaller hoop. Press into place. Tighten the screw to hold the fabric firmly. If the fabric grain is distorted in the hoop, remove the top hoop and adjust the fabric.

Needles

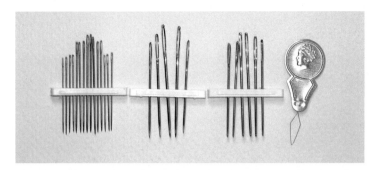

From left: embroidery needles, sizes 5–10; chenille needles, sizes 18–22; tapestry needles, sizes 18–21; and a needle threader.

Embroidery needles (also known as crewel needles) have a sharp point and long eye to hold multiple thread strands or ribbon. Chenille needles also have a sharp point, but a larger body and eye for working with heavier threads and yarns. Tapestry needles have a blunt point, a thick body, and a large eye. Chenille and embroidery needles are also used for ribbon work.

Choose the needle with the smallest eye you can comfortably thread. A needle threader is invaluable for guiding multiple stranded threads through the eye. The needle should make a hole in the fabric just large enough for the thread to pass through; a needle that is too large will mar the fabric.

Practice cloth

Always practice a stitch on a scrap of fabric before sewing on fashion fabric; some embroiderers call this practice piece a "doodle cloth." A doodle cloth will remind your fingers of the stitch steps and length, so you can start your sewing with perfected stitches and fewer guide markings.

PREPARING THE FABRIC FOR STITCHING

Mark the stitching line or pattern on the fabric. Mark stitch lengths along the stitching line if needed before hooping the fabric. If the marked line is not straight when the fabric is hooped, pull the fabric straighter or re-hoop.

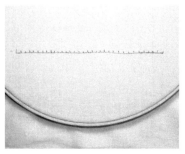

Starting and finishing

There are several ways to start and finish embroidery stitches. Shown here are techniques for knotting and creating a waste knot.

USING A KNOT

Knotting the yarn is not normally recommended for embroidery; knots add bulk and make a shiny spot on the right side when ironed over. However, unknotted thread work on clothing will unravel easily, making knotless work impractical.

KNOTTING

1 Working on the wrong side, knot the thread 3in (7.5cm) from the end (see Knotting Thread Ends, p. 29) and begin sewing. Keep the thread tail clear of all the stitching.

2 After sewing a line of stitches you will need to secure the end of the thread. Working on the wrong side, knot the thread close to the base fabric.

3 Weave the needle and thread through the last two stitches. This will keep the thread tail neatly contained and prevent unraveling.

4 Cut the thread. Return to the beginning of the line of stitches. Thread the thread tail through a large-eyed needle.

5 As in Step 3, weave the thread through the first two stitches and then cut the thread tail.

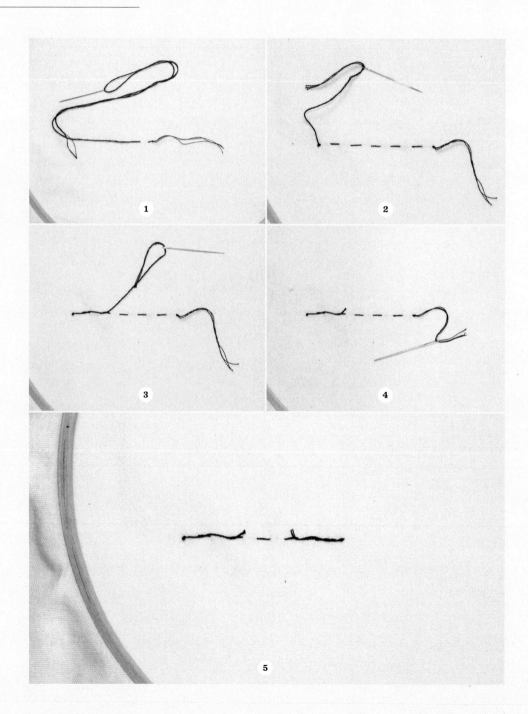

WASTE KNOT OR STITCH AWAY (AWAY STITCH)

1 When you are using a dense stitch like satin stitch, you can use the waste-knot or stitch-away technique. Make a knot in the thread, then make a small stitch on the right side of the fabric, away from the area of work. Alternatively, just make a small backstitch without the knot. (Here a small stitch has been made to the right of the flower petal.)

2 After making the first few stitches, cut the thread leading to the knot or small backstitch.

3 Remove the knot or small stitch and continue stitching over the thread tail.

4 To finish, working on the wrong side, weave the thread through a few stitches before cutting it.

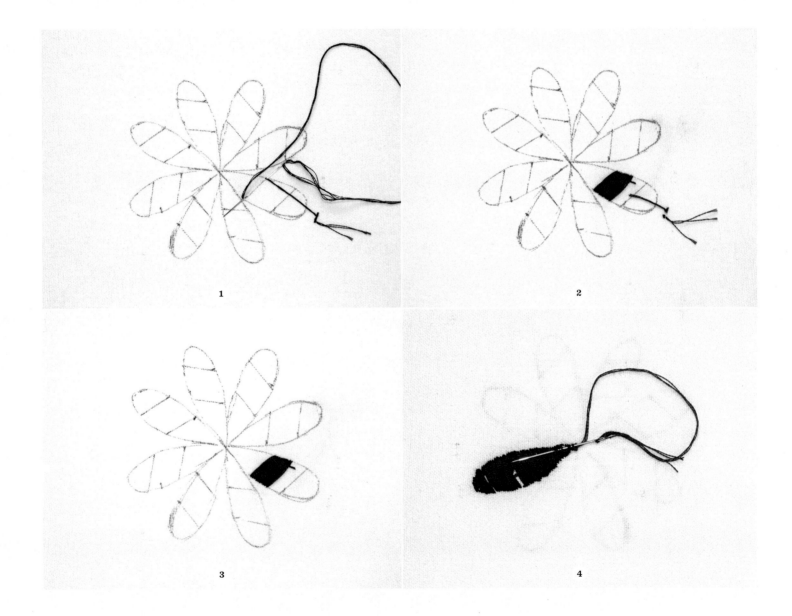

Running stitch / Damask stitch

Running stitch is the most basic of all embroidery stitches; it forms a dashed line of stitches sewn from right to left. Since half of the thread is on the wrong side of the fabric, use an opaque base fabric, or be prepared for the shadows of the stitches on the wrong side to show through on the right side.

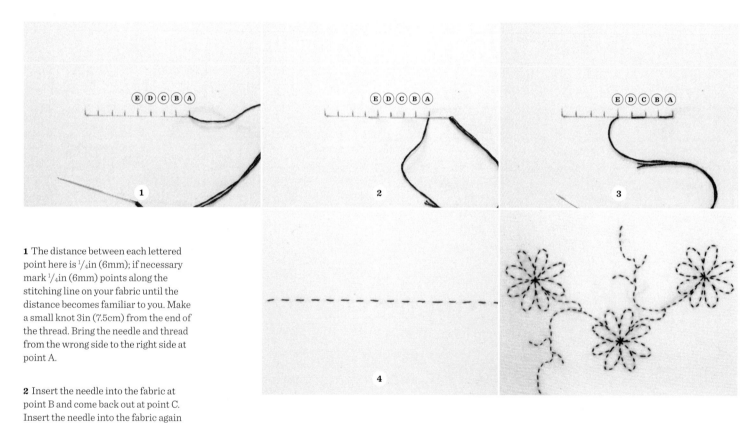

1 The distance between each lettered point here is ¹/₄in (6mm); if necessary mark ¹/₄in (6mm) points along the stitching line on your fabric until the distance becomes familiar to you. Make a small knot 3in (7.5cm) from the end of the thread. Bring the needle and thread from the wrong side to the right side at point A.

2 Insert the needle into the fabric at point B and come back out at point C. Insert the needle into the fabric again at point D and come back out at point E.

3 Pull the thread all the way through. Repeat Steps 2–3. Check that all the stitches are even and follow the stitching line. Knot the thread (see Knotting Thread Ends, p. 29).

4 The finished line of running stitches.

VARIATION

Lines of running stitches can be used to create different patterns, such as the brick pattern shown here.

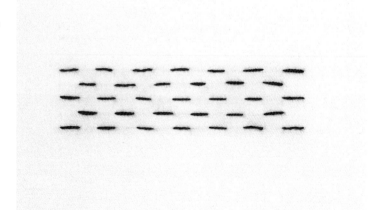

Backstitch / Point de sable

Backstitch forms a solid line of stitches sewn from right to left.

1 The distance between each lettered point here is ¼in (6mm); if necessary mark ¼in (6mm) along the stitching line on your fabric until the distance becomes familiar to you. Make a small knot 3in (7.5cm) from the end of the thread. Bring the needle and thread from the wrong side to the right side at point A.

2 Insert the needle into the fabric at point B and come back out at point C. Pull the thread through.

3 Insert the needle at point B and come out at point D, skipping past point C.

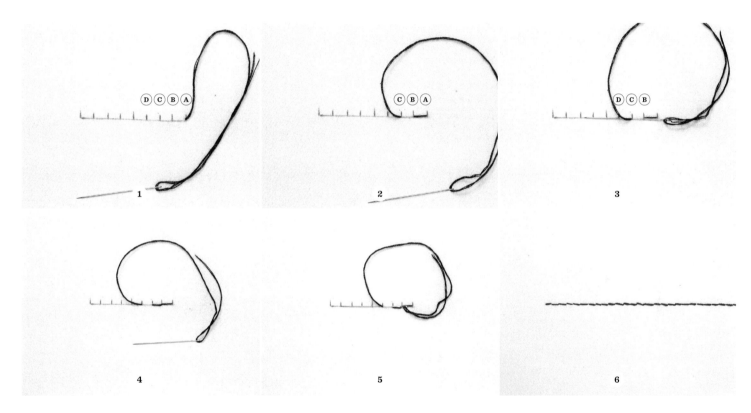

4 Pull the needle and thread through.

5 Continue inserting the needle at the front of the previous stitch and coming out two stitch lengths later. Check the stitching to make sure all the stitches are even and follow the stitching line. Knot the thread (see Knotting Thread Ends, p. 29).

6 The finished line of backstitches.

Wrapped backstitch / Whipped backstitch

Wrapped backstitch provides a lovely way to blend thread colors, producing a candy cane striped effect. It can also be used to even out irregular stitching, as the whipping blurs the in and out points of the base stitches; you can wrap a short stitch just once, but wrap a longer stitch twice to make all the stitches appear to be the same length.

1 After sewing a line of foundation backstitches, bring the needle with a second, contrasting thread to the right side of the base fabric at the beginning of the stitching line. Guide the needle under the first foundation stitch, without catching any of the foundation stitch thread. Pull the thread through.

2 Guide the needle under the next foundation stitch, again without catching any of the foundation stitch thread. Pull the thread through. The thread will wrap around the foundation stitch, creating the candy cane stripe.

3 Continue wrapping the foundation stitches. If you are wrapping a long line of backstitches, knot the wrapping stitch thread on the wrong side of the fabric every 3–4in (7.5–10cm); this will prevent the entire line of stitches from being distorted if the threads are accidently snagged. Check that all the stitches are even and follow the stitching line. Knot the thread (see Knotting Thread Ends, p. 29).

4 The finished line of wrapped backstitches.

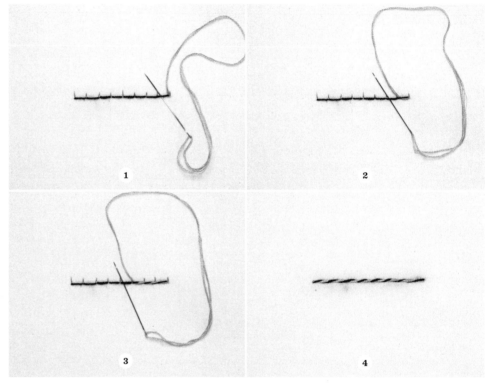

Stem stitch / Crewel stitch / South Kensington stitch / Stalk stitch

Stem stitch, worked from left to right, forms a denser line of stitching than backstitch, as each ¼in (6mm) of the stitching line is covered by two overlapping stitches. Stem stitch works well for sewing curved lines and filling in odd shapes.

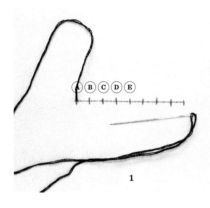

1 The distance between each lettered point here is ¼in (6mm); mark the increments along your stitching line until the distance becomes familiar to you. Make a small knot 3in (7.5cm) from the end of the thread. Bring the needle and thread from the wrong side to the right side at point A.

2 Insert the needle into the fabric at point C and come back out at point B. With each stitch, angle the needle upward from right to left, keeping the standing thread (the thread coming out of the fabric from the previous stitch) beneath the work area. This will keep the stitches identical.

3 Pull the thread all the way through.

4 With the thread coming from point B, insert the needle into the fabric at point D and come back out at point C, above the earlier stitch.

5 Pull the thread all the way through. Repeat Steps 4–5. Check that all the stitches are even and follow the stitching line. Knot the thread (see Knotting Thread Ends, p. 29).

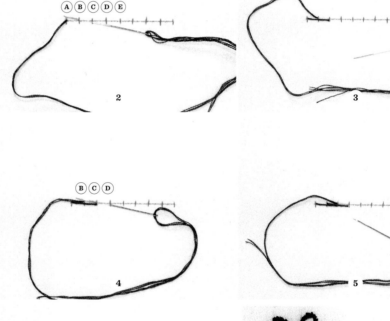

6 The finished line of stem stitches.

VARIATION

This sequence of stitches can also be worked with the new stitch sliding in below the previous stitch. Angle the needle down from right to left and keep the standing thread above the work area.

Chain stitch / Tambour stitch / Point de chainette / Twisted chain stitch

Chain stitch, made up of small, intertwined loops of thread, can be used along a curved line or as a heavy outline stitch.

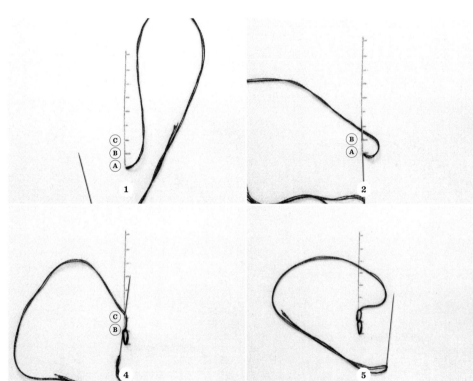

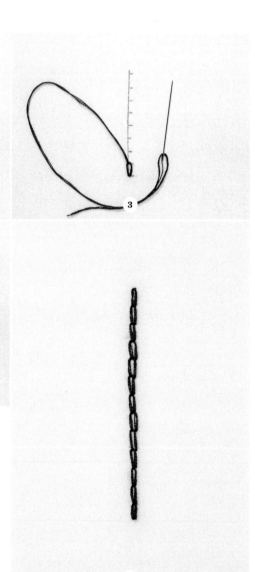

1 The distance between each lettered point here is ¹/₄in (6mm); mark the increments along your stitching line until the distance becomes familiar to you. Make a small knot 3in (7.5cm) from the end of the thread. Bring the needle and thread from the wrong side to the right side at point A.

2 Insert the needle into the fabric just to the left of point A and come back out at point B. Hook the thread under the tip of the needle, passing the thread from right to left. You can pass the thread from left to right, but be consistent in direction each time.

3 Pull the thread through, forming the first loop of the chain.

4 Insert the needle just to the left of point B, inside the loop, and come back out at point C. Again, hook the thread under the tip of the needle, passing the thread from right to left.

5 Pull the needle and thread through, forming the second loop of the chain. Repeat Steps 3–4 until the chain is complete. Check that all the stitches are even and follow the stitching line. Knot the thread (see Knotting Thread Ends, p. 29).

6 The finished line of chain stitches.

VARIATION

Twisted chain stitch is stitched in the same fashion as chain stitch, but the thread is passed under the needle from left to right, causing the loop to twist.

1 Insert the needle into the fabric just to the left of point A and come back out at point B. Hook the thread under the tip of the needle, passing the thread from left to right.

2 Pull the needle and thread through, forming the first loop of the twisted chain. Repeat Steps 1–2 until the twisted chain is complete.

3 Twisted chain stitch on the left and plain chain stitch on the right.

Chain stitch also forms the basis of lazy daisy stitch or detached chain stitch (see Ribbon Embroidery, p. 330).

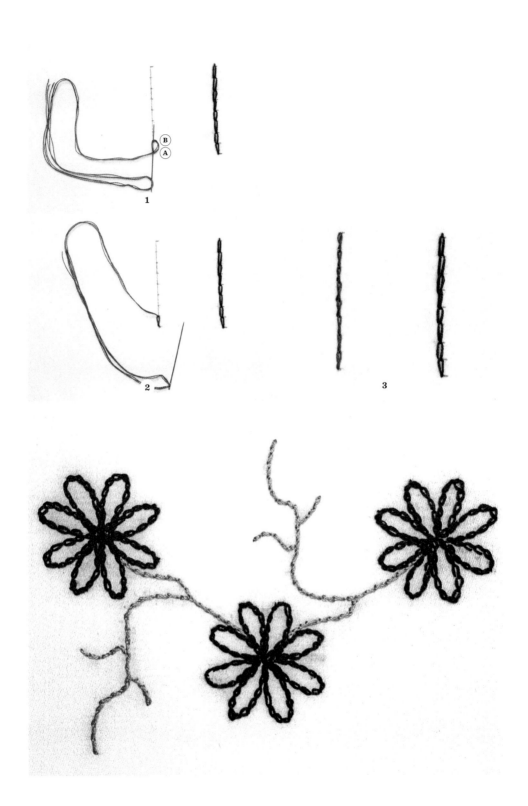

Cross stitch / Sampler stitch / Berlin stitch / Point de marque

Cross stitch can be worked in two different ways: sewing a row of backward-sloping stitches (\\\) along a row and then returning along the row with forward-sloping stitches (///), or sewing a row of combined stitches in the form of an X. Here the backward- and forward-sloping stitch method is shown.

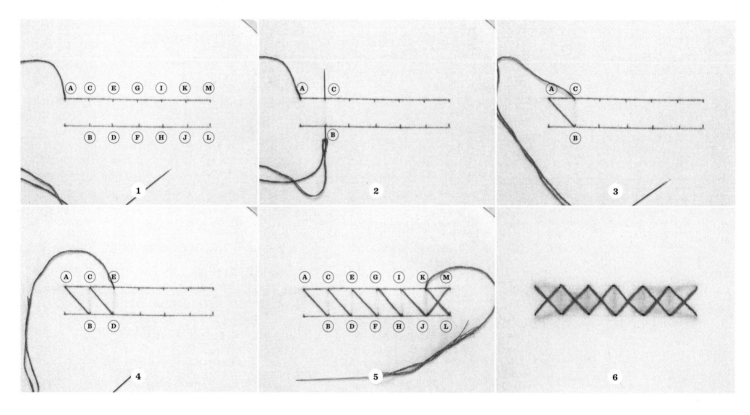

1 The distance between each lettered point here is ¼in (6mm); mark the increments along your stitching lines until the distance becomes familiar to you. Make a small knot 3in (7.5cm) from the end of the thread. Bring the needle and thread from the wrong side to the right side at point A.

2 Insert the needle into the fabric at point B and come back out at point C.

3 Pull the thread all the way through.

4 Insert the needle into the fabric at point D and come back out at point E.

Pull the thread all the way through. Repeat to the end of the stitching lines. When properly sewn, a ladder of stitches will appear on the wrong side.

5 Bring the needle and thread to the right side at point M, insert the needle into the fabric at point J, and come back out at point K. Pull the thread all the way through. Repeat back toward point A. A double ladder of stitches will now appear on the wrong side. Check that all the stitches are even and follow the stitching line. Knot the thread (see Knotting Thread Ends, p. 29).

6 The finished row of cross stitches.

VARIATION

Cross stitch can also be worked with a space between each of the crosses.

Herringbone stitch / Catch stitch / Mossoul stitch / Persian stitch / Russian stitch / Russian cross stitch / Plaited stitch / Witch stitch

Herringbone stitch, also commonly known as the catch stitch and widely used for garment hems, works well as a border stitch or as a filling stitch when densely sewn.

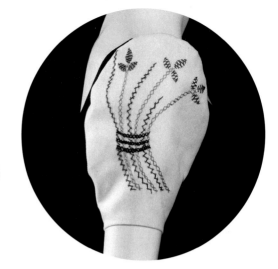

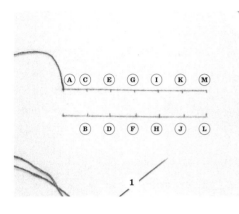

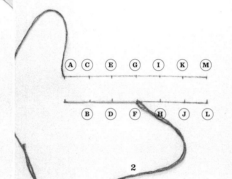

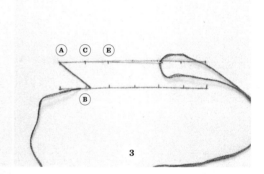

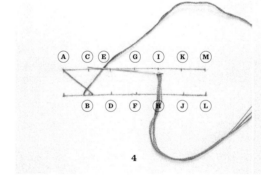

1 The distance between each lettered point here is ¹/₄in (6mm); mark the increments along your stitching lines until the distance becomes familiar. Make a small knot 3in (7.5cm) from the end of the thread. Bring the needle and thread from the wrong side to the right side at point A.

2 Insert the needle into the fabric just to the right of point B, coming out an equal distance to the left of point B, making a small stitch. Tuck the standing thread under the tip of the needle before pulling it all way through. You can let the standing thread lay over the top of the needle, but be consistent each time.

3 Pull the thread all the way through. Insert the needle into the fabric just to the right of point E, coming out an equal distance to the left of point E, making a small stitch.

4 Again, tuck the standing thread under or over the tip of the needle before pulling the thread all way through. Repeat Steps 3–4. When properly sewn, a ladder of stitches will appear on the wrong side. Check that all the stitches are even and follow the stitching line. Knot the thread (see Knotting Thread Ends, p. 29).

5 The finished line of herringbone stitches.

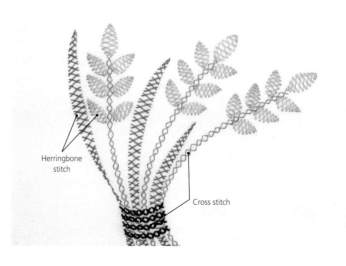

Herringbone stitch

Cross stitch

Feather stitch / Briar stitch / Plumage stitch

Feather stitch, as the name suggests, produces a feathery interweaving of thread. The tips can be spaced widely apart or tightly together, producing a transparent or opaque web of stitches.

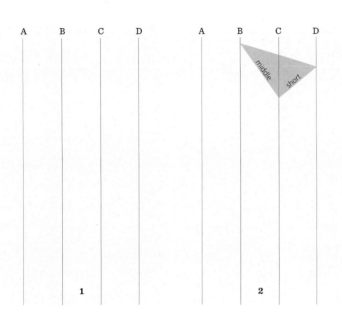

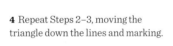

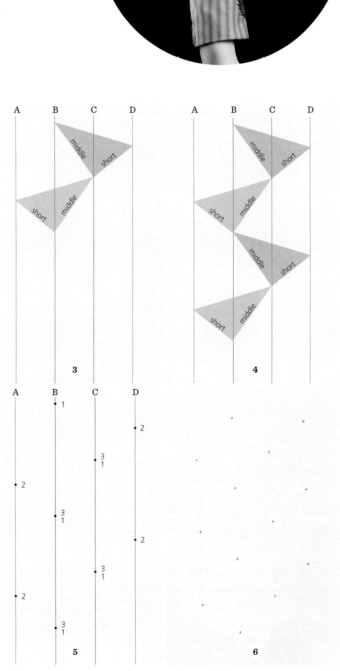

1 Make a pattern. Draw four equally spaced lines and label them A, B, C, and D. Here the lines are 6³/₄in (17cm) long and 1in (2.5cm) apart.

2 Draw a triangle with three unequal sides and angle it slightly between lines B, C, and D, with the longest side between B and D. Here the sides are: 1¹/₂in (3.8cm), 1³/₈in (3.5cm), and a top of 2in (5cm). Mark where the triangle touches the lines.

3 Copy the triangle, flip it over, and position it so that the triangles touch on line C and the other corners sit on lines A and B. Note that the middle-length side of the triangle stays between the two center lines. Mark where the new triangle touches the line.

4 Repeat Steps 2–3, moving the triangle down the lines and marking.

5 Label the marks as shown.

6 Transfer the dots of the pattern to the fabric.

7 Make a small knot 3in (7.5cm) from the end of the thread. Bring the needle and thread from the wrong side to the right side at line B, point 1. Insert the needle into the fabric at line D, point 2.

8 Bring the needle and thread back out at line C, point 3, keeping the thread under the tip of the needle.

9 Pull the thread all the way through.

10 Insert the needle into the fabric at line A, point 2. Come back out at line B, point 3, keeping the thread under the tip of the needle.

11 Pull the thread all the way through. Note that the needle goes to the wrong side of the fabric in the outside column and returns to right side of the fabric in the nearest inside column. Repeat Steps 10–11.

12 The finished feather stitch.

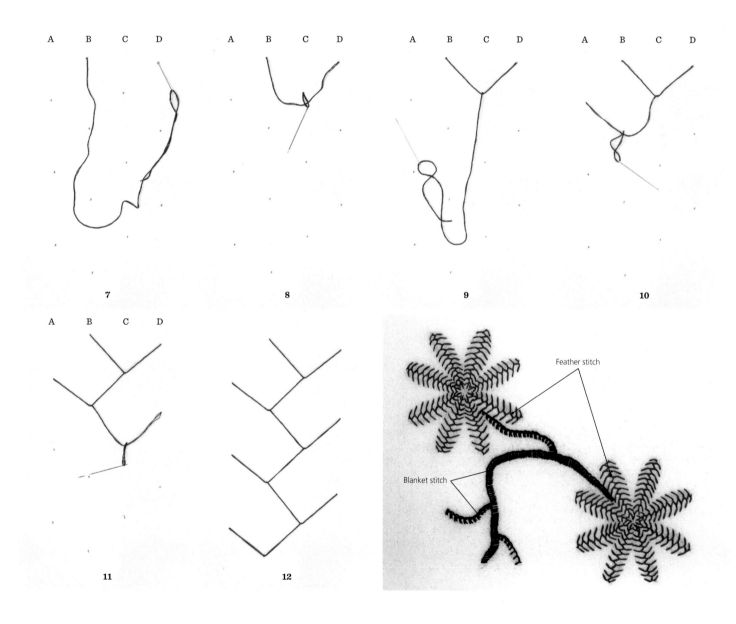

Blanket and buttonhole stitches

Blanket stitch, traditionally used to edge blankets, is a good border stitch and can also be used as a filling stitch. When sewn without space between the stitches, blanket stitch is called buttonhole stitch. Buttonhole stitch makes a dense line of stitches.

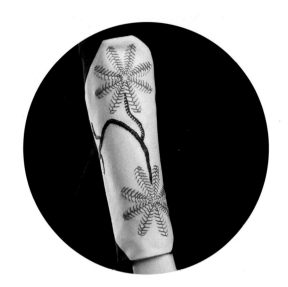

Blanket stitch

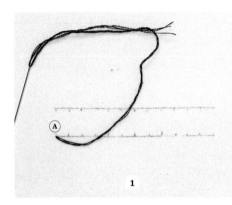

1

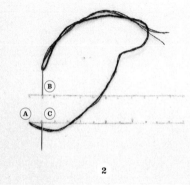

2

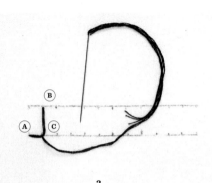

3

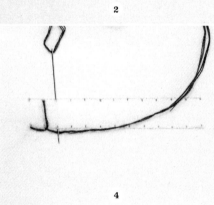

4

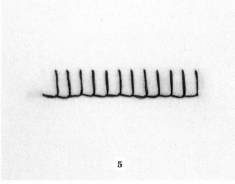

5

1 Make a small knot 3in (7.5cm) from the end of the thread. Bring the needle and thread from the wrong side to the right side at point A.

2 Insert the needle into the fabric at point B, then come back out at point C, catching the standing thread under the tip of the needle at C.

3 Pull the thread all the way through.

4 Repeat Steps 2–3.

5 A row of blanket stitches.

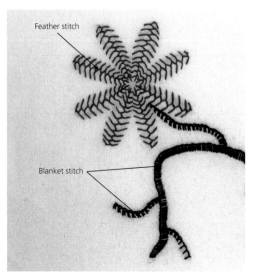

Feather stitch

Blanket stitch

Buttonhole stitch

If you are using buttonhole stitch to finish a buttonhole, place the looped edge along the centerline of the buttonhole.

1 You can sew buttonhole stitches around a piece of card stock to keep them the same height.

2 A row of buttonhole stitches.

3 A buttonhole hand-sewn with pearl cotton #5, which is stronger than embroidery floss and better able to endure the rubbing of a button.

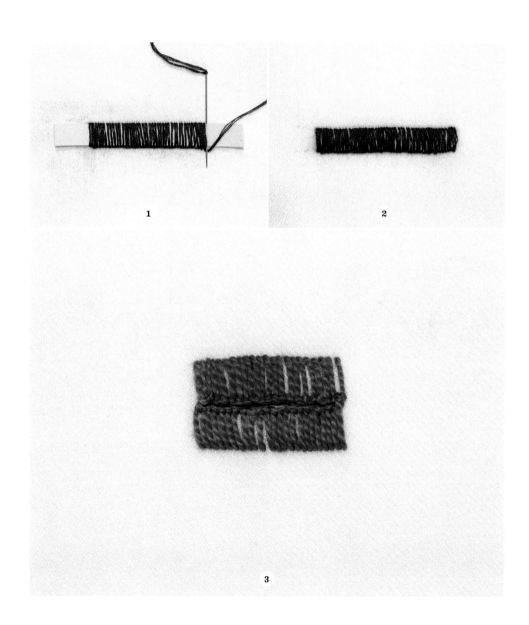

Satin stitch

Satin stitch is a filling stitch, as opposed to an outlining stitch. With this stitch, the threads are laid side by side until the shape is filled in.

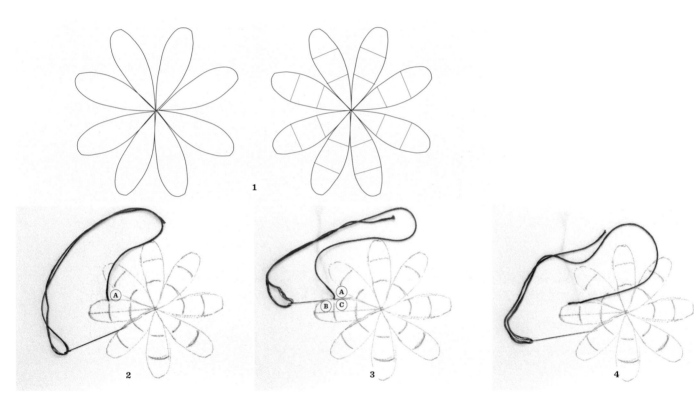

1 Transfer your pattern to the fabric (see Transferring Patterns, pp. 18–23). The flower petals in this design are quite large, so rather than make long, unattractive stitches, each petal has been divided into three portions.

2 Make a waste knot (see p. 295) or make a small knot 3in (7.5cm) from the end of the thread. Bring the needle and thread from the wrong side to the right side at point A.

3 Insert the needle into the fabric at point B, then come back out at point C, which is right next to point A.

4 Pull the thread all the way through.

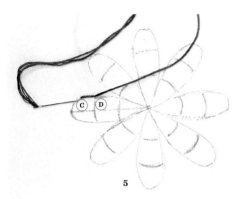

5

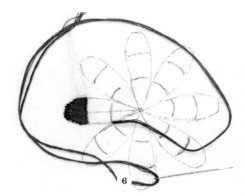

6

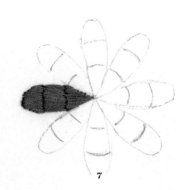

7

5 Insert the needle next to the previous stitch, at point C, coming out again next to where you just started, at point D. To see where to put the needle next you can lay the thread down on the fabric next to the previous stitch. The thickness of thread will indicate where the next stitch should be placed. Repeat Steps 3–5 until the shape is filled.

6 The first section completed. Sew the remaining sections in the same manner.

7 The first petal completed.

Long-and-short stitch

Satin stitch

VARIATION

Large petals can be divided in any manner. Here the petals were divided on a slant, which is a standard embroidery technique.

Long-and-short stitch

Long-and-short stitch is actually two stitches—one long and one short—repeated and interwoven to create a seamless blending of the stitches. This filling stitch is perfect for shading or subtle color changes within a shape.

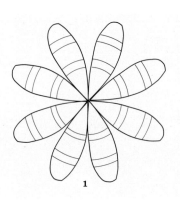

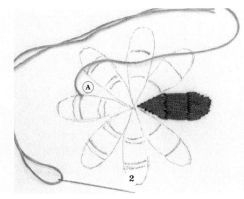

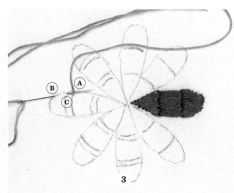

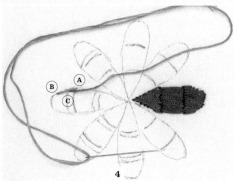

1 Transfer your pattern to the fabric (see Transferring Patterns, pp. 18–23). To make the characteristic long and short stitches, add a double line at each division of the petal: the black line in subsequent photos marks the boundary for the short stitches and the blue line marks the boundary for the long stitches.

2 Make a waste knot or make a small knot 3in (7.5cm) from the end of the thread. Bring the needle and thread from the wrong side to the right side at point A on the blue line.

3 Insert the needle into the fabric at point B, making a long stitch. Come back out at point C on the other end of the black boundary line to start a short stitch.

4 Pull the thread all the way through, finishing the first long stitch and getting ready for the first short stitch.

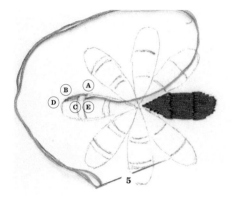

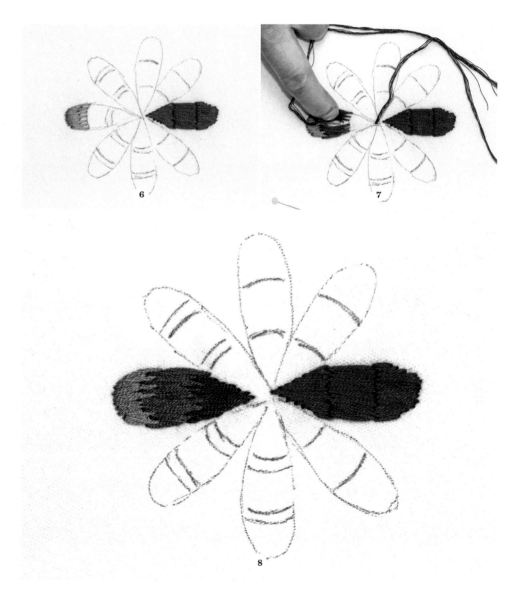

5 Insert the needle next to the previous stitch, at point D. Pull the thread all the way through, finishing the first short stitch. The next stitch, a long stitch, will start at point E.

6 Repeat Steps 3–5 until the first section is filled in.

7 When adding the next layer of stitches, in addition to following the long-and-short pattern, if you cheat the needle just past the boundary line, interweaving the new and old threads, the layering of the thread will be more subtle.

8 The left-hand petal is filled with long-and-short stitch and the right-hand petal with satin stitch in three sections. Choose the end result that will best suit your design.

Chinese knot / Peking knot / Forbidden knot / Blind knot

Wrapping the thread around the needle and plunging the needle back into the fabric creates a knot stitch. Spaced out or clustered together, knotted stitches add texture and shading to a design. Chinese knots are the smallest of the knotted stitches as they are made with only one loop of thread wrapped around the needle.

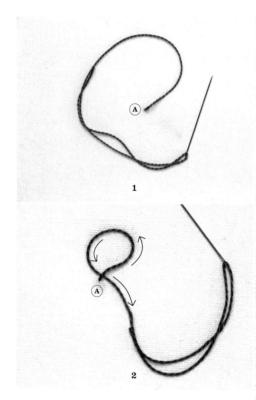

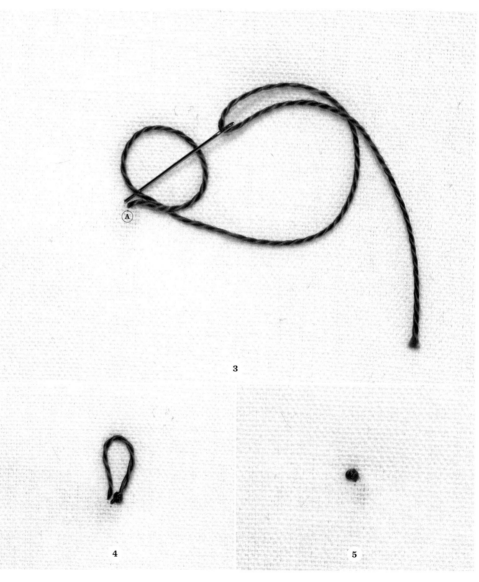

1 Make a small knot 3in (7.5cm) from the end of the thread. Bring the needle and thread from the wrong side to the right side at point A.

2 Make a loop with the thread from point A. Slide the needle under the standing thread at point A.

3 Working from the top of the loop, guide the needle over the thread on the right and under the thread on the left and insert the needle into the fabric next to point A.

4 Pull the thread gently. The knot will form at point A. Continue pulling the extra thread to the wrong side.

5 The completed Chinese knot.

French knot / Knotted stitch / Twisted knot stitch / French dot stitch / Wound stitch

French knots can be small or large, depending on how many times the thread is wrapped around the needle.

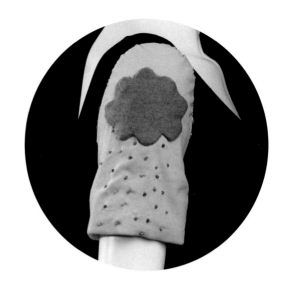

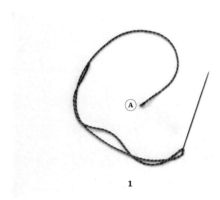

1

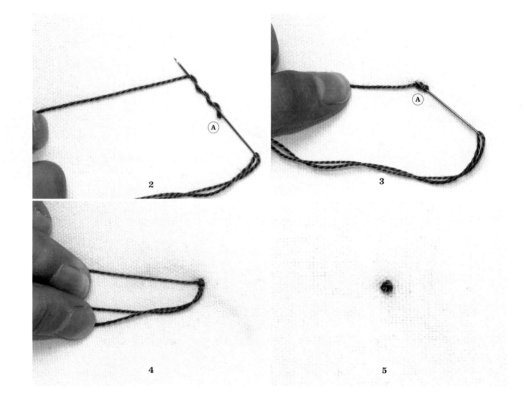

2

3

4

5

1 Make a small knot 3in (7.5cm) from the end of the thread. Bring the needle and thread from the wrong side to the right side at point A.

2 Place the tip of the needle near point A. Wrap the thread around the tip of the needle several times, keeping tension on the thread coming off the tip of the needle. You can wrap the thread around clockwise or counterclockwise, as long the wrapping direction is consistent throughout the design.

Here the thread is wrapped around the tip of the needle three times. To increase the size of the knot, wrap the thread around the needle more times.

3 While keeping tension on the thread, insert the needle into the fabric next to point A and slide the thread wraps down the needle. Do not let the wraps get out of order or overlap, as that will interfere with making the French knot.

4 While keeping tension on the thread, pull the needle through the fabric and continue pulling until the wraps are held tightly against the fabric, forming the knot.

5 The completed French knot.

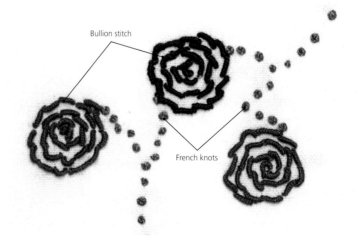

Bullion stitch

French knots

Bullion stitch / Coil stitch / Grub stitch / Worm stitch / Porto Rico rose stitch

Bullion stitch features thread coiled around a base thread. The coiled thread adds bulk and texture to the stitch, raising it above the fabric surface. Bullion stitch is often sewn with metallic threads on ecclesiastical pieces or with wool yarn, making luxurious roses.

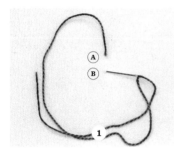

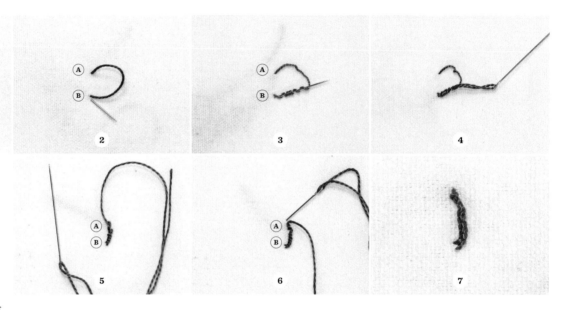

1 Make a small knot 3in (7.5cm) from the end of the thread. Bring the needle and thread from the wrong side to the right side at point A. Insert the needle back into the cloth at point B, a stitch length away.

2 Leaving a small loop of thread between points A and B, bring the tip of the needle to the right side of the fabric just next to point B.

3 Wrap the thread from the loop around the tip of the needle enough times to fill the space between points A and B (the stitch) with wrapped thread. Here the thread has been wrapped seven times.

4 Pull the needle and all the thread through the thread wraps, settling the wraps onto the fabric surface. Do not let the wraps get out of order or overlap, as that will interfere with the look of the bullion knot.

5 The wraps should fill the space between points A and B. If the stitch needs to be rounded or stand proud of the fabric, add additional thread wraps to overfill the stitch space.

6 Insert the needle just next to point A, pulling all the excess thread to the wrong side.

7 The completed bullion stitch.

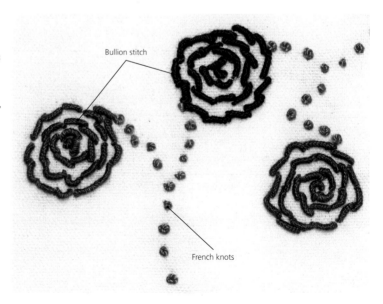

Bullion stitch

French knots

Shisha / Mirror work

Shisha work, the art of sewing small mirrors to fabric, is based on techniques originally perfected in northern India. Popular in the hippie era of the 1960s, these little mirrors add sparkle to a garment. They are made of mica, glass, or plastic and are available in a variety of shapes and sizes. The basic technique for attaching shisha consists of three rounds of stitching. Further decorative techniques can then be used, including twisted buttonhole stitch (see p. 317).

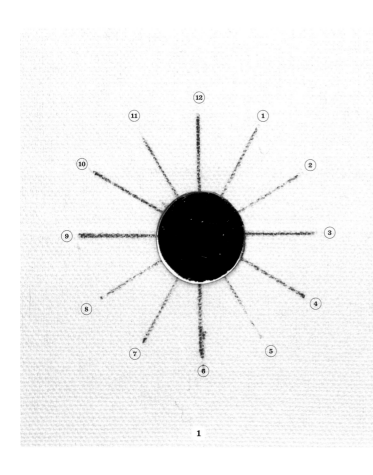

1

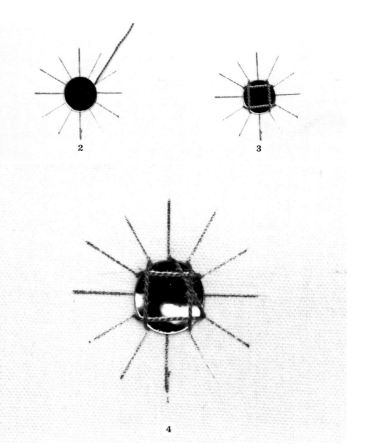

2

3

4

1 Sand down the mirror edges using an emery board or sandpaper so that the sharp edges do not cut through the threads. Use a little dab of glue to hold the mirror in place while you are sewing; try a craft glue or E6000™ glue. The stitching will hold the mirror in place once it is complete. Draw a clock around the mirror to guide your sewing.

2 Make a small knot 3in (7.5cm) from the end of the thread. Bring the needle and thread from the wrong side to the right side at 2 o'clock.

3 Exit at 10 o'clock. Enter at 8, exit at 4; enter at 5, exit at 1; enter at 11, exit at 7. This makes a square across the face of the mirror and completes the first round of anchoring stitches.

4 Round two of the anchoring stitches creates another square across the mirror face, but with the corners at different points. Enter at 12, exit at 4.

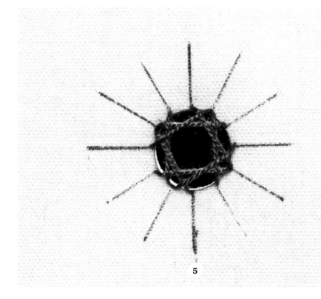

5

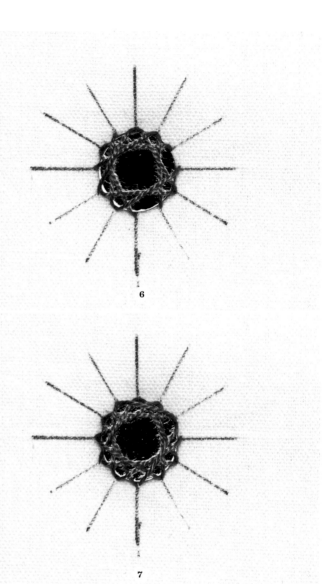

6

7

5 Enter at 6, exit at 10; enter at 9, exit at 1; enter at 3, exit at 7. This completes the second round of stitching, making the second square anchoring the mirror to the fabric.

6 Round three of anchoring stitches creates another square at a third set of points. Enter at 8, exit at 12; enter at 9, exit at 5; enter at 6, exit at 2. Enter at 3, weave the thread under one of the other threads, and then exit at 11. The third round of stitching completes the third square.

7 Every hour mark of the clock should have two threads forming a corner of one of the squares. The mirror is firmly held in place by the three squares. You can stop here or continue with a decorative round of stitching, such as twisted buttonhole stitch (see opposite).

Shisha / Mirror work with buttonhole stitch

After a shisha mirror has been anchored to fabric, a decorative buttonhole stitch can be sewn over the anchoring threads. Based on blanket stitch, buttonhole stitch has multiple steps; here it is demonstrated in a straight row before being shown in the round.

TWISTED BUTTONHOLE STITCH

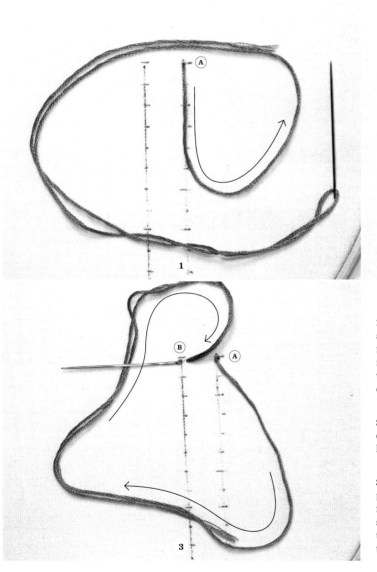

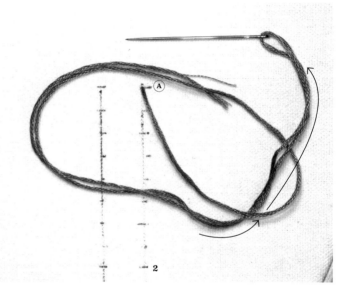

1 Draw two lines about 1in (2.5cm) apart. Make a small knot 3in (7.5cm) from the end of the thread. Bring the needle and thread through from the wrong side at point A. Circle the thread counterclockwise from point A.

2 Guide the needle under the thread circle. Pull the thread to form a Chinese knot at point A (see p. 312).

3 Circle the thread clockwise from point A. With the tip of the needle facing away from point A, make a small stitch at point B. Guide the needle over the thread circle. Gently pull the thread to create a blanket stitch (see p. 306).

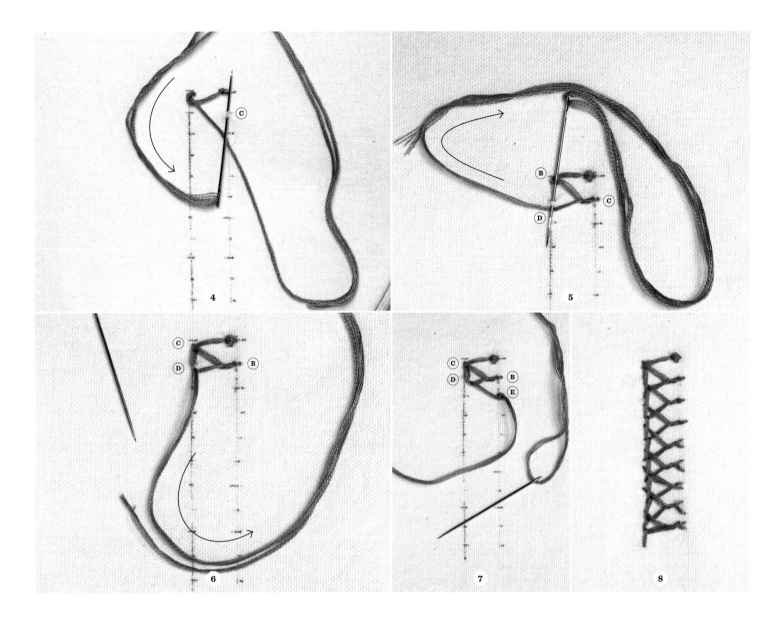

4 Loop the thread around in a counterclockwise direction and make a small stitch at point C, guiding the needle over the thread. This makes a twisted stitch, rather than a knot, at point C.

5 Loop the thread in a clockwise direction. Guide the needle down through the knot at point B, then make a small stitch at point D, and, finally, guide the needle over the thread coming from point C. There should be a triangle with a twisted top between points B, C, and D.

6 Loop the thread around in a counterclockwise direction.

7 Make a small stitch at point E, guiding the needle over the thread, as in Step 4. Repeat Steps 4–6 until you have a line of triangles with twisted tops.

8 A completed row.

TWISTED BUTTONHOLE STITCH AROUND A SHISHA MIRROR

After learning this stitch, you can sew it in the round, over the anchoring stitches surrounding the mirror.

1 To sew this variation of buttonhole stitch over a shisha mirror, first build the basic mirror cage (see pp. 315–16). Using the same thread, or a new thread, bring the needle and thread out at 12.

2 Guide the needle over and then under all the stitches on the mirror at 12, leaving a loop.

3 Guide the needle through the loop, making a Chinese knot.

4 Lead the thread away from the mirror.

5 Circle the thread in a counter-clockwise direction. With the point of the needle facing away from the mirror, make a small stitch $^{3}/_{16}$ in (5mm) away from the mirror edge. Guide the needle over the thread.

6 Gently pull the thread to create a blanket stitch (see Step 3, p. 317).

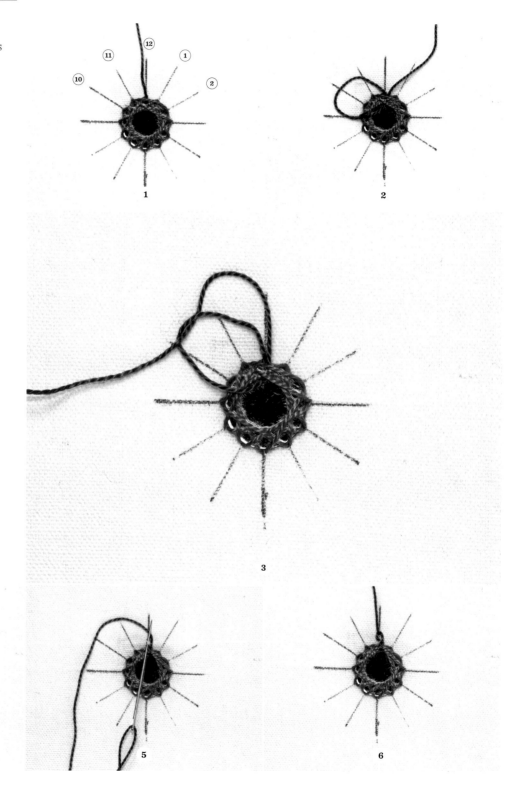

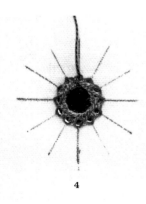

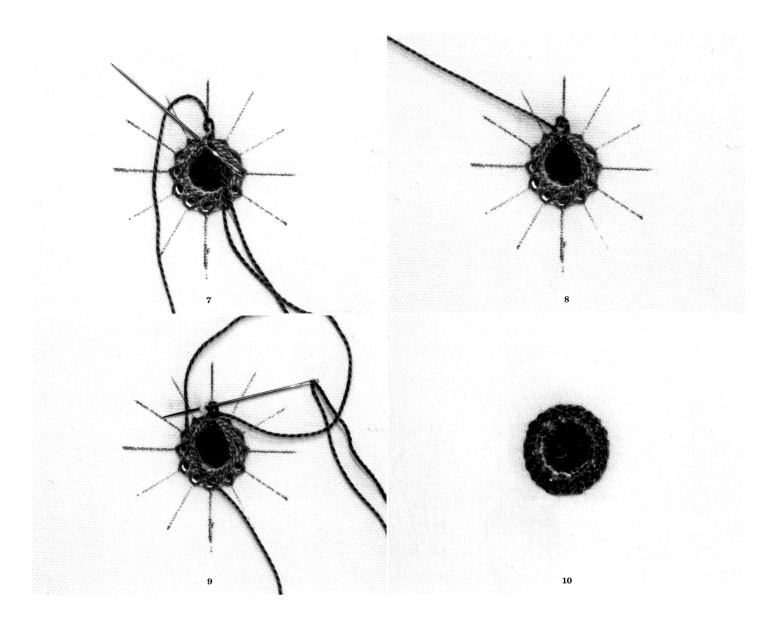

7 Loop the thread around in a counterclockwise direction and guide the needle under all the thread on the mirror, next to the previous stitch, and then over the circled thread.

8 Pull to make a twisted stitch (see Step 4, p. 318).

9 Loop the thread in a clockwise direction. Guide the needle through the knot at 12, make a small stitch in the fabric, and, finally, guide the needle over the thread coming from the mirror. When the thread is pulled tight it will form the base of the triangle (see Step 5, p. 318). Repeat Steps 5–9 until the mirror is encircled with stitches that cover the anchoring squares.

10 The completed shisha mirror.

Couching

Couching is often used to lay delicate metallic threads on the surface of a piece of embroidery; this technique avoids pulling the threads through the fabric, which can cause them to fray. Large threads, yarns, strings, and trims that are difficult to pass repeatedly through a base fabric can also be couched.

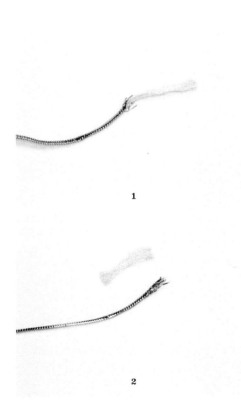

1

2

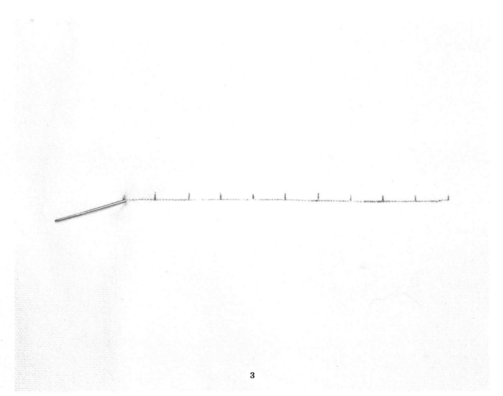

3

Here a piece of gold string with a polyester filler is couched to the base fabric. Before the couching begins, the end of the string is passed through a small hole in the base fabric and anchored to the wrong side of the fabric. To reduce the bulk of the string as much as possible before it is passed through the fabric, the filler may be removed from the center of the string.

1 Push back the outer casing of the string so that it gathers slightly, exposing the filler.

2 Cut off a piece of the filler and smooth out the casing.

3 Working on the right side of the base fabric, make a small hole for the end of the string to go through to the wrong side. Using a blunt, thick tapestry needle, poke the needle tip between the fibers of the fabric at the starting point of your stitching line. Work the needle back and forth to create a hole without breaking any fibers. You can use an awl to create a larger hole, but be careful not to break the fibers; the aim is just to push them aside.

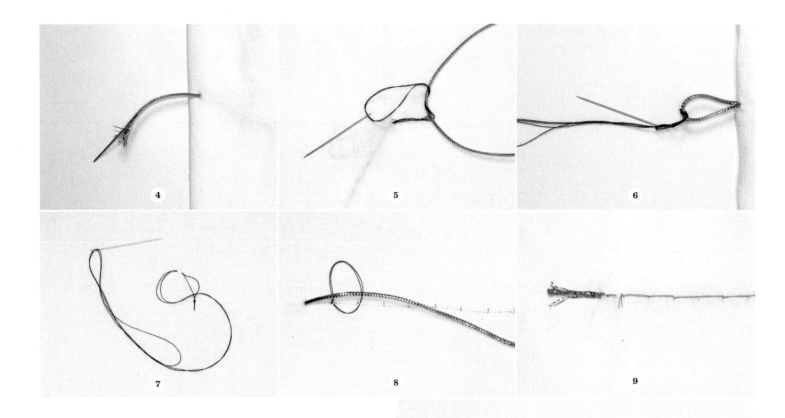

4

5

6

7

8

9

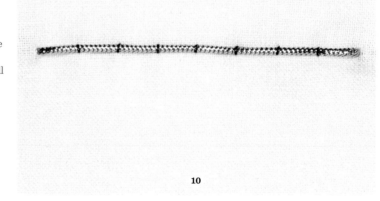

10

4 Thread the string onto the tapestry needle and bring the beginning of the string through to the wrong side. Massage the fabric fibers back to close the hole around the string. Leave the tapestry needle on the string to act as a toggle and help prevent the string end from being pulled to the right side.

5 If the string will not go through when threaded onto the tapestry needle, you can use the lasso method. Bring a needle and thread through the hole to the right side. Wrap the thread twice around the string and insert the needle back into the hole.

6 From the wrong side grasp the needle and the thread tail and gently pull until the string pops through. Unwrap the thread from the string.

7 Make a small knot 3in (7.5cm) from the end of a contrasting or matching thread on the wrong side of the fabric, or, using knotted doubled thread, make a small stitch from the wrong side.

Slide the needle and thread between the two threads near the knot. Pull the thread taut to form a secondary knot.

8 Bring the needle and thread up to the right side of the fabric. Loop the thread over the string, then return the needle and thread to the wrong side, close to where you started. Gently pull the needle and thread down, pulling the string down to rest on the fabric's surface. Repeat until you are one stitch length from the end of the string. Create a hole and take the string end to the wrong side, as in Steps 3–6.

9 Sew the string ends to the fabric with a slip stitch.

10 The gold string couched with contrasting thread to the fabric surface.

Couching in a spiral

1 To make a couched spiral, draw a clock on the base fabric. Use a tapestry needle and an awl to open the hole in the center to insert the end of the string (see Step 3, p. 321).

2 Here a doubled length of string was used to increase the bulk of the trim, so the two ends of the trim were threaded through the hole to the wrong side of the base fabric.

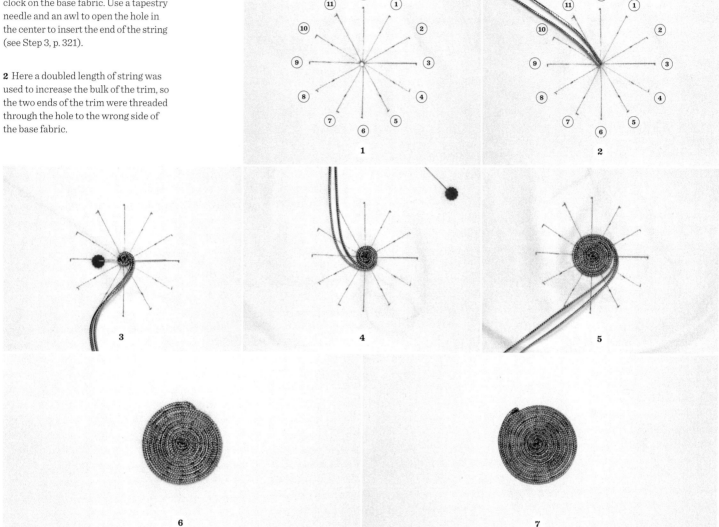

3 Working with the doubled piece of string, wrap the strings in a clockwise spiral, beginning with just a few revolutions. Insert a pin through the side of the strings to hold the spiral together as you work.

4 Couch the strings to the fabric with thread just at 12, 3, 6, and 9 o'clock for the first few rounds. If you couch at every mark at the beginning, the couching threads will obscure the strings.

5 As the spiral gets bigger, increase the couching to every hour mark.

6 Continue wrapping the strings and couching them until the spiral is complete. Tuck the ends of the strings under the previous rows or take them back through the fabric to the wrong side. Secure the ends of the strings (see Step 9, opposite).

7 The same string couched with a matching thread.

Ribbon embroidery can quickly produce a large swathe of dramatic color or a delicate spray of whimsy. It is traditionally used on lingerie, where its forte for creating three-dimensional flowers makes it a popular choice. However, taking the trouble to create a more contemporary design can add a unique statement to your garment.

Most of the basic stitches practiced by thread embroiderers will also work well in ribbon embroidery. In addition, there are a few stitches that are specific to the technique, or worked in a special way: ribbon stitch, long-and-short ribbon stitch, lazy daisy stitch, coral stitch, rosebud stitch, and spider web rose stitch.

3.14
Ribbon embroidery

With the vast array of ribbons that are now available, in a multitude of colors, widths, and materials, ribbon embroidery can be used to highlight any area of a garment, from a collar or neckline to a hem.

Ribbons

Ribbon embroidery is traditionally created with soft, fine silk ribbons as they are easily folded, looped, and pierced by a sharp needle. Chenille and embroidery needles are used for ribbon embroidery as their eyes are large enough to carry the ribbons.

To test whether a ribbon is suitable for ribbon embroidery, thread the ribbon through a needle and, doubling back, pull needle and ribbon through the ribbon. If it is hard to pull the needle through the ribbon, or the needle creates a large hole in the ribbon, that ribbon is not suitable for ribbon embroidery.

Ribbon widths are measured in millimeters. The standard widths for those used in ribbon embroidery are 2mm, 3mm, 4mm, 7mm, and 13mm.

Silk ribbons are available on small cards, on spools, or loose by the yard. If you iron a length of ribbon, roll it onto a cardboard tube covered with clean muslin to keep it flat.

The delicate ribbons suitable for ribbon embroidery will degrade as you use them, so cut them in short lengths of 12–18in (30–46cm) to keep the ribbon in good condition.

Testing ribbons for suitability in ribbon embroidery: The pink silk ribbon on the left is easily pierced by the needle, while the purple polyester ribbon on the right requires effort to pierce, and the needle leaves a large hole in the ribbon. The purple polyester ribbon will not work well for ribbon embroidery and is better suited for another project.

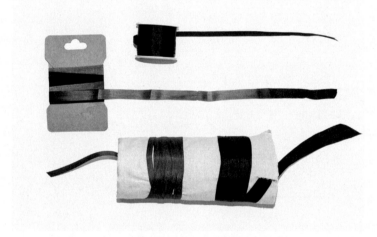

Keep ribbons straight by wrapping them on a spool, card, or muslin-covered tube.

2mm	
3mm	
4mm	
7mm	
13mm	

Standard ribbon widths for ribbon embroidery.

KEEPING THE TENSION RELAXED

As you work, keep your ribbon tension relaxed; if the tension is too high, the ribbon will stretch and look like regular thread. Use your thumb or a blunt tapestry needle to help keep the ribbon flat and plump.

Knotting the ribbon

1 Thread the end of the ribbon through a needle. Fold under the raw end of the ribbon at the other end. Guide the needle through the center of the two layers of ribbon.

2 Gently pull the length of the ribbon through the doubled ribbon end.

3 The completed knot.

Locking the ribbon on the needle

1 Some sewers like to lock the needle on the ribbon tip, which is the same process as knotting the ribbon. Thread the ribbon through the needle and slide it down by 2–3in (5–7.5cm). Pierce the ribbon near the end with the needle tip.

2 Pull the needle all the way through. A small knot will form at the end of the needle eye.

3 The needle with the ribbon knotted and locked in place.

Long-and-short ribbon stitch

This is the same stitch as long-and-short stitch (see pp. 310–11), but using two colors of silk ribbon, with the ribbons held flat and then twisted for variation. Here the stitch is used to create a simple flower.

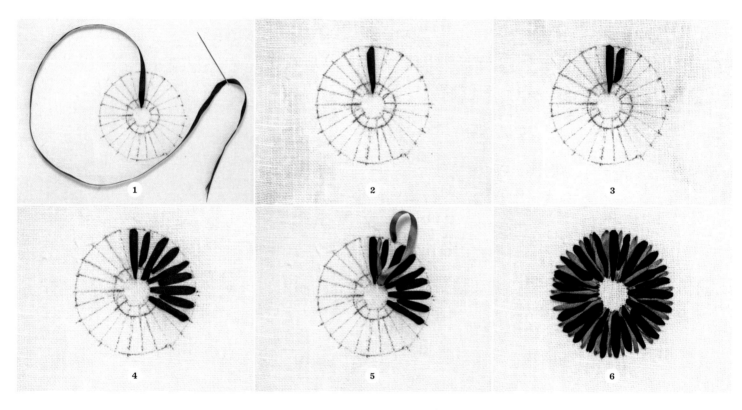

1 Transfer your design to your fabric (see Transferring Patterns, pp. 18–23). Make a small knot at the end of the ribbon (see p. 327). Bring the needle and ribbon from the wrong side to the right side at the starting point.

2 Smooth the ribbon along the sewing guideline. Insert the needle into the fabric and gently pull the ribbon through to the wrong side, making sure that the ribbon remains flat and untwisted. A blunt tapestry needle can be used to smooth or fluff the ribbon into place.

3 Make the next, short, stitch in the same fashion, making sure the ribbon is flat on both the right and wrong sides of the fabric.

4 Repeat Steps 2–3.

5 To add more dimension to the flower, introduce a second ribbon. Bring the second ribbon to the right side and twist the ribbon several times before reinserting the needle and ribbon back into the fabric. Keep the ribbon flat on the wrong side.

6 The completed flower.

Ribbon stitch

This stitch is used to create a petal with a small curl at the outer edge. The curl will be more three-dimensional if you use a springy organza ribbon, as shown here; if you use a soft silk ribbon, the curl will narrow slightly at the tip.

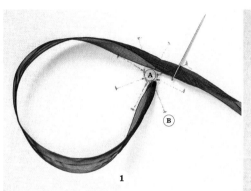

1

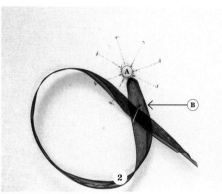

2

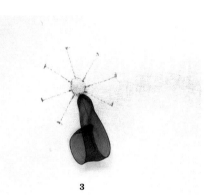

3

4

5

1 Transfer your design to your fabric (see Transferring Patterns, pp. 18–23). Make a small knot at end of the ribbon (se p. 327). Bring the needle and ribbon from the wrong side to the right side at point A.

2 Lay the ribbon along the line extending beyond point B. Insert the needle at point B. Gently pull the needle and ribbon through the base ribbon and the fabric.

3 As the ribbon is pulled through the base ribbon, a small curl will develop.

4 Pull the ribbon through just enough to create a sizable curl at the outer edge. A crochet hook or toothpick inserted through the curl will prevent it from being pulled down too much as the petal is worked.

5 The completed flower.

Lazy daisy stitch / Detached chain stitch

Lazy daisy stitch is a variation of chain stitch (see pp. 300–301).

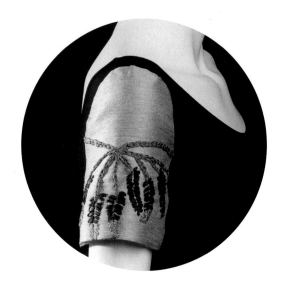

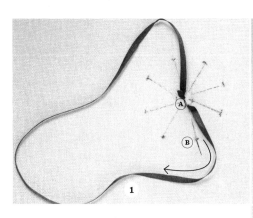
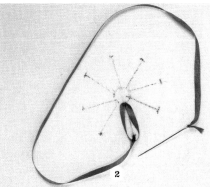
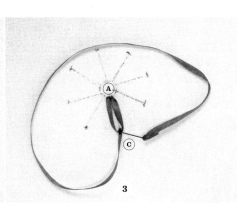

1 Transfer your design to your fabric (see Transferring Patterns, pp. 18–23). Make a small knot at the end of the ribbon (see p. 327). Bring the needle and ribbon from the wrong side to the right side at point A. Insert the needle back into the fabric just to the left of point A and come back out at point B. Hook the ribbon under the tip of the needle, passing the ribbon from the right to the left. You can also pass the ribbon from left to right, but you must be consistent in the direction you choose.

2 Gently pull the ribbon through the fabric at point B until you have a loop.

3 Insert the needle and ribbon on the outside of the loop, at point C, to anchor it in place.

4 The completed lazy daisy flower.

Coral stitch / Beaded stitch / Snail trail

Coral stitch is a running stitch with a knot at the end.
This stitch makes a lovely vine for flowers.

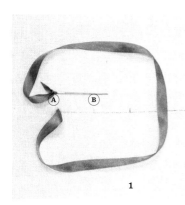

1

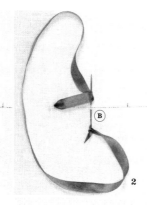

2

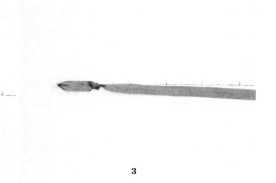

3

1 Transfer your design to your fabric
(see Transferring Patterns, pp. 18–23).
Make a small knot at the end of the
ribbon (see p. 327). Bring the needle
and ribbon through from the wrong
side to the right side at the starting
point A. Point B is the end of this stitch,
and the beginning of the next stitch.

2 Make a small vertical stitch at point
B. Wrap the ribbon over the tip of the
needle. Gently pull the needle and
ribbon through to form a small knot
at point B.

3 The first coral stitch completed.
Repeat Step 2.

4 A line of coral stitches.

4

Rosebud stitch

This little bud is made from four stitches that overlap at their bases. Using variegated ribbon adds an extra dimension to the bud.

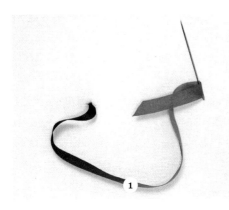

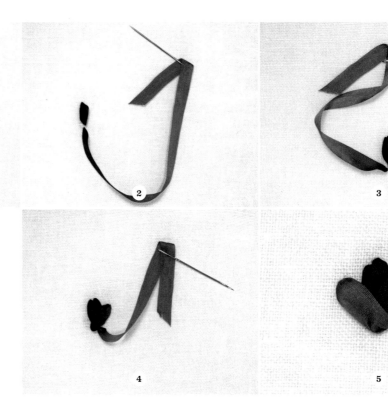

1 The center of the bud is given form by stitching two petals, one on top of the other. Start by creating the under petal. Make a small knot at the end of the ribbon (see p. 327). Bring the needle and ribbon to the right side of the fabric just below where the top of the center petal will sit.

2 Make a small downward stitch to form the under petal. Bring the needle and ribbon to the right side just below the bottom of the under petal. Pull the edges of the ribbon up and out to slightly inflate the under petal.

3 Make another stitch directly over the under petal to form the over petal; this pair of stitches should look like one puffy center petal. Bring the needle and ribbon through the fabric slightly to the left of the petal, ready for the third stitch. Inflate the second stitch as in Step 2.

4 The third stitch crosses over the center petals from left to right. Bring the needle and ribbon to the right side on the right of the petals, ready for the fourth and final stitch. The final stitch crosses over the right-hand and center petals to finish. Knot the ribbon on the wrong side.

5 The finished rosebud.

Spider web rose stitch

A spider web rose consists of two parts: a pointed star base that serves as a web for ribbon to be woven through, and the weaving ribbon that forms the rose petals.

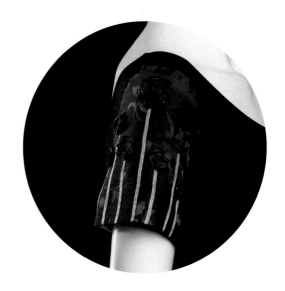

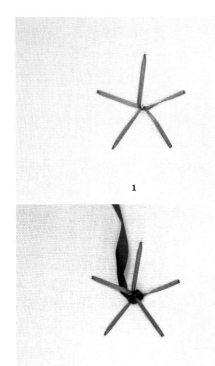

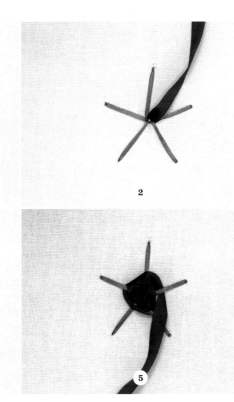

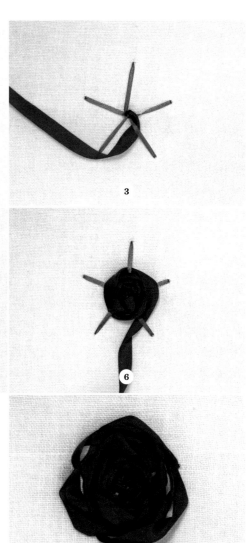

1 Make a small knot (see p. 327) at the end of a thin base ribbon (shown here in green for clarity). Create a five-point star: start with a feather stitch (see pp. 304–5) for a three-point star, then add two more arms for a five-point star.

2 Make a small knot at the end of the main ribbon (see p. 327). Bring the main ribbon up through the center of the star.

3 Weave the ribbon over one arm of the star and then under the next arm. Allow the ribbon to billow out slightly between the arms.

4 Twist the ribbon while weaving it around the web to add texture to the rose.

5 Continue wrapping the ribbon under and over the arms.

6 To finish the spider web rose, insert the end of the ribbon through the fabric and knot on the wrong side.

7 The finished spider web rose.

Ribbons can be used to make bows, cockades, and flowers, each of which can be simple or intricate in style. An extravagant bow on the back of a simple gown can add an element of surprise and sophistication. Ribbons, folded and pleated into intricate patterns and motifs, can be used to make a unique trim on the edge of a jacket, skirt, or dress.

One of the wonderful things about ribbons is that they are almost always woven with selvages on both edges— there are exceptions, of course—which means no raveling or hemming before you start your project. Ribbons come in hundreds of fabrics, colors, patterns, and widths.

3.15
Decorative ribbons

When creating ribbon embellishments, there is no right or wrong ribbon choice. Small changes in technique can create very different results from even a limited ribbon palette, as you will see in this chapter.

Ribbon width (RW)

Ribbon width (RW) can be measured by the inch or in millimeters, and occasionally by the old French method of lignes. A ruler or tape measure with both inches and millimeters is a handy tool when shopping for and working with ribbons.

Many of the folding techniques in this chapter use an RW measurement. Two ways to measure the width of a ribbon are shown below.

TWO METHODS FOR MEASURING RW

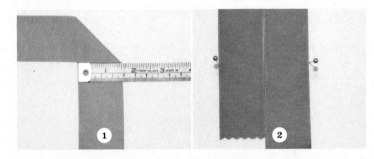

1 Fold the ribbon across itself at a 45° angle and measure from selvage to selvage. Folding the ribbon ensures you are not at an angle and gives you an edge to align the tape measure with.

2 Lay the ribbon on a pin board, place a pin on either side, remove the ribbon, and measure the space. Here a measurement for 2 RW is being taken.

Top row: Five fans made from ⅞in (2.3cm) wide grosgrain ribbon.
Bottom row: Five fans made from 1½in (3.8cm) wide grosgrain ribbon.
Both sets of fans were folded using the same proportions: each fold in the fan was ½ RW, and the spacing between the fans was 1 RW.

Making a folding pattern or gauge

Making a folding pattern or gauge is highly recommended. Patterns can be made from oak tag, manila folders, card stock, or quilting template plastic. Do not use colored paper as the paper dye may run when pressed or steamed.

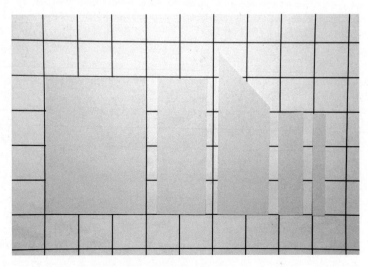

Patterns made of oak tag for 1½in (3.8cm) ribbon.
From the left: 2 RW, 1 RW, 1 RW angled, ½ RW, ¼ RW.

Preparing ribbon

Always press your ribbon before you start any technique; it should be crease-free and preshrunk. If the ribbon has a built-in texture, just lightly steam it with the iron to preshrink it. To prevent the ribbons ends from fraying, there are three options: cut them at a 45° angle, cut straight across with pinking shears or a wavy rotary cutter, or sew straight across with very small stitches of 1mm (25 spi) to lock the yarns together.

If the right ribbon for the project is not available, make some rouleau tubes out of fabric, press them flat, and treat them as ribbon (see pp. 140–41).

HIDING THE THREAD TAILS

After the ribbons have been folded, pressed, and sewn in place, knot the threads, leaving the thread tails fairly long. Short tails will stick up, but if they are longer they can be twisted and hidden in a ribbon fold.

Ribbon choices

Ribbons are made from acetate, cotton, grosgrain, jute, lace, organza, polyester, satin, silk, velvet, and tulle, to name just a few fabrics and weaves. Some ribbons are "wired," which means they have thin wires threaded through the selvage that can be helpful when forming a specific shape; they can easily be pulled out if not needed. If you decide to keep the wire, be very gentle with it as it can break inside the ribbon, leaving you with a snapped edge rather than a malleable selvage. If you decide to remove the wire, tease the end out of the ribbon until you can grasp it and pull it out. If the wire breaks somewhere along the length of the ribbon, just find a new wire end—the wired section will be stiffer than the wireless part—tease it out of the ribbon right there, and start pulling again.

Consider both right and wrong sides of a ribbon when shopping; both sides are usually exposed in a finished embellishment. Double-faced satin ribbon is satin on both sides; single-faced satin ribbon is satin on one side only. Printed ribbons are only printed on one side. Woven-design ribbons have the design woven through them, but the reverse is often in opposite colors from the front. Ombre ribbons are dyed in multiple colors, fading from one color to the next. Picot-edged ribbons have a small loop trim woven onto the selvage.

As when choosing fabric, consider the hand of the ribbon before embarking on a project. A lush velvet ribbon will make a lovely fat bow, and a slinky silk ribbon will gather into a tiny rosebud, but that velvet ribbon cannot gather tightly enough to make a tiny rosebud, and the silk ribbon is not bulky enough to make a big bow that stands proud of the garment.

Two-loops bow

This is a simple, demure flat bow.

MATERIALS

To create a bow 2in (5cm) wide x 9$\frac{1}{2}$in (24cm) long:
• 64.5cm (25$\frac{1}{2}$in) of ribbon, 2in (5cm) wide

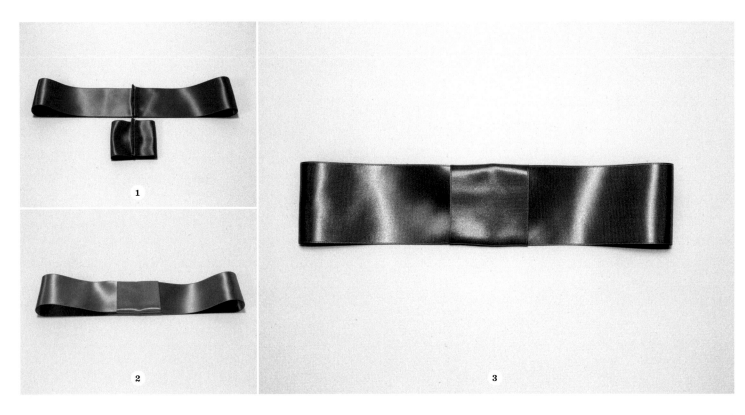

1 Cut the ribbon into one piece 21in (53cm) long, and one piece 4$\frac{1}{2}$in (11.5cm) long or 2 RW plus $\frac{1}{2}$in (1.3cm) seam allowance.

Fold both pieces of ribbon in half, wrong sides together. Sew a French seam in both pieces of ribbon, making two separate loops.

2 Turn the ribbons right side out to turn the seams to the inside. Slide the large loop through the small loop. Secure the large loop to the small loop with small stitches.

3 The completed bow.

Butterfly bow

This generous bow is based on a variation of the two-loops bow.

MATERIALS

To create a bow 7$^{1}/_{2}$in (19cm) wide x 9$^{1}/_{2}$in (24cm) long:
• 67$^{1}/_{2}$in (170.5cm) of double-faced satin ribbon, 2in (5cm) wide

1 Cut the ribbon into three pieces 21in (53cm) long, and one piece 4$^{1}/_{2}$in (11.5cm) long or 2 RW plus $^{1}/_{2}$in (1.3cm) seam allowance.

Fold all four pieces in half, wrong sides together, and sew a French seam in each piece.

2 Turn all four loops so that the French seam is inside. Arrange the long pieces so that the French seam is in the middle. Sew a gathering stitch across each long piece next to the seam.

3 Gently gather each ribbon through the center.

4 Slide all three large loops through the small loop. When you are happy with the arrangement of the large loops, secure them to the small loop with small stitches.

5 The completed bow.

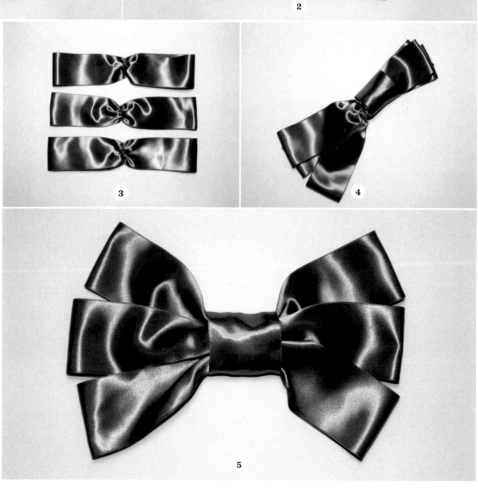

Stepped bow

This multitiered flat bow looks complicated but is surprisingly easy to make.

MATERIALS

To make a bow 11in (27.5cm) long x 2in wide (5cm):
• 60in (150cm) of double-faced satin ribbon, 2in (5cm) wide

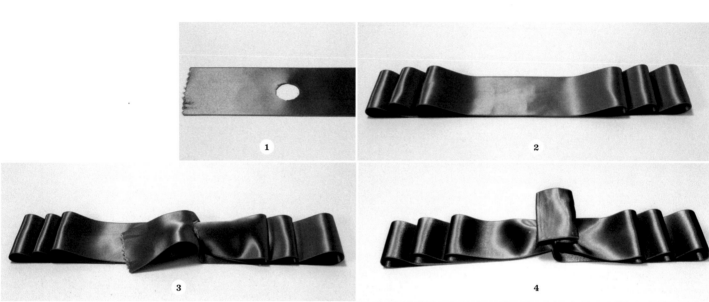

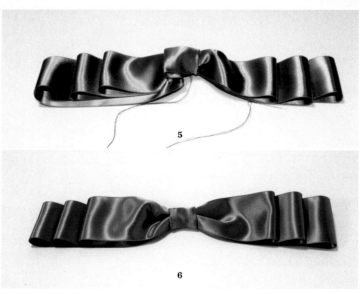

1 Measuring 3in (7.5cm) from one end, cut a hole in the center of the ribbon $^3/_4$in (2cm) in diameter.

2 Fold the ribbon in a stack, with the hole in the bottom layer. The bottom layer should measure 11in (27.5cm) long, the middle layer should be 10in (25cm) long, and the top layer should be 9in (22.5cm) long.

Tuck the end of the ribbon under the top layer to hide the raw end; it should reach to the center of the loops.

3 Pick up one end of the stacked loops and thread them through the hole in the center of the ribbon on the bottom layer. The beginning tail of the ribbon will now be on top.

4 Fold the exposed tail to cover the raw end and the hole, pleating the tail if desired.

5 Pull the selvages of the tail piece to the wrong side to form the center knot. Sew the selvages together on the wrong side of the bow. Secure the large loops to the center knot with small stitches.

6 The completed bow.

Fans

Fans are made with a series of folds that are pressed in the same direction. The basic folding technique illustrated here is the basis for all the folded ribbons in this chapter.

MATERIALS

To make fans $2^5/8$in (6.5cm) long, with $3/4$in (2cm) between motifs:
• Grosgrain ribbon, $1^1/2$in (3.8cm) wide
• $1/4$ RW pattern, measuring $3/8$in (1cm) wide x 3in (7.5cm) long
• $1/2$ RW pattern, measuring $3/4$in (2cm) wide x 3in (7.5cm) long

1 Using the $1/4$ RW pattern as a guide, make three stacked folds, pressing each fold separately into mountains and valleys (see Mountain and Valley Folds box, p. 79). For the first fold, place the pattern on the ribbon and fold the left-hand tail over to the right. Press.

2 For the second fold, remove the pattern and place it on top of the first fold, then fold the tail back to the left. Press. This counts as one completed "stacked fold."

3 Continue until you have three stacked folds, which create one fan.

4 Measure $1/2$ RW from the last fan fold using your oak tag pattern before starting the next fan fold.

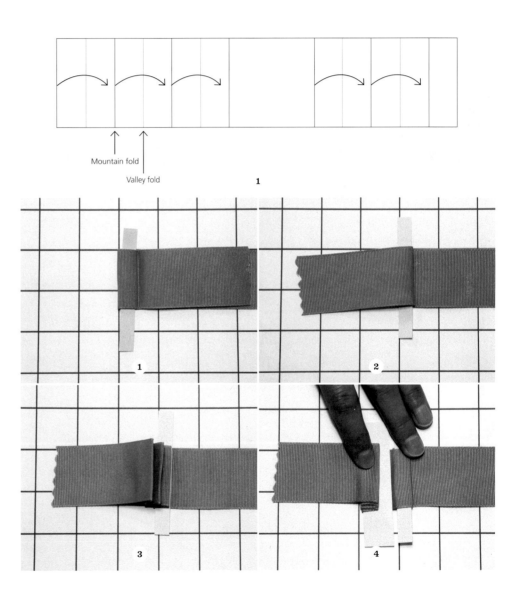

Mountain fold

Valley fold

1

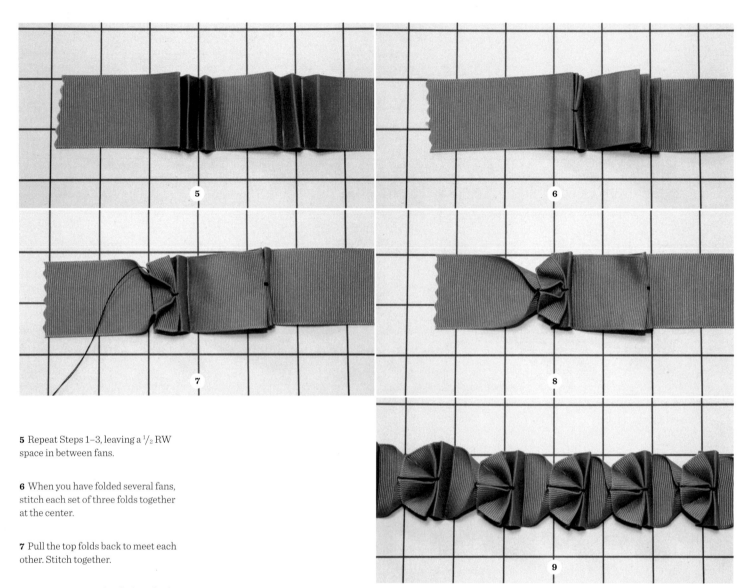

5 Repeat Steps 1–3, leaving a $^{1}/_{2}$ RW space in between fans.

6 When you have folded several fans, stitch each set of three folds together at the center.

7 Pull the top folds back to meet each other. Stitch together.

8 Repeat Steps 1–7 for the length of the ribbon.

9 The completed fans.

VARIATION

Fans will take on a different character when made from different types of ribbon. Here two fans are made in a strip of frayed dupioni silk.

Two-fold motifs / Inverted box pleats

This folding pattern creates round motifs. Each motif uses $3^{7}/_{8}$in (10cm) of ribbon.

MATERIALS

To make a 6in (15cm) strip of six motifs, with $^{3}/_{8}$in (1cm) between motifs, and $1^{3}/_{4}$in (4.5cm) unpleated at each end:
• $28^{3}/_{4}$in (74cm) of grosgrain ribbon, $1^{1}/_{2}$in (3.8cm) wide
• $^{1}/_{4}$ RW pattern, measuring $^{3}/_{8}$in (1cm) wide x 3in (7.5cm) long
• $^{1}/_{2}$ RW pattern, measuring $^{3}/_{4}$in (2cm) wide x 3in (7.5cm) long

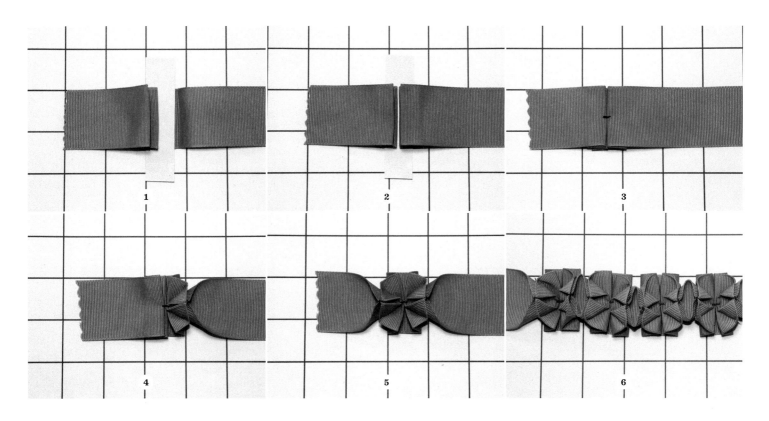

1 2 3

4 5 6

1 Using the $^{1}/_{4}$ RW pattern as a guide, make two stacked folds, pressing each fold separately (see Fans, Steps 1–3, p. 341). Use the $^{1}/_{2}$ RW pattern to measure to the start of the next set of folds.

2 Make two $^{1}/_{4}$ RW folds facing the other folds. The folds should meet in the center.

3 Stitch all four folds together at the center; this will create one motif.

4 Open the pleats to create the motifs: pull the top folds back to meet each other on one side. Stitch together.

5 Repeat Step 4 on the other side.

Repeat Steps 1–5 for additional motifs, folding and pressing all the creases for the length of the ribbon before opening the pleats to create the motifs.

6 Completed motifs.

VARIATION

Vary the placement of the motifs along the ribbon to create different effects. Here multiple motifs are spaced 2in (5cm) apart.

Four-fold motifs and variations

By changing the number of folds, the spacing between the folds, or the size of the folds, the variations of a basic four-fold motif are infinite.

MATERIALS

To make a 10in (25.4cm) strip of four motifs, with ³⁄₄in (2cm) between motifs:
• 24¹⁄₄in (62cm) of grosgrain ribbon, 1¹⁄₂in (3.8cm) wide
• ¹⁄₄ RW pattern, measuring ³⁄₈in (1cm) wide x 3in (7.5cm) long
• ¹⁄₂ RW pattern, measuring ³⁄₄in (2cm) wide x 3in (7.5cm) long

Four-fold motifs

This folding pattern creates round motifs with ¹⁄₄ RW or more between them. The example shown here has ¹⁄₂ RW between each motif. Each motif uses 5¹⁄₂in (14cm) of ribbon.

1 Using the ¹⁄₄ RW pattern as a guide, make four folds (see Fans, Steps 1–3, p. 341), pressing each fold separately so that they stand up from the table.

2 Stitch the four folds together at the center top.

3 Pull the top folds back to meet each other. Stitch together.

4 Completed motifs with ¹⁄₂ RW between each motif.

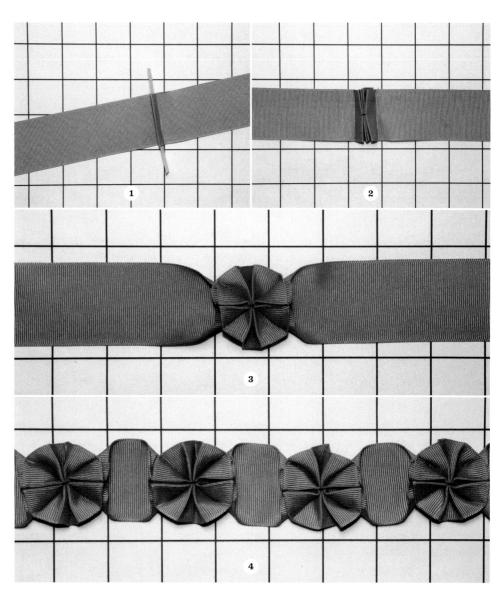

Six-fold motifs

This folding pattern creates dense, square motifs. Each motif uses
6in (15cm) of ribbon.

MATERIALS

To make a $7^{1}/_{2}$ in (19cm) strip of three motifs, with 1in (2.5cm) between motifs,
and $1^{3}/_{4}$ in (4.5cm) unpleated at each end:
• $23^{1}/_{2}$ in (60cm) of grosgrain ribbon, $1^{1}/_{2}$ in (3.8cm) wide
• $^{1}/_{4}$ RW pattern, measuring $^{3}/_{8}$ in (1cm) wide x 3in (7.5cm) long
• $^{1}/_{2}$ RW pattern, measuring $^{3}/_{4}$ in (2cm) wide x 3in (7.5cm) long

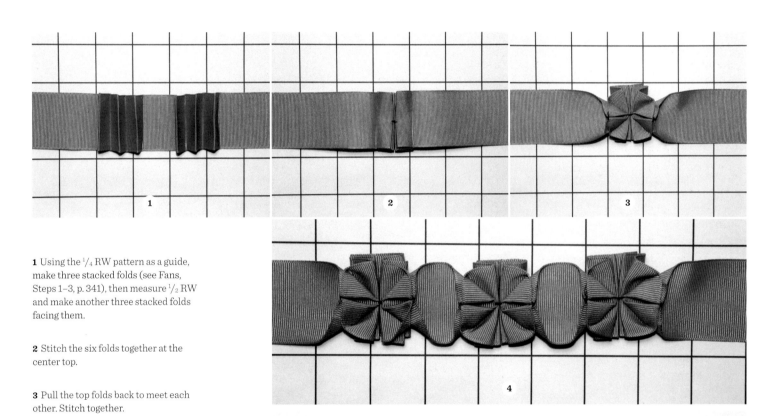

1 Using the $^{1}/_{4}$ RW pattern as a guide,
make three stacked folds (see Fans,
Steps 1–3, p. 341), then measure $^{1}/_{2}$ RW
and make another three stacked folds
facing them.

2 Stitch the six folds together at the
center top.

3 Pull the top folds back to meet each
other. Stitch together.

4 Completed motifs with $^{1}/_{2}$ RW
between each motif.

VARIATIONS

Fold back the middle fold to create
a more three-dimensional motif,
as shown in the top row, center
two motifs.

Decrease the space between motifs to
dramatically change the look, as in the
bottom row.

Diamonds

This folding pattern creates a geometric motif. Each full diamond with a half diamond on either side uses 9in (23cm) of ribbon.

MATERIALS

To make a $6^3/_4$ in (17cm) strip of four full, continuous diamond motifs:
• 36in (92cm) of grosgrain ribbon, $1^1/_2$ in (3.8cm) wide
• $^1/_2$ RW pattern, measuring $^3/_4$ in (2cm) wide x 3in (7.5cm) long

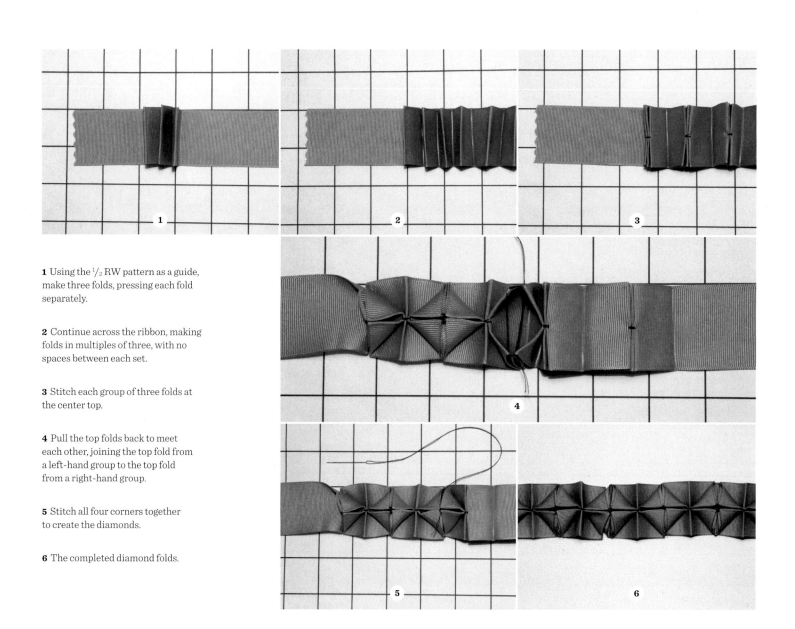

1 Using the $^1/_2$ RW pattern as a guide, make three folds, pressing each fold separately.

2 Continue across the ribbon, making folds in multiples of three, with no spaces between each set.

3 Stitch each group of three folds at the center top.

4 Pull the top folds back to meet each other, joining the top fold from a left-hand group to the top fold from a right-hand group.

5 Stitch all four corners together to create the diamonds.

6 The completed diamond folds.

Prairie points

Prairie points are easy and efficient to make with ribbon because the ribbon is already cleanly finished with selvage edges.

MATERIALS

To make a 17in (43cm) strip of nine double points:
• 36in (92cm) of satin ribbon, ⁷⁄₈in (2.3cm) wide
• 1 RW pattern cut off at one end at a 45° angle

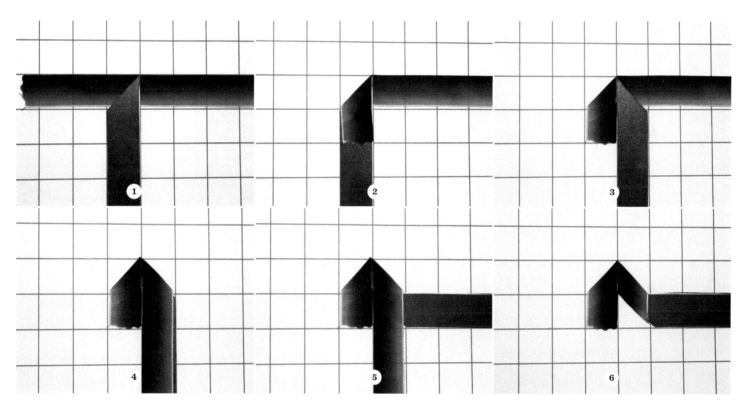

1 Place the 45° pattern perpendicular to the ribbon, with the point aiming up and the long edge facing to the right.

2 Fold the ribbon end down over the angled pattern. Press.

3 Remove the pattern and turn it over. Place the pattern parallel to the selvage of the ribbon from the first fold, with the point aiming up and the long edge facing to the left.

4 Fold the ribbon down and over the pattern piece, keeping the ribbon's selvages right next to each other. Press.

5 Remove the pattern piece, turn it over, and rotate it 90°. Place the pattern under the ribbon, with the point aiming left and the long edge facing up.

6 Wrap the ribbon under the pattern, making sure the ribbon's selvages are even with the pattern's sides. Press.

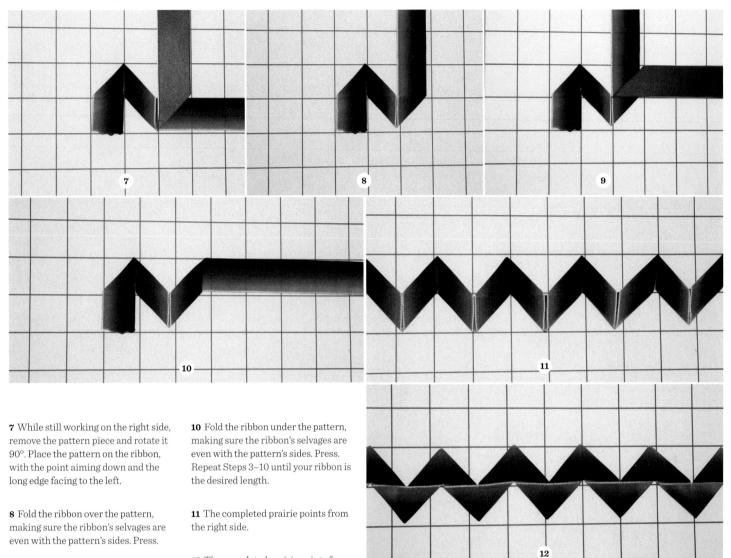

7 While still working on the right side, remove the pattern piece and rotate it 90°. Place the pattern on the ribbon, with the point aiming down and the long edge facing to the left.

8 Fold the ribbon over the pattern, making sure the ribbon's selvages are even with the pattern's sides. Press.

9 Remove the pattern piece, turn it over, and rotate it 90°. Place it on the ribbon with the point aiming left and the long edge facing down.

10 Fold the ribbon under the pattern, making sure the ribbon's selvages are even with the pattern's sides. Press. Repeat Steps 3–10 until your ribbon is the desired length.

11 The completed prairie points from the right side.

12 The completed prairie points from the wrong side.

VARIATION

To create shark's teeth, start with a strip of prairie points, wrong side up. Fold the lower points up so that the tips are the same height as the upper points. Press. When folded properly, the points will interlock.

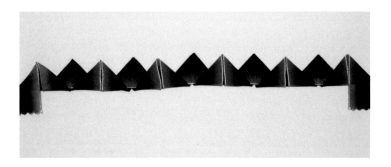

Star points

Star points are often used in cockades, but they also have many other uses. Ribbon choice can make a big difference to the look of a star point: grosgrain ribbons feature a ribbed texture but can be unwieldy, while a smaller, wired ombre ribbon gives a more delicate result.

MATERIALS

For a star of 4$^{1}/_{4}$in (10.8cm) diameter, using 4 RW for each point:
• 72in (183cm) of grosgrain ribbon, 1$^{1}/_{2}$in (3.8cm) wide; or 24in (61cm) of wired ribbon, $^{7}/_{8}$in (2.3cm) wide
• 1 RW pattern cut off at a 45° angle

Folding pattern: Right side   Folding pattern: Wrong side

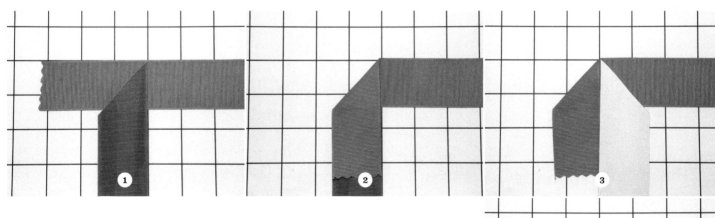

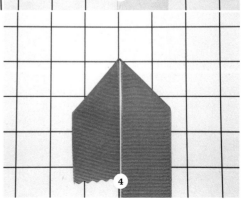

1 Place the 45° pattern on the ribbon, with the point aiming up and the long edge facing to the right.

2 Fold the ribbon end down over the angled pattern. Press.

3 Remove the pattern and turn it over. Place the pattern parallel to the selvage of the ribbon from the first fold, with the point aiming up and the long edge facing to the left.

4 Fold the ribbon down and over the pattern piece, keeping the ribbon selvages right next to each other. Press.

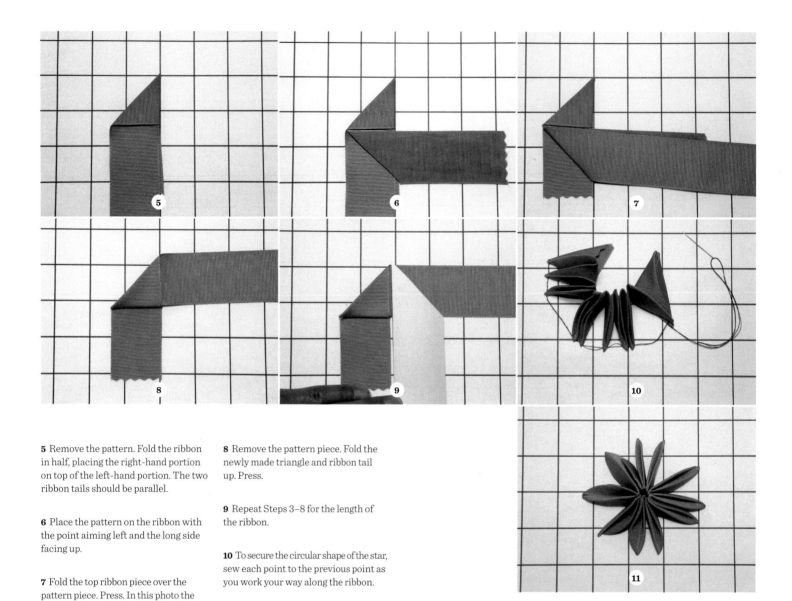

5 Remove the pattern. Fold the ribbon in half, placing the right-hand portion on top of the left-hand portion. The two ribbon tails should be parallel.

6 Place the pattern on the ribbon with the point aiming left and the long side facing up.

7 Fold the top ribbon piece over the pattern piece. Press. In this photo the ribbon is slightly askew to show the pattern piece beneath.

8 Remove the pattern piece. Fold the newly made triangle and ribbon tail up. Press.

9 Repeat Steps 3–8 for the length of the ribbon.

10 To secure the circular shape of the star, sew each point to the previous point as you work your way along the ribbon.

11 Gently gather all the points together to form the center of the star. Tuck the ends of the ribbon into the first and last folds.

VARIATIONS

To make a softer star, do not press the folds as you work the folding pattern.

If you use wired ribbon, the wire will hold each fold of the star without pressing.

Gathered ribbons

Ribbons can be sewn together and then gathered to create unique trims.

MATERIALS

Assorted ribbons of different widths and textures

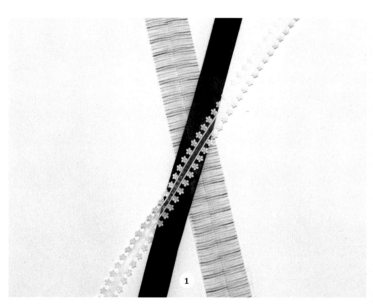

1 Lightly crease each of the ribbons in half lengthwise with your finger or using a low-temperature iron.

2 Stack the ribbons in the desired order and pin them together, matching the creases. Sew gathering stitches down the crease (see Machine Gathering Stitch, p. 25). Gather the ribbons to the correct length.

3 The completed gathered ribbon.

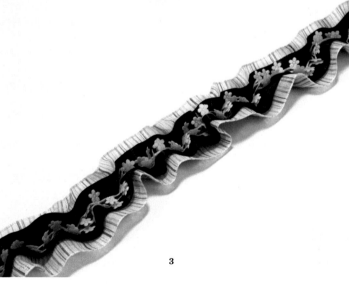

Tiny rosebuds, generous camellias, fringed carnations, bell-shaped foxgloves—all can embellish your garment. Flowers made in ribbon or fabric can be fast and simple or more complex, depending on which flower, technique, and textile you choose. The flower can be modeled closely on the original, a stylized version of the original, or entirely a product of your imagination. This section covers basic techniques of flower making: small ribbon and fabric widths, tightly gathered petals, limited embellishment. You can, however, can create small subtle flowers, large robust blooms, or anything in between, and you can vary the color palette to encompass many different varieties of flower.

3.16
Flowers

Flowers can be made of ribbon or fabric. Ribbon has two selvage edges, so your flower will have a clean-finished edge and a neat underside. Ribbons also come in many fabrics, textures, widths, and colors (see Ribbon Choices, p. 337).

Fabric can be cut and folded so the exposed edge is clean finished, but a double thickness of fabric may make the flower bulky. Fabric can also be frayed to create a fringed edge (see Fringe, p. 202); just make sure the fabric will not continue to fray or the flower may fray away to nothing. Textured and printed fabrics make lovely flowers, adding an extra design dimension to the petals.

Once the basic flower is created, consider adding further embellishments: beads, buttons, embroidery, purchased stamens, real seedpods. Leaves and stems can add realism or link flowers together. Adding snaps to the bottom of a flower, or mounting several flowers on buckram, will allow them to be removed when the garment is cleaned.

Peony *(Paeonia)*

This big, full flower is similar to a real peony, but could be any large flower with multiple petals. It is made by one of the simplest of techniques: a single piece of ribbon is gathered by hand along one edge before being wound into a spiral shape.

MATERIALS

To create a peony 3¹/₂in (9cm) wide:
• 44in (112cm) of double-faced satin ribbon, 1³/₈in (3.5cm) wide

1 Starting at the outer edge of your ribbon, sew gathering stitches diagonally down to the inner edge.

2 With the last stitch ending on the right side of the ribbon, bring the needle to the wrong side of the ribbon and start your next stitch next to the selvage.

3 This "turning stitch" over the edge of the ribbon will help form the center of your flower.

4 Sew gathering stitches along the inner edge of the piece of ribbon.

5 If you are making a large flower, sew the gathering stitches in several sections. This will give you better control of your gathering. Each time you end one section and start a new one, leave a 2–3in (5–7.5cm) thread tail.

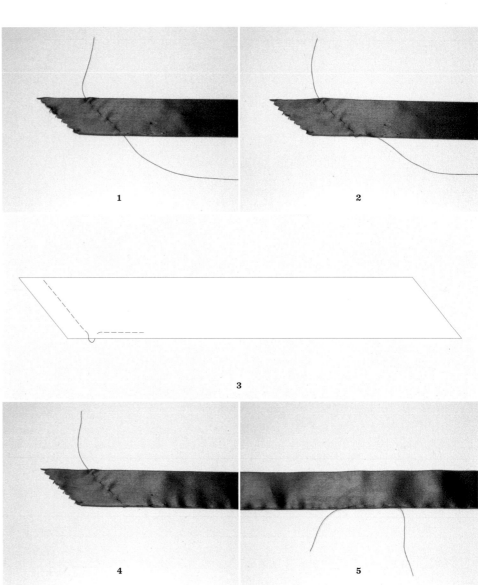

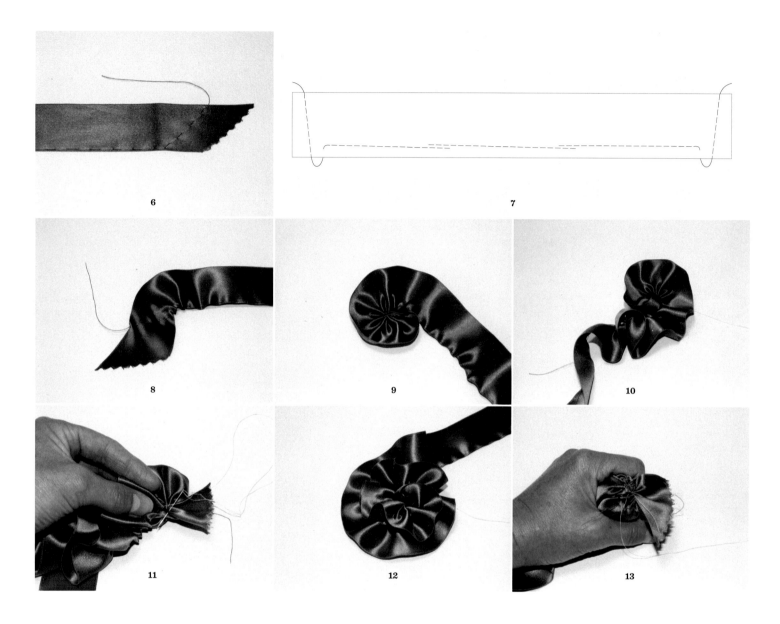

6 Two inches (5cm) before the end of your ribbon, bring your needle to the wrong side of the ribbon, make a turning stitch, and then stitch diagonally at 45° up to the top edge of the ribbon. Leave a thread tail.

7 The diagram shows the different sections of stitching.

8 Pull gently on the diagonal stitching at the start of the ribbon to form the center of the flower.

9 Continue to pull gently on the gathering thread; the ribbon will begin to curl up. Do not pull too hard: you want to create a spiral, not circles.

10 Working with small sections at a time, gather up the ribbon and arrange the gathers into a pleasing shape.

11 Secure the layers of gathers by stitching them together, just above the selvage and the gathering thread. Here the green thread is the gathering thread, and the yellow thread is being used to stitch the gathers into the flower shape.

12 Keep checking the flower on the right side to make sure it looks good, and continue gathering and tacking the ribbon.

13 As the flower grows thicker, you may need to hold it tightly to see where to stitch the gathers.

SEWING GATHERING STITCHES BY MACHINE

You can sew the gathering stitches on ribbon flowers by hand, but sewing them by machine also works well (see Machine Gathering Stitch, p. 25). Follow the stitching pattern illustrated in Step 7. You will not need a turning stitch if you are sewing by machine.

14 Finally, the diagonal stitching across the end of the ribbon will neatly pull the gathers to a close. Use the ribbon tails to camouflage any hole in the center of your flower.

15 The bottom of the flower with the two beginning and ending ribbon tails pulled out of the way to reveal the stitching.

16 The finished flower on the wrong side, unconstricted.

17 The finished flower on the right side.

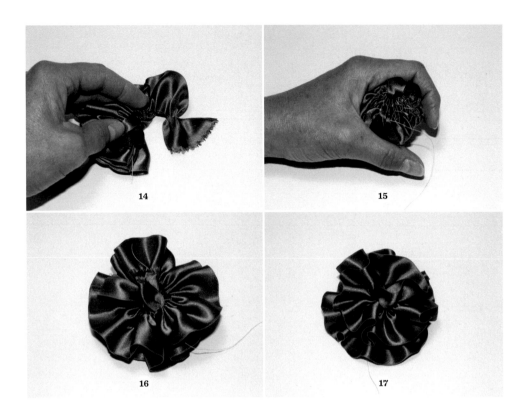

FINISHING TOUCHES

Add leaves to your flower to complete the design (see pp. 380–82).

You may also want to insert stamens into the center of your flower (see pp. 384–87), or create a yo-yo to cover the wrong side of the flower and any stitching that may be visible (see p. 389).

Carnation *(Dianthus)*

This soft, gathered flower can be made to look like a newly opening tight bud or an older, blowsy bloom simply by adjusting the amount by which it is gathered.

MATERIALS

To create a carnation 3¹/₂in (9cm) wide:
• 55in (140cm) of bias-cut, raw-edged silk ribbon, 1¹/₂in (3.8cm) wide

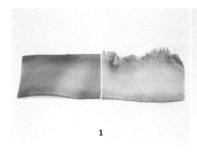

1

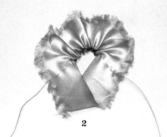

2

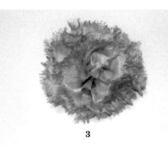

3

4

1 Although technically not ribbon, as there is no selvage on either side, raw-edged silk is cut on the bias and sold as "silk ribbon." Any bias strip can be fringed; just brush the edge with a small, stiff brush: a nail brush or suede brush works well. The "ribbon" is shown in its original state on the left, and brushed into a fringe on the right.

2 Once you have frayed the edge, follow the directions for making a peony (see pp. 354–56). Gather the ribbon by hand.

3 A loosely gathered, frayed ribbon drawn up into a carnation.

4 Gather the same ribbon more tightly to create a more compact-looking flower.

FINISHING TOUCHES

Add a stem to your flower to complete the design (see p. 383).

Rosette

This is a two-layer flower with a distinctive center, created with ribbon that has been folded lengthwise and then gathered.

MATERIALS

To create a rosette 2in (5cm) wide:
• 7½in (19cm) of ribbon, 1½in (3.8cm) wide

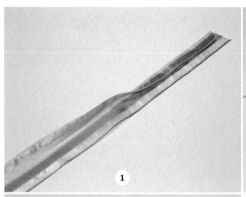

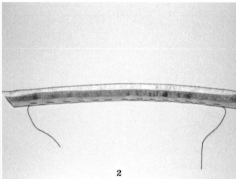

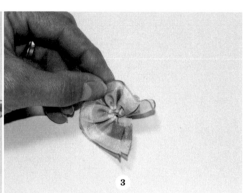

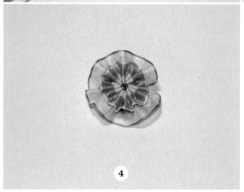

1 Divide the width of the ribbon into three and then fold one third of the ribbon lengthwise. Press.

2 Sew gathering stitches along the folded edge.

3 Gather up the ribbon and knot the gathering threads. Using a thread tail, sew the two ends of the ribbon together.

4 The completed rosette.

FINISHING TOUCHES

Add leaves to your flower to complete the design (see pp. 380–82). You may also wish to add stamens or centers (see pp. 384–87).

Twinned flowers

These flower pairs are quick and fun to make. Use a ribbon that has different colors on each side to add subtle variations to your design.

MATERIALS

To create a pair of flowers 4³/₄in (12cm) wide:
• 21in (53cm) of polyester ribbon, 1¹/₂in (3.8cm) wide

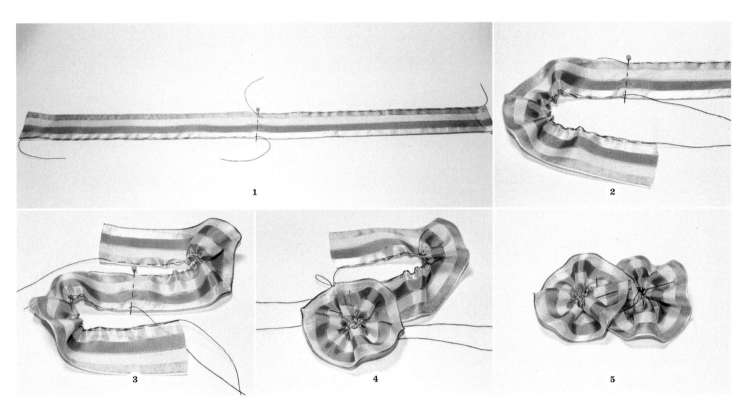

1 Fold the ribbon in half across its width to find the halfway point and mark with a pin. Sew gathering stitches along one side of the ribbon to the halfway point, leaving long thread tails at both ends. Turn the ribbon around and stitch along the opposite selvage on other half.

2 Start to gather the ribbon on one thread.

3 Repeat with the other side.

4 Continue gathering the first side until it forms a flower shape. Wrap the threads around the pin to hold the gathers in place.

5 Repeat with the other side, adjusting the gathering threads until you are satisfied with the figure-of-eight shape.

6

7

6 Pull the thread tails to the wrong side of the ribbon and secure. Fold one end of the ribbon under the figure of eight and secure. Fold the other end under itself twice to create a clean hemmed edge. Stitch the folded edge to the figure of eight to secure in place.

7 The completed pair of flowers.

FINISHING TOUCHES

Add stamens or centers to your flowers (see pp. 384–87). You can also add leaves (see pp. 380–82).

Foxglove (Digitalis)

Foxgloves have small, tubular blossoms that increase in size down the stalk, which suit ribbon available in multiple widths. Picot-edged ribbons add a delicate trim to the blossoms. Bell flowers (*Campanula*) and wisteria (*Wisteria*) can also be made with this technique.

MATERIALS

To create a tubular flower $1^{1}/_{2}$in (3.8cm) wide:
• 2 RW of picot-edged, double-faced satin ribbon, plus $^{1}/_{2}$in (1.3cm) seam allowance

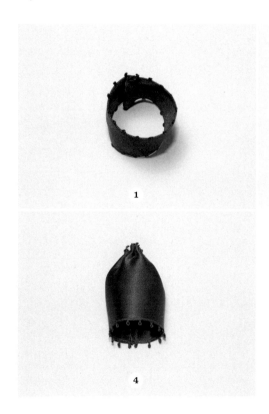

1

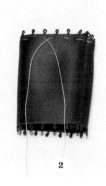

2

3

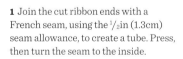

4

1 Join the cut ribbon ends with a French seam, using the $^{1}/_{2}$in (1.3cm) seam allowance, to create a tube. Press, then turn the seam to the inside.

2 Hand-sew gathering stitches around the top of the tube.

3 Gather tightly, then knot the gathering threads.

4 The completed flower.

FINISHING TOUCHES

Add a stem to your flowers (see p. 383).

Plum blossom *(Prunus domestica)*

The U-petal technique is the basis for many flowers, including plum blossom, pansies (*Viola*), primroses (*Primula*), impatiens (*Impatiens*), and aubrietia (*Aubrieta*). The ungathered ribbon side becomes the petal's outer edge, and the gathered side the inner edge.

MATERIALS

To create a flower 3½in (9cm) wide:
• 22in (56cm) of striped polyester ribbon, 1½in (3.8cm) wide, or 14 RW plus 1in (2.5cm) seam allowance

1 Make a simple pattern if you are making more than one flower of the same size. Each pattern represents one petal in the flower.

2 Starting at the outer edge of the ribbon, sew gathering stitches diagonally down to the inner edge. This line will be one side of a "mountain." The angle of the stitching line will be dictated by the width of the mountain's base (see Step 5).

With the last stitch ending on the right side of the ribbon, bring the needle to the wrong side of the ribbon and start your next stitch next to the selvage. This will create a "turning stitch."

3 Each large petal of the flower should be at least 2 RW long; here the "valley," which will become the large petal and where the gathering stitches are placed, is 2 RW or 3in (7.5cm) long. Sew along the bottom edge of the ribbon.

4 Place another turning stitch at the end of the valley, then sew diagonally up to the outer edge of the ribbon, place another turning stitch at the edge of the ribbon, and sew diagonally down to the inner edge of the next petal to form a "mountain." The mountain base in the sample is 1 RW (1½in or 3.8cm) wide.

1

2

3

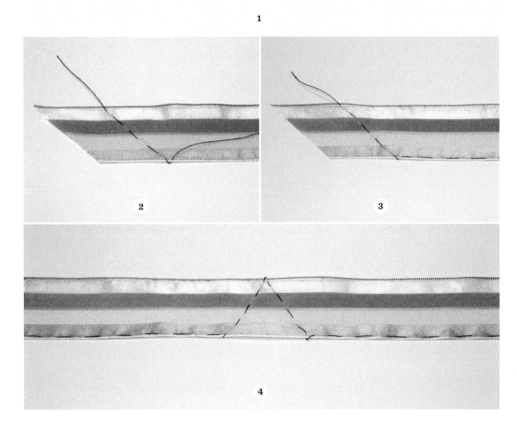

4

5 This diagram shows the stitching lines for one petal.

6 Repeat Steps 2–4, the valley and mountain stitching sequence, starting with the turning stitch, for each petal. End the stitching sequence at a mountain peak. The number of valleys will be equal to the number of petals. Here there are five valleys and five mountains (counting the mountain formed when you join the two ends of the ribbon together).

7 Pulling gently on the gathering thread causes an "earthquake": it pulls the thread straight and gathers the ribbon into petals. The valleys will become large petals and the mountains will become small, inner petals. Here, the first valley erupts to become the first large petal.

8 The first mountain collapses to become a smaller, inner petal.

9 The second valley becomes the second large petal and the second mountain collapses to become the second small petal.

10 Continue gathering until all five large petals are formed.

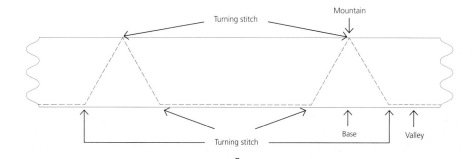

5

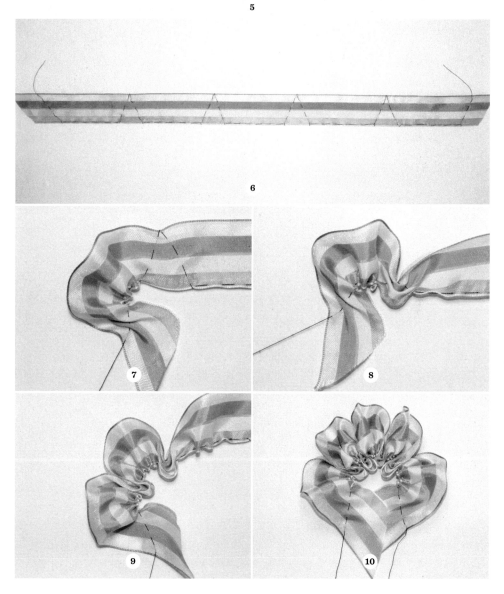

6

7

8

9

10

11 Twist the thread tails around a pin to temporarily secure the gathers, then spread the gathers equally among the petals.

12 Bring the pins/gathering threads together, creating the circular flower.

13 When you are satisfied with the flower shape, secure the gathering threads with a small knot.

14 Pull the petals up to access the two ribbon ends beneath.

15 Sew the two ribbon ends together.

16 A completed five-petal flower.

FINISHING TOUCHES

Add leaves, stems, and stamens or a center to give further dimension to your flower (see pp. 380–87).

VARIATION

1 Add more petals to make a pansy or other flowers. Changing the length of the valleys will change the size of your petals. Again, this ribbon is divided into five valleys and mountains, but the valleys here are 3 RW across the base and the mountains are 1 RW at the base (see Step 2 photo, right).

2 The left-hand flower is made with smaller valleys (2 RW) and has more distinct outer petals, while the right-hand flower has larger valleys (3 RW) that have resulted in nearly indistinguishable outer petals.

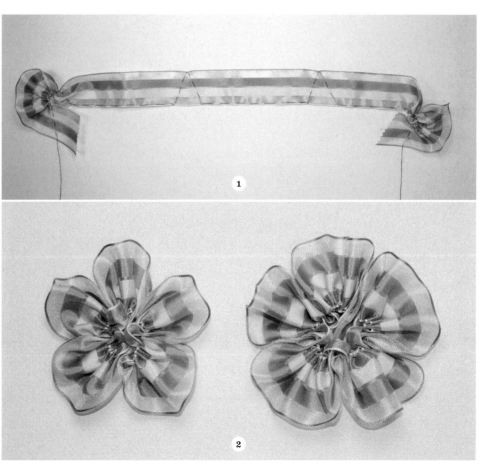

Pansy (Viola)

A pansy has five petals: two at the top, one at each side, and one at the bottom with a slight beard. You can make the beard, or any pair of petals, in a different color, as shown here.

MATERIALS

To create a pansy 4in (10cm) wide:
• For the two side petals and beard, 22in (56cm) of ombre silk ribbon, 1½in (3.8cm) wide, or 14 RW plus 1in (2.5cm) for seam allowance
• For the two top petals, 11½in (29cm) of silk organza ribbon in a complementary color, 1½in (3.8cm) wide, or 7 RW plus 1in (2.5cm) for seam allowance

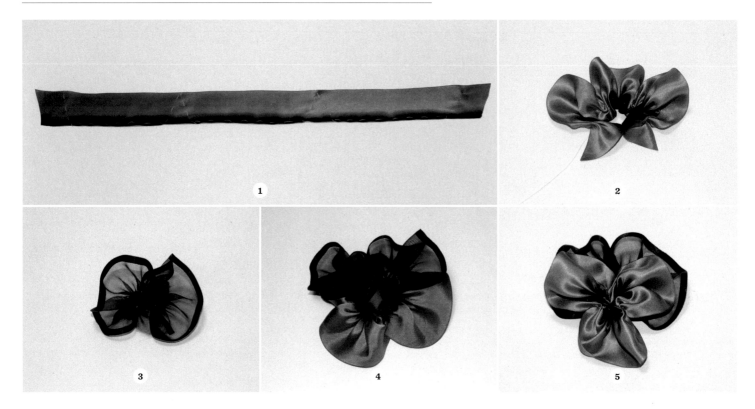

1 Using the U-petal technique (see Plum Blossom, Steps 1–4, p. 362), sew three petals. In this sample, each petal is 3 RW or 4½in (11.5cm) long, measured in the valley, and the base of each mountain is ⅔ RW or 1in (2.5cm) wide.

2 Gather the ribbon to form the three petals, then sew the ribbon ends together to form a circle.

3 Make a complementary-colored ribbon into the top two petals.

4 Working on the wrong side, slide the ribbon ends of the two top petals around the ribbon ends of the other three petals.

5 Looking at the right side of the pansy, move the contrasting petals around until they sit properly with the other petals. Sew the two ribbons together.

FINISHING TOUCHES

Add leaves and a stem to your flower (see pp. 380–82).

Geranium (*Pelargonium*)

Geraniums, poppies (*Papaver*), and globeflowers (*Trollius*) are good examples of flowers that can be made with the L-shaped ribbon technique. Short pieces of ribbon are sewn together and gathered to produce individual overlapping petals. This works well with ombre ribbon: the petals will change color from center to edge.

MATERIALS

To create a flower 3in (7.5cm) wide:
• Multiple pieces of 6 RW ombre taffeta ribbon, each 6in (15cm) long x 1in (2.5cm) wide

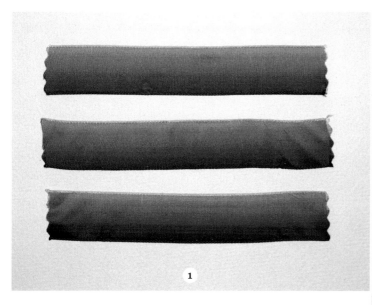

1 Cut the ribbon into 6 RW lengths, one piece for every petal.

2 Lay two ribbon pieces at right angles to each other, overlapping the ends by 1 RW, to form an L shape. Pin together. Repeat with the next piece of ribbon to form a U shape.

Starting at top of the L, stitch diagonally across the width of the ribbon. Make a turning stitch at the ribbon edge and then stitch across the valley (see Plum Blossom, Steps 2–3, p. 362) of the piece of ribbon.

Stitch diagonally across the elbow of the L, joining the two pieces of ribbon. Continue stitching along the valley of the central ribbon piece, then stitch diagonally across the second elbow and along the right-hand valley of the U.

3 Pulling gently on the thread, gather the ribbon into petals.

4 Continue to pull on the thread until all three petals are formed.

5 When you are happy with the shape of the petals, wrap the thread tails around a pin to hold the gathers. Knot the gathering threads and sew the petals into the flower shape.

6 Add stamens or a center to complete your flower (see pp. 384–87).

VARIATION

1 Add as many ribbon pieces as you wish, varying the size and/or colors of the ribbons. Here, seven pieces of ribbon are sewn together to make seven petals.

2 Gently gather the ribbon, creating a spiral of petals.

3 The completed seven-petal flower.

Fringe bells *(Shortia soldanelloides)*

This flower uses a paper circle as a pattern, which can be any size. Depending on the ribbon width and the size of circle, the flower works well sitting flat like a daisy (*Bellis*) or hanging down like a daffodil (*Narcissus*). The fringe bells shown use thin ribbon for clarity, but wider ribbon will make a fuller flower.

MATERIALS

To create a flower 6in (15cm) wide:
- Piece of paper
- Thumbtack
- 56in (142cm) of long ribbon, ¼in (6mm) wide, but do not cut the ribbon from the spool until Step 5

1

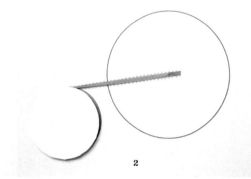

2

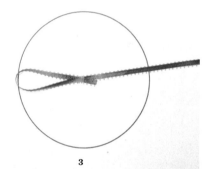

3

1 Draw a circle with a diameter of 6in (10cm) on the piece of paper. Place the thumbtack in the center of the circle with the point sticking up. You can stick the thumbtack through from the back of the paper and tape it in place on the back.

2 Fold the raw end of the ribbon under twice to create a hem and push onto the thumbtack. Pull the ribbon tail out to one side.

3 Using the circle edge as a guide, fold the ribbon's tail back across the circle, anchoring the ribbon on the thumbtack. Note that the ribbon is anchored on the thumbtack slightly off center: this will direct the petals around the circle as you work.

4 Fold the ribbon's tail back across the circle, anchoring the ribbon on the thumbtack, again slightly off center to create a second loop.

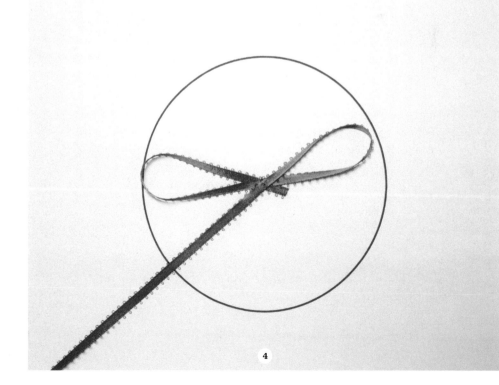

4

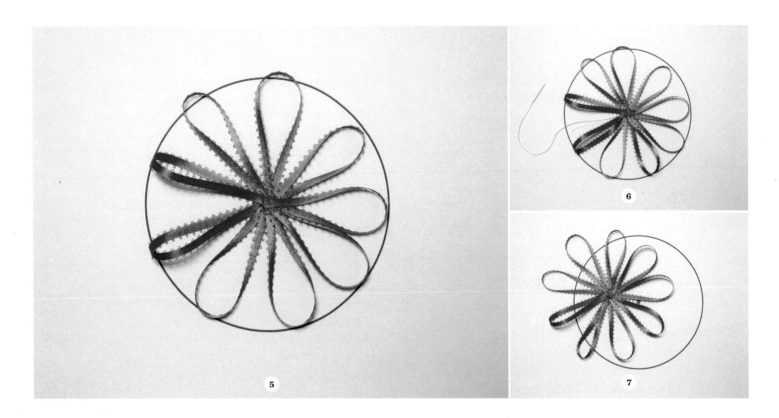

5

6

7

5 Repeat Steps 3–4 until the flower looks full. Cut the ribbon's tail, leaving ¹/₂in (1.3cm). Fold ¹/₄in (6mm) of raw end under twice to create a clean finish. Press with your fingers. Place the folded end on the thumbtack.

6 While keeping the ribbon on the thumbtack, carefully push a threaded needle through the center of the flower (here green thread is used for clarity). Make a small stitch to secure all the ribbon layers in place. Lift the flower off the thumbtack and add a few more stitches to secure the flower.

7 The completed flower.

FINISHING TOUCHES

Add stems (see pp. 383), or add a foxglove-style blossom (see p. 361) in the center.

Dior rose

This popular fabric rose was made famous by the designer Christian Dior, who clustered the roses at the waists of his dresses and massed them on the backs of his gowns.

MATERIALS

To create a flat, open rose 5in (12.5cm) wide, and a smaller bud 2in (5cm) wide:
• ¹/₂yd (0.5m) of fabric, such as heavy silk organza (used here); any type of fabric can be used, but thick fabric will not gather easily, so you may wish to skip the small petals

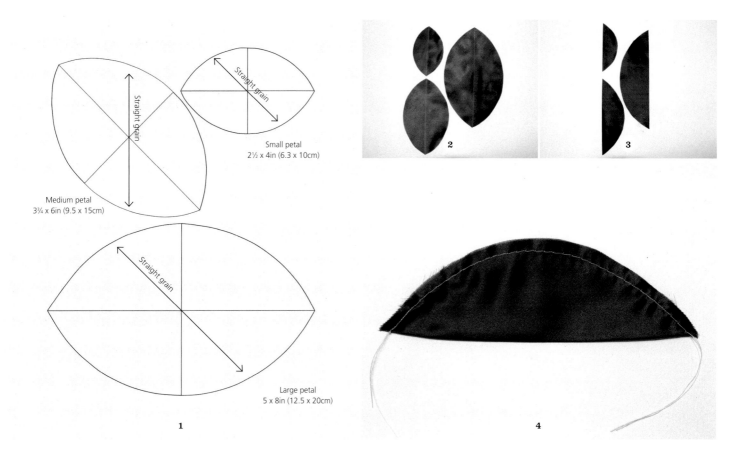

Small petal
2½ x 4in (6.3 x 10cm)

Medium petal
3¾ x 6in (9.5 x 15cm)

Large petal
5 x 8in (12.5 x 20cm)

1 Copy and cut out the paper patterns.

2 Cut out at least two of each petal size, paying particular attention to the grain markings on the patterns. The sample here is made with three each of the small- and medium-sized petals and four large-sized petals.

3 Fold all the rose petals in half along the long centerline.

4 Using a ¹/₄in (6mm) seam allowance, start sewing with a very small stitch of 1.5mm (15 s.p.i.), for ¹/₄in (6mm). With the needle down, change stitch length to 5mm (5 s.p.i.). Sew the rest of the petal edge in the long stitch length.

The short stitch length will lock the thread to the petal, so you do not have to knot the thread tails on that end of the petal. The long stitches will be the gathering stitches.

CHANGING THE STITCH LENGTH

When changing stitch length on the sewing machine, always leave the needle down in the fabric. If the needle is up when you change the length, it will make a thread nest on the wrong side.

5 Gather the first small petal and knot the thread ends. Gather the other two small petals, but leave the threads of these unknotted.

6 Wrap the first small petal around your finger to form the center of the rose.

7 Wrap a second petal around the first petal, being careful to offset the start of the second petal by a third or a half of a petal to create a more realistic-looking flower.

8 Once you are happy with the shape of the rose center, knot the gathering thread of the second petal. Hand-sew the two petals together. Here, the yellow thread secures the petals.

9 Wrap the third small petal around the growing rose center. Tighten or loosen the gathering threads to make the petal fit with your first two petals.

The small petals should create one or two rows of petals, depending on how you position them. Knot the gathering thread and then sew the third petal to the bud.

10 Add the medium petals in the same way.

11 Be careful to keep the gathering stitching and seam allowances aligned at the bottom of the rose. Each time you change petal sizes, the first petal will seem very large and you will want to slide the seam allowance farther down to make it smaller, but all petals should be aligned along the raw edges.

12 Continue adding petals in increasing sizes until the rose looks complete.

13

14

13 The completed rose viewed from the side.

14 The completed ten-petal rose.

FINISHING TOUCHES

Add leaves (see pp. 380–82) and stamens or a center to your flower (see pp. 384–87).

VARIATION

1 Make small rose buds by using just the small and medium petals. Two small and three medium petals were used to make this bud.

2 The finished rose and rose bud.

1

2

Poinsettia (Euphorbia pulcherrima)

Poinsettias, lilies (*Lilium*), and clematis (*Clematis*) are some of the flowers you can make using the triangle-petal technique. Silk organza or Ultrasuede® Light are good fabric choices for triangle-petal flowers, as they do not fray; the petals are cut out and gathered into a flower.

MATERIALS

To create a flower 4in (10cm) wide:
• ¹⁄₂yd (0.5m) of lightweight organza
• Paper pattern of an isosceles triangle

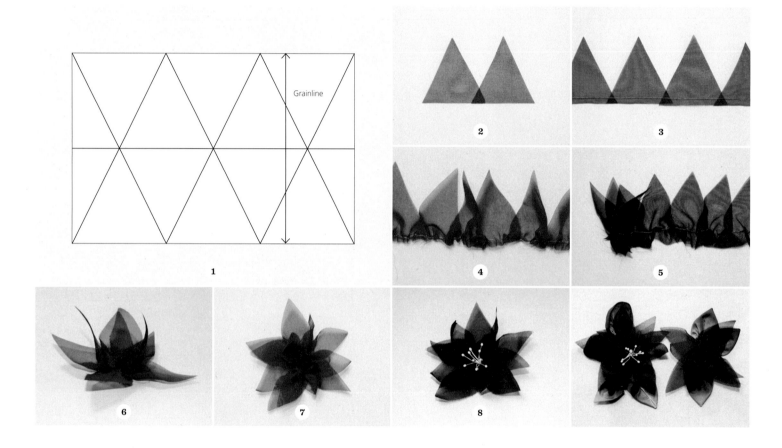

1 Cut out a series of identical isosceles triangles. Here, one flower is made with eight petals (Step 7), and one is made with twelve petals (Step 8). When cutting from fabric, be sure to cut the bases of the triangles on the straight or cross grain to minimize fraying on all edges.

2 Lay the triangles in a line, overlapping the bases by ¹⁄₄–¹⁄₂in (6mm–1.3cm).

3 Stitch the triangles together with a ¹⁄₂in (1.3cm) seam allowance, using a long basting stitch. If a smaller seam allowance is used, the stitches may pull out of the fabric as the petals are being gathered.

4 Gently gather the triangles. Knot one end of the gathering threads: this will be your beginning petal.

5 Gently pull the gathering thread and adjust the gathers until you are satisfied with the shape of the flower center.

6 Leave the other end of the threads unknotted until the flower is completed so the gathers can be adjusted. Sew the petals together as you work, gathering, twisting, and sewing the petals into a flower.

7 The finished poinsettia made with eight petals.

8 The finished poinsettia made with twelve petals. Add stamens or centers to complete the flower (see pp. 384–87).

FINISHING TOUCHES

Add leaves to your flower (see pp. 380–82).

Camellia *(Camellia)*

This flower features gathered scalloped petals and should be made with a sturdy fabric, such as the silk duchess satin used here or blanket binding. Marigolds (*Tagetes*) and gardenias (*Gardenia*) can also be made using this technique.

MATERIALS

To create a flower 5in (12.5cm) wide:
• Piece of fabric, 4in (10cm) wide x 86in (218cm) long, folded in half lengthwise—press the lengthwise fold or leave it soft

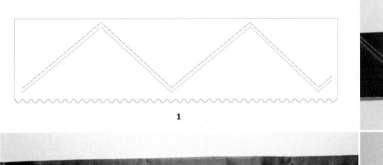

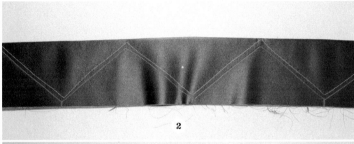

1 Mark a pattern of triangles on your fabric. Each valley will become a flower petal. The flower here has 14 petals.

2 Using a small stitch length of 1.5mm (15 spi), stitch along the lower line, pivoting at each mountain top and valley bottom. (Here, the stitches were sewn in green thread for clarity.)

Next, change the stitch length to a long basting stitch of 5mm (5 spi). Sew ¼in (6mm) above the previous stitching line. Be careful not to stitch off the edge of the fabric, and to keep the stitching line continuous. (Here, this second line of stitches was sewn in white thread.)

3 Trim away below the line of small stitches (sewn here in green thread).

4 Gently pull on the gathering thread, which will straighten the stitching line and create scalloped petals above the stitching line.

5 The scallops may spiral around the thread, so be careful to straighten them before twisting them into a flower shape.

6 Twist the petals into a spiral shape to create the flower before sewing the layers of the flower together.

7 The completed flower.

FINISHING TOUCHES

Add stamens or a center to your flower (see pp. 384–87).

Hollyhock (Alcea)

This dense flower can be made from any fabric cut on the bias, and expanded to any size. Hollyhocks are made with densely gathered fabric; gather the fabric more lightly to make petunias (*Petunia*).

MATERIALS

To create a flower 4in (10cm) wide:
- 34in (86cm) of bias-cut fabric, 3¹⁄₂in (9cm) wide, folded to 1³⁄₄in (4.5cm) wide
- 30in (76cm) of bias-cut fabric, 3in (8cm) wide, folded to 1¹⁄₂in (4cm) wide
- 28 in (71cm) of bias-cut fabric, 1¹⁄₂in (4cm) wide, folded to ³⁄₄in (2cm) wide

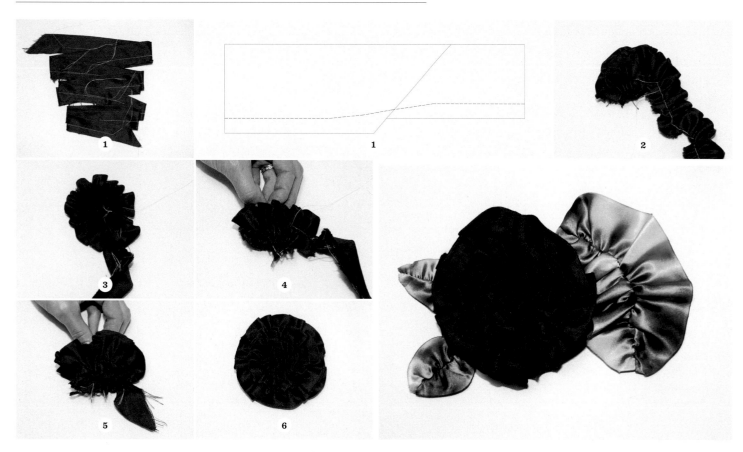

1 Cut the bias strips. The length and width can be altered to suit your design. Sew the strips together to form one long piece. Fold the strip in half lengthwise, with the joining seam allowances hidden inside. Press. At each join, trim away just a little bit of the seam allowance on the larger bias strip to make a gradual change from the wider strip to the narrower strip, as shown in the diagram.

Sew each section of the bias strip with a long basting stitch ¹⁄₂in (1.3cm) from the raw edge, creating the gathering stitches for the next step (see Machine Gathering Stitch, p. 25). Overlap the basting stitches for 2in (5cm) from one section to the next.

2 Gently gather the first section of bias strip. Twist into a spiral shape to form the flower. Secure the layers of gathered bias strip by stitching them together, just above the gathering thread.

3 Repeat Step 2 with the next section of bias strip.

4 Keep the raw edges of the seam allowances aligned as you gather each section.

5 The bottom of the completed flower. Pull the fabric tail over the bottom to cover the seam allowances, or trim the fabric tail away and cover the seam allowances with a yo-yo (see p. 389).

6 The completed flower.

FINISHING TOUCHES

Add leaves to your flower (see pp. 380–82).

Folded rose / Baltimore rose / Cabbage rose

For this flower, ribbon anchored to a cone of buckram (a loosely woven, stiffened cotton or linen cloth) is folded twice to make each petal. The lushness of the petals depends on the tightness of the folds.

MATERIALS

To create a rose 3¼in (8cm) wide:
• Piece of buckram
• 36in (91.5cm) of double-faced satin ribbon, 1½in (3.8cm) wide

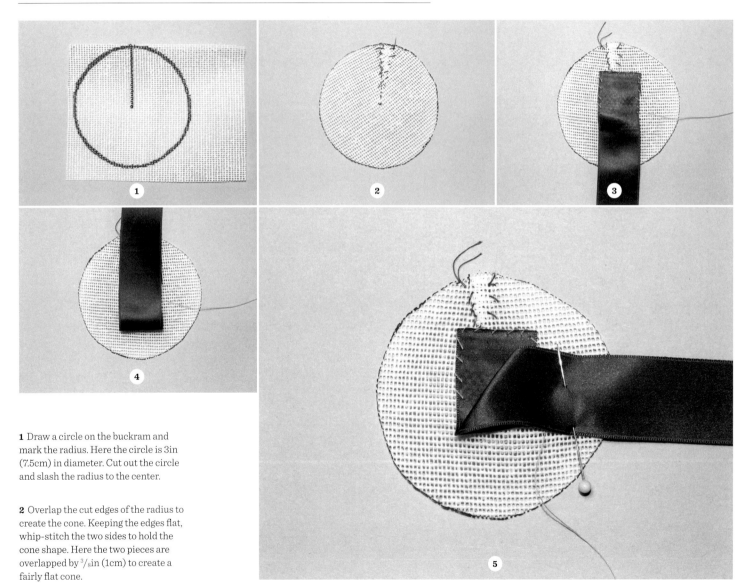

1 Draw a circle on the buckram and mark the radius. Here the circle is 3in (7.5cm) in diameter. Cut out the circle and slash the radius to the center.

2 Overlap the cut edges of the radius to create the cone. Keeping the edges flat, whip-stitch the two sides to hold the cone shape. Here the two pieces are overlapped by ³⁄₈in (1cm) to create a fairly flat cone.

3 Fold under the raw end of the ribbon and place the end of the ribbon over the tip of the cone. Sew the ribbon to the buckram on three sides, leaving the ribbon's tail free.

4 Fold the ribbon back over the stitched section at a 90° angle.

5 Fold the ribbon at a 45° angle toward the thread tail, exposing a bias fold of the ribbon. Pin to the buckram.

6 Finish the first petal by sewing across the ribbon, anchoring only the top layer of ribbon, using the ribbon beneath as a stitching guide. Pull the thread tail straight out from the ribbon.

7 Fold the ribbon across the stitched section at a 90° angle.

8 Fold the ribbon at a 45° angle toward the thread tail, making another bias fold in the ribbon. Pin to the buckram.

9 Finish the second petal by sewing across the ribbon, anchoring only the top layer of ribbon, using the ribbon beneath as a stitching guide. Pull the thread tail straight out from the ribbon.

Repeat Steps 7–9 until you reach the end of the first row of petals.

10 After you complete the first row of petals around the center, adjust the angle of the folds to allow you to create more petals as you work the second row, starting here with the sixth petal. Continue until you reach the edge of the buckram or the end of the ribbon.

11 As you reach the edge of the buckram—here the 18th petal—note how the angle of the folds has become less acute to make the petals wider.

12 When the buckram is full, fold the ribbon's tail to the underside and stitch it to the buckram.

13 The completed flower.

VARIATION

---

1 If you decide your flower is finished before you reach the edge of the buckram, you can trim the buckram; just be careful not to snip any stitches.

2 The wrong side of the flower, with the buckram trimmed away.

3 The completed flower with the buckram trimmed away.

Finishing touches

Once you have created your flowers, use these elements to complete the design.

Curved leaves

MATERIALS

To create a leaf 2in (5cm) long and 1^1/$_2$in (3.8cm) wide:
• 2 RW of hand-dyed silk ribbon, 1^1/$_2$in (3.8cm) wide

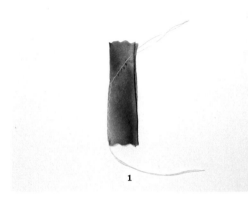

1

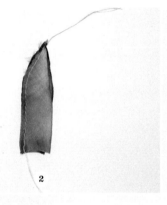

2

3

1 Fold the ribbon in half lengthwise, right sides together. Press. Using a long machine gathering stitch or hand stitch, sew a curve across the top of the ribbon from the top of the outside edge and then down to the bottom of the folded edge.

2 Trim away the ribbon above the curved stitching line.

3 Gently gather the leaf. Knot the threads, but do not cut them. Open the leaf, arrange the gathers and then gently press. Use the thread tails to help you hold the leaf in the proper shape while pressing.

4 Turn the very tip and the bottom of the leaf under to hide the raw edges.

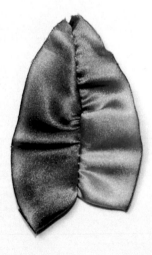

4

Prairie point leaves

These directions are for single leaves, but you can also make a string of leaves (see Prairie Points, pp. 347–48).

MATERIALS

To create a leaf 1¼in (3cm) long and 1in (2.5cm) wide:
• 4 RW of ribbon for each leaf; here 5in (12.5cm) of iridescent silk ribbon, 1¼in (3cm) wide, is used

1 Divide the ribbon in half. Fold half the ribbon's tail down at a 45° angle.

2 Fold down the other half also at a 45° angle. Press.

3 Turn the ribbon over. Machine or hand-sew across the bottom of triangle with a long gathering stitch.

4 Gently gather the ribbon to create the leaf. Knot the threads.

VARIATION

Experiment with different ribbons for effect. Here, these prairie point leaves have been made from ombre dyed ribbon.

Boat leaves

Long boat leaves can be intertwined with flowers.

MATERIALS

To create a leaf 5in (12.5cm) long and 3in (7.5cm) wide:
• 20in (50cm) of iridescent hand-dyed silk ribbon, 1¹/₂in (3.8cm) wide, cut into two pieces each 10in (25cm) long or folded in half

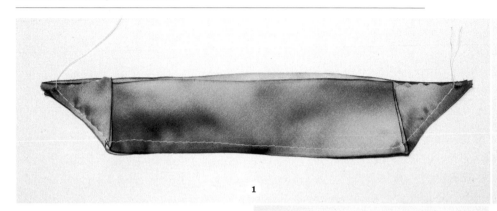

1

2

3

4

1 Place the two pieces of ribbon with right sides together. Fold up both corners at a 45° angle. Machine- or hand-sew a long gathering stitch from the top corner down to the bottom, along the bottom, and then up to the other top corner.

2 Gently gather the ribbon to the desired length. Knot the threads but do not cut them.

3 Open the leaf, arrange the gathers, and then gently press. Use the thread tails to help you hold the leaf in the proper shape while pressing.

4 The completed boat leaf.

U-petal leaves

Use the U-petal technique (see Plum Blossom, Steps 1–4, p. 362) to create clusters of leaves. Shown here is a three-leaf cluster made from grosgrain ribbon.

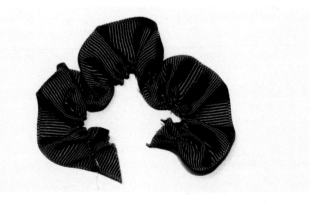

Stems

Hand-dyed ribbons or fabrics provide good color variations along a stem.

MATERIALS

A length of ribbon or a strip of fabric

This length of hand-dyed ribbon has been hand-pleated and twisted to give it texture and depth. Use steam from the iron to set the twists and pleats.

This length of grosgrain ribbon was folded in half lengthwise, then machine-stitched in a wavy pattern. Moving the ribbon on the machine bed while stitching introduces an uneven tension to the ribbon, which causes it to buckle slightly. Stitch with a light green thread, or a color that coordinates with the flower.

Seedpods

Seedpods are made in the same way as foxgloves (see p. 361), but both ends are gathered and the pod is stuffed. The picot edging on the ribbon adds a lovely ruffled finish to the pod.

MATERIALS

To create a pod 1in (2.5cm) round:
• 2 RW plus seam allowances of picot-edged, ombre silk ribbon, 1¹/₂in (3.8cm) wide

1

2

3

1 Fold the ribbon in half, right sides together. Using a ¹/₄in (6mm) seam allowance, sew along the raw edges. Turn the tube right side out and press.

2 Hand-sew a line of gathering stitches ¹/₈in (3mm) from both selvages.

3 Gently gather one end and knot the threads. Stuff the tube with a cotton ball or similar filling. Gently gather the other end and knot the threads.

4 The completed seedpod.

4

Stamens and centers

Stamens and centers can be made of almost anything you wish:
buttons, sequins, beads, purchased stamens, ribbon, or found seeds,
for example.

BEADS AND SEQUINS

Sew sequins in the center of your flower, either
singly or in a pattern of multiple sequins.

Beads can also be sewn on singly or in multiples.

PURCHASED STAMENS

Stamens are available in a wide range of colors and sizes.

1 You can purchase a bundle of stamens and select the number you wish to use.

2 Or buy a pre-arranged set of stamens in a stem.

3 If you purchase a set of stamens on a stem, you can also select the number you wish to use by thinning the stamens. Simply unwrap the stem and remove the unwanted pieces.

4 To use the stamens, fold them in half and tie them together with thread. Thread a needle onto the thread.

5 Guide the needle and thread through the center of the flower from the right side. Pull the stamens into position.

6 When the stamens are properly arranged, sew the thread ends to the wrong side of the flower.

RIBBON

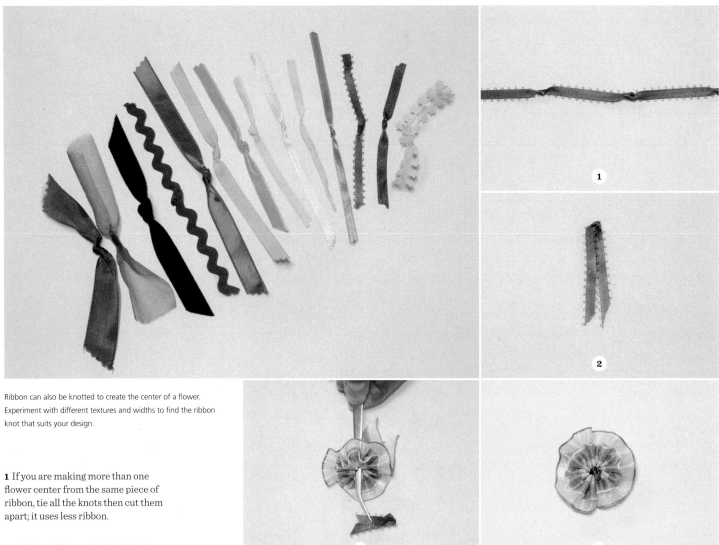

Ribbon can also be knotted to create the center of a flower. Experiment with different textures and widths to find the ribbon knot that suits your design.

1 If you are making more than one flower center from the same piece of ribbon, tie all the knots then cut them apart; it uses less ribbon.

2 Fold the ribbon in half with the knot at the top.

3 Pull the ribbon tails through the center of the flower from the right side with tweezers.

4 The completed flower with a pink ribbon knot for the center.

VARIATION

1 For a larger flower, tie a double knot to increase the size of the center (single knot on the left and double knot on the right).

2 A flower with a double-knotted ribbon for the center.

FRINGED FABRIC

A strip of fabric can be fringed to look like the pistils found in many flowers, such as poppies and old-fashioned roses.

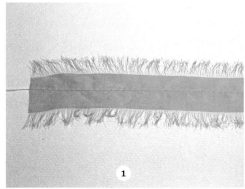

1 Cut a strip of fabric. Fringe both sides (see Basic Fringe, p. 202). Sew gathering stitches down the center of the strip.

2 Fold the strip along the gathering stitches. Press.

3 Gather the strip into a small circle. Secure the circle shape with stitches and add it to a flower.

4 The fringed center in a flower.

Sewing flowers and leaves to buckram

To fix flowers and leaves into a permanent bouquet, you will need to sew them to some buckram (a loosely woven, stiffened cotton or linen cloth).

1 Create an arrangement of flowers and leaves on a piece of buckram. Individually lift each piece and place a piece of double-sided sticky tape on the wrong side of the flower or leaf. Stick it back down on the buckram.

2 Carefully turn the flowers and buckram over. Pin each piece to the buckram from the wrong side. Remove the pieces of sticky tape.

3 Sew the flowers and leaves to the buckram from the wrong side, working from the center to the edges, shown here in blue thread.

4 Trim away as much buckram as you can. Round off all the corners, but leave enough buckram to keep the petals and leaves from flopping over, and to keep the whole arrangement stable.

Slip-stitch around the edge of the buckram, changing thread to match the colors of the flowers and leaves. Add a snap or pin back to the buckram to attach the bouquet to a garment.

5 The finished bouquet.

Yo-yos

Yo-yos can be used to cover the seam allowance at the back of a flower. Sewing a snap into the yo-yo will allow you to remove the flower from the garment for cleaning.

MATERIALS

- Silk organza or lining fabric are nice to use because they are not bulky, but any fabric will work
- #6 snap ($^3/_8$in or 1cm)

1 Cut a circle twice the size of the finished yo-yo; here the circle is $1^1/_2$in (3.8cm) in diameter.

2 Make a small hole for the ball of the snap to go through. Using a blunt, thick tapestry needle, poke the needle tip between the fibers of the fabric at the starting point of your stitching line. Work the needle back and forth to create a hole without breaking any fibers. Insert the ball of the snap into the hole.

3 Working on the wrong side, sew the ball half of the snap into the center of the yo-yo, with the ball itself protruding through the fabric. This yo-yo will be bigger than the snap as it will cover the seam allowance on the bottom of the flower, too.

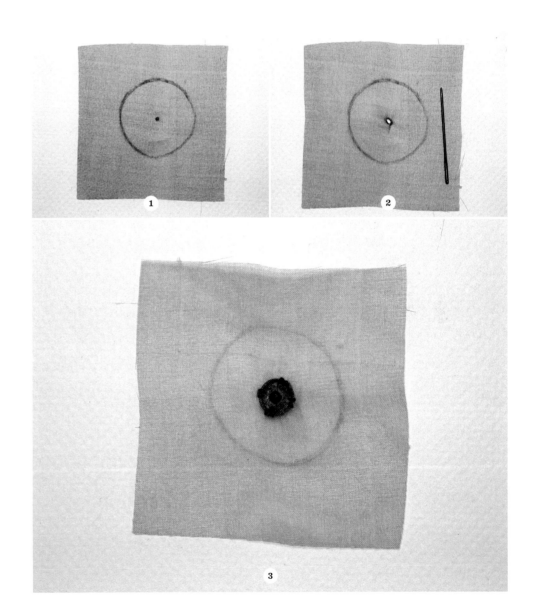

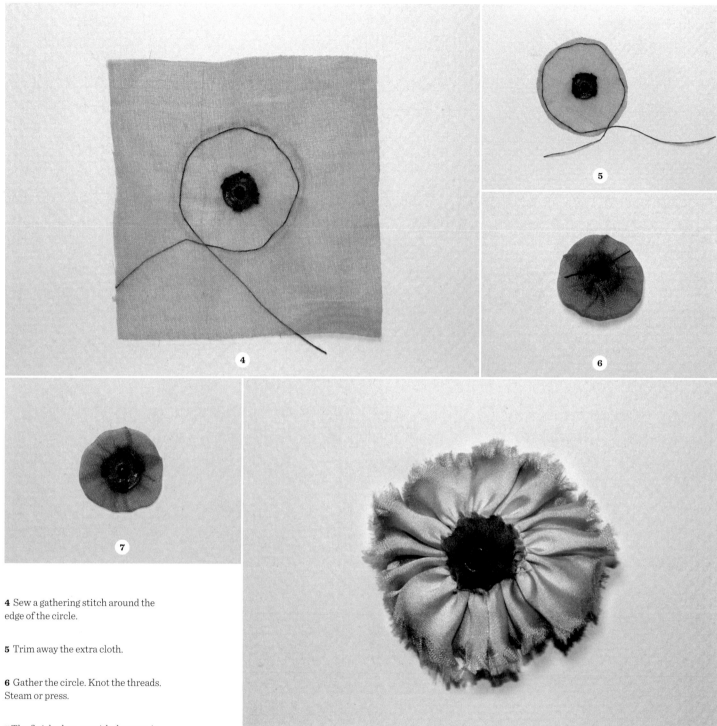

4 Sew a gathering stitch around the edge of the circle.

5 Trim away the extra cloth.

6 Gather the circle. Knot the threads. Steam or press.

7 The finished yo-yo with the snap in the center.

8 Sew the yo-yo onto the bottom of the flower. Cover the other half of the snap and sew onto the garment. If you make the yo-yo in green fabric, it will look like part of the flower stem.

Covered snaps

Cover a snap in matching fabric to camouflage it, or cover it in contrasting fabric to make a feature out of a closure.

1 Draw two circles on your fashion fabric approximately 1.5 to 2 times the diameter of the snap.

2 Before cutting out the circles, hand-sew a line of gathering stitches just inside the edge of the circles. Cut out the circles.

3 Place the ball part of the snap in the center of one of the fabric circles and the socket part in the other. Make sure the ball and the socket are both facing down into the fabric.

4 Draw up the fabric using the gathering stitches, keeping the snap centered in the circle. Do not draw the fabric completely taut around the snap: leave a little slack to allow the ball to snap into the hole through the fabric. Knot the gathering threads. After the two parts of the snap have been pressed together a couple of times, the ball should poke through the fabric. Sew both parts of the snap onto the garment.

5 The finished covered snaps.

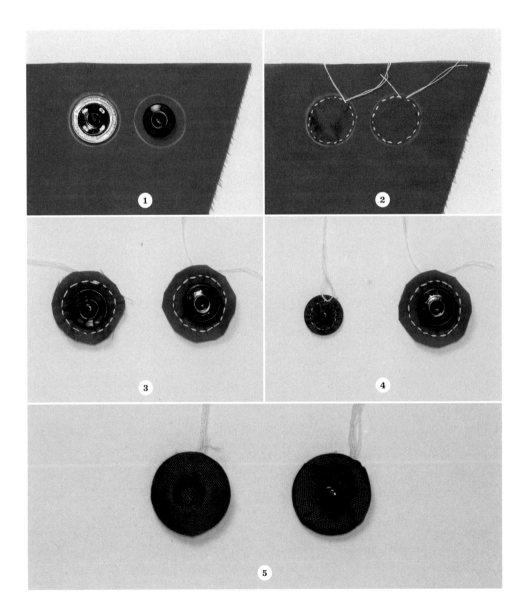

Glossary

Anchoring stitch Formed of two small stitches, sewn one on top of the other, instead of a knot at the beginning or ending of a line of stitches, similar to a *backstitch*.

Appliqué The art of layering one or more fabrics upon a base fabric to create design. From the French, "applied."

Backing fabric A fabric placed behind fashion fabric to add strength and stability, or to protect the back of the fashion fabric from friction. Backing fabrics are commonly used with trapunto (see pp. 116–17) and corded quilting (see pp. 118–21).

Backstitch A single extra stitch made going backwards instead of a knot at the beginning or ending of a line of stitches, similar to an *anchoring stitch*. Also an *embroidery* stitch (see p. 297) and a *basting* stitch.

Basting A series of large, temporary stitches sewn to hold two or more layers of fabric together, or to hold a trim in place before the final sewing. Basting is useful when the fabric layers shift too easily against each other, when pins cause the fabric to be lumpy, and when right and left sides (e.g., of sleeves) must match and you need to double-check fabric placement.

Batting A fluffy fiber product made of cotton, silk, wool, or polyester, used between two layers of fabric to provide loft and/or warmth.

Bias The bias line runs at 45° to the straight *grainline* (45° from the selvage and 45° from the straight raw edge) of a piece of fabric. The bias grain is more malleable and stretchy than straight and cross grains, which can be an asset.

Blind hem stitch A machine-sewn stitch in which a curved needle is inserted sideways into the fabric, picking up only a few threads of the fabric to create a nearly invisible stitch. One of the features of this stitch is that if you pull on one end of the thread, the entire seam will unravel; this can be good or bad.

Bobbin A small, round machine part, made of metal or plastic, that holds the lower thread in a sewing machine. Metal bobbin cases have a tensioning device for the thread built into them; plastic bobbins rely on tensioning devices built into the sewing machine.

Bobbin thread The lower thread in a sewing machine, which passes through a tensioning device before taken up by the needle thread in the "thread race" to form a stitch. See also *needle thread*.

Buckram A loosely woven fabric, stiffened with pyroxylin or sizing, used for backing flower corsages and stiffening curtain headers. Buckram can be purchased in 3, 4, 20, up to 60in (7.5, 10, 50, up to 150cm) widths.

Cockade A circular knot or arrangements of ribbons, often used to trim a hat.

Cord Any sort of round trim. Rat-tail cord is a cord that is smooth, shiny and ³/₃₂in (2mm) wide.

Cording A strand of filler (e.g., yarn, string, or cotton cable) that is covered with fashion fabric. The seam allowances of cording are turned to the inside to make a smooth fashion-fabric-covered strand (see p. 150).

Cordonette A yarn or thread used to outline the clothwork motifs in lace.

Dart A triangle-shaped tuck used for fitting garments. Most darts radiate from the bust area or the waist.

Edgestitching Stitching along the edge of a pleat, hem, or other garment detail to anchor a folded edge or draw attention to the edge.

Embroidery The art of fancy stitching to decorate fabric with thread. Embroidery can be sewn by hand or by machine.

Feed dogs The two rows of small teeth on the bed of a sewing machine surrounding the hole the needle enters with each stitch. The feed dogs grab the (lower) fabric and move it along the stitching path.

Finger-pressing The pressing open of a seam or along a fold of fabric with your fingers; the warmth and pressure of your fingers serve as a gentle, lightweight iron.

Finished edge The final edge of a garment as it lies against the body: e.g., a neckline edge, the edge of a cuff, the lowest edge of a pant hem.

French seam A seam that is sewn twice to enclose the raw edges of the seam allowance. This seam treatment is useful with sheer fabrics when the raw edge of the fabric would be unsightly and/or with fabrics that unravel easily. To make a French seam, assuming a ¹/₂in (1.3cm) seam allowance:

1. Match the seam allowances wrong sides together. Sew the seam at ¹/₄in (6mm). Press the seam as sewn.

2. Trim the seam allowance to ¹/₈in (3mm).

3. Open the fabric up, exposing the seam allowance as a ridge. Push the seam allowance to one side of the stitching line; press. Fold the fabric, right sides together, along the stitching line, to hide the seam allowance inside. Press again, making sure the seam line is at the edge of the fold.

4. Sew at ¹/₄in (6mm). Press the seam as sewn. Open up the fabric to expose the new seam on the wrong side of the fabric. Press the enclosed seam allowance to one side if needed.

Galloon A wide, double-edged lace made in various widths. A double-edged, highly decorative braid is also called a galloon.

Grading seam allowances A technique to reduce bulk. Trim the seam allowance closest to the body to ¹/₈in (3mm) and the seam allowance farther away from the body to ³/₁₆in (5mm). The seam allowance closest to the outside of the garment is longer and covers the shorter seam allowance.

Grainlines The straight grain of a fabric follows the direction of the vertical *warp* yarns running the length of the fabric, parallel to the *selvage*. The cross grain follows the horizontal *weft* yarns running the width of the fabric.

Hotfix The glue inside the back of rhinestones, crystals, nailheads, and studs. The glue is melted with an iron or Hotfix applicator, permanently attaching the trims to the fashion fabric.

Invisible thread Also known as monofilament. A polyester or nylon thread in "Clear " or "Smoke" colors, used in sewing machines when a colored thread would distract from the embellishment.

Mitering The joining of two fabric strips in a diagonal seam. The angle of the diagonal can be obtuse or acute.

Muslin An inexpensive cotton plain-weave fabric, which can be "natural" or bleached. Muslin is good cloth to practice with, as it is relatively cheap; be sure to preshrink it before use, either by washing or ironing it.

Needle thread The upper thread in a sewing machine, which is passed through a set of spring tension disks and along the take-up arm and other guides before finally being threaded through the needle. The needle thread then passes through a hole in the throat plate of the sewing machine to form a loop in the thread race and engage with the *bobbin thread* to form a stitch.

Notches Small snips made within the seam allowance of a pattern and the fashion fabric. Matching the notches of one garment piece to the notches of another garment piece should ensure that the pieces can be accurately sewn together.

Oak tag A stiff but flexible paper, the same as that used to make Manila file folders. Oak tag is undyed, so it can be steamed or wetted without leaching colour onto fashion fabric. Also, oak tag will not break down when wetted, making it ideal for folding and pressing tucks (see p. 48) and pleats (see p. 64).

Off grain Refers to a fabric that has been skewed during weaving or rolling after weaving, such that the *warp* and *weft* yarns do not cross each other at 90°, but at some other angle. Sometimes this can be corrected by wetting the fabric and pulling it to realign the yarns to their proper places.

Also, a pattern can be placed off grain, meaning that the pattern is not properly aligned with the straight grain of the fabric, resulting in the garment piece being cut off grain and then hanging from the body unevenly.

Press cloth A cloth, made of silk organza or thin cotton, placed on top of fabric before pressing with an iron. The press cloth will keep the fashion fabric from scorching or becoming shiny from too much contact with the metal soleplate of the iron. A damp press cloth will make additional steam, which is helpful when setting creases and pleats.

Pressing (soft/hard) Soft pressing is the first pass with an iron when making pleats: a very light touch of steam from an iron held above the fabric. This allows you to check that the pleats are even and straight before hard pressing.

Hard pressing is the second pass with an iron, when a damp *press cloth*, along with lots of steam and pressure from the iron, are used to set the pleats.

Raw edge The unfinished edge of a fabric.

Running stitch A stitch sewn with a quick in-and-out motion of the needle and thread. Running stitch can be used for basting, sewing seams, or embroidery, depending on the stitch length and thread used.

Seam allowance The portion of the fabric outside of the seam lines.

Seam line Another name for the stitching line or the line where the stitches should go.

Selvage The finished woven edge at either side of a bolt of fabric, created when the shuttle carrying the *warp* thread finishes one row of weaving and turns to go back in the other direction for the next row.

Serger A sewing machine that cuts and binds the seam allowance using three, four, or five threads, depending on the machine.

Standing thread The thread coming out of the fabric from the previous stitch.

Staystitching Medium-sized machine stitches sewn along a seam line to stabilize, and sometimes mark, the seam line. For example: a neckline should always be staystitched to prevent it from stretching while the collar or facing is attached. Since a neckline is nearly a circle, some part of the seam line is on the bias, part is on the cross grain, and part is on the straight grain; each of these sections will stretch differently as the neckline is handled. The staystitching will prevent the fabric from stretching where the stitches are sewn.

Steaming Done using an iron or a steamer to shrink fabric, set a seam or a pleat, or smooth out a wrinkle. When using an iron, hold the iron just above the fabric and saturate the fabric with steam until it is just damp. Gently adjust the fabric as needed, steam again, and then do not move the fabric until it is completely dry.

Stitch in the ditch A technique usually used with a bias binding. This last line of stitching should disappear from view when completed.

1. Fold and sew the bias binding as directed on pp. 133–34. The bias binding on the wrong side should be $^{1}/_{8}$in (3mm) longer than on the right side. When you pin through the bias binding's edge, the pins should catch the bias binding on the wrong side but not catch the bias binding on the right side (see Step 10, p. 134).

2. While looking at the right side of the bias binding, place the bound raw edge to your right, with the rest of the project to your left. Move the project to the sewing machine and place it so that machine's needle is just to the left of the seam line. Stitch right next to the seam line, catching the bias strip on the wrong side but being very careful to not catch it on the right side. When you finish sewing, this last line of stiches should be snugged right up to the folded bias strip on the right side and holding the edge of the bias strip in place on the wrong side. Press.

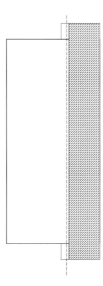

Style line A seam line used for style rather than for the fit of a garment.

Tailor's tacks Loose, temporary placement stitches made in doubled thread with unknotted ends to mark a point on the fabric. Unlike some other marking tools and techniques, tailor's tacks leave no marks behind. To make a tailor's tack:

1. Thread a needle with a long, doubled thread.

2. Make two small stitches, one on top of the other, through one layer of the fabric, where the mark needs to be.

3. Cut the thread, leaving 2in (5cm) thread ends behind.

Thread tail The thread end trailing behind the beginning of a line of stitches.

Thread tracing A line of basting stitches hand-sewn to trace the outline of a garment piece.

Throat plate The smooth piece of metal on a sewing machine's flat "bed" that the *feed dogs* and needle go through. Sometimes the throat plate has a very small hole for the needle to go through, which makes a very good straight stitch. A zigzag stitch requires a large hole in the throat plate, as the needle moves from right to left and back to make each stitch.

Tunneling Occurs when one of the threads in a zigzag stitch pulls too tightly, causing the fabric or trim to become concave. Tunneling can be prevented by loosening the thread tensions of the zigzag stitch, or by adding a layer of interfacing or tissue paper above or below the fabric or trim, which adds stiffness to the stitch path, forcing the thread to shape the stitch without tunneling.

Turning bead The bottom bead in a line of beads in a beaded fringe. When making beaded fringe, the fringe's thread comes down from the fabric or ribbon through a line of beads, through the turning bead at the bottom, makes a U-turn, and then travels back up through the same line of beads, back to the fabric or ribbon. (See p. 237.)

Turning stitch Primarily used in gathering ribbons for flower embellishments. When hand-sewing the gathering, stitch diagonally down to the ribbon's selvage; the last stitch should end with the needle and thread on the wrong side of the ribbon. Bring the needle to the right side of the ribbon and start your next stitch next to the selvage. The stitch coming from the wrong side to the right side is the turning stitch.

Twill tape Fabric tape, made of cotton or polyester, named for its distinctive twill-weave pattern of over two, under one. The diagonal woven pattern is very stable, making twill tape perfect for inserting into seams to add strength and prevent stretching without adding bulk.

Underlining A layer of fabric placed directly beneath fashion fabric to add strength, reduce transparency, or prevent rough fabric scratching skin. Underlining is usually grid-basted to the fashion fabric so the two layers can be treated as one layer. Interfacing and lining are some of the other layers that can be added to a garment.

Warp and weft The two yarns used to weave a piece of fabric. The vertical warp yarn runs the length of the fabric, parallel to the *selvage*. The horizontal weft yarn runs from left to right, and then back again. (See Bias, p. 128, for more information.)

Resources

Books

Appliqué

Sheila Sturrock, *Celtic Knotwork Designs*. Lewes, East Sussex: Guild of Master Craftsman Publications, 1997.

Rose Verney, *The Appliqué Book: A Guide to the Art and Craft of Appliqué*. New York: Alfred A. Knopf, 1991.

Philomena Wiechec, *Celtic Quilt Designs*. Saratoga, Calif.: Celtic Design, 1980.

Beads

Connie Long, *Embellish Chic: Detailing Ready-to-Wear*. Newtown, CT: Taunton Press, 2002.

Carole Rodgers, *Beading Basics*. Iola, WI: Krause Publications, 2006.

Larkin Jean Van Horn, *Beading on Fabric: Encyclopedia of Bead Stitch Techniques*. Loveland, CO: Interweave Press, 2006.

Bias

Lydia Chen, *Chinese Knotting: Creative Designs that Are Easy and Fun*. Boston, MA: Tuttle, 2003.

Distinctive Details: Great Embellishment Techniques for Clothing. A Threads book. Newtown, CT: Taunton Press, 1995.

Braids

Jacqui Carey, *200 Braids to Twist, Knot, Loop, or Weave*. Loveland, CO: Interweave Press, 2007.

Peter Owen, *The Book of Decorative Knots*. New York: Lyons & Burford, 1994.

Decorative ribbons

Nancy Nehring, *Ribbon Trims*. Newtown, CT: Taunton Press, 1999.

Mary Brooks Pickens, *Old-Fashioned Ribbon Trimmings and Flowers*. Mineola, NY: Dover Publications, 1993.

Woman's Institute of Domestic Arts and Sciences, *Ribbon Trimmings: A Course in Six Parts*. Pleasant Hill, CA: Sloane Publications, 1992.

Design

100 Dresses. New York: Costume Institute, Metropolitan Museum of Art; New Haven: Yale University Press, 2010.

Rosemary Crill, Jennifer Wearden, and Verity Wilson, *Dress in Detail from Around the World*. London: V&A Publishing, 2002.

Fashion: The Definitive History of Costume and Style. New York: DK Publishing, 2012.

Akiko Fukai, ed., *Fashion: A History from the 18th to the 20th Century; Collection of the Kyoto Costume Institute*. London: Taschen, 2002.

Avril Hart and Susan North, *Seventeenth and Eighteenth-Century Fashion in Detail*. London: V&A Publishing, 2009.

Sadao Hibi and Motoji Niwa, *Snow, Wave, Pine: Traditional Patterns in Japanese Design*. Translated by Jay W. Thomas. New York: Kodansha International, 2007.

Lucy Johnston, *Nineteenth-Century Fashion in Detail*. London: V&A Publishing, 2009.

Harold Koda and Andrew Bolton, *Chanel*. New York: Metropolitan Museum of Art; New Haven: Yale University Press, 2005. Exhibition catalogue.

Richard Martin and Harold Koda, *Haute Couture*. New York: Metropolitan Museum of Art, 1995. Exhibition catalogue.

Richard Martin and Harold Koda, *Orientalism: Visions of the East in Western Dress*. New York: Metropolitan Museum of Art, 1994. Exhibition catalogue.

Lesley Ellis Miller, *Balenciaga*. London: V&A Publishing, 2007. Exhibition catalogue.

Astrida Schaeffer, *Embellishments: Constructing Victorian Detail*. Rye, NH: Great Life Press, 2013.

Sharon Sadako Takeda et al., *Fashioning Fashion: European Dress in Detail, 1700–1915*. Los Angeles: Los Angeles County Museum of Art; DelMonico Books, 2010. Exhibition catalogue.

Claire Wilcox and Valerie Mendes, *Modern Fashion in Detail*. London: V&A Publications; Woodstock, NY: Overlook Press, 1991.

Claire Wilcox and Valerie D. Mendes, *Twentieth-Century Fashion in Detail*. London: V&A Publishing, 2009.

Embroidery / Ribbon embroidery

Amy Carroll and Dorothea Hall, *Embroidery*. The Pattern Library. New York: Ballantine Books, 1981.

Melinda Coss, *Reader's Digest Complete Book of Embroidery*. Pleasantville, NY: Reader's Digest, 1996.

Judith Baker Montano, *Elegant Stitches: An Illustrated Stitch Guide and Source Book of Inspiration*. Lafayette, CA: C&T Publishing, 1995.

Lynette Mostaghimi, *Countryside Needlecraft Source Book*. London: Anaya, 1992.

Deanna Hall West, *An Encyclopedia of Ribbon Embroidery Flowers: 121 Designs*. San Marcos, CA: American School of Needlework, 1995.

Feathers

Ann Albrizio and Osnat Lustig, *Classic Millinery Techniques: A Complete Guide to Making and Designing Today's Hats*. Asheville, NC: Lark Books, 1998.

Maureen Reilly and Mary Beth Detrich, *Women's Hats of the Twentieth Century: For Designers and Collectors*. Atglen, PA: Schiffer Publishing, 1997.

Flowers

Helen Gibb, *The Secrets of Fashioning Ribbon Flowers: Heirlooms for the Next Generation*. Iola, WI: Krause Publications, 1998.

Candace Kling, *The Artful Ribbon: Beauties in Bloom*. Lafayette, CA: C&T Publishing, 1996.

General sewing

Carol Laflin Ahles, *Fine Machine Sewing: Easy Ways to Get the Look of Hand Finishing and Embellishing*. Newtown, CT: Taunton Press, 2001.

Connie Amaden-Crawford, *A Guide to Fashion Sewing*, 6th edition. New York: Fairchild Publications, 2015.

Charlotte Mankey Calasibetta and Phyllis Tortora, *The Fairchild Dictionary of Fashion*, 3rd edition. New York: Fairchild Publications, 2003.

Georgina O'Hara Callan and Cat Glover, *The Thames & Hudson Dictionary of Fashion and Fashion Designers*, revised, expanded, and updated edition. London and New York: Thames & Hudson, 2008.

Roberta Carr, *Couture: The Art of Fine Sewing*. Portland, OR: Palmer/Pletsch, 1993.

Jane Conlon, *Fine Embellishment Techniques: Classic Details for Today's Clothing*. Newtown, CT: Taunton Press, 1999.

Cy DeCosse, *Sewing for Special Occasions: Bridal, Prom and Evening Dresses*. Singer Sewing Reference Library. Minnetonka, MN: Cy DeCosse Inc., 1994.

Sandy Hunter, *Heirloom Sewing for Today: Classic Materials, Contemporary Machine Techniques*. New York: Sterling Publishing, 1997.

Susan Khalje, *Linen and Cotton: Classic Sewing Techniques for Great Results*. Newtown, CT: Taunton Press, 1999.

N. Marie Ledbetter and Linda Thiel Lansing, *Tailoring: Traditional and Contemporary Techniques*. Englewoods Cliffs, NJ: Prentice-Hall, 1981.

Lynda Maynard, *The Dressmaker's Handbook of Couture Sewing Techniques*. Loveland, CO: Interweave Press, 2010.

Tomoko Nakamichi, *Pattern Magic*. London: Laurence King Publishing, 2010.

Reader's Digest, *New Complete Guide to Sewing: Step-by-Step Techniques for Making Clothes and Home Accessories*. Pleasantville, NY: Reader's Digest, 2002.

Claire Shaeffer, *Claire Shaeffer's Fabric Sewing Guide*, 2nd edition. Cincinnati, OH: Krause Publications, 2008.

Colette Wolff, *The Art of Manipulating Fabric*. Iola, WI: Krause Publications, 1996.

Lace

Judyth L. Gwynne, *The Illustrated Dictionary of Lace*. London: Batsford; Berkeley, CA: LACIS Publications, 1997.

Susan Khalje, *Bridal Couture: Fine Sewing Techniques for Wedding Gowns and Evening Wear*. Iola, WI: Krause Publications, 1997.

Rosemary Shepherd, *Lace Classification System*. Sydney, Australia: Powerhouse Museum, 2003. https://www.powerhousemuseum.com/pdf/research/classification.pdf

Rosemary Shepherd, *Powerhouse Museum Lace Collection: Glossary of Terms*. Sydney, Australia: Powerhouse Museum, 2003. https://www.powerhousemuseum.com/pdf/research/glossary.pdf

Quilting

Mary S. Parker, *Sashiko: Easy and Elegant Japanese Designs for Decorative Machine Embroidery*. Asheville, NC: Lark Books, 1999.

Sashiko: Traditional Japanese Quilt Designs. Tokyo: Nihon-Vogue, 1989.

Quilting – Seminole

Cheryl Greider Bradkin, *Basic Seminole Patchwork*. Mountain View, CA: Leone Publications, 1990.

Smocking

Chris Rankin, *Creative Smocking: Contemporary Design, Traditional Techniques*. Asheville, NC: Lark Books, 2003.

Erica Wilson, *Erica Wilson's Smocking: All You Need to Know to Create Your Own Designs in This Traditional English Craft*. New York: Scribner, 1983.

Tassels

Kenneth D. King, *Designer Techniques: Couture Tips for Home Sewing*. New York: Sterling Publishing, 2002.

Websites

Anne Selby
anneselby.com
Website of UK silk accessory designer Anne Selby. Her arashi shibori collections are excellent inspiration, and her webshop stocks equipment for arashi shibori pleating.

Gütermann
www.guetermann.com
Website of the sewing-thread manufacturer. Contains information on products and where to buy them, as well as some patterns available for free download.

Henry's Buttons
henrysbuttons.co.uk
Dedicated to the heritage craft of making Dorset buttons. Includes a shop and tutorials.

Ian's Shoelace Site
www.fieggen.com/shoelace
The ultimate lacing guide. The site is focused on shoelaces, but the lacing styles can be adapted for couture lacing.

The Lace Guild
www.laceguild.org
Website of the Lace Guild, based in Stourbridge, West Midlands, UK. Contains information on the origins and history of lace, videos about lace making, and photographs and discussion of many different types of lace.

Lynne McMasters
lynnmcmasters.com
Instructions for making period costumes by designer Lynne McMasters. See especially her articles on feather ornaments.

Swarovski Magazine
www.crystals-from-swarovski.com/magazine
Includes current trends on crystals in fashion.

Your Wardrobe Unlock'd
yourwardrobeunlockd.com
Excellent collection of resources on general sewing and historical costume making.

Supplies

General

M & J Trimming (US)
www.mjtrim.com
Trims, ribbons, rhinestones, beads, buttons, sewing supplies.

Sewing Parts Online (US)
www.sewingpartsonline.com
Sewing machine parts, notions, needles, manuals, thread.

Fabrics

Apple Annie Fabrics (US)
www.appleanniefabrics.com
Fabrics, notions.

Borovick Fabrics Ltd (UK)
borovickfabrics.com
Fabrics, feather boas.

Fabrics and Fabrics (US)
fabrics-fabrics.com
Fabrics, lace.

Gorgeous Fabrics (US)
gorgeousfabrics.com
Fabrics, notions.

Linton Tweeds (UK)
www.lintondirect.co.uk
Supplied Chanel with tweeds, can supply you too!

MacCulloch & Wallis Ltd. (UK)
www.macculloch-wallis.co.uk
Fabric, thread, trims.

NY Elegant Fabrics (US)
nyelegant.com
Fabrics, lace, notions.

Trims and embellishments

Of the Earth (US)
www.custompaper.com/earthsilk
Hand-dyed silk ribbons.

Fancy Feather (US)
fancyfeather.com
Feathers.

Moonlight Feather (US)
www.moonlightfeather.com
Feathers.

Playtime (US)
www.rhinestones.com/index.html
Rhinestones.

The Satin Cord Store (US)
www.satincord.com
Cords in many colors for making braids and knots.

Sposabella Lace (US)
sposabellalacenyc.com
The ultimate lace shop.

Index

Credits

Garment designs

Bodice designs by Amy Ozay
pp. 35, 44, 59, 83, 92, 127, 143, 160, 191, 210, 213, 228, 249, 273, 285, 325, 335, 353

Bodice designs by Ellen W. Miller
pp. 105, 177

Sleeve designs by Catherine Burkey
pp. 242, 287, 298, 299, 300, 304, 310, 312, 313, 314, 328, 329, 330, 331

Sleeve designs by Ellen W. Miller
pp. 296, 297, 303, 306, 308, 330, 331

Sleeve designs by Edward Phillips
pp. 36, 37, 38, 39, 42, 43, 47, 49, 51, 52, 53, 56, 61, 66, 69, 71, 72, 73, 74, 78, 80, 84, 85, 86, 89, 94, 95, 97, 108, 112, 116, 118, 122, 133, 138, 140, 144, 149, 150, 153, 155, 157, 169, 170, 173, 174, 175, 181, 182, 188, 193, 194, 195, 196, 197, 198, 199, 202, 203, 206, 207, 210, 218, 220, 222, 223, 224, 225, 227, 236, 237, 238, 239, 241, 246, 247, 250, 256, 258, 266, 267, 271, 275, 276, 278, 279, 280, 281, 328, 329, 340, 341, 343, 344, 347, 349, 351, 354, 358, 359, 361, 362, 366, 367, 369, 371, 374, 375, 376, 377

Illustrations and photographs

All photographs by Ellen W. Miller, except where otherwise noted.

p. 32: Madeleine Vionnet (French, 1876–1975), dress (detail), c. 1926. Red silk crepe. Brooklyn Museum Costume Collection at The Metropolitan Museum of Art, New York; Gift of the Brooklyn Museum, 2009; Gift of Mr. and Mrs. Mitchell Ittelson, 1965 (2009.300.3846) © 2017. Image copyright The Metropolitan Museum of Art/Art Resource/Scala, Florence
p. 124: House of Givenchy (French, founded 1952), evening dress (detail), early 1960s. Metallic thread, feathers, silk. The Metropolitan Museum of Art, New York; Gift of Mrs. John Hay Whitney, 1974 (1974.184.1a–c) © 2016. Image copyright The Metropolitan Museum of Art/ Art Resource/Scala, Florence
p. 214 (bottom left): Lepas/Shutterstock.com
p. 214 (bottom right): Olgysha/Shutterstock.com
p. 215 (top left): Aksenova Natalya/Shutterstock.com

Bodice and sleeve photographs by Tracy Aiguier
pp. 6, 34, 36 (top), 38 (top), 39 (top), 41 (top), 42 (top), 43 (top), 44, 47, 49, 51 (top), 52 (top), 53, 56 (top), 58, 61, 66 (top), 69 (top), 71 (top), 72 (top), 73 (top), 74 (top), 78 (top), 80 (top), 82, 84 (top), 85 (top), 86 (top), 89 (top), 92, 94 (top), 95 (top), 97 (top), 104, 106 (top), 108 (top), 112 (top), 116 (top), 118 (top), 122 (top), 126, 133 (top), 135 (top), 138 (top), 140 (top), 142, 144 (top), 149 (top), 150 (top), 152 (top), 153 (top), 155 (top), 157 (top), 160, 169 (top), 170 (top), 173 (top), 174 (top), 175 (top), 176, 181 (top), 182 (top), 188 (top), 190, 193 (top), 194 (top), 195 (top), 196 (top), 197 (top), 198 (top), 199 (top), 200, 202 (top), 203 (top), 206 (top), 207 (top), 208 (top), 210 (top), 212, 218 (top), 220 (top), 222 (top), 223 (top), 224 (top), 225 (top), 226 (top), 227 (top), 228 (top), 236 (top), 237 (top), 238 (top), 239 (top), 242 (top), 243 (top), 246 (top), 247 (top), 248, 249 (top), 256 (top), 258, 266 (top), 267 (top), 271 (top), 272, 275 (top), 276 (top), 278 (top), 279 (top), 280 (top), 281 (top), 284, 287 (top), 288 (top), 289 (top), 290, 296 (top), 297 (top), 298 (top), 299 (top), 300 (top), 302 (top), 303 (top), 304 (top), 306 (top), 308 (top), 310 (top), 312 (top), 313 (top), 314 (top), 315 (top), 321 (top), 324, 328 (top), 329 (top), 330 (top), 331 (top), 332 (top), 333 (top), 334, 338 (top), 339 (top), 340 (top), 341 (top), 343 (top), 344 (top), 347 (top), 349 (top), 351 (top), 352, 354 (top), 357 (top), 358 (top), 359 (top), 361 (top), 362 (top), 366 (top), 367 (top), 369 (top), 371 (top), 374 (top), 375 (top), 376 (top), 377 (top)

Diagrams by Jane Levin
pp. 24, 25, 27, 46, 47, 48, 49, 50, 51, 52, 53, 54, 60, 61, 62, 63, 64, 65, 66, 67, 68, 69, 70, 78, 79, 80, 95, 106, 107, 117, 119, 122, 123, 128, 129, 130, 131, 133, 135, 146, 178, 179, 184, 186, 230, 234, 235, 236, 237, 238, 239, 240, 243, 247, 250, 251, 254, 255, 287, 288, 304, 310, 341, 344, 354, 355, 362, 363, 371, 374, 375, 376

Acknowledgements

Thank you to Jonathan, Abigail, Benjamin and Audrey Miller, Bill and Mary Wasserman, Abby Tonry, Peggy Imbrie, Andrea Wasserman, Diane Kupelnick, Amy Ozay, Martha Palaza, Roseanna Ansaldi, Edward Phillips, Jane Levin, Catherine Burkey, Diane Covert, Tracy Aiguier, Louise Cushing, Lisa Micheels, James Hannon, and Anne Townley and Jodi Simpson.

Thank you also to the staff at Playtime, Cambridge Quilt Stop, NY Elegant Fabrics, and Sposabella Lace who thought this book sounded "cool" and like something they would like to read.

You encouraged, taught, inspired, aided, pushed, abetted, and helped me throughout the long process of creating this book.